Smart Grid Security

Smart Grid Security
Innovative Solutions for a Modernized Grid

Edited by

Florian Skopik

Paul Smith

ELSEVIER

AMSTERDAM • BOSTON • HEIDELBERG • LONDON
NEW YORK • OXFORD • PARIS • SAN DIEGO
SAN FRANCISCO • SINGAPORE • SYDNEY • TOKYO

Syngress is an Imprint of Elsevier

SYNGRESS.

Acquiring Editor: Chris Katsaropoulos
Editorial Project Manager: Benjamin Rearick
Project Manager: Mohana Natarajan
Designer: Mark Rogers

Syngress is an imprint of Elsevier
225 Wyman Street, Waltham, MA 02451, USA

Notices

Knowledge and best practice in this field are constantly changing. As new research and experience broaden our understanding, changes in research methods, professional practices, or medical treatment may become necessary.

Practitioners and researchers must always rely on their own experience and knowledge in evaluating and using any information, methods, compounds, or experiments described herein. In using such information or methods they should be mindful of their own safety and the safety of others, including parties for whom they have a professional responsibility.

To the fullest extent of the law, neither the Publisher nor the authors, contributors, or editors, assume any liability for any injury and/or damage to persons or property as a matter of products liability, negligence or otherwise, or from any use or operation of any methods, products, instructions, or ideas contained in the material herein.

British Library Cataloguing-in-Publication Data
A catalogue record for this book is available from the British Library

Library of Congress Cataloging-in-Publication Data
A catalog record for this book is available from the Library of Congress

ISBN: 978-0-12-802122-4

Contents

List of Contributors

Stylianos Basagiannis
United Technologies Research Centre, 4th floor Penrose Wharf, Cork, Ireland

Menouer Boubekeur
United Technologies Research Centre, 4th floor Penrose Wharf, Cork, Ireland

Rohan Chabukswar
United Technologies Research Centre, 4th floor Penrose Wharf, Cork, Ireland

Paul De Hert
Vrije Universiteit Brussel (VUB), Research Group on Law, Science, Technology
and Society (LSTS), Belgium

Ivo Friedberg
Centre for Secure Information Technologies (CSIT), Queen's University Belfast,
UK; Austrian Institute of Technology, Vienna, Austria

Robert W. Griffin
RSA – the Security Division of EMC, Ireland

Martin Hutle
Fraunhofer AISEC, Germany

Karl H. Johansson
ACCESS Linnaeus Centre, KTH Royal Institute of Technology, Stockholm,
Sweden

Markus Kammerstetter
Automation Systems Group, Vienna University of Technology, Austria

BooJoong Kang
Centre for Secure Information Technologies (CSIT), Queen's University
Belfast, UK

Dariusz Kloza
Vrije Universiteit Brussel (VUB), Research Group on Law, Science, Technology
and Society (LSTS), Belgium

Friederich Kupzog
Austrian Institute of Technology, Vienna, Austria

Lucie Langer
Austrian Institute of Technology, Vienna, Austria

Zhendong Ma
Austrian Institute of Technology, Vienna, Austria

Peter Maynard
Centre for Secure Information Technologies (CSIT), Queen's University
Belfast, UK

Kieran McLaughlin
Centre for Secure Information Technologies (CSIT), Queen's University
Belfast, UK

Gavin McWilliams
Centre for Secure Information Technologies (CSIT), Queen's University
Belfast, UK

Paul Murdock
Landis+Gyr, Switzerland

Silvio La Porta
EMC Research Europe

Henrik Sandberg
ACCESS Linnaeus Centre, KTH Royal Institute of Technology, Stockholm,
Sweden

Sakir Sezer
Centre for Secure Information Technologies (CSIT), Queen's University
Belfast, UK

André Teixeira
ACCESS Linnaeus Centre, KTH Royal Institute of Technology, Stockholm,
Sweden

Niels van Dijk
Vrije Universiteit Brussel (VUB), Research Group on Law, Science, Technology
and Society (LSTS), Belgium

Yi Yang
Centre for Secure Information Technologies (CSIT), Queen's University,
Belfast, UK

Foreword

In an attempt to reduce our dependence on environmentally-damaging fossil fuels and to increase the longevity of installed power infrastructures, there has been a significant drive towards energy efficiency and a greater use of renewable energy sources. To support these goals, the electricity grid is being transformed into a so-called *smart grid*. At the core of the smart grid are increased monitoring and control capabilities, primarily in medium- and low-voltage networks, that are supported by Information and Communication Technology (ICT) and Supervisory Control and Data Acquisition (SCADA) systems. An example use of these systems is to support dynamic voltage control strategies that enable the deployment of volatile Distributed Energy Resources (DERs), such as photovoltaics, without the need for installing new and expensive grid capacity.

To date, much of the attention on the smart grid has focused on the smart meter and the Advanced Metering Infrastructure (AMI) – an important part of the smart grid that, for the moment, is largely used for fine-grain electricity consumption measurement and billing. There are limited pilot deployments of more advanced and operationally critical smart grid applications, such as for voltage control and power flow optimisation. We can expect a wider adoption of these applications based on the success of these pilots. Consequently, ICT and SCADA systems, as part of the smart grid, will play an increasingly operationally critical role in future electricity distribution networks; cyber-attacks to these systems could have a significant societal impact.

Alongside these smart grid developments, a number of cyber-attacks have targeted industrial control systems and energy sector organisations. The motivation for these attacks is varied, and includes industrial espionage and causing damage to physical plant. For the moment, the latter is the exception, and can require difficult to acquire expertise and in-depth knowledge of the target. Meanwhile, attack tools and methods are, on the one hand, becoming commoditised, lowering the barrier of entry for their use, and on the other hand, increasingly sophisticated and difficult to detect.

This combination of factors makes addressing the cybersecurity of the smart grid a timely and important issue, and forms the motivation for this book.

Because of the drive to deploy smart meters, the primary security concern for smart grids has related to ensuring the privacy of consumers. This is an important issue and has rightly received attention. In addition to the privacy concerns that stem from smart metering, other smart grid use cases, such as demand-response applications, and security solutions themselves introduce privacy and data protection problems. Consequently, in this book, we address privacy and data protection issues, but do not major on them. Rather, we cover a range of issues that relate to ensuring the security and resilience of the smart grid, with chapters focusing on topics from assessing cybersecurity risk through to operational security aspects.

Ensuring the security and resilience of the smart grid is a necessarily multi-disciplinary endeavour, requiring expertise in information security, industrial control systems (security), power systems engineering, control theory, and social and legal aspects, for example. For the most part, the chapter authors are participating in the multidisciplinary EU-funded SPARKS project. Without their willingness and enthusiasm for this project, and their subject knowledge, this book would not have been possible. As editors, we are grateful for their significant contribution.

Finally, a word on the intended readership of the book: we foresee the book being useful to forward-looking smart grid practitioners, such as Distributed Systems Operators and solutions providers, who are concerned about security and are interested in learning about state-of-the-art solutions, both in practice and applied research. Similarly, we suggest the book has value for academics and post-graduate students that are beginning their studies in this important area, and are seeking to get an overview of the research field. As editors, we have encouraged the chapter authors to follow a "bath-tub" approach to the depth of knowledge required to read each chapter, i.e., the start and end of each chapter should be approachable and give high-level insights into the topic covered, whereas the core content of the chapter may require more attention from the reader, as it focuses on details.

Florian Skopik and Paul Smith, Vienna 2015

Introduction

The Smart Grid is considered to be a key technology to prepare electric energy infrastructures for the challenges of upcoming decades. Strong pressure to change from an electrical energy system that was mostly based on fossil sources towards a system with a considerably high share of renewable forms of energy has caused significant effects on the power grid infrastructure. With large quantities of distributed renewable energy resources to be connected in electricity distribution grids and the potential for a strong growth in demand caused by electric vehicles, it is required to make most efficient use out of existing infrastructure by means of information and communication technologies (ICT). Monitoring and control systems that in the past were exclusively used on the transmission backbone level are spreading into distribution grids. With this, significant parts of one of the largest technical infrastructures built by mankind become online in the sense that real-time data is available and remote actions can be performed not only on wide areas but also in deep detail. With progress of automation into medium and low voltage distribution grids, the number of automated nodes in the system can increase by factor thousand to million depending on region and circumstances.

Electrical and ICT interoperability is the base for the smooth operation of any type of Smart Grid. Whenever ICT is introduced, cyber security needs to be addressed. Given the diversity in different Smart Grid approaches and the interdisciplinary character of the topic that covers even more than electrical engineering, computer science, socio-economics, social sciences, there is no straight-forward blueprint for Smart Grid security. The situation is not made easier by the fact that there are already existing ICT and security solutions for power grid operation that need to be scaled or re-designed for future requirements. For this reason, this book takes a deep look into ICT systems for power grid operation today and tomorrow. Not only the societal importance, but also risks and central technical counter-measures against cyber-attacks on Smart Grids are discussed with respect to existing infrastructure and also future development paths.

1.1 WHAT IS A SMART GRID?

What is a Smart Grid and what precisely does it do? With the concept of Smart Grids becoming more and more mature, this question is no longer that hard to answer as it was a few years ago. The European energy regulators (ERGEG, 2009) define: *A smart electrical grid is defined as an electrical grid, which can integrate the behaviour and actions of all connected users in a cost effective way – including producer, consumer and actors, which are both producer and consumer – to ensure a resource-saving and economically efficient electrical network with less losses, high quality, great security of supply and high technical safety.* Based on a communication and control network (ICT) of affected actors, electricity production should be coordinated and demanded in a more effective way. Generally speaking, the Smart Grid provides an ICT infrastructure, which allows interaction among participants of the power grid, specifically those connected to the so-called distribution level, i.e. the part of the power grid that brings energy to the end users at 230 V up to a few ten kV. The basic concept of a common communication infrastructure was formulated by a number of researchers around 2005 and has not changed since then. The infrastructure is used by different applications in a number of use cases in a synergetic fashion. The more relevant these applications are, the more likely it is that the existing conventional ICT infrastructure (if existent) is extended to form something one can call a Smart Grid. The type and relevance of Smart Grid applications vary over time and region. One can however say that the boost of renewable forms of energy has created a set of special requirements for electrical distribution grids, making some applications relevant that were previously not discussed for a conventional grid. This is especially true for Europe. In other parts of the world, motivations can be different. In the U.S., for instance, one major driver for Smart Grids is the ageing power grid infrastructure and the need for online condition monitoring. In China, the term Smart Grid is often interpreted differently. Here, the challenge is to transport electricity over large distances and reliably provide it to large areas with a very high population density. A similar situation can also be found in India.

1.2 THE STRUCTURE OF A SMART GRID SYSTEM

In order to establish a better understanding about the most important structural areas of the Smart Grid, we adopt here the layers and zones proposed by (CCESGCG, 2014), to draw a very first sketch[1] of a Smart Grid (see Figure 1.1). Notice, since the Smart Grid in its current form is primarily associated with energy distribution facilities (and less with generation and transmission, where ICT has been already widely adopted), there are mainly the three relevant domains – Distribution, Distributed Energy Resources (DER) and Customer Premises – depicted.

Starting from the top of the image, first of all there are diverse **Market Platforms** that serve different purposes, predominantly long-term to short term energy trading. **Energy trading** entities are connected to these market platforms. Concepts like aggregators or **virtual power plants** are also included here that collect a number of smaller units in a pool and trade their common flexibility on markets. Staying on the left side of the image, distribution system operation takes place in the **Network**

[1]This picture will be further elaborated in the coming chapters.

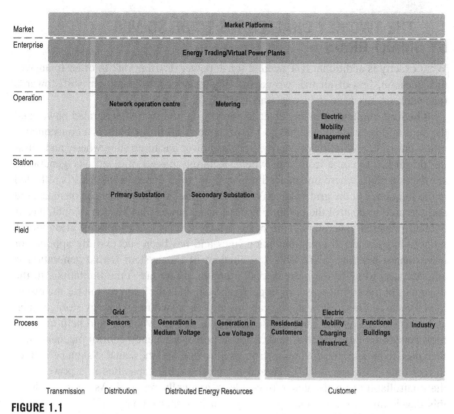

FIGURE 1.1

Aggregated Smart Grid component overview.

Operation Centre. Also **Metering** is a task of many Distribution System Operators, so the relevant databases and accounting systems for smart meters can be found here. These systems interact with the Enterprise level mostly by exchanging load and generation forecasts for the distribution level. Further down the stream, **Primary and Secondary Substations** can be found. Primary substations connect transmission and medium voltage grids, secondary substations are the interface between medium and low voltage grids. Most primary substations and (today) typically a few large secondary substations are connected with the Network Operation Centre by automation systems. A few **Grid Sensors** at critical points outside of substations can also be part of this automation infrastructure.

Connected to this distribution system are the **generators** (Distributed Energy Resources Domain) and loads (Customer Domain). Generators can be connected to medium of low voltage depending on their power rating (some MW vs. some kW). The demand side can be structured in **Residential Customers**, **Electric Mobility Charging** Infrastructure, **Functional** (i.e. smart) **Buildings** and **Industry**. For each of these areas, Smart Grid IT interfaces and standards are typically different.

1.3 THE TWO KEY CHALLENGES TO BE SOLVED BY SMART GRIDS

What exactly is additional ICT needed for in power distribution? In order to answer this question, first of all the two central challenges of the paradigm shift towards renewable energy need to be explained.

The first challenge: In any electric power grid, the sum of generated power and the sum of consumed power has to be the same at all times. This is a consequence of the law of conservation of energy. Surplus power has to go somewhere, and missing power has to come from somewhere. Rotating masses of electricity generators are the first place where imbalanced power flows to or comes from. This is reflected in the frequency of the grid voltage. Variations of the grid frequency can be measured and are used to control the output power of large power plants, such as coal, gas or nuclear powered generators. This basic principle of our transmission grids works without any dedicated communication lines and has been successfully applied for more than a hundred years. One key element of this system is that generation is adjusted according to the current load situation. There are some limitations in the dynamics of the output power of large plants, which is the main reason for the use of load forecasts. These allow day-ahead power plant scheduling. Energy storage, such as hydro storage plants, can provide additional power dynamics and help to avoid high generation peaks. The aforementioned power-frequency control mechanism is then used to balance the deviations from the forecast and the actual system behaviour in real time. However, with more and more renewable capacities in a power grid, the controllability on the generation side is gradually reduced. As an example of this development, the German power system had approximately 75% controllable generation in 2009. Plans for 2020 indicate that this share will reduce down to 50% (Dena-Netzstudie, 2010) and less in the upcoming years. This means that in order to maintain the ability to balance the grid in any weather situation, either conventional capacities have to be maintained or controllability is sought elsewhere, especially on the demand side of the system. This challenge is not too severe in the European interconnected grid today, but its significance will grow with time. In this regard, the Smart Grid is a means to gain and manage load flexibility.

The second challenge: The above description of power grid balancing includes a simplification: maintaining the power balance does not only mean that the strict mathematical sum of generated power is the same as the sum of consumed power in the overall grid. In practice, there is a grid infrastructure that transports the power from A to B, and this infrastructure has its limits. Dealing with line limits is well-known in transmission grid operation. Trans-European energy trading is often challenging the European interconnected transmission infrastructure and appropriate technical and market mechanisms are in place to deal with such situations. However, since renewable energy sources are mainly integrated in the distribution level and not on the transmission level, due to the low energy density of renewable forms of energy (except large hydro and concentrated offshore wind), distribution grids are now the scene of congestions. Here, the limitations are essentially line power ratings and operational voltage bands. But while transmission grids are well-monitored and controllable, distribution grids are operated blindly in large parts. They are statically designed and dimensioned according to pre-calculated worst -case utilisation situations, which in the past was an appropriate and efficient approach. In Austria, for example, 75 895 secondary substations and 1 060 primary substations were in operation on the distribution level in December 2012 (e-control, 2014). While the 1 060 primary stations can be assumed to be automated and monitored, the majority of the 75 895 secondary substations are manually operated stations. In order to collect measurements from these stations, a technician has to visit them. Consequently, the current "visibility" of the distribution grid is in the magnitude of 2%. Dealing with congestions in such a system is challenging, but urgent. In a number of places, distribution grids are already reaching capacity according to conventional planning rules, and reinforcements have to be made in order to host more renewable energy sources. Avoiding congestions by worst-case dimensioning as it was done in the past is a very expensive option. An alternative is to invest in monitoring and control in the distribution grid infrastructure. This is where the Smart Grid comes into practical operation for the first time.

1.4 SMART GRID APPLICATIONS AND THEIR CRITICAL NATURE

From these two central challenges, the most relevant smart grid applications can be derived. Obviously, a large variety of implementation alternatives exist for all of these applications, therefore this overview should be seen as non-exhaustive.

1. **Monitoring of distribution grids** – as shown above, one of the primary goals is to increase the transparency of distribution grid operation, i.e. increase the monitoring capabilities. The International Energy Agency (IEA) describes in its "Technology Roadmap Smart Grids" the missing technologies in the distribution domain that are required for smart grid deployment: "Automated re-closers, switches …, remote controlled distributed generation and storage, transformer sensors, wire and cable sensors" (IEA, 2011). While some of these relate to the second smart grid application described next, most relate to monitoring. Integration of additional sensors into existing infrastructure is expensive, and is only done by distribution grid operators when an additional benefit is obvious. Transportation of monitoring data is one of the core functions of smart grid ICT. Sensors can be dedicated grid sensors, mostly situated in transformer substations or at critical points in the grid. However, also smart energy meters have the potential to reveal essential data for grid operation and planning.

2. **Advanced control of distribution grids** – Technical barriers for renewable integration have been a major driver for smart grid research and development for advanced control approaches in recent years, resulting in a number of concepts and products. The dominant technical barrier is that line voltage levels

rise with the number of distributed generators. Generally, four approaches can be distinguished to address this problem. Communication and control in these approaches is a core smart grid application.

   a. Grid reinforcement: building of new lines or transformer stations. This option is usually not economically viable for the case of voltage problems, and is better suited to solve line overloads.

   b. Transformer or line-based techniques: here, components such as on-load tap changers or alternative continuous techniques are used to change the voltage on a selected line or in a selected network segment. These approaches consist of a hardware component (e.g. a transformer with switchable windings) and an associated control algorithm. While hardware components are available as products today (for a long time at the medium voltage level, and more recently at the low voltage level), control algorithms are still subject to research. Existing products such as "intelligent secondary transformers" come with simple controllers that are typically based on local measurements only.

   c. Generator-based techniques: here, the unit causing a voltage rise is also used to keep this rise within limits. This can either be achieved by reactive power (Q) management or (as a last resort) by shedding of active power (P) (Hambley, 2004). State of the art Photovoltaic inverters are equipped with selectable Q(U), P(U) as well as Q(P) and $\cos\varphi(U)$ characteristics. Again, these characteristics are usually controlled based on local measurements in the inverter. Remote control of these parameters is possible for some products; however, no widely accepted standardized way to achieve this has been defined yet.

   d. Combinations of the two approaches b) and c) discussed above

3. **Ancillary services from network participants on the distribution level –** the term ancillary service (Rebours et al., 2007) relates to services that are provided by power network participants (typically large power plants) that are required to ensure the safe and reliable operation of the system. Frequency control, reactive power control or voltage control are examples of ancillary services. Since a considerable share of generation is shifting into distribution grids, connected generators on the distribution level will increasingly have to provide such services. Ancillary services can also be provided by energy consumers (active management of load flexibility). It is a likely scenario that so-called Virtual Power Plants (Pudjianto et al., 2007) or aggregators will gather many small units (generators, loads, storages) and generate ancillary services from the pool of resources, increasing reliability and efficiency. Management processes and communication between individual units and their aggregators, as well as from ancillary service providers to service consumers can be seen as an application for smart grid ICT.

It can be seen from this list of applications that Smart Grid functionality takes a very critical role in the provision of electrical energy once applied. Already today, power grid operation is heavily dependent on ICT. With Smart Grid systems in place, the complexity and also the number of possible channels for cyber-attacks increase. Attacks targeting the distribution infrastructure do not necessarily aim only to cause power blackouts. They start from manipulating energy bills, blackmailing, power disruptions using Smart Meter-integrated switches, damage of distribution or customer equipment, up to effects on transmission grids with extensive consequences.

1.5 CHALLENGES IN SMART GRID SECURITY

Securing the Smart Grid is a challenging task for a number of reasons. First of all, the developments described above result in a significantly increased scale and complexity of ICT systems for distribution grids, including new devices, new control loops and especially a closer coupling of grid automation with "end-user" and third-party systems. This leads to an erosion of conventional technical and organisational boundaries because of increased openness. In particular, there is a strong need for interoperability between different subsystems that were previously isolated. Additionally, a rapidly changing threat landscape and the increasing sophistication of cyber-attack methods, such as Advanced Persistent Threats (APTs), create a demand for novel security solutions. Existing mature security solutions are largely focused on ICT systems, so they are not readily applicable to the cyber-physical nature of the Smart Grid.

In addition, some important cultural challenges have to be handled. The current focus in power grid design is mostly on safety and fault tolerance. Here, additional security might even be counterproductive, prohibiting that an emergency-off signal will reach its destination in time with advanced authentication and integrity checks in place. In fact, the organisational bodies dealing with power engineering and security were in most cases two separate worlds in the past and have had different languages and motivation. With a limited security budget, solutions need to be well-justified and targeted. However, in a world of complex and changing security guidance and standards landscape (see e.g. ISO 27000, IEC 62443, ANSI/ISA 99, NIST 7628, SGIS, ENISA, …) it is very difficult to judge which is the most useful solution and what should it target. Also testing the security level of the existing system is a challenge itself, since the power grid in its whole functionality cannot simply be copied to an isolated version which can be attacked for testing purposes. Advanced modelling and validation solutions are required for this.

One issue, well known since the emergence of the first Smart Grid concepts, is that of the very different lifetime expectations of power hardware and ICT components. Equipment is expected to function for much longer in the field for power systems. While the ICT lifecycle is 3 years; power equipment is assumed to work for 10, 20 or even 40 years. A lot can change in 3 years, but what will happen in 10 or 20 years? Do we have to assume the availability of post quantum computer crypto methods for smart meters, as quantum computers may become a reality within the typical lifetime of a meter or other equipment? Related to this, there is the additional issue of vendor lock-ins and cost for patches to known and potentially critical vulnerabilities, and the licensing arrangements that are in place to be part of these patch cycles. Last but not least, it is the task of the system designers to address upcoming privacy concerns, especially in the context of Smart Metering.

In order to illustrate these challenges, let us assume a given Smart Grid shall be secured against cyber-attacks. The first question in order to solve this task might be: **Which ICT system has to be secured?** The answer is that we are currently talking about a moving target. It is not yet entirely clear how the future system will look like. Additionally, the migration path from today's systems to a future Smart Grid solution is still subject to discussion and will not be the same for different system operators. Therefore, it is essential to find techniques to grasp the subject of analysis, the Smart Grid of the coming years. One approach that has proven to be adequate is to make use of Smart Grid Architectures. Mainly motivated by interoperability concerns, the clustering of Smart Grid components and their interaction has already been studied and documented even before it is finally decided which solutions will be installed in the field. With some adaptions, these architecture models can be used as a stable target for security analysis.

A second question might be: **Against what kind of attacks shall the system be secured?** Fortunately, due to experience from other fields of IT and automation systems, the threat landscape and the different kinds of attacks that can be expected from remote cyber-attacks to actual physical attacks can be drawn. However understanding the attack methods and the development of new attack techniques is an ongoing race between attackers and defenders.

Once these main points are settled, it should be considered, **what could be the effect of an attack?** In order to judge in which areas it makes most sense to invest in additional security, it is necessary to evaluate where in the system the risk for an attack is high and the effects of a potential attack are critical. Developing a structured risk catalogue is one possible solution, but a highly interdisciplinary work, since experts from IT, automation, power grid and energy economy are required. When looking even deeper and not only estimating but even simulating the effects of a cyber-attack, it makes sense to take a control system view on Smart Grids and model the cyber-attack as false data injection into power grid control loops.

1.6 THE STORYLINE OF THIS BOOK

After the introduction, the storyline of this book continues as follows:

Chapter 2 studies the importance of data privacy in context of the emerging Smart Grid. It elaborates on the social challenges of Smart Grids as well as legal implications and provides a sophisticated overview of regulatory approaches that are being prepared to address related challenges.

Then, Chapter 3 takes a deeper look into the different types and potential impacts of cybersecurity threats to Smart Grids, focusing on different Smart Grid domains in three comprehensive case studies. The challenges of risk assessment in future power grids are reflected, and different risk assessment frameworks proposed to date are discussed, including their applicability to smart grids.

Based on the structured threat overview, Chapter 4 dives deeper into the "physical aspects" of smart grid security, such as the physical attack vectors against critical equipment and basic protection measures. A particular emphasizes is placed on so-called physical uncloneable functions (PUFs), which promise a solution to many physical attacks against key components.

After the discussion of security mechanisms of physical components, Chapter 5 focuses on the security of communication links between components. For this purpose, it provides a comprehensive overview of the most important communication protocols, applied in the Smart Grid, and their features. This is the basis to discuss concrete attacks, such as spoofing, injection, replay and man-in-the-middle attacks, and then comes up with feasible counter measures, specifically in context of mentioned communication standards.

Chapter 6 specifically deals with the application of technologies discussed before in industrial control systems (ICSs). Specifically, feedback control loops are a core component in the Smart Grid, as they enable the efficient utilization of the physical infrastructure and its resources. As the number control loops in the Smart Grid increases, the cyber security challenges faced by ICSs become increasingly important within the Smart Grid's context. To highlight such novel challenges, the chapter provides an overview of the envisioned control loops in future Smart Grids, and discusses the potential impact of cyber threats targeting critical Smart Grid functionalities. As a case study, false-data injection attacks on power transmission networks are considered.

Eventually, after surveying threats and attack methods on different levels and in varying dimensions of the Smart Grid, Chapter 7 provides an overview about applicable current and future security architectures. It further elaborates on the adoption of Smart Grid Security architecture methodologies, defines a concrete Smart Grid security architecture, and outlines a way of moving from a basic architecture to an actual security design.

An often undervalued aspect of security is the overall development lifecycle. A sound security design and architecture as well as sophisticated security technologies only address one part of the challenge. To ensure security in the Smart Grid, from development via roll-out to operation and eventually de-commissioning, proven development processes and management are needed to minimize or eliminate security flaws, vulnerabilities, and weakness induced in the whole product lifecycle. Chapter 8 therefore looks into security considerations in all phases of the Smart Grid's life cycle. It outlines industrial best practices and research activities, and describes a system development life cycle process with existing and emerging methods and techniques for Smart Grid security.

Assuming a robust architecture for Smart Grid security is in place and defensive mechanisms against the threats and attacks outlined in the previous chapters are deployed, there is still the chance that an attack eludes these mechanisms. Thus, Chapter 9 deals with all aspects of operational security. It presents an operational model for effective management of security capabilities that enables discovery of security issues, analysis of those issues to determine whether and how to respond, and remediation or recovery for those issues that require action to be taken.

Chapter 10 concludes the book by reviewing outlined security solutions in this work under real-world circumstances; specifically, intrusion detection systems, smart meter authentication and key management using Physical Unclonable Functions, security analytics and resilient control algorithms. Furthermore, this chapter deals with evaluation use cases of security tools applied in smart grid infrastructure test-beds, anticipated experimental results from the use-cases and conclusions about the successful transitions of security measures to real world smart-grid operations are also part of this chapter.

REFERENCES

CEN-CENELEC-ETSI Smart Grid Coordination Group (2014). Reports in response to Smart Grid Mandate M/490. Available at http://www.cencenelec.eu/standards/Sectors/SustainableEnergy/SmartGrids/Pages/default.aspx.

Dena-Netzstudie, I. I. (2010). Integration erneuerbarer Energien in die deutsche Stromversorgung im Zeitraum 2015-2020 mit Ausblick 2025. Berlin, Germany, Nov.

e-control, http://www.e-control.at/de/statistik/strom/bestandsstatistik, last visited 03/2014.

European Regulators' Group for Electricity and Gas (December 2009). Position Paper on Smart Grids. An ERGEG public consultation paper.

Hambley, A. R. (2004). *Electrical Engineering*. Pearson.

IEA (2011). *Technology Roadmap Smart Grids*. International Energy Agency.

Pudjianto, D., Ramsay, C., & Strbac, G. (2007). Virtual power plant and system integration of distributed energy resources. *Renewable power generation, IET*, *1*(1), 10–16.

Rebours, Y. G., Kirschen, D. S., Trotignon, M., & Rossignol, S. (2007). A survey of frequency and voltage control ancillary services—Part I: Technical features. Power Systems. *IEEE Transactions*, *22*(1), 350–357.

Assessing the European Approach to Privacy and Data Protection in Smart Grids. Lessons for Emerging Technologies[a]

2

Dariusz Kloza, Niels van Dijk, and Paul De Hert[b]

Vrije Universiteit Brussel (VUB), Research Group on Law, Science,
Technology and Society (LSTS), Belgium

2.1 INTRODUCTION

In order to keep pace with environmental, societal and technological developments presently foreseen, energy would need to be generated, distributed, used, recycled, managed and governed in different ways (Achenbach, 2010, pp. 3–7). Smart grids represent a possible response with the promise of numerous environmental and energy-efficiency benefits, among others (Clastres, 2011). At the same time, however, they are capable of invading the inviolability of the most privacy-sensitive place – the home (Cuijpers & Koops, 2013). In the last decade, smart grids have been deployed throughout the world, from Canada and United States, through Europe, to China. In some countries, due to their invasiveness, their deployment caused public outrage, e.g. in the Netherlands or

[a] We would like to thank Irina Baraliuc, Monika Kokštaitė, Lucas Melgaço, Kjetil Rommetveit and Tomas Wyns for an exchange of ideas. This paper is based on research projects: (1) EPINET (*Integrated Assessment of Societal Impacts of Emerging Science and Technology from within Epistemic Networks*; 2012-2015; http://epinet.no), co-funded by the European Union under its 7th Framework Programme for Research and Technological Development, and (2) "*A risk to a right? Exploring a new notion in data protection law*", co-funded by the Research Foundation – Flanders (FWO) (2015-2017). The contents are the sole responsibility of the authors and can in no way be taken to reflect the views of any of these funding agencies.

[b] Dariusz Kloza is researcher at Vrije Universiteit Brussel (VUB), Research Group on Law, Science, Technology and Society (LSTS) and at VUB's Institute for European Studies (IES), dariusz.kloza@vub.ac.be; Dr. Niels van Dijk is researcher at VUB-LSTS and at Radboud Universiteit Nijmegen (RU), Institute for Computing and Information Sciences (iCIS), niels.van.dijk@vub.ac.be; Prof. Dr. Paul De Hert is co-director of VUB-LSTS and professor at Tilburg University (TiU), Tilburg Institute for Law, Technology, and Society (TILT), paul.de.hert@uvt.nl.

California (Cuijpers & Koops, 2008).[1] In others, their roll-out has been crafted to, more or less, minimise some of their negative impacts, e.g. in Ontario (cf. e.g. Cavoukian et al., 2010; Cavoukian, 2012; Information and Privacy Commissioner of Ontario, 2011). This experience shows that the question of the sacrosanctity of the home is one of the first concerns to be duly taken into consideration while deploying smart grids.

In this chapter, we would like to sketch societal challenges posed by smart grids, and in particular those related to surveillance, and – subsequently – to critically assess the approach of the European Union (EU) to addressing them. We first use the Dutch example of smart meters roll-out to illustrate that smart grids constitute a complex socio-technical phenomenon, and first and foremost, can be used as a surveillance tool (sections 2-3). Second, as the treat of abusive surveillance, to which we limit this chapter, is frequently framed in the language of privacy and personal data protection, we briefly introduce relevant legal frameworks of the EU (section 4) in order to demonstrate how smart grids interfere with these notions (section 5). Third, although the said frameworks solved some issues, they still left a number of open questions. Thus the EU has experimented with adding, on top of them, a "light" regulatory framework for personal data protection in smart grids, of which a data protection impact assessment (DPIA) can be seen as a core element. Having overviewed this development in section 6, we attempt to critically assess it in a subsequent section. We analyse the choice of regulatory instruments, their scope, focus, quality and effectiveness, among others. We conclude, in section 8, that the DPIA framework, chosen as the main means to solve the threat of abusive surveillance in smart grids, is rather a missed opportunity.

This chapter takes a predominantly legal perspective and is written from the European standpoint. We use the term "smart grids" as comprising the smart grid itself (i.e. the whole network), smart meters (i.e. tools installed at households) and smart metering systems (i.e. the infrastructure processing data from a smart meter). Throughout this chapter one can find not only an in-depth analysis of the deployment of smart grids in the EU, but also a broader reflection on the kind of assessments that modern democracies with comprehensive fundamental rights, e.g. to personal data protection, need when challenged by emerging technologies. In our conclusion we will therefore end with two recommendations on assessment and governance of these technologies in general. We observe a need for *inclusive*, *easy* to use and *flexible* impact assessments, satisfying certain quality criteria.

2.2 THE DUTCH CASE STUDY: A SMART GRID ROLL-OUT THAT NEGLECTED INDIVIDUAL INTERESTS

Driven, *inter alia*, by the promised benefits of smart grids, since the early 2000s the EU has embarked on an ambitious policy of increasing the efficiency of the energy use in the Union. This has been presented as a part of bigger goals concerning the protection of environment, combatting climate change and fostering the development

---

[1]Cf. http://www.wijvertrouwenslimmemetersniet.nl and http://stopsmartmeters.org.

of an internal market. It has resulted in the adoption of a series of legally binding instruments, including the 2006 Energy Efficiency Directive, the so-called 2009 Third Energy Package and the 2012 New Energy Efficiency Directive.[2] As a result, among many initiatives, each European household shall be equipped with an advanced measuring instrument (AMI), better known as a smart meter, provided the cost-benefit analysis is positive. As a directive is a supranational legal instrument binding the Member States as to the goals, but leaving them the means of achieving them, it needs to be implemented into the national legal system. The government of one of the EU Member States, the Netherlands, took this obligation very seriously.

While the legal framework was still taking shape, in 2008 the Dutch government tabled in the national parliament, *Staten-Generaal der Nederlanden*, two proposals to amend the Electricity and Gas Acts, both from 1998.[3] The proposals provided for:

> *the mandatory introduction of so-called smart meters in every Dutch household. Not accepting the installation of a smart meter was made punishable as an economic offence, sanctioned with a fine of up to 17,000 euro or imprisonment for a maximum of 6 months. The smart meter would record and forward to the network operators […] data about consumers' energy consumption at detailed interval periods, namely hourly measurements for gas and quarter-hourly measurements for electricity. These data would be forwarded to the energy suppliers, who would then use these data to provide consumers with detailed information about their energy consumption, so that the consumers could adapt their energy-consuming behaviour accordingly.*
>
> *Besides the measuring and communication functionalities, the initial Dutch proposals also included signaling, switching and regulatory functions. The signaling function enables the network operator to detect energy quality remotely. The switching function enables network operators to remotely switch energy capacity off and on, in order to deal with fraudulent or non-paying customers, or in case of disasters. Finally, the regulatory function entails the possibility to add options to the meter so that it can carry out additional supportive functions (Cuijpers & Koops, 2013, pp. 269–293).*

Not surprisingly, the Dutch data protection authority (*College Bescherming Persoonsgegevens*), the local consumers' association (*Consumentenbond*), as well as the society at large, raised concerns with the proposals. Not only the set of

---

[2]Cf. *inter alia*, Directive 2006/32/EC of the European Parliament and of the Council of 5 April 2006 on energy end-use efficiency and energy services and repealing Council Directive 93/76/EEC; OJ L 114, 27.04.2006, pp. 64–85; Directive 2009/72/EC of the European Parliament and of the Council of 13 July 2009 concerning common rules for the internal market in electricity and repealing Directive 2003/54/EC, OJ L 211, 14.08.2009, pp. 55–93; Directive 2009/73/EC of the European Parliament and of the Council of 13 July 2009 concerning common rules for the internal market in natural gas and repealing Directive 2003/55/EC, OJ L 211, 14.08.2009, pp. 94–136; Directive 2012/27/EU of the European Parliament and of the Council of 25 October 2012 on energy efficiency, amending Directives 2009/125/EC and 2010/30/EU and repealing Directives 2004/8/EC and 2006/32/EC, OJ L 315, 14.11.2012, pp. 1–56.
[3]Parliamentary Documents, Second Chamber 2007/08, 31 320, No. 2; Parliamentary Documents Second Chamber 2007/08, 31 374, No. 2.

functionalities of a smart meter proposed in the law would severely invade the sanctity of the home (Cuijpers & Koops, 2013, pp. 269–293), but also the process of rolling them out lacked democratic standards, and in particular public consultation (Hoenkamp et al., 2011, pp. 280–282).

After the bills had been passed in the Second Chamber (*Tweede Kamer*), the *Consumentenbond* commissioned a study to test whether the proposed smart metering legislation was in conformity with the European Convention on Human Rights (ECHR),[4] in particular with its Art 8 that guarantees the right to private and family life. A true revolt against the roll out of smart meters further fuelled the need for this study.[5] The final report issued by the Tilburg University in October 2008 changed the course of the bills (Cuijpers & Koops, 2008).

While the *Tweede Kamer* basically ignored the concerns of the Dutch data protection watchdog,[6] the concerns of consumers and their association actually did make a change. When the report reached the Dutch First Chamber (*Eerste Kamer*), this political body threatened to reject the bill altogether unless the government would introduce an amendment, a *novelle*.[7]

> *A major change enhancing the privacy-friendliness of the Dutch smart metering landscape concerns cancelling the obligatory roll-out of smart meters. The* novelles *explicitly grant end users the right to refuse a smart meter, without risking a fine or imprisonment, as the sanction is lifted. Besides declining a smart meter, consumers are offered a possibility to request the operator to 'administratively shut down' the smart meter. This means that a grid operator will stop reading measuring data of an end user. A grid operator is legally obliged to honour this request.*
>
> *A second considerable improvement for privacy is a clarification and codification of the terms and conditions under which personal data can be processed by the parties involved in the process of energy supply. The collection of end-user metering data by the grid manager and energy suppliers is now explicitly tied to their legally prescribed tasks, such as billing by suppliers and network management by the grid operator. This is a refinement of the rules regarding the processing of measuring data. Previously, only the conditions under which grid operators were allowed to transfer measuring data of end users to suppliers were laid down. The conditions now in place regarding the collection and use of such data by grid operators provide more checks and balances to protect the privacy of consumers.*
>
> *The Dutch Parliament was satisfied with the privacy improvement of making the smart meters voluntary. The Second Chamber passed the* novelles *in*

---

[4]European Convention on Human Rights (ECHR), Rome, 4 November 1950, ETS 5.

[5]Cf. *supra*, note 1.

[6]College bescherming persoonsgegevens, *Wijziging van de Elektriciteitswet 1998 en de Gaswet ter verbetering van de werking van de elektriciteits- en gasmarkt (31 374)*, Den Haag, 17 June 2008. https://cbpweb.nl/sites/default/files/downloads/adv/z2008-00769.pdf

[7]In the Dutch constitutional system, the upper house can only accept or reject a bill. It might, however, request the relevant minister to introduce an amendment. If so, the bill returns to the lower house that subsequently votes the amended version (Cuijpers & Koops, 2013).

November 2010 and the First Chamber accepted the original smart metering bills, including the amendments made by the novelles, *in February 2011 (Cuijpers & Koops, 2013, pp. 269–293).*

As a result, the Netherlands perhaps currently has in place the most privacy- and personal data protection friendly legislation on smart meters. This has been achieved largely because the initially neglected interests of consumers – i.e. privacy and their voice in its governance – have been, after a long debate, eventually taken into consideration. The lesson learnt here is that (Cuijpers & Koops, 2013, pp. 289–293; Hoenkamp et al., 2011, pp. 281–282):

1. privacy and personal data protection concerns, especially the inviolability of the home, are of utmost importance,
2. voice needs to be given to the public at large while deploying smart grids,
3. these concerns need to be considered at the early stage of the roll-out, and
4. neglecting them will significantly flaw such a roll out in a given jurisdiction.

2.3 THE SMART GRID: A SOCIALLY COMPLEX PHENOMENON WITH A SURVEILLANCE DIMENSION

Let us now reflect on the substantive nature of the problem in question, that is, why is the protection of the inviolability of the home so important? Are not smart grids a facility that allows more control and choice? Advocates claim that benefits of smart grids are plentiful. Individuals might wish to be offered a wider variety of tariffs that depend on detailed meter readings (i.e. dynamic pricing), they might wish to sell the energy produced themselves by their solar panels to the grid or they might wish to ask for some energy-efficiency advice services.[8] Individuals can remotely manage their energy usage, e.g. by turning lights on and off at a given hour while on holidays in order to prevent a burglary. (There is also this fictional story of watching a pet left at home during the daytime.)[9] Statistical information produced by smart meters might help energy companies manage the grid better, e.g. preventing blackouts or reducing energy load during times of peak demand (i.e. demand-response). From the perspective of the society at large, it has been already reported that the police in the United States, having some reasonable suspicion, request metering information from utility companies to discover indoor marijuana-growing operations. "If a growing operation is inside, the utility records reveal far higher energy use than at comparable homes because of the high-wattage bulbs

---

[8]Cf. http://www.enerbyte.com. Discontinued services included Microsoft Hohm or Google PowerMeter.

[9]In a Belgian TV advertisement, the electricity provider Electrabel in 2012 launched an advertising campaign in which Kito, a dog, uses home appliances while his masters are outside the house. Yet the dog does not realize that his masters watch his activities via an on-line platform connected to a smart meter and that they are able to remotely control the usage of energy. To the great disappointment of the dog, at a certain moment they turn off the electricity as the dog abuses its usage. Cf. https://www.youtube.com/watch?v=bTvUuLnOsjc

needed for growing" (Narciso, 2011; Vijayan, 2011). Finally, the deployment of smart grids is believed to benefit environmental and climate change goals (e.g. by the reduction of greenhouse gas emissions and widespread use of renewable energy sources) as well as economic objectives (e.g. by reducing procurement through dynamic pricing strategies and optimisation of transmission costs) (cf. although critically, Clastres, 2011).[10]

The source of the privacy problem is the smart meter as a part of a smart grid. Certain functionalities of these meters can severely invade the inviolability of, as Koops and Cuijpers put it, "the most privacy-sensitive place – the home" (2013, p. 269). In practical terms, a digital meter that is capable of reading the use of electricity of each home appliance with a heavy granularity, of transmitting this information to various entities in a long and blurred energy supply chain and, consequently, allowing these entities to make and execute decisions based on such information – gives a strong insight into what is happening at home and allows for the control of inhabitants.

For example, research recently conducted at the Münster University of Applied Sciences demonstrated that it is possible to know what programme or movie was watched on a TV only from the analysis of information acquired from a smart meter:

> *Having gained some experiences with 653 content files and some days of recorded program broadcast, we could state that detection of movies produced for cinema projectors was almost always a feasible task while many TV studio productions (e.g. talk shows, news) are difficult or impossible to identify when played as recorded content. […]*
>
> *The successful test results affirm our belief that movie/TV content identification via fine-grained smart meter data is possible. […]*
>
> *We have demonstrated that particular information available on appliances in the household via its detailed power profile allow a fine-grained analysis of the appliance's behavior. Taking measurements at an interval of two seconds is sufficient to enable the identification of a television program or audiovisual content if favorable conditions are in place (e.g. no major interference of other appliances for minutes long). Our research has shown that the electricity usage profile with a $0.5s^{-1}$ sample rate leads to an invasion into a person's private sphere regarding his TV watching habits. Five minutes of consecutive playing of a movie is in many cases sufficient to identify the viewed content by analyzing the smart meter power consumption data (Greveler et al., 2012, pp. 10–15).*

Such detailed information about one's daily life and habits might interest many people. As the US-based Electronic Frontier Foundation once observed:

> *it's not hard to imagine a divorce lawyer subpoenaing this information, an insurance company interpreting the data in a way that allows it to penalize customers, or criminals intercepting the information to plan a burglary. Marketing companies*

---

[10]But, on the other hand, smart grids might negatively impact human health, cf. electromagnetic hypersensitivity (Barringer, 2011), and economic well being, cf. raising energy prices (Cornish, 2012). However, a detailed analysis thereof lies outside the scope of this chapter.

will also desperately want to access this data to get new intimate new insights into your family's day-to-day routine – not to mention the government, which wants to mine the data for law enforcement and other purposes (Tien, 2010).

Furthermore, an energy company can switch off supply if someone defaults, even unintentionally (Anderson & Fuloria, 2010) or cyberspies can penetrate electrical grids and leave behind "software programs that could be used to disrupt the system" (Gorman, 2009).

Information gathered that way, combined with the functionalities of smart grids, are the first prerequisites for exercising control and influence over those who stay or happen to be at home. These characteristics construct smart grids as a surveillance tool: they make it possible to direct a "focused, systematic and routine attention to personal details for the purposes of influence, management, protection or detection" (as surveillance is classically defined) (Lyon, 2007, p. 14). The French word "surveillance"[11] literally means "to watch over" and one could watch others because she *cares*, i.e. she is "concerned for their safety; lifeguards at the edge of swimming pool might be an example" (Lyon, 2007, pp. 13–14). Or she could *control* others, i.e. watch over those "whose activities are in some way dubious or suspect; police officers watching someone loitering in a parking lot would be an example" (Lyon, 2007, pp. 13–14). As surveillance always has some ambiguity, its two main purposes exemplified above – *care* and *control* – might equally bring advantages and disadvantages, might correspondingly be socially desirable or not as well as might be exercised in a socially acceptable or unacceptable way (Lyon, 2007, p. 14).

The foregoing shows that the individual and collective promised benefits of smart grids need to be balanced in the light of the threat of *abusive* surveillance. "This is what the world is for: making electricity" (MGMT, 2007) versus "I'm expected to behave as if nothing ever happened, but it's hard for me to do this because I feel I'm always being watched" (Atwood, 2009, p. 23). Both interests at stake – the benefits of smart grids and the protection against abusive surveillance practices – are legitimate and the problem here is about finding the thin red line between these two.

Note that the need for this balancing also has to do with other threats than those posed by surveillance. Smart grids have the character of an emerging "large technical system" that also incorporates a whole series of non-technical elements, thus constituting a complex socio-technical phenomenon. Moreover, in their current form, smart grids are still just "a set of promises, expectations and visions that shape innovation" and these promises "are at least partly speculative".[12] These visions raise numerous issues concerning, *inter alia*, environment, climate change, state security, economic well being, ethics or – as we have been discussing – surveillance.[13] To give the reader an impression of this complexity, we share our attempt to draw up a list of many of these concerns in a form of a word cloud (Fig. 2.1). Moreover, the fact that smart grids

---

[11]From French: *sur-* ("over") + *veiller* ("to watch").

[12]Jeroen van der Sluijs intervention at *The future of social robustness of smart electricity networks in Europe*, EPINET project's workshop, 16-17 January 2013, Hilversum, the Netherlands.

[13]Ibid.

FIGURE 2.1

An attempt to map societal concerns posed by smart grids.

technologies do not come in a single shape or configuration – thus each technical design would have a different impact on each of these societal concerns – only adds to this complication.

In result, this makes it difficult to comprehensively assess their societal consequences and, in result, regulate these technologies. This situation is related to the classical Collingridge dilemma:

> *The social consequences of a technology cannot be predicted early in the life of the technology. By the time undesirable consequences are discovered, however, the technology is so much part of the whole economics and social fabric that its control is extremely difficult. This is the dilemma of control (Collingridge, 1980, p. 11).*

Our analysis limits itself to the question of abusive surveillance of smart grids. And even here, it is clear that privacy and personal data protection, although constituting one of the main issues, do not exhaust all the societal concerns that smart grids might raise. In other words, the problem is much bigger than just these two issues.

2.4 PRIVACY AND PERSONAL DATA PROTECTION IN THE EUROPEAN LEGAL ORDER

This threat of abusive surveillance is often best framed in the language of ethics, or particularly in the language of privacy and personal data protection (cf. Lyon, 2007, p. 180).[14] Privacy is frequently seen as a notion setting constitutional limits that shield the individual against the public authorities and other powers, therefore warranting her a certain level of *opacity* (De Hert & Gutwirth, 2009). And because surveillance is primarily about control, looking at it through the prism of privacy allows controlling those who control.

This constitutional function of privacy, however, does not tell us what privacy is or does. In a classic formulation, "the idea of privacy embraces the desire to be left alone, free to be ourselves – uninhibited and unconstrained by the prying of others" (Wacks, 2010, p. 30). Privacy is a broad concept, comprising a wide range of individual interests, from thoughts and feelings, to associations, to data and image, to communications; this list is not exhaustive and cannot be. As the conceptualisation

---

[14] Again, we note that "Lyon argues that privacy is also inadequate to capture all of the negative effects of surveillance, since other civil liberties concerns, in addition to privacy, are implicated in new technologies of surveillance. For example, the use of surveillance technologies may inhibit individuals' freedom of assembly or freedom of expression due to a "chilling effect" that discourages individual participation in social movements or public dissent activities. In relation to profiling via data mining, Schreurs et al. discuss a right of non-discrimination [...]; Coleman and McCahill argue that the use of surveillance technologies often reinforces existing social positions, particularly positions of marginalisation along the lines of race, class, gender, sexuality and age. Surveillance technologies may impinge upon individuals' freedom of movement, in a clear example of Lyon's notion of social sorting. [...] In addition to these civil liberties concerns around the negative effects on individuals, [...] individuals also have a right to security" (Finn & Wright, 2012, p. 186; refernces omitted).

of privacy matured, it became clear that one of the aspects of this "being left alone" – i.e. the one concerning *information* relating to an individual, directly or indirectly – requires separate attention. In other words, the concept of "data protection" was created (cf. De Hert & Gutwirth, 2009; Finn et al., 2013; Gellert & Gutwirth, 2013; González Fuster, 2014; Kokott & Sobotta, 2013).

Although these two concepts – privacy and personal data protection – safeguard similar interests, i.e. the political private sphere, they do so differently. Privacy, as we explained above, limits the use of power as a tool of *opacity*, whilst personal data protection channels the legitimate use of power, imposing a certain level of *transparency* and accountability (Gutwirth & De Hert, 2006, pp. 61–104). One of the practical consequences of this distinction is a possibility that a given measure could be perfectly in line with the data protection principles, but – at the same time – could still be infringing individual's privacy. For example, in the famous case of *S. and Marper vs. the United Kingdom* (2004) the European Court of Human Rights found that despite biometric data processed for criminal prevention purposes "were retained on the basis of legislation allowing for their indefinite retention" (§113) their retention "constitute[d] a disproportionate interference with the applicants' right to respect for private life and cannot be regarded as necessary in a democratic society" (§125).[15]

From the legal viewpoint, both concepts – privacy and personal data protection – are in the European legal order conceptualized as fundamental rights. Three overlapping systems ensure their protection.[16] First, within the Council of Europe – a human rights-oriented regional organisation, currently comprising 47 European countries – the European Convention on Human Rights (ECHR) provides for the right to respect for private and family life, safeguarding four main interests: private life, family life, home and correspondence.[17] The European Court of Human Rights (ECtHR), by its case law, interprets the rights enshrined in the Convention, ensures their observation and – subsequently – has derived the protection of personal data from the protection of privacy. From the headquarters of this Court in the Alsatian capital, this system is commonly referred to as "Strasbourg system". In parallel, under the auspices of the Council of Europe, two binding international legal instruments safeguarding personal data have been adopted: Convention 108 and the Additional Protocol thereto (181).[18]

The second system is that of the EU. The Charter of Fundamental Rights (CFR) has explicitly recognized privacy and personal data protection as two separate yet interrelated rights.[19] While Art 7 CFR copies almost literally the contents of the right

---

[15]ECtHR, *S. and Marper vs. the United Kindgom*, judgment (grand chamber) of 4 December 2008, applications nos. 30562/04 and 30566/04.

[16]All these three systems overlap as all EU Member States are also contracting parties to the European Convention on Human Rights (as well as to the Convention 108) and all constitutions concerned protect privacy and personal data in one or another way.

[17]Art 8 ECHR, cf. *supra*, note 4.

[18]Convention for the Protection of Individuals with regard to Automatic Processing of Personal Data, Strasbourg, 28 January 1981, ETS 108 (*hereinafter*: Convention 108); Additional Protocol to the Convention for the Protection of Individuals with regard to Automatic Processing of Personal Data regarding supervisory authorities and transborder data flows, Strasbourg, 8 November 2001, ETS 181.

[19]Charter of Fundamental Rights of the European Union, OJ C 326, 26.10.2012, pp. 391–407.

to privacy from the Strasbourg system, Art 8 CFR not only introduces a new right, but also sets forth the main principles of personal data protection.

Article 7 – Respect for private and family life
Everyone has the right to respect for his or her private and family life, home and communications.

Article 8 – Protection of personal data
1. *Everyone has the right to the protection of personal data concerning him or her.*
2. *Such data must be processed* fairly *for* specified purposes *and on the* basis *of the consent of the person concerned or some other legitimate basis laid down by law. Everyone has the* right of access *to data which has been collected concerning him or her, and the* right to have it rectified.
3. *Compliance with these rules shall be subject to* control *by an independent authority.*[20]

The Court of Justice of the EU (CJEU) is, in this regard, similarly tasked as its Strasbourg counterpart. And again, because of the seat of the EU highest court, this system is referred to as "Luxembourg system".

Art 8 CFR reflects some of the main principles of personal data protection, known from the mid-1970s. There are various ways of classifying them and Bygrave, for example, categorizes them as: (1) fair and lawful processing, (2) minimality, (3) purpose specification, (4) information quality, (5) data subject participation and control, (6) disclosure limitation, (7) information security, and (8) sensitivity (2002, pp. 57–69). The 1995 Data Protection Directive and the Fair Information Practice Principles constitute their landmark codifications, while the most recent systematisation is the 2013 revision of the Organisation for Economic Co-operation and Development's (OECD) Guidelines on the Protection of Privacy and Transborder Flows of Personal Data (1980).[21]

In order to respond to the technological developments and societal challenges, since January 2012 the EU data protection framework is undergoing a substantial reform process (cf. e.g. De Hert & Papakonstantinou, 2012; Kuner, 2012).[22]

The third system is a national one, i.e. virtually all constitutions of Western liberal democracies protect the right to privacy and/or personal data protection in one or another way. Rooted in international human right law (i.e. the first two systems),

---

[20]Emphasis added.

[21]Directive 95/46/EC of the European Parliament and of the Council of 24 October 1995 on the protection of individuals with regard to the processing of personal data and on the free movement of such data, OJ L 281, 23.11.1995, pp. 31–50 (*hereinafter*: 1995 Data Protection Directive); Privacy Act of 1974, Pub. L. No 93-579 (Dec. 31, 1974), 5 U.S.C. §552a (1974); Recommendation of the Council concerning Guidelines governing the Protection of Privacy and Transborder Flows of Personal Data (2013), C(80)58/FINAL, as amended on 11 July 2013 by C(2013)79.

[22]European Commission, Proposal for a Regulation of the European Parliament and of the Council on the protection of individuals with regard to the processing of personal data and on the free movement of such data (General Data Protection Regulation), Brussels, 25 January 2012, COM(2012)11 final.

privacy (and data protection) at a national level are constitutional basic rights. These rights were not formulated as a directive for public authorities, but as direct and effective rights for individuals (Gutwirth, 2002).

However, privacy and personal data can be protected not only by legal means. A number of extra-legal "tools" – i.e. methodologies, best practices and standards, among others – have been developed to supplement the former. It all started with Privacy Enhancing Technologies (PETs) in early 1990s (van Blarkom et al., 2003), went through Privacy by Design (PbD) (cf. e.g. Cavoukian, 2013), Legal Protection by Design (Hildebrandt, 2013), and – most recently – included privacy impact assessments (PIAs) (De Hert et al., 2012; Wright & De Hert, 2012); this list is not exhaustive. These "privacy protection tools" are not meant to replace the legal means of protection discussed above, but rather to supplement and support them. However, they are slowly being integrated into legal systems and are acquiring the status of enforceable obligations for public authorities, organizations and corporations. For example, the pending EU data protection reform would introduce a duty to conduct a form of PIA in certain situations.[23]

2.5 PRIVACY TESTING AND DATA PROTECTION TESTING OF SMART GRIDS

Depending on the actual technical design, smart grids can have a profound negative impact on both the right to privacy and the right to personal data protection. Here the distinction between these two rights becomes crucial as it creates a double-test: all technologies should be first looked at from the angle of privacy. Then, and only if a technology survives the privacy testing, the test can be turn to personal data protection. Of course, this is a conceptualisation, but it responds to a gut feeling: first we need to decide what kind of technologies we do not want in our society, then we need to determine the rules that should be respected when using technologies that we want in our society. First the big question, then the fine-tuning.[24]

Speaking about privacy, this fundamental right offers probably the most broad protection of individual interests,[25] but is not an absolute one[26] – it could be legally interfered with, provided three conditions are cumulatively satisfied. As a result, one's privacy is limited, but such a limitation is considered lawful. (Or, broadly speaking, ethically and socially acceptable, as each legal system reflects axiological

---

[23]Cf. Art 33 of the General Data Protection Regulation (*supra*, note 22), introducing a data protection impact assessment (DPIA).
[24]Cf. in the context of regulating biometrics, e.g. De Hert, 2013, pp. 369–414; Gutwirth, 2007, pp. 61–65.
[25]Cf. *supra*, sec. 4.
[26]An example of absolute human right could be the prohibition of torture, i.e. under no circumstances a person can be tortured.

values of a given culture.) In the Strasbourg system, any limitation on the exercise of this right must be:

1. prescribed by law (criterion of legality),
2. necessary in democratic society (necessity) and proportionate to the legitimate aim pursued (proportionality), implying there is no alternative, less intrusive solution, and
3. serve at least one of the certain public interests: national security, public safety, economic well-being of the country, prevention of disorder or crime, protection of health or morals, and protection of the rights and freedoms of others (legitimacy).

While it is quite easy to enact the smart grids legal framework (i.e. to fulfil the first criterion), it is much more difficult to assess whether their interference with the right to privacy can be justified (i.e. necessity, proportionality and legitimacy). This begs a number of questions, such as (De Hert & Kloza, 2011, p. 194):

1. Do smart grids contribute to the economic well-being of the country?
2. Do they contribute to energy savings, energy efficiency, reduction of greenhouse gas emissions and a more competitive energy market?
3. Is such an interference proportionate to the aim pursued?
4. Are there any less invasive alternatives?
5. Is there a good "proportional" reason to send detailed metering data outside the consumer's home?
6. Why allowing third parties to look at metering data if smart grids are presented as predominantly consumer-friendly and consumer-serving?

Speaking about personal data protection, it spells out the conditions for the use of these data. The mere fact of processing them in smart grids makes the whole data protection legal framework applicable thereto. This framework regulates a wide range of activities performed on personal data: "collection, recording, organization, storage, adaptation or alteration, retrieval, consultation, use, disclosure by transmission, dissemination or otherwise making available, alignment or combination, blocking, erasure or destruction"[27] or, in other words – their "processing". The concept of personal data is very broad and encompasses "any information relating to an identified or identifiable natural person". An identifiable person is "one who can be identified, directly or indirectly, in particular by reference to an identification number or to one or more factors specific to his physical, physiological, mental, economic, cultural or social identity".[28]

Despite the data protection framework fully applies to smart grids and even though it solves a lot of problems, a number of open questions are left. These include, among others (De Hert & Kloza, 2011; Goel et al., 2015):

1. Who, among the various actors involved in an energy supply chain – i.e. generators, transmission system operators (TSOs), distribution system

---

[27]Art 2(b) of the 1995 Data Protection Directive.
[28]Art 2(a) of the 1995 Data Protection Directive.

operators (DSOs), market suppliers, metering operators and energy service entities – is a data *controller* and who is a data *processor*? The former determines the purposes and means of the processing and the latter processes personal data on behalf of the former. However, it is a sole responsibility of a *controller* to ensure full application of the data protection law as only she would be held accountable for that. The distinction between these two might be, however, blurred and so could be their accountability.

2. What information processed within smart grids constitute "personal data"? Undoubtedly, among the vast categories of information that such system processes, some information could be purely of a technical nature, i.e. certain information gathered from metering, generation, distribution or transmission, e.g. measured values like voltage. Yet other information would relate "to an identified or identifiable natural person", or – in other words – would constitute personal data. The latter category includes, *inter alia*, identification information of the customer and metering data necessary for billing. There is no exhaustive list of such personal categories of information, e.g. they can even include anonymised, pseudonymised or aggregated data if it is normally technically possible to track these data back to their source. The distinction between "technical" and personal data is furthermore not clear-cut, i.e. it depends on the actual configuration of a smart grid. Each time it needs to be checked whether a piece of information can be linked to an individual.

3. What is the relevant legal basis for the processing of personal data? While a free, explicit, written, prior and unambiguous consent seems to be the most preferred one, other legal bases could include: (a) negotiation and/ or performance of a contract to which an individual is party, (b) a legal obligation or (c) a legitimate interest of the controller (Knyrim & Trieb, 2011, pp. 121–128).[29]

4. What personal data can be collected and for exactly what purposes?

5. For which purpose and for how long personal data should be stored (retained)? E.g. information acquired from a smart meter interests energy chain companies for efficient network maintenance. Certain information must be retained in order to compute the energy bill. Sometimes customers could get a tax break (deduction) if they change their energy consumption patterns. Thus such information must be normally stored until the elapse of the statute of limitations, i.e. usually 3-5 years. Some third party companies might offer added value services, such as energy advice. Law enforcement agencies might be interested in access to records on energy consumption for investigation and crime prevention purposes. The state itself, as a regulator, might be interested in data retention for policy-making purposes. Each of these purposes would require separate consideration.

6. How an individual could exercise her rights (e.g. information, access and objection) as a data subject?

---

[29] Art 7 of the 1995 Data Protection Directive.

7. How to ensure security and confidentiality of personal data processing?

8. What means – other than legal – could be employed to ensure the effective protection of personal data? How should they be implemented?

2.6 REGULATING SMART GRIDS IN EUROPE: A "LIGHT" APPROACH TO PERSONAL DATA PROTECTION

2.6.1 SUPPLEMENTING THE LEGALLY BINDING DATA PROTECTION FRAMEWORK

The Dutch case gave the EU an impetus to look closely at the privacy and personal data protection challenges raised by smart grids and to appropriately address them. Since 2009, i.e. since the enactment of the Third Energy Package, these issues became a concern as equally as important as the cost-benefit analysis, technical specifications, cyber-security or environmental protection, among others.

As the EU is empowered to enact binding secondary laws solely in the field of personal data protection (and not in the field of privacy),[30] the Union opted for supplementing the existing binding data protection framework with a "light" regulatory approach to personal data protection. The 1995 Data Protection Directive proved to be sufficiently clear and satisfactory at a general level, but – in the context of smart grids – it required some tailoring down (De Hert & Kloza, 2011, p. 196). In other words, this "light" regulatory approach was meant to answer some of the open questions.[31]

In this context, the European Commission, the executive body (i.e. the government) of the EU, in 2009 established the Smart Grids Task Force, consisting of four experts groups and one of them was charged with providing regulatory recommendations for privacy, data protection and cyber-security in smart grid environment (EG2).[32] Based on the work of this Task Force, in 2012 the European Commission issued a recommendation on the roll out of smart grid and smart metering systems.[33]

The 2012 Recommendation addresses three main issues: (1) personal data protection, (2) cost-benefit analysis, and (3) common minimum functional requirements of smart meters. With regard to the first aspect, it clearly states the 1995 Data Protection Directive applies and clarifies its application to the nature and needs of smart grids (§§ 16, 18-29). It further suggests six "tools" for achieving an adequate level of personal data protection: data protection by default and by design (§§ 10-14), privacy certification (§ 15), Privacy Enhancing Technologies (PETs), in particular anonymisation and encryption; and Best Available Techniques (BATs) (§ 17).

---

[30]Art 16 of the Treaty on the Functioning of the European Union (TFEU).

[31]Cf. *supra*, sec.5.

[32]Cf. http://ec.europa.eu/energy/en/topics/markets-and-consumers/smart-grids-and-meters/smart-grids-task-force

[33]European Commission, *Recommendation of 9 March 2012 on preparations for the roll-out of smart metering systems*, 2012/148/EU, OJ L 73, 13.03.2012, pp. 9–22 (*hereinafter*: the 2012 Recommendation).

However, the most important tool seems to be a data protection impact assessment (DPIA) (§§ 4-9).

Although the 2012 Recommendation is the core of this "light" regulatory approach, it has been supplemented by a series of opinions, guidelines and studies. Subsequently the process of DPIA template development was concluded by another of the Commission's recommendation[34] (Fig. 2.2). All these *supplement* (not *replace*) the existing, legally binding personal data protection framework. At the end of the day, this complex approach is confusing and difficult to use in practice.

2.6.2 A DATA PROTECTION IMPACT ASSESSMENT FRAMEWORK IS THE CORE ELEMENT

2.6.2.1 The First Regulatory Experiment: The RFID PIA Framework

The choice of an impact assessment as a "tool" to support and supplement the legal means for the protection of privacy and personal data in smart grids predominantly builds on the hopes reposed in a similar impact assessment framework for radio-frequency identification (RFID) applications (2011).[35] For the sake of clarity, in 2009 the EU started its experiment with a "light" regulatory approach to address privacy and personal data protection problems in emerging surveillance solutions. The RFID was the first technology targeted.[36] A model was developed in which the European Commission issues a recommendation that suggests, *inter alia*, stakeholders to develop a privacy and/or data protection impact assessment framework to be subsequently sent for an opinion and/or endorsement by the Art 29 Working Party, the EU advisory body on personal data protection, and then to be widely used by the industry in the Member States.

The results of this first experiment are far from satisfactory: we have a nonbinding (a recommendation) and non-exhaustive (personal data protection only) normative instrument[37] – that at the end of the day – helps very little to protect these two rights and that almost no industry stakeholder follows.[38] Despite such results and the danger it creates for the protection of personal data, the EU has enthusiastically opted for analogous model for smart grids.

Yet the early enthusiasm for such an analogy cooled immediately. Spiekermann initially argued that "the RFID PIA is generic enough to be adaptable to other technologies of the Internet of Things. It can be taken as a starting point or even a blueprint for how to do privacy impact assessments generally" (Spiekermann, 2012,

---

[34]Cf. *infra*, note f.

[35]Privacy and Data Protection Impact Assessment Framework for RFID Applications, 12 January 2011.

[36]However, there is a vivid debate on whether personal data protection regulation should remain technology-neutral or not. Cf. e.g. Hildebrandt & Tielemans, 2013.

[37]A normative legal instrument contains norms and rules shaping behaviour, regardless if compulsory or not.

[38]Cf. *infra*, note 51.

				the binding framework
Council of Europe	Art 8 ECHR (privacy) Convention 108 + Additional Protocol 181 (data protection) ECtHR case law	*national constitutional systems*		
European Union	Art 7 CFR (privacy) Art 8 CFR & Art 16 TFEU (data protection) CJEU case law			
	1995 Data Protection Directive			
opinions	WP29 opinion on smart metering[a] EDPS opinion on 2012 Recommendation[b] ENISA opinions on cyber-security[c] 1st WP29 opinion on DPIA template[d] 2nd WP29 opinion on DPIA template[e]	**2012 Recommendation** *DPIA framework* *data protection by design* *data protection by default* *privacy certification* *Privacy Enhancing Technologies* *Best Available Techniques*	normative instruments	the EU "light" regulatory approach
studies	common functional requirements[g] cost-benefit analysis guidelines[h]	**2014 Recommendation**[f]		

FIGURE 2.2

Mapping the EU regulatory framework for personal data protection in smart grids.

Note:
[a]Art 29 Working Party, *Opinion 12/2011 on smart metering*, Brussels, 4 April 2011, 00671/11/EN, WP 183.
[b]European Data Protection Supervisor, *Opinion on the Commission Recommendation on preparations for the roll-out of smart metering systems*, Brussels, 8 June 2012.
[c]European Network and Information Security Agency (ENISA), *Smart Grid Security. Recommendations for Europe and Member States*, 1 July 2012; idem, *Appropriate security measures for smart grids. Guidelines to assess the sophistication of security measures implementation*, 6 December 2012.
[d]Art 29 Working Party, Opinion 04/2013 on the Data Protection Impact Assessment Template for Smart Grid and Smart Metering Systems ('DPIA Template') prepared by Expert Group 2 of the Commission's Smart Grid Task Force, Brussels, 22 April 2013, 00678/13/EN, WP205.
[e]Art 29 Working Party, *Opinion 07/2013 on the Data Protection Impact Assessment Template for Smart Grid and Smart Metering Systems ('DPIA Template') prepared by Expert Group 2 of the Commission's Smart Grid Task Force*, Brussels, 4 December 2013, 2064/13/EN, WP209.
[f]European Commission, *Recommendation of 10 October 2014 on the Data Protection Impact Assessment Template for Smart Grid and Smart Metering Systems*, 2014/724/EU, OJ L 300, 18.10.2014, pp. 63–68 (*hereinafter*: the 2014 Recommendation).
[g]European Commission, *A joint contribution of DG ENER and DG INFSO towards the Digital Agenda, Action 73: Set of common functional requirements of the smart meter*, Brussels, October 2011. http://ec.europa.eu/energy/gas_electricity/smartgrids/doc/2011_10_smart_meter_funtionalities_report_full.pdf
[h]European Commission, Joint Research Centre, Institute for Energy and Transport, *Guidelines for conducting a cost-benefit analysis of Smart Grid projects*, Report EUR 25246 EN, Petten 2012. http://ses.jrc.ec.europa.eu/sites/ses.jrc.ec.europa.eu/files/publications/guidelines_for_conducting_a_cost-benefit_analysis_of_smart_grid_projects.pdf; idem, *Guidelines for Cost Benefit Analysis of Smart Metering Deployment*, Report EUR 25103 EN, Petten 2012. http://ses.jrc.ec.europa.eu/sites/ses/files/documents/guidelines_for_cost_benefit_analysis_of_smart_metering_deployment.pdf

pp. 323–346). However, very soon the Art 29 Working Party observed that the risk approach used should thus be more specific to the (industrial) sector:

> *The DPIA Template lacks sector-specific content. Both the risks and the controls listed in the template are of generic nature and only occasionally contain industry-specific guidance – best practice that could be genuinely useful. In a nutshell: the risks and controls do not reflect industry experience on what the key concerns and best practices are.*[39]

Furthermore, a representative of the European Data Protection Supervisor's office, when referring to these technologies, stated that smart grids are *very different networks* from those implied in the RFID, since they deal with critical infrastructure and very big players, which is a different ball-game from having little chips in items in the supermarket. The differences between technologies, or rather, between technological networks or contexts of innovation, necessitate differences in assessment approaches and formats (van Dijk & Gunnarsdóttir, 2014, p. 35). "It is important to strike a balance between a generic assessment methodology vs. a technological sector-specific methodology. [...] Each assessment process should partly be tailored to the specificity of the technological network of concern" (van Dijk & Rommetveit, 2015, pp. 7-8). This thus requires the assessment method to be sufficiently flexible. Important criteria for taking account of network-specificity could include the number and size of actors, complexity and type of technology, amount of societal concerns connected as well as specific types of risk and control.

Despite these shortcomings, in general terms, impact assessments in the field of privacy are considered appropriate means to address contemporary challenges thereto, despite their novelty and relative immaturity.[40] Building on the positive experience of environmental impact assessments (EIAs), launched in 1960s, the growing interest in privacy impact assessments (PIA) started in mid-1990s and was caused by public distrust in emerging technologies in general, by the robust development of privacy-invasive tools, by a belated public reaction against the increasingly privacy-invasive actions of both public authorities and corporations, as well as by a natural development of rational techniques for managing different types of risks for and by organisations (Clarke, 2009, p. 124; Davies & Wolf-Phillips, 2006, p. 57; De Hert et al., 2012, p. 5). Furthermore, impact assessments have shifted the attention from reactive measures towards more anticipatory instruments, in the belief in the rationale of an "ounce of prevention" (Bennett & Raab, 2003, p. 204). However, they are flexible tools and much of their efficacy and efficiency depends on their actual implementation.

A PIA is usually defined as "a process for assessing the impacts on privacy of a project, policy, programme, service, product or other initiative and, in consultation

---

[39]Art 29 Working Party, *Opinion 04/2013 on the Data Protection Impact Assessment Template for Smart Grid and Smart Metering Systems ('DPIA Template') prepared by Expert Group 2 of the Commission's Smart Grid Task Force,* Brussels, 22 April 2013, 00678/13/EN, WP205, p. 8.
[40]For a brief overview of various types of impact assessments, cf. e.g. Clarke, 2014.

with stakeholders, for taking remedial actions as necessary in order to avoid or mi-nimise the negative impacts" (De Hert et al., 2012, p. 5). Wright advocates that PIA benefits can be:

> *[...] described as an early warning system. It provides a way to detect potential privacy problems, take precautions and build tailored safeguards before, not after, the organisation makes heavy investments. The costs of fixing a project (using the term in its widest sense) at the planning stage will be a fraction of those incurred later on. If the privacy impacts are unacceptable, the project may even have to be cancelled altogether. Thus, a PIA helps reduce costs in management time, legal expenses and potential media or public concern by considering privacy issues early. It helps an organisation to avoid costly or embarrassing privacy mistakes (Wright, 2012, p. 55).*

Opponents of PIA criticize it as an unnecessary cost, adding to the bureaucracy of decision-making and as something that will lead to delays in implementing a project. There is a risk that if a PIA policy were too burdensome for organizations, it would be performed perfunctorily, i.e. like a "tick-box" exercise, and it would thus be less effective than, e.g. audit practices carried out voluntarily (De Hert et al., 2012, p. 9).

2.6.2.2 The Second Regulatory Experiment: The DPIA Framework for Smart Grids and Smart Metering Systems

The second regulatory experiment started when the European Commission recom-mended stakeholders to develop a DPIA template to be subsequently sent for an opinion by the Art 29 Working Party. The mandate of EG2 was renewed and the group was charged with the development of the said template.[41] While the first ver-sion (April 2013) did not meet the Working Party's expectations,[42] the second one did (December 2013).[43] The template was officially made public in October 2014[44] and followed by a Commission's recommendation on the use thereof (the 2014 Rec-ommendation).[45]

In its introduction, the DPIA template presents an overview of the rationale, scope, benefits and success factors of the DPIA process (Fig. 2.3), and discusses the stakeholders that need to be involved in such a process. These include TSOs, DSOs, energy generators, energy market suppliers, metering operators, energy services or-ganisations as well as – to a certain extent – consumers (i.e. individuals). It suggests a particular risk management methodology, built on a relevant handbook issued by

---

[41]Cf. *supra*, sec. 6.1.

[42]Cf. *supra*, note d.

[43]Cf. *supra*, note e.

[44]Data Protection Impact Assessment Template for Smart Grid and Smart Metering systems, 18 March 2014. http://ec.europa.eu/energy/sites/ener/files/documents/2014_dpia_smart_grids_forces.pdf

[45]Cf. *supra*, note f.

the *Commission Nationale de l'Informatique et des Libertés* (CNIL), the French data protection authority (CNIL, 2012). However, it does not preclude the application of other methodologies. In its final part, the template offers a form that could be filled in while preparing the final report of the DPIA process, supplemented by a glossary, "privacy and data protection targets" and a list of possible controls.

In its main part, the template offers a detailed guidance on performing the DPIA, foreseeing the following steps:

Step 1 – Pre-assessment and criteria determining the need to conduct a DPIA
    Criterion 1: Processing of personal data
    Criterion 2: Classification of data controllers and data processors
    Criterion 3: Impacts on rights and freedoms
    Criterion 4: Timing and motivation to perform a DPIA
    Criterion 5: The nature of the system/application
    Criterion 6: Legal basis and public concerns
    [other]

Step 2 – Initiation
    The DPIA team
    Resources needed

Step 3 – Identification, characterisation and description of Smart Grid systems / applications processing personal data
    The use case
    System information
    Description of primary and supporting assets of the system

Step 4 – Identification of relevant risks
    Threats identification for each feared event

Step 5 – Data protection risk assessment
    Impact of feared events
    Likelihood of threats
    Final risk level/value priority

Step 6 – Identification and recommendation of controls and residual risks
    Assessment of implemented and planned controls
    Risk treatment
    Residual risks and risks acceptance
    Resolution

Step 7 – Documentation and drafting of the DPIA report

Step 8 – Reviewing and maintenance

FIGURE 2.3

The DPIA process for smart grid and smart metering systems (Cf. *supra*, note f).

As mentioned earlier, the publication of the DPIA template was complemented by the 2014 Recommendation,[46] specifically addressing how to use this template and what steps would be taken to evaluate it. This recommendation invites the EU Member States to encourage data controllers to apply the DPIA template (§ 3), to stimulate and support its dissemination and use (§ 4), to complement its application with Best Available Techniques (BATs) (§ 5) and to consult national data protection authorities (DPAs) on DPIA, prior to the commencement of personal data processing (§ 7). It next introduces a test phase in which the efficiency and efficacy of the current DPIA template will be evaluated (§§ 9-13).[47] It further introduces a public inventory of DPIAs actually conducted (§ 14). The Recommendation concludes by a revision clause (§§ 15-17).

2.7 THE EU "LIGHT" REGULATORY APPROACH TO PERSONAL DATA PROTECTION IN SMART GRIDS: AN EVALUATION

As smart grids are a surveillance tool, such a threat needs to be appropriately addressed. The EU has focused on personal data protection and opted, in the first place, for legal means, supplementing the generally applicable legal framework that is already in place by a "light" regulatory approach.

However, we question the appropriateness of such a move for the following reasons.

1. **Not only law regulates**

   The EU has chosen *legal* means to address the question of protecting personal data in smart grids. To this end, it has supplemented the legally binding data protection laws (hard law), already in place, by a set of non-binding recommendations, guidelines and opinions (soft law) (Fig. 2.2). However, not only law regulates.

   There is a wide repertoire of tools and techniques that are used in regulating social behaviour (Morgan & Yeung, 2007, p. 79). Based upon the "modality" of control primarily in operation,[48] Lessig's influential "pathetic dot theory" distinguishes four constraints that regulate human behaviour: law, market, social norms and architecture (code) (Lessig, 2006, pp. 121–125). Acknowledging that no scheme of classification is watertight, Morgan and Yeung more or less agree with Lessig, but they differentiate five methods of regulation: command and control, competition and economic instruments, consensus, communication and techno-regulation (code) (Morgan & Yeung, 2007, pp. 79–149) (Fig. 2.4). Each of these "modalities" can influence each other, each of them produces the best effects in different contexts, and each of them has their own advantages and disadvantages.

---

[46]Cf. *supra*, note f.

[47]The two-year test phase started in March 2015. Cf. https://ec.europa.eu/energy/en/test-phase-data-protection-impact-assessment-dpia-template-smart-grid-and-smart-metering-systems

[48]This does not preclude the fact that frequently these "modalities" are *introduced* by legal means.

Morgan & Yeung			Lessig
command & control	hard law	lex perfecta lex plus quam perfecta lex minus quam perfecta lex imperfecta	law
consensus	soft law	templates self-regulation co-regulation codes of conduct	
economic instruments & competition		charges taxes subsidies emission trades	market
communication		naming & shaming naming & faming guidelines methodologies	
techno-regulation		architecture computer software	architecture (code)
			social norms

FIGURE 2.4

Mapping regulatory techniques. In grey highlighted have been instruments chosen to regulate personal data protection in smart grids in the EU.

It needs to be emphasized, however, that regulation is primarily a concept of a political, not of a legal nature as it enables the completion of a well-defined political agenda (Gutwirth et al., 2008, pp. 193–194). In Lessig's model, regulatory goals are achieved by choosing an "optimal mix" from this repertoire of "modalities". But such a choice will always raise political questions of efficiency and legitimacy (Morgan & Yeung, 2007, p. 80), as well as the danger of instrumentalisation of these "modalities", in particular of the law, which risks becoming a "servant of politics" (cf. de Vries & van Dijk, 2013; Gutwirth et al., 2008, pp. 193–218).

Within the legal domain, many authors have put into question the efficiency of existing mechanisms in addressing the challenges to the protection of personal data in the digital era. Having questioned the specific laws currently in place, some suggest looking at other branches of law, such as environmental law, for inspiration (cf. e.g. Hirsch, 2006; Kloza, 2013; van Dijk et al., 2015). Others suggest "privacy protection tools", such as PETs or certification schemes.[49] Those are good steps, but more is needed. Thus far, not much attention has been paid to means that lie outside the legal domain, with a view to achieve more efficient protection of personal data. One can think, e.g. of corporate transparency with a strong focus on data protection issues (i.e. "naming and faming" or "naming or shaming") (De Hert & Kloza, 2014), funding agencies requiring an impact

---

[49]Cf. *supra*, sec. 5.

assessment report before subsidies could be obtained (cf. Wright, 2011, p. 127) or even tax exemptions, subsidies or other financial inventiveness for those who pioneer in the observance of personal data protection.

When it comes to addressing smart grids challenges in the EU, it seems that possibilities other than law to address this very problem have not been explored nor used. Therefore, attention should be given to the choice and combination of other means that could regulate behaviour. This will have to be done by careful consideration of the constraints of the different practices in which these "regulators" of behaviour are brought about.

2. **Focusing solely on personal data protection is not enough**
Smart grids are a complex and highly invasive surveillance solution that touches upon many societal values.[50] Ethical principles, and among them personal data protection, are only a fistful of them. Therefore, it is difficult if not impossible to properly address all societal challenges raised by smart grids by focusing *solely* on personal data protection. A DPIA framework is good only for data protection problems; nothing less, nothing more.

When it comes to surveillance technologies, Raab and Wright have already observed the limits of a classical impact assessment focusing solely on personal data protection (information privacy). They have argued that "its nearly exclusive focus on privacy" neglects "a range of other individual and societal values, rights or freedoms that may be impacted by surveillance" (Raab & Wright, 2012, p. 378; cf. also Wright & Raab, 2012). Furthermore, policy-makers promoting a DPIA framework as a sole and ultimate solution to the problem at stake convey a wrong message to the industry, and to the society at large, that the framework is a magical tool solving all problems. This way, a few steps back in the level of protection are taken.

Therefore, we would have liked to see a *holistic* and *systematic* solution, acknowledging the social complexity of the problem at stake. Speaking more concretely, a methodology for assessing smart grids against a wide variety of societal concerns should have been put in place. An initiative to develop a framework for assessing their impacts on personal data protection is only a first good step.

3. **A "light" regulatory approach will not solve the problem**
Even assuming (dangerously) that a DPIA framework were an adequate solution to the problem at stake, the said framework, as of now, is of a voluntary nature (i.e. soft law). Being lawyers, we tend to believe that if something were not compulsory, it would never happen. (Imagine the consequences of a criminal code being voluntary: you are brought to justice only if you want it.) This is particularly valid for big industry that is confronted with societal values such as personal data protection. Bayley and Bennett rightly have once observed that "the likelihood of PIAs being conducted is related to the degree of policy compulsion to conduct them and to accountability for their completion" (2012,

---

[50]Cf. *supra*, sec. 3.

p. 182). The experience of the EU RFID PIA framework only confirms that a handful of PIAs have been made since its introduction in 2009 and we see no much chance of changing it.[51]

Therefore, we would have liked to see certain elements of this regulatory framework being compulsory, i.e. to have been introduced by hard law with sanctions for non-compliance. At the end of the day, we have a fundamental right at stake that concerns the protection of the most privacy-sensitive place, the home (Cuijpers & Koops, 2013, p. 269).

There is a hope with the EU reform of its data protection framework. The new General Data Protection Regulation, expected to enter into force in 2017, would introduce a compulsory DPIA in certain situations.[52] The new law would provide for just a "legal hook" for an impact assessment, but further specifications would be dealt with later on.[53] This might remedy this particular problem, but it should have been devised earlier. Further change will be brought about by the evaluation and revision clauses in the 2014 Recommendation.

4. Shortcomings in the regulatory process

A number of issues concerning the regulatory process deserve some attention. First, the whole process of the development of the smart grids DPIA template did not meet transparency conditions, necessary in a democratic society. The work was carried out behind closed doors, the stakeholders selected arguably did not meet the criteria of representativeness and there were no public consultations of the draft template.

Second, in the first regulatory experiment, the European Commission recommended that the EU RFID PIA framework be sent to the Art 29 Working Group for an "endorsement". However, the first draft thereof was stunningly rejected and – willing to avoid the history repeating itself – for the smart grids counterpart, the Commission recommended the DPIA template to be sent just for an "opinion". This did not prevent the Art 29 Working Party to spectacularly reject the first draft too. The second draft was accepted, although we have our own reservations towards this piece of work of the Working Party. Furthermore, the 2012 Recommendation did not foresee any evaluation nor follow up, but this was rectified in the 2014 Recommendation. All these pertain to a conclusion that the process was not democratic enough and did not fulfil criteria of a good law making process.

Third, the pending reform of the EU data protection framework seems not to have been taken into consideration, despite the fact it started, more or less, in parallel with the work on the DPIA template. It is true that the outcome of the

---

[51]Cf. European Commission, *Implementation of the Recommendations on Privacy and Data Protection issues in Applications supported by RFID – Monitoring study. Final Report,* N 30-CE-0206743/00-33 Lot 4, Brussels, 21 December 2012 (unpublished); French National RFID Center, Convergent Software Ltd, *RFID Privacy Impact Assessment Software,* 2014. http://rfid-pia-en16571.eu
[52]Art 33 of the General Data Protection Regulation (*supra*, note 22).
[53]Marie-Hélène Boulanger, intervention at the seminar: *Implementation of the RFID Privacy Impact Assessment (PIA) Framework. Towards a coherent European Approach*, Brussels, 8 February 2012.

reform is difficult to predict at the time of writing (March 2015), however, it is clear that new law would pay special attention to the use of impact assessments. For the sake of legal certainty, it would provide specific conditions for their conduct. In particular, the proposed law gives voice to the stakeholders in the DPIA process, a thing that is deliberately neglected in the DPIA template. In our opinion, for the sake of the higher level of protection as well as for simple efficiency, the text of the proposed reform and the surrounding debate should have guided the development of the DPIA template.

Fourth, the patchwork of regulatory instruments that constitutes this "light" regulatory approach, itself supplementing the legally binding framework, is too complicated (cf. Fig. 2.2). From the industry viewpoint, the very need for most organisations is the availability of practical and pragmatic tools to conduct an impact assessment, which do not require a long introduction (De Hert et al., 2012, p. 9).

Finally, the DPIA template is full of terminology errors and editorial mistakes. A few examples: first, it confuses "privacy" with "data protection", often using the former to refer to the latter. Second, "industrial consumer" does not exist – a consumer could be only a natural person (cf. p. 11).[54] Third, there are flaws in the referencing system. It shall suffice to say that the 1995 Data Protection Directive is cited in many different ways, including even a simple link to the official Eur-Lex database (cf. e.g. footnote no. 14). At the end of the day, nobody took the trouble to copy-edit the template professionally – it is just a Microsoft Word document, using the simplest styles.

5. **The DPIA template focuses on the industry and neglects the consumer**
Any smart grids technology could constitute a severe invasion into the privacy of a household, understood broadly. Therefore, given the societal impacts as well as societal importance of smart grids, it would have been expected that the primary focus of a DPIA framework would be on protecting the interests of the individual in the first place. Economic benefits of particular societal groups (e.g. industry) cannot take precedence over concerns such as the most fundamental rights or safety and security of the society at large. The Dutch experience has already shown that "smart metering is up for failure when the technical and commercial aspects are considered to be more important than the interests of the end users" (Hoenkamp et al., 2011, p. 269).

The first draft of the DPIA framework focused its analysis on the interests of the industry, only indirectly affecting an individual. This has been heavily criticised by the Art 29 Working Party and was remedied in the second draft, by adding Section 3.4.1.4 ("Threats that might jeopardise personal data"; even

---

[54]Consumer "means any *natural* person who […] is acting for purposes which are outside his trade, business, craft or profession"; emphasis added. Cf. Art 2(1) of the Directive 2011/83/EU of the European Parliament and of the Council of 25 October 2011 on consumer rights, amending Council Directive 93/13/EEC and Directive 1999/44/EC of the European Parliament and of the Council and repealing Council Directive 85/577/EEC and Directive 97/7/EC of the European Parliament and of the Council, OJ L 304, 22.11.2011, pp. 64–88.

though listing those threats non-exhaustively). It, however, still shows the tendency.

Furthermore, the template – in its final version – explicitly states that the "role of the consumer is rather passive" (p. 11) during the assessment process, naturally adding in the same vein that the "consumer is of course no beneficiary of DPIA" (p. 10). If one looks at the steps of a foreseen DPIA process, there is no "stakeholder involvement".

This abandonment of consumers can be easily explained. Organisations would like to rely only on the expert's knowledge in risk management, and they do not expect added value from the involvement of laymen's wisdom. From this point of view, the whole stakeholders engagement usually only causes delays and costs (i.e. time, money, manpower). Furthermore, organisations do not want to risk revealing any commercially sensitive information that becomes explicit during these assessment processes, given that no proper public consultation can be made "if not all the cards are on the table" (De Hert, 2012, p. 75).

In a canonical model of risk management, a stakeholder, including an individual, is at the core of the whole assessment process. This is no different when it comes to an impact assessment. She should be identified, informed about the project under assessment, her views should be sought and subsequently duly taken into consideration (De Hert et al., 2012, p. 15). One could ask a question why? First, from a broader viewpoint, individual participation in decision-making lies at the core of the democratic society (Kloza, 2013, pp. 123–126). In particular, from the deliberative democracy viewpoint, the idea of legitimate decision-making issues from the public deliberations of citizens and not merely from elections (Bohman & Rehg, 1997, p. ix). It is a way to supplement traditional forms of democracy by advocating for the involvement of citizens in decision-making in ways other than electoral (Tanasescu, 2009, p. 15).

Second, Hildebrandt highlights the place of science in democracy:

Taking democracy serious means that the scientists and engineers that produce hybrids like RFID systems, genetic tests or technologically enhanced soldiers should be obligated to present their case to the public that is composed of those that will suffer or enjoy the consequences. ... When funding and developing specific technologies these publics should have the opportunity to voice their opinion, co-determining the direction of research as well as the introduction of such artifacts into everyday life infrastructures. Different types of technology assessment (TA) have been developed to involve lay persons into the early stages of technological design ... often entailing citizen participation (Hildebrandt, 2008).

Third, there is a strong business case for public participation, as it constitutes an integral element of corporate responsibility. A company should be aware of, and responsive to, the demands of its stakeholders, including employees, customers, suppliers and local communities (Blowfield & Murray, 2011, p. 207). By engaging stakeholders a company can reduce costs, gain public trust and support, avoid activism and escape negative public reaction or loss of reputation, among others.

The fourth and the last argument links the previous three: public participation contributes to informed decision-making with a view to improve its quality. In particular, engaging stakeholders helps to discover risks and impacts that might not otherwise be considered. It is a way to gather fresh input on the perceptions of the severity of risks and on possible measures to mitigate them (Wright, 2012, p. 58). In complex and uncertain situations, it can overcome the incompleteness of scientific knowledge as the management of risks cannot solely be based upon technical knowledge.[55] In other words, the public may have information, ideas, views or values that had not been previously considered or had been regarded as relatively minor (Wright, 2012, p. 58). The public may also be able to suggest alternative courses of action to achieve the desired objectives or may have some suggestions for resolving complex issues (Wright & Mordini, 2012, p. 397).

The 2012 Recommendation explicitly states that a DPIA should contain "an assessment of the risks to the rights and freedoms of data subjects […], taking into account the rights and legitimate interests of data subjects and persons concerned". It is a suggestion to balance the legitimate needs of various stakeholders, but such a balancing cannot be properly conducted without engaging those who could be directly or indirectly affected by an envisaged project. The DPIA framework ignores this condition and thus it can be said to be inconsistent even with the 2012 Recommendation on which it is based.

6. **Here "privacy" is understood in terms of risk assessment, without explaining how to make sense of "privacy risks"**
   It could well be argued that the DPIA template shifts the conception of privacy and data protection towards more narrow conceptions taken from computer security. The whole DPIA methodology has too quickly become based on a probabilistic risk assessment methodology, without reflecting on the consequences of doing this. One immediate effect is that of the bypassing of legal practice.

   This becomes apparent in the DPIA template that, for instance, speaks about a "data protection risk assessment" (Fig. 2.5) in which the concept of privacy has become incorporated into a risk management approach as a new source of risk, called "privacy risks". In order to determine these risks, three types of "data protection threats" will have to be identified: confidentiality, integrity and availability of the data. This grouping is based on information security

---

[55]This follows the logic of the precautionary principle, well established in environmental law. According to the 15th principle of the 1992 Rio Declaration: "where there are threats of serious or irreversible damage, lack of full scientific certainty shall not be used as a reason for postponing cost-effective measures to prevent environmental degradation." Cf. United Nations, *Rio Declaration on Environment and Development*, Rio de Janeiro, 3-14 June 1992; http://www.un.org/documents/ga/conf151/aconf15126-1annex1.htm; also e.g. Wright, Gellert, Gutwirth, & Friedewald, 2011.

3.5. Step 5 - Data Protection Risk Assessment

Level of identification + prejudicial effects	Severity/impact
< 5	1. Negligible
= 5	2. Limited
= 6	3. Significant
> 6	4. Maximum

Supporting asset vulnerabilities + risk source capabilities	likelihood
< 5	1. Negligible
= 5	2. Limited
= 6	3. Significant
> 6	4. Maximum

Feared events	Threat ID	Related Privacy targets	Affected assets	Impact	Likelihood	Risk Level
Feared event 1						
Feared event 2						
Feared event 3						

FIGURE 2.5

Step 5 – Data Protection Risk Assessment – of the DPIA template for smart grids.

vocabulary and has little to do with data protection in the legal sense, apart from the case, of course, where data protection law refers to data security.[56]

As a subsequent methodological step, the likelihood of the occurrence of these threats and the severity of the harm or impact on the individual will have to be calculated in probabilistic terms in order to determine the risk level (Fig. 2.5). Very little guidance is provided as to quantification and calculation of such probabilities, especially as they relate to broad qualitative concepts as "the identity and privacy of data subjects and human rights and liberties" (p. 27). These issues might well be side effects of too unreflectively basing the whole DPIA process on this security risk assessment methodology.

Moreover, barely any discussion or reflection has taken place on the consequences of uniting the vocabularies of rights and risks in this new

---

[56]Cf. Art 17 of the 1995 Data Protection Directive, Art 30 of the General Data Protection Regulation, *supra*, note 22; cf. sections 3.4.1 ff of the DPIA template.

notion of assessing the "risks to the rights" of individuals. This is all the more remarkable, considering that both concepts originate in very different domains of law and risk management with very different meanings. When we want to take seriously the notion of *privacy* risk, these DPIA approaches would benefit greatly from the lessons drawn from legal practices in dealing with concepts like "procedure", "risk", "probability" and "harm" (van Dijk et al., 2015).

7. **Risk management and legal compliance checks are not the same things, yet they overlap**

The risk management approach to DPIAs can be seen as a reaction against the original way of doing a PIA, like the PIA framework for RFID technologies, or guidance documents in Canada, New Zealand or Australia (cf. Clarke, 2009, pp. 123–135). These approaches consisted of a legal compliance check, to ensure that one is okay with the data protection principles in a given jurisdiction. This approach was criticized for not being sufficiently methodologically sound and for merely consisting of a tick-box exercise. Risk management was proposed as a solution for these problems.[57] As it was argued in the section above, this approach might have well moved too rashly and unreflectively away from legal issues in its search for a solid methodological framework, by too eagerly framing all the issues at stake in terms of the vocabularies of risk and security.

A more equilibrated approach might thus be required. Possible solutions would be to either treat risk assessment and legal compliance as separate exercises that both need to be performed subsequent (or in parallel) to each other, or to integrate both exercises in one process. In the latter case there should be more eye for legal detail, for instance, by adding a column to the DPIA template to specify which expertise should minimally be required for dealing with which questions. Otherwise the legal dimensions personal data protection run the risk of being subsumed in the risk and security framework as in the present DPIA models and templates.

What will also have to be explored is a third way that more explicitly relates these two positions to each other and addresses some of the problems mentioned above. This third way can be summarized in the possibility of taking the "DPIA as a court for upstream adjudication" (van Dijk et al., 2015). The idea here is of using lessons and characteristics taken from fair trial procedures in a court of law as a way to structure DPIA processes. From this perspective, the steps of assessing risks and checking for legal compliance could then be related to each other in the way that questions of fact are connected with questions of law in court proceedings, where they are worked out in constant interaction with each other.[58] Within such proceedings, both risk experts and legal experts are thus assigned their respective roles and interactions. Furthermore, due legal process also assigns a crucial role for the participation of the parties who will be

---

[57]Cf. *supra*, note 39.
[58]Here a legal compliance check would fit in as a first step, although legal qualification comprises more than a mere checklist.

affected by these data processing technologies – the individuals – according to the principles of fair trial. This approach thus integrates the approaches of legal compliance (legal qualification) and risk assessment (factual proof) into the framework of due legal process with stakeholders participation.

2.8 CONCLUSION: DPIA TESTING IS A FIRST GOOD STEP BUT A MORE INCLUSIVE, EASY TO APPLY AND FLEXIBLE SOLUTION IS NECESSARY

2.8.1 A MISSED OPPORTUNITY?

Smart grids constitute a socially complex phenomenon that is difficult to regulate. They raise a range of issues, from environmental concerns to the problem of abusive surveillance. With regard to the latter, to which we limit our chapter, the Dutch case demonstrates that, in order to achieve a successful roll-out of smart grids, relevant privacy and personal data protection concerns must be duly taken into consideration; this should be achieved in a dialogue with society at large and as early as possible. This lesson, to some extent, has influenced EU policy-making, in which the existing, binding data protection framework was supplemented by a "light" regulatory approach.

Section 7 of this chapter has provided a critical discussion of this EU "light" regulatory approach. Should it then be considered a missed opportunity? We would answer "yes". First and foremost, although this approach has answered some of the open questions about personal data protection,[59] from a broader perspective, the sole focus on a single, fundamental right is not sufficient to adequately address the social complexity of smart grids. Put simply, there is a number of other concerns that need to be tackled as well. Personal data protection is a catchy notion and it is too bad that it drew all of the attention of the European regulator.[60] Second, despite addressing some of the consequences of a surveillance tool, this "light" regulatory approach lacks compulsion (i.e. it is based on a non-binding recommendation), which would be normally required, to a reasonable extent, when the stakes are that high. Technically speaking, the whole patchwork of recommendations, opinions, studies and guidelines – already built upon a legally binding framework – is rather difficult to navigate and use. Modalities of regulation other than law were not taken into consideration. Eventually, the core element of this approach, i.e. the data protection impact assessment (DPIA) framework, developed behind closed doors, contains some serious methodological flaws. These predominantly concern: neglecting the interests and the voice of the individuals in the assessment process, being based upon

---

[59]Cf. *supra*, sec. 5.

[60]We acknowledge, however, that other means *do* regulate certain other aspects of smart grids, thus solving some of the societal concerns that this technology poses. For example, environmental law does provide for an environmental impact assessment (EIA) to be conducted for certain elements of smart grids. Cf. Council Directive 85/337/EEC of 27 June 1985 on the assessment of the effects of certain public and private projects on the environment, OJ L 175, 05.07.1985, pp. 40–48 (as amended).

a precipitated risk management methodology that does not take into account the legal complexities involved in assessing "privacy risks" as well as linking risk management with legal compliance check.

These reflections on the EU DPIA framework for smart grids can also be used for drawing up lessons for the assessment and governance of emerging technologies in general. Therefore, we conclude this chapter with two more general recommendations.

2.8.2 RECOMMENDATION 1: THE GOVERNANCE OF EMERGING TECHNOLOGIES SHOULD CAREFULLY COMBINE REGULATORY STRATEGIES

From a technical viewpoint, the governance of emerging technologies should *also* employ means of regulation outside the legal domain, that is – in Lessig's classification – market, social norms and architecture (code). Despite law playing here a vocal role, a *careful* combination of regulatory modalities, which takes due account of the specific way of working of each of these, can produce better effects than employing just one of them. For example, the very obligation to conduct a certain type of impact assessment in some situations in a particular manner could (and, in most situations, would) be introduced by law. However, there are plenty of other regulatory methods to ensure a wide application of such assessments (as discussed in Section 7.1).

Furthermore, speaking about impact assessments for emerging technologies, much of their success would depend on a continuous interaction between assessors and relevant public authorities. This is "communication" in Morgan and Yeung's terms (cf. Fig. 2.4). These authorities should promote and facilitate impact assessments by providing expertise, guidance and advice as well as – possibly – by reviewing and providing feedback on (selected) impact assessments that have been actually carried out (cf. De Hert et al., 2012, pp. 21–22). Data controllers should be incentivised and guided to tailor the assessment process to the specificity of the technological field at stake.

2.8.3 RECOMMENDATION 2: IMPACT ASSESSMENTS OF EMERGING TECHNOLOGIES SHOULD BE INCLUSIVE, EASY TO USE AND FLEXIBLE

The choice of an impact assessment as such as a means to evaluate societal challenges of emerging technologies seems to be an appropriate one and a tool such as a DPIA framework is a first good step. However, we would have liked to see a carefully designed, *inclusive* solution that systematically attempts to address – in cooperation with stakeholders – as many of these challenges as possible. Such a solution should remain *easy* to use, i.e. an efficient method that does not create too much trouble nor costs (time, money, manpower) for all the actors involved, and *flexible*, i.e. giving an option to adjust the framework to the particular needs of a given emerging technology and to integrate with other types of impact assessments or risk management areas, if necessary.

This inclusivity ensures – first and foremost – the *completeness* of the process, both in terms of societal concerns assessed and of stakeholders involved. It further increases the democratic legitimacy, corporate responsibility and the robustness of decision-making quality of technology development. Second, best results are guaranteed only with a sufficiently flexible method, fitting to the needs of a particular emerging technology, sponsors thereof and stakeholders concerned. In other words, no one-size-fits-all. Such flexibility further allows to strike a balance between generic assessment principles and the specifics of the technological network in question. Lastly, the easier an impact assessment method is to apply, the more eagerly and widely it would be followed.

The "toolbox" of available impact assessments can suggest at least two relevant impact assessment types that better satisfy the condition of inclusiveness. One of them could be a *societal impact assessment* (SIA). This methodology is defined as "the evaluation of the intended and unintended risks, externalities and consequences of technologies, policies, programs, and systems. Impacts can be project specific ones relating to costs or staffing, but the emphasis on *societal* brings in issues such as way of life, political systems, the environment, health, disability, rights, and more. As a result, a SIA is a means of accounting for a wide range of concerns and stakeholders" (Galdon Clavell, 2014, p. 2). The SIA approach relies on a four-part conceptual framework composed of *desirability*, *acceptability*, *ethics*, and *data management*. These categories capture key concepts that are necessary for assessment of emerging technologies (Galdon Clavell, 2014, p. 3).

Another option would be a *technology assessment* (TA). It is a scientific, interactive, and communicative process that aims to contribute to the formation of public and political opinion on societal aspects of science and technology (van Est & Brom, 2012, p. 306).

> TA has to deliver (as comprehensively and unbiased as possible) information on the technological and scientific aspects of the issue that is at stake (e.g. features of technology, results/or problems of scientific risk assessment, economic costs, eco-balances, etc.). A description of the problem or issue at stake would be incomprehensible without describing the societal aspects: TA has to deliver knowledge about relevant actors (their interests, values etc.) and possible social conflicts that can evolve around the technology under consideration. On the grounds of a proper description of the scientific and technological aspects and in connection with a description of the social environment (debate, actors), TA has to analyse the policy aspects of the problem; i.e. has to consider the restrictions and opportunities of policy making and has to develop policy options, such as exploring politically viable ways for problem solving (legislation, R&D funding, action plans). At the end, it has to again evaluate policy options with regard to possible side-effects (e.g. social conflicts) they might produce (TAMI Project, 2004, p. 60).

These two tools, obviously, do not exhaust the whole catalogue of impact assessment types that are inclusive, both with regard to societal concerns assessed and participating stakeholders. The selection available is even bigger when we think that these tools come with various methodologies, each with its own advantages and disadvantages. Yet, at the end of the day, the particular type, name or methodology of an impact assessment does not matter that much as long as it satisfies the quality criteria vested thereupon.

On a more concrete level, a few lessons for a good impact assessment framework can be drawn from two regulatory experiments – the RFID PIA framework and the smart grids DPIA template. It should be tailored to each specific field of emerging technologies (i.e. it should be sector-specific), has to be created in a democratic, transparent and participatory manner, has to reflect the state-of-the-art in the field, must pay due attention to safeguarding – in the first place – individual interests, and must give voice to the society at large. Its scope should reflect the societal challenges of the emerging technology under scrutiny; in most cases, it will be always more than just personal data protection. Such impact assessment would bring fruit only when it is widely applied and therefore lawyers here usually think about some form and level of compulsion.[61] Last but not least, such an assessment requires the use of an appropriate risk management methodology, which is separate from legal compliance checks, but interacts therewith, and takes into account lessons from legal practices in dealing with the relevant concepts used for assessing societal impacts.

ACRONYMS

AMI	advanced measuring instrument
BAT	Best Available Techniques
CFR	Charter of Fundamental Rights (of the European Union)
CJEU	Court of Justice of the European Union
CNIL	*Commission nationale de l'informatique et des libertés*
DPA	data protection authority
DPIA	data protection impact assessment
DSO	Distribution System Operator
ECHR	European Convention on Human Rights
ECtHR	European Court of Human Rights
EDPS	European Data Protection Supervisor
EIA	environmental impact assessment
ENISA	European Union Agency for Network and Information Security
EU	European Union
IA	impact assessment
JRC	Joint Research Centre [of the European Commission]
PbD	Privacy by Design
PETs	Privacy Enhancing Technologies
PIA	privacy impact assessment
R&D	research and development
RFID	Radio Frequency Identification
SIA	societal impact assessment
TA	technology assessment
TSO	Transmission System Operator
WP29	Art 29 Working Party

[61] Cf. however, *infra*, at 8.3.

REFERENCES

Achenbach, J. (2010). The 21st Century Grid. *National Geographic Magazine*, July. http://ngm.nationalgeographic.com/print/2010/07/power-grid/achenbach-text.

Anderson, R., & Fuloria, S. (2010). Who Controls the off Switch? *Smart Grid Communications (SmartGridComm), 2010 First IEEE International Conference on Smart Grid Communications.* doi:10.1109/SMARTGRID.2010.5622026.

Atwood, M. (2009). *Cat's Eye.* London: Little Brown Book Group.

Barringer, F. (2011). New Electricity Meters Stir Fears. *New York Times*, 31 January, p. A12. http://www.nytimes.com/2011/01/31/science/earth/31meters.html.

Bayley, R., & Bennett, C. (2012). Privacy impact assessments in Canada. In P. de Hert & D. Wright (Eds.), *Privacy impact assessment.* Dordrecht: Springer. doi:10.1007/978-94-007-2543-0.

Bennett, C., & Raab, C. D. (2003). *The governance of privacy: Policy instruments in global perspective.* Burlington: Ashgate Publishing.

Blowfield, M., & Murray, A. (2011). *Corporate responsibility.* Oxford: OUP.

Bohman, J., & Rehg, W. (1997). *Deliberative democracy: Essays on reason and politics.* Cambridge: MIT Press.

Bygrave, L. A. (2002). *Data protection law: Approaching its rationale, logic and limits.* The Hague, New York: Kluwer Law International.

Cavoukian, A. (2012). *Operationalizing privacy by design: A guide to implementing strong privacy practices.* Toronto: Information and Privacy Commissioner. https://www.privacybydesign.ca/content/uploads/2013/01/operationalizing-pbd-guide.pdf

Cavoukian, A. (2013). *Privacy by design.* Toronto: Information and Privacy Commissioner. http://www.ipc.on.ca/images/Resources/2009-06-23-TrustEconomics.pdf.

Cavoukian, A., Polonetsky, J., & Wolf, C. (2010). SmartPrivacy for the Smart Grid: embedding privacy into the design of electricity conservation. *Identity in the Information Society*, 3, 275–294.

Clarke, R. (2009). Privacy impact assessment: its origins and development. *Computer Law & Security Review*, 25(2), 123–135.

Clarke, R. (2014). *Approaches to impact assessment.* http://www.rogerclarke.com/SOS/IA-1401.pdf

Clastres, C. (2011). Smart grids: another step towards competition, energy security and climate change objectives. *Energy Policy*, 39, 5399–5408.

CNIL. (2012). *Methodology for privacy risk management. How to implement the Data Protection Act* (pp. 1-31). Paris: CNIL. http://www.cnil.fr/fileadmin/documents/en/CNIL-ManagingPrivacyRisks-Methodology.pdf.

Collingridge, D. (1980). *The social control of technology.* New York: St. Martin's Press.

Cornish, D. (2012). *The case against smart meters.* Wired.

Cuijpers, C., & Koops, B.-J. (2008). *The "smart meters" bill: a privacy test based on article 8 of the ECHR* (p. 39). http://www.consumentenbond.nl/morello-bestanden/pdf-algemeen-2008/onderzoek_UvT_slimme_energi1.pdf.

Cuijpers, C., & Koops, B.-J. (2013). Smart metering and privacy in Europe: lessons from the Dutch case. In S. Gutwirth, R. Leenes, P. De Hert, & Y. Poullet (Eds.), *European data protection: coming of age* (pp. 269–293). doi: 10.1007/978-94-007-5170-5_12.

Davies, K. G., & Wolf-Phillips, J. (2006). Scientific Citizenship and good governance: implications for biotechnology. *Trends in Biotechnology*, 24(2), 57–61.

De Hert, P. (2012). A human rights perspective on privacy and data protection impact assessments. In D. Wright, & P. De Hert (Eds.), *Privacy impact assessment* (pp. 33–76). Dordrecht: Springer.

De Hert, P. (2013). Biometrics and the challenge to human rights in Europe. Need for regulation and regulatory distinctions. In P. Campisi (Ed.), *Security and privacy in biometrics* (pp. 369–413). Dordrecht: Springer. doi:10.1007/978-1-4471-5230-9_15.

De Hert, P., & Gutwirth, S. (2009). Data protection in the Case Law of Strasbourg and Luxemburg: Constitutionalisation in Action. In S. Gutwirth, Y. Poullet, P. Hert, C. Terwangne, & S. Nouwt (Eds.), *Reinventing data protection?* (pp. 3–44). Dordrecht: Springer. doi:10.1007/978-1-4020-9498-9_1.

De Hert, P., & Kloza, D. (2011). The challenges to privacy and data protection posed by smart grids. In E. Schweighofer, & F. Kummer (Eds.), *Europäische Projektkultur als Beitrag zur Rationalisierung des Rechts. Tagungsband des 14. Internationalen Rechtsinformatik Symposions IRIS 2011* (pp. 191–196). Vienna: Osterreichische Computer Gesellschaft.

De Hert, P., & Kloza, D. (2014). Corporate transparency is crucial, but it must also become far more meaningful. *The PrivacySurgeon*. http://www.privacysurgeon.org/blog/incision/corporate-transparency-is-crucial-but-it-must-also-become-far-more-meaningful/

De Hert, P., Kloza, D., & Wright, D. (2012). *Recommendations for a privacy impact assessment framework for the European Union*. Brussels – London. http://piafproject.eu/ref/PIAF_D3_final.pdf.

De Hert, P., & Papakonstantinou, V. (2012). The proposed data protection regulation replacing Directive 95/46/EC: A sound system for the protection of individuals. *Computer Law & Security Review*, *28*(2), 130–142.

De Vries, K., & van Dijk, N. (2013). A bump in the road. Ruling out law from technology. In M. Hildebrandt, & J. Gaakeer (Eds.), *Human law and computer law: Comparative perspectives SE - 5, 25* (pp. 89–121). Dordrecht: Springer. doi:10.1007/978-94-007-6314-2_5.

Finn, R. L., & Wright, D. (2012). Unmanned aircraft systems: Surveillance, ethics and privacy in civil applications. *Computer Law & Security Review*, *28*(2), 184–194.

Finn, R. L., Wright, D., & Friedewald, M. (2013). Seven types of privacy. In S. Gutwirth, R. Leenes, P. de Hert, & Y. Poullet (Eds.), *European data protection: Coming of age* (pp. 3–32). Dordrecht: Springer. doi:10.1007/978-94-007-5170-5_1.

Galdon Clavell, G. (2014). *Methodology for the assessment of societal impacts in technology development* (p. 21). Bercelona (work in progress).

Gellert, R., & Gutwirth, S. (2013). The legal construction of privacy and data protection. *Computer Law & Security Review*, *29*(5), 522–530.

Goel, S., Hong, Y., Papakonstantinou, V., & Kloza, D. (2015). *Smart grid security*. Dordrecht: Springer. doi: 10.1007/978-1-4471-6663-4

González Fuster, G. (2014). *The emergence of personal data protection as a fundamental right of the EU*, Dordrecht: Springer. doi:10.1007/978-3-319-05023-2.

Gorman, S. (2009). Electricity grid in U.S. Penetrated by spies. *The Wall Street Journal*, http://www.wsj.com/articles/SB123914805204099085.

Greveler, U., Justus, B., & Loehr, D. (2012). Multimedia content identification through smart meter power usage profiles. http://www.nds.rub.de/media/nds/veroeffentlichungen/2012/07/24/ike2012.pdf.

Gutwirth, S. (2002). *Privacy and the information age*. Lanham: Rowman & Littlefield Publishers.

Gutwirth, S. (2007). Biometrics between opacity and transparency. *Annali dell'Istituto Superiore Di Sanita*, *43*, 61–65.

Gutwirth, S., & De Hert, P. (2006). Privacy, data protection and law enforcement. Opacity of the individual and transparency of power. In E., Claes, A., Duff, S., Gutwirth, (Eds.), *Privacy and the criminal law* (pp. 61-104). http://works.bepress.com/serge_gutwirth/5/.

Gutwirth, S., De Hert, P., & De Sutter, L. (2008). The trouble with technology regulation from a legal perspective. Why Lessig's "optimal mix" will not work. In R. Brownsword, & K. Yeung (Eds.), *Regulating technologies* (pp. 193–218). Oxford: Hart Publishers.

Hildebrandt, M. (2008). Legal and technological normativity: more (and less) than twin sisters. *Techné*, *12*(3).

Hildebrandt, M. (2013). Smart energy collective. Legal protection by design in the smart grid. *Privacy, data protection & profile transparency*, http://works.bepress.com/mireille_hildebrandt/42/.

Hildebrandt, M., & Tielemans, L. (2013). Data protection by design and technology neutral law. *Computer Law and Security Review*, *29*(5), 509–521.

Hirsch, D. D. (2006). Protecting the inner environment: What privacy regulation can learn from environmental law. *Georgia Law Review*, *41*(1), 1–63.

Hoenkamp, R., Huitema, G. B., & de Moor-van Vugt, A. J. C. (2011). The neglected consumer: The case of the smart meter rollout in the Netherlands. *Renewable Energy Law and Policy (RELP)*, *4*, 269–282.

Information and Privacy Commissioner of Ontario. (2011). *Operationalizing privacy by design: The Ontario smart grid case study*. https://www.ipc.on.ca/images/Resources/pbd-ont-smartgrid-casestudy.pdf

Kloza, D. (2013). Public voice in privacy governance: Lessons from environmental democracy. In E., Schweighofer, A., Saarenpää, & J., Böszörmenyi, (Eds.), *KnowRights 2012 Proceedings* (pp. 80–97). Vienna: Osterreichische Computer Gesellschaft.

Knyrim, R., & Trieb, G. (2011). Smart metering under EU data protection law. *International Data Privacy Law*, *1*(2), 121–128.

Kokott, J., & Sobotta, C. (2013). The distinction between privacy and data protection in the jurisprudence of the CJEU and the ECtHR. *International Data Privacy Law*, *3*(4), 222–228.

Kuner, C. (2012). The European Commission's proposed data protection regulation: A Copernican Revolution in European Data Protection Law. *Privacy and Security Law Report*, 1–15.

Lessig, L. (2006). *Code Version 2.0*. http://www.codev2.cc/download+remix/

Lyon, D. (2007). *Surveillance studies: An overview*. Cambridge: Wiley.

MGMT. (2007). *Electric feel*.

Morgan, B., & Yeung, K. (2007). *An introduction to law and regulation: text and materials*. Cambridge: Cambridge University Press.

Narciso, D. (2011). Police seek utility data for homes of marijuana-growing suspects. *The Columbus Dispatch*.

Raab, C. D., & Wright, D. (2012). Surveillance: Extending the limits of privacy impact assessment. In D. Wright, & P. de Hert (Eds.), *Privacy impact assessment* (pp. 363–383). Springer. doi:10.1007/978-94-007-2543-0_17.

Spiekermann, S. (2012). The RFID PIA – Developed by industry, endorsed by regulators. In D. Wright, & P. De Hert (Eds.), *Privacy impact assessment* (pp. 323–346). Netherlands: Springer. doi:10.1007/978-94-007-2543-0_15.

TAMI Project. (2004). *Technology assessment in Europe: Between method and impact. Final Report*. doi:10.2310/7070.2004.0053a.

Tanasescu, I. (2009). *The European Commission and interest groups: Towards a deliberative interpretation of stakeholder involvement in EU policy-making*. Brussels: VUB Press.

Tien, L. (2010). New "smart meters" for energy use put privacy at risk. *Deeplinks*. https://www.eff.org/deeplinks/2010/03/new-smart-meters-energy-use-put-privacy-risk.

Van Blarkom, G., Borking, J., & Olk, J. (2003). *Handbook of privacy and privacy-enhancing technologies. The case of Intelligent Software Agents*. The Hague: College Bescherming Persoonsgegevens.

Van Dijk, N., Gellert, R., & Rommetveit, K. (2015). A risk to a right? Beyond data protection risk assessments. *Computer Law & Security Review, (submitted)*.

Van Dijk, N., & Gunnarsdóttir, K. (2014). *Disciplinary orientations and method | Inter-disciplinary approximations and distantiations*. Epinet Project. http://eprints.lancs.ac.uk/74259/1/EPINET_WP2_D22.pdf

Van Dijk, N., Rommetveit K. (2015), *A Risk to a Right? Cross-Cutting Lessons for Data Protection Impact Assessments, Summary of findings and policy recommendations*, EPINET project. http://epinet.no/sites/all/themes/epinet_bootstrap/documents/dpia_report.pdf.

Van Est, R., & Brom, F. (2012). Technology assessment, analytic and democratic practice. *Encyclopedia of Applied Ethics, 4*, 306–320. doi:10.1016/B978-0-12-373932-2.00010-7.

Vijayan, J. (2011). Will the smart grid become law enforcement's new best friend? *Computerworld*.

Wacks, R. (2010). *Privacy: A very short introduction*. Oxford: OUP.

Wright, D. (2011). Should privacy impact assessments be mandatory? *Communications of the ACM, 54*(8), 121. doi:10.1145/1978542.1978568.

Wright, D. (2012). The state of the art in privacy impact assessment. *Computer Law & Security Review, 28*(1), 54–61.

Wright, D., & De Hert, P. (Eds.). (2012). *Privacy impact assessment*. Dordrecht: Springer. doi:10.1007/978-94-007-2543-0.

Wright, D., Gellert, R., Gutwirth, S., & Friedewald, M. (2011). Minimizing technology ricks with PIAs, precaution, and participation. *IEEE Technology and Society Magazine, 30*(4), 47–54.

Wright, D., & Mordini, E. (2012). Privacy and ethical impact assessment. In D. Wright, & P. Hert (Eds.), *Privacy impact assessment* (pp. 397–418). Dordrecht: Springer. doi:10.1007/978-94-007-2543-0_19.

Wright, D., & Raab, C. D. (2012). Constructing a surveillance impact assessment. *Computer Law and Security Review, 28*(6), 613–626.

The Evolution of the Smart Grid Threat Landscape and Cross-Domain Risk Assessment

3

Lucie Langer* and Markus Kammerstetter†

*Austrian Institute of Technology, Vienna, Austria;
†Automation Systems Group, Vienna University of Technology, Austria

3.1 INTRODUCTION

Future intelligent power grids will make extensive use of information and communication technology (ICT) to enable the integration of renewable energy sources and to optimise energy management efficiency. End-users will be connected to the grid via smart gateways for electricity billing and demand-side management, and novel grid components such as smart secondary substations will contain a considerable amount of ICT-enabled functionalities to support intelligent energy management. This transformation introduces a significantly larger cyber-attacks surface compared to conventional power grids, which use ICT in a much more isolated fashion. Cyber-attacks to the grid's underlying ICT infrastructure can have a negative impact on the power grid, either intentionally with the power infrastructure being the main target, or as a side-effect. Examples for possible attacks are smart meter tampering with the purpose of reducing electricity bills fraudulently, spoofed or biased measurement data causing a misinterpretation of the current system status and leading to wrong control commands, or even concerted attacks targeting various critical system components to cause major disruptions. A successful attack can have negative consequences both for customers (in terms of security of supply), and for grid operators or energy providers, such as financial loss or loss of reputation, possibly involving regulatory fines; disruptions of the grid and black-outs affecting whole districts; cascading effects affecting other critical infrastructures such as transport or healthcare; or safety issues to the point of serious injuries or deaths. The degree of damage caused by a cyber-attack towards the power grid depends very much on the skills and resources of the attacker(s). Recent events have shown that attacks on industrial control systems are becoming increasingly sophisticated (see callout box).

A Security Response released by Symantec (Symantec, 2014b) describes a 2013 cyber-attack campaign on European and U.S. energy companies for spying purposes, which was launched by a group of attackers referred to as the "**Dragonfly**" group (also known as "Energetic Bear") in early 2013. The top five countries with active infections have been Spain, the U.S., France, Italy, and Germany. Dragonfly uses Remote Access Tool (RAT) type custom-made malware to obtain access and control of compromised computers. Infection was accomplished by means of spear phishing through targeted spam e-mail with malicious pdf attachments, and watering hole attacks via compromised energy-related websites. Additionally, malware was inserted in legitimate software packages which could be downloaded from the websites of three different vendors of industrial control systems software. The different types of attacks show that the Dragonfly group has strong technical and strategic capabilities. This campaign follows in the footsteps of **Stuxnet** (Falliere et al., 2011), which was the first publicly known malware targeting industrial control systems. Whilst Stuxnet was tailored to sabotage the Iranian nuclear programme, Dragonfly appears to have a "much broader focus with espionage and persistent access as its current objective with sabotage as an optional capability if required" (Symantec, 2014a).

Cyber-attacks can only be successful if a **threat** (such as a Trojan horse enabling malicious remote access to a system) correlates with a suitable **vulnerability** of an exposed system component (such as an unpatched software bug). A contributing factor is that smart grid ICT technology providers and utilities have limited experience with these new technologies, and may push new products onto the market which have not undergone an adequate quality assurance process, thus potentially exhibiting severe security vulnerabilities. Additional time pressure is created by the EU energy market legislation in the Third Energy Package (Annex I.2 to Directive 2009/72/EC of the European Parliament and of the Council, 2009), which requires a roll-out target of 80% market penetration for smart metering systems by the year 2020, provided that a long-term cost-benefit analysis has proven positive[1]. At the same time, common baselines or minimum security requirements for smart grid components do not exist on a European level (for country-specific regulations see for example the Smart Meter Protection Profiles developed by the Germany Federal Office for Information Security (2013b, 2013c). Eventually, smart grid components may be rolled out on a large scale without clearly defined security requirements to be followed.

A precondition of defining appropriate security requirements, and therefore a necessary step to secure future energy supply, is a thorough assessment of the risk posed by cyber-attacks. This involves learning the vulnerabilities of specific system architectures or components, and the threats posed by external attackers as well as insiders, system failures, or natural disasters. Infrastructure providers and utilities must know which parts of their infrastructures are most critical and

---

[1]In Germany, for example, this cost-benefit analysis has shown that smart meters are only economically justified for consumers with a yearly consumption of 6000 kWh and more; see Report from the Commission (2014) for the results of the evaluations in the different EU member states.

therefore require protection most importantly. Of course, future events cannot be predicted with certainty. However, it is possible to identify the system components that, due to their characteristics, their location or configuration, expose the greatest vulnerabilities, which, could lead to large-scale outages or disruptions of the grid when exploited (IEEE, 2014). The findings can subsequently be used to decide on the measures and investments to be taken in order to increase grid resilience. However, the design, implementation, and deployment of secure smart grid systems must still be carried out in a cost-effective manner. A clear picture of the risk attached to different parts of the system can help utilities and manufacturers to prioritise the measures, and to define appropriate protection levels for smart grid assets.

3.2 SMART GRID ARCHITECTURES: THE BASICS

Threats and vulnerabilities apply to *smart grid assets*, i.e. valuable resources such as hardware components, systems, processes, or specific pieces of information (see Section 8.2.3 of ISO/IEC 27005, 2011). To help the reader comprehend the concepts introduced in the remainder of this chapter, a basic understanding of the structure and the functionalities of a (smart) power grid is required. Therefore, a brief overview of existing smart grid reference architectures including a high-level description of the main smart grid building blocks is provided in this section. Chapter 7 provides a more detailed view on smart grid architectures.

The development of different ICT architecture models in the smart grid domain over the past few years was mainly motivated by the need to gain an overview of the existing standardisation landscape, and to clearly specify the interfaces of new smart grid components to existing systems. Cybersecurity was only a driver in some of these architecture developments. The predominant motivation has been to achieve interoperability through a structured approach. The following overview lists relevant international approaches for smart grid ICT architectures and shows their practical value, without claiming to be exhaustive.

3.2.1 GRIDWISE INTEROPERABILITY CONTEXT-SETTING FRAMEWORK

The U.S. *GridWise initiative* is driving the coordination and harmonisation of smart grid activities among different stakeholders from industry and government. The *GridWise Architecture Council (GWAC)* is focusing on interoperability between technologies and systems and standardisation needs, and has published a guideline for smart grid interoperability (2007). It defines eight layers for which interoperability between different organisational or technical units in a smart grid should be considered, grouped into three categories: *technical interoperability, informational*

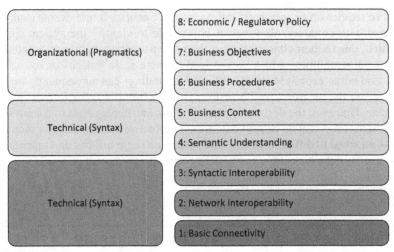

FIGURE 3.1

GridWise Interoperablity Layers (2007).

interoperability, and (iii) *organisational interoperability* (see Figure 3.1). These layers also form the basis of subsequent architecture models such as the NIST and the M/490 framework, explained below.

3.2.2 NIST SMART GRID FRAMEWORK

In the *Energy Independence Security Act* of 2007, the *National Institute of Standards and Technology (NIST)* was appointed primary responsible for defining a framework to support smart grid interoperability in the United States. In its *Smart Grid Conceptual Reference Model* (2010), NIST divides the smart grid into seven building blocks or *domains* (Bulk generation, Transmission, Distribution, Customer, Service Provider, Operations, and Markets), and identifies interfaces among domains and corresponding actors. Together, the GridWise interoperability layers and NIST domains define a space in which existing and future smart grid ICT systems and protocols can be clearly assigned. This allows identifying areas in which missing standards have to be established.

3.2.3 SMART GRID ARCHITECTURE MODEL AND EU MANDATE M490

In the past years, the European standardisation institutions *CEN, CENELEC* and *ETSI* have developed a *Smart Grid Reference Architecture* for Europe as part of their response to the *EU Smart Grid Mandate M/490*[2] (CEN-CENELEC-ETSI

---

[2]The M/490 Mandate has been issued in March 2011 to be finalised by the end of 2012. The need for another iteration was decided upon in 2012, initiating a second phase of the Mandate, which has been finalised at the end of 2014.

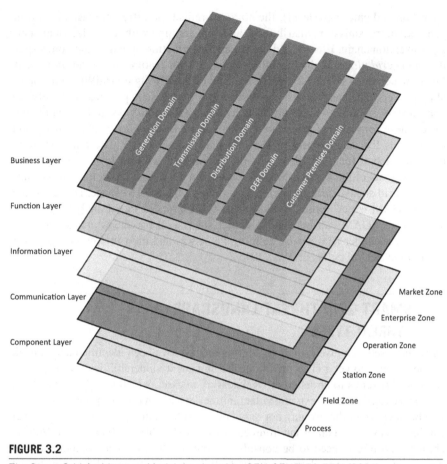

FIGURE 3.2

The Smart Grid Architecture Model developed by CEN-CENELEC-ETSI (2014).

Smart Grid Coordination Group, 2014), which is the European equivalent to the U.S. NIST Smart Grid Framework (2010). The NIST Conceptual Model was adapted for the European market to obtain a European Conceptual Model. The major difference between both models is that, for the European variant, a Distributed Energy Resources (DER) domain was introduced which captures small distributed generators to reflect their important role for the European market. In addition to the European Conceptual Model, the CEN-CELENELC-ETSI Smart Grid Reference Architecture framework defines the Smart Grid Architecture Model (SGAM), see Figure 3.2. It is a three-dimensional model that supports smart grids use-case definition and representation of interoperability viewpoints both for current and future (smart) grid implementations. SGAM is defined by *zones*, *domains*, and *interoperability layers*. Whilst the *zones* are derived from the typical layers of a hierarchical automation system (from field via process, station towards operation and enterprise level), the *domains* reflect the different stages of power generation, transmission, distribution, and consumption within the electrical energy conversion chain. Electrical domains and information management zones span the *smart grid plane*. In the third dimension, SGAM features five *interoperability layers* which are a condensed version of the originally eight GridWise interoperability layers. The base layer is the *component layer*, where physical and software components are situated. On top of that, communication links and protocols between these components are located in the *communication layer*. The *information layer* holds the data models of the information exchanged. The *function layer* holds the actual functionalities, and the uppermost *business layer* describes the business goals of the system. SGAM was originally defined to help identify gaps in smart grid standardisation by locating them in the SGAM space. However, the use of SGAM is not limited to that purpose. In terms of threat analysis and risk assessment, SGAM can be used to depict smart grid use cases and automation architectures under analysis by defining the assets and their interconnections for each of the SGAM cells (ENISA, 2013).

3.3 SMART GRID THREAT LANDSCAPE

3.3.1 THREAT TYPES

Once the assets in a given smart grid infrastructure have been identified and valued, the next step is to get a clear picture of the immanent vulnerabilities and threats. A *vulnerability* refers to an inherent weakness of an asset, which may be exploited; a *threat* takes advantage of existing vulnerabilities to cause harm to one or more assets. In a broader sense, threats may not only be caused by deliberate human actions, but can have also accidental or environmental causes (ISO/IEC 27005, 2011). Vulnerabilities and threats need to be considered both for the technical components and the relevant organisational processes. In the following, the focus will be on technical threats and vulnerabilities applicable to information and components in the smart grid. For threats emerging from organisational procedures and processes, the reader is referred, for example, to the catalogues developed by the German Federal Office for Information Security (2013a).

The main challenge when determining the threats and vulnerabilities of a given system is to draw a complete picture. Although exhaustiveness is hard (if not impossible) to achieve, a systematic, methodical approach helps to minimise the risk of overlooking any important aspects. Different threat modelling techniques have been proposed to date, such as attack trees (Schneier, 1999) or *STRIDE*, which is an acronym for *Spoofing, Tampering, Repudiation, Information Disclosure, Denial of Service, and Elevation of Privilege* (Hernan et al., 2006). A systematic threat and vulnerability analysis is also an important factor of secure system design, and, as such, an integral part of the Secure Development Lifecycle, see Chapter 8. For existing (smart) grid infrastructures, the actual characteristics of the system under evaluation should be taken into account, including any security measures already in place. A powerful means to detect practical vulnerabilities of existing components is to perform a security (or penetration) test, see Chapters 4 and 5.

For smart grids, different collections of threats and vulnerabilities have been proposed to date. The *European Union Agency for Network and Information Security (ENISA)* has conducted a study on the most important smart grid threats, mapping them to smart grid assets, and taking into account the capabilities of possible adversaries (ENISA, 2013). It concludes with a good practice guide, which shows how smart grid security controls from existing standards can provide protection against the identified threats. The following threat groups are suggested by ENISA (2013, p.10):

- Natural disaster
- Damage or loss of IT assets
- Outages
- Nefarious activity or abuse
- Deliberate physical attacks
- Unintentional data damage
- Failures or Malfunction
- Eavesdropping, interception, or hijacking
- Legal

The U.S. *National Electric Sector Cybersecurity Organization Resource (NESCOR) Technical Working Group 1 (TWG1)* has developed a set of cybersecurity failure scenarios for the smart grid (NESCOR, 2013). Here, a *failure scenario* is an event in which a certain harm occurring to smart grid cyber assets has a negative impact on the electrical grid (generation, transmission, or delivery of power). The harmful event is due to certain vulnerabilities exploited or triggered by matching threats (both intentional attacks and unintentional failures, errors or disasters). The vulnerabilities identified in the failure scenarios are categorised into 23 classes which are a subset of the vulnerability classes from NISTIR 7628 Vol. 3 (2014). The failure scenarios are organised in six functional categories, corresponding to the domains identified in the NIST Smart Grid Framework (2010):

- *Advanced Metering Infrastructure (AMI)*. Systems that enable information near real-time pricing and load exchange between smart meters and utility business systems (NIST, 2010).
- *Distributed Energy Resources (DER)*. Small-scale decentralised systems that either provide power to, or store power from the distribution grid.
- *Wide Area Monitoring, Protection, and Control (WAMPAC)*. Systems that support wide-area applications, related mainly to synchrophasor technology and the devices that generate, receive, and utilise synchrophasor data (NESCOR, 2012).
- *Electric Transportation (ET)*. Systems relating to supply and management of Electric Vehicles (EV).

- *Demand Response (DR)*. Systems related to management of customer energy consumption in response to supply conditions such as grid balance or market prices (NIST, 2010).
- *Distribution Grid Management (DGM)*. Components and applications for managing and optimising networked distribution systems.

In addition, there are failure scenarios in a seventh category called *Generic*, which includes cross-cutting failure scenarios that may impact several of these functional categories. For each of the failure scenarios, the relevant vulnerabilities, impacts, and mitigation strategies are described. Potential impacts include power loss, equipment damage, human casualties, revenue loss, violations of customer privacy, and loss of public confidence. TWG1 also developed methods for prioritising the failure scenarios, and performed a ranking of the scenarios according to impact and likelihood (see Section 3.4.1). Table 3.1 lists the top-ranked NESCOR failure scenarios (NESCOR, 2013). It shows that, in many cases, problems that are well-known from the ICT world are also key vulnerabilities of smart grids, such as lack of authentication leading to unauthorised access or privilege elevation, and poor system design or configuration (e.g. weak passwords, unnecessary services or interfaces). Additionally, the specifics of the smart grid as a cyber-physical system have to be considered; for example, cybersecurity issues affecting safety mechanisms in an unwanted way, or poor anomaly detection mechanisms that fail to meet the requirements of this specific area of application.

Eventually, any generic collection of threats or vulnerabilities, such as (ENISA, 2013) or (NIST, 2014), can only provide a starting point to help stakeholders in assessing a specific instantiation of the smart grid (sub-)system, taking into account the given infrastructure with its real-world systems, their configurations and interdependencies. The theoretical assessment should, whenever possible, be complemented with a practical assessment in the form of a security analysis or penetration test. Details can be found in Chapter 8.

3.3.2 THREAT AGENTS

Threats are posed by certain *threat agents*. These are classes of related actors that could cause a risk to manifest by exploiting or triggering a given vulnerability, either as the only cause or as a contributing factor. Compared to the terms *attacker* or *adversary* which suggest a malicious intent, a threat agent also covers unintended errors, accidents, or natural disasters. Table 3.2 shows the most important smart grid threat agents, which can be found in similar form for example in (ENISA, 2013) and (NESCOR, 2013).

The urgency of a threat depends to a great extent on the capabilties, resources, and motivation of the threat agent (or *attacker*, as a malicious intent is presumed in the following). Therefore, it is important to consider potential attackers for instance by defining an *attacker model* for the system that is subject to a threat analysis, i.e. the *Target of Evaluation (TOE)*. The attacker model specifies the type of access an

Table 3.1   Top-ranked NESCOR Failure Scenarios (NESCOR, 2013)

ID	Failure Scenario	Description of Failure Scenario and Potential Impacts
AMI.1	Authorised Employee Issues Invalid Mass Remote Disconnect	Employee of the utility issues harmful command sequence (e.g. remote disconnect) to large number of smart meters, potentially causing temporary blackouts and loss of reputation for the utility provider (insider attack).
DER.1	Inadequate Access Control of DER Systems Causes Electrocution	Attacker gets access through the user interface (due to poor system implementation or configuration, or lacking authentication mechanisms) and disables anti-islanding protection in DER settings, potentially causing physical damage to DER system or electrocution of utility field crew member.
WAMPAC.1	Denial of Service Attack Impairs NTP Service	Unavailability or malfunction of timestamping service (caused by Denial of Service (DoS) attack, unnecessary traffic flows, or poor implementation or configuration) causes incorrect timestamps on PMU measurements, leading to wrong or delayed control commands, potentially causing grid imbalance, overload or tripping of lines, and equipment damage.
WAMPAC.6	Communications Compromised between PMUs and Control Centre	Wide area network (WAN) components under attack (e.g. through lack of authentication and poor anomaly detection mechanisms) inhibit WAN communication; same potential impacts as with scenario *WAMPAC.1*.
Generic.1	Malicious and Non-malicious Insiders Pose Range of Threats	Threats posed by insiders (malicious, bribed, socially engineered), due to lack of authentication which allows unauthorised access or privilege elevation.
Generic.2	Inadequate Network Segregation Enables Access for Threat Agents	Attacker gains unauthorised access to control systems network via compromised business network (due to lack of network segregation); wide range of potential impacts from minor incidents to large-scale disruptions or outages.
Generic.3	Portable Media Enables Access Despite Network Controls	Asset compromised through portable media device carrying malware or counterfeit firm- or software (facilitated by lack of authentication, unnecessary services or interfaces, and poor implementation or configuration); same potential impacts as with scenario *Generic.2*.

attacker has on the TOE. In general, attackers can be classified into *internal* and *external*. An external attacker has limited access to the TOE and is typically constrained to the communication interfaces. Compared to that, an internal attacker is more powerful due to wider access facilities to the TOE, and might, for instance, have physical access to the TOE with non-privileged rights. A proper definition of the

Table 3.2 Important Smart Grid Threat Agents, cf. (ENISA, 2013) and (NESCOR, 2013)

Threat Agent	Description
Nation states	Seeking to gain information or cause harm for strategic or political reasons.
Terrorists	Organisations or individuals motivated by religious, ideological or political reasons.
Economic Criminals	Organisations or individuals motivated by financial revenue or competitive advantage (e.g. cyber criminals, industrial spies).
Malicious criminals	Organisations or individuals seeking to cause harm (e.g. disgruntled employees).
Activists	Groups or individuals motivated socially or politically (e.g. hacktivists expressing protest or civil disobedience).
Recreational criminals	Individuals seeking entertainment or self-promotion (e.g. hackers, crackers).
Hazards	Natural disasters, accidents, human errors, degradation.

attacker model is mandatory as it also determines the *attack surface*. As a result, the attacker model has to correspond to the environment the TOE is employed in. In general, there is a trade-off between attacker capabilities and the security that can be achieved within a system. If the attacker has privileged access rights and full control over the TOE (including physical access), most security mechanisms can be circumvented easily. On the other side, if the attacker model is too limited, the analysis results will not cover real-world scenarios.

3.3.3 ATTACK VECTORS

A practical smart grid instance typically comprises many different systems from various manufacturers and utility-specific solutions. It is thus not possible to conduct a threat analysis based on an abstract and generalised model of the instantiated smart grid, as the result of this analysis would not reflect the utility's actual installation. Instead, it is important to consider the technical and utility-centric smart grid details as well. From a high-level view, a smart grid instance typically adheres to a common architecture model. For instance, considering two different utilities, both could have a smart metering system comprising smart meter devices in the customer's premises, data concentrators in between, and a Meter Data Management (MDM) system at the top that is integrated with other systems (e.g. an SAP-based billing system). However, whilst one utility might employ strictly separated physical networks for metering and for grid operation, the other one could have decided to save costs and use the existing control network for both systems. From a security perspective, this configuration difference accounts for a significant increase of the risk that otherwise well-protected systems in the grid operation network become targets of attacks originating from the metering network, which is more easily accessible.

Ultimately, the attack surface is based on the attacker model and depends on the access capabilities of the attacker. For instance, if the attacker model corresponds to an external attacker who can communicate with the TOE system over a given communication port, then the attack surface covers all TOE functions that can be reached through the communication port, whilst TOE functions that are only available through local access are not within the reach of the attacker. A viable methodology to discover potential unauthorised entry points to an existing system are *attack vectors*. The general idea of attack vectors is to find potential paths an attacker (according to the attacker model) could take to successfully enter and compromise a system (Hansman & Hunt, 2005).

The first step usually involves the identification of technical communication interfaces, technologies, and system locations of the TOE system. An architecture model that includes the necessary information (i.e. system locations, communication technologies, etc.) can help to determine possible access points for an attacker. For instance, a smart meter device in the customer's premises is fully accessible to an external attacker (i.e. the customer). This renders it prone to physical attacks such as firmware readout or the extraction of key material and credentials. Similarly, the meter communication network the smart meter is attached to (i.e. the power line communication network) is also easily accessible to the attacker. In contrast, a substation protection switch connected to a physically separated communication network is by far less easy to access if only external attackers are considered. The likelihood of an attacker being able to access these networks increases if wireless technologies are employed. At the end of the analysis conducted in this step, the result is a ranked list of individual access points to the considered smart grid systems, providing an overview of the initial attack surface from an accessibility perspective. The ranking is affected by the effort which the attacker has to invest to not only access, but also utilise the devices or communication interfaces. For instance, a wireless link relying on state-of-the-art protection mechanisms (i.e. a cryptographic Virtual Private Network (VPN) setup protecting the confidentiality, integrity, availability, authenticity and freshness) can still be easily accessed by an attacker over the air, but it will be dramatically harder to actually utilise the network as the attacker (in case of an external attacker model) does not have the necessary key material to also access the VPN inside the wireless link. As a result, the ranking for wireless link attack surface should consider the VPN protection mechanism.

It is also possible to combine the attack considerations for different systems. For instance, if potential attack vectors shall be considered for a smart metering data concentrator inside a physically secure location, the attack vectors are considered for the data concentrator first. As the data concentrator is typically connected to a Power Line Communication (PLC) network connected to a high number of smart meter devices, the attack vector over these interfaces should be considered as well. The results of the attack vector analysis on the PLC network and the smart meter are then combined with the according attack vectors on the data concentrator. The analysis results in potential attack vectors on each of the systems under consideration, where attack vectors involving easier accessibility are more critical compared to attack vectors involving protection mechanisms that would first need to be overcome by the attacker.

3.3.4 CASE STUDIES

This section discusses the most important cybersecurity threats and attack vectors in smart grids, focusing on the AMI, WAMPAC and DGM domains defined by the NIST Smart Grid Framework (2010) and used in the NESCOR failure scenarios (2013), see also Section 3.3.1.

3.3.4.1 Advanced Metering Infrastructure (AMI)

This case study features a utility that has deployed a single-manufacturer smart metering infrastructure comprising smart meters at the customer's premises, data concentrators, an AMI headend system and an MDM system. Details of the setting and the configuration of these systems are provided in the following to allow for a comprehensive assessment of potential attack vectors.

The smart meter is typically located in the customer premises. It has multiple communication interfaces: the uplink employs a proprietary PLC system, which, according to the manufacturer, uses state-of-the-art encryption technologies. Besides the PLC communication interface, there is an optical interface for the configuration and maintenance of the smart meter. Access to the optical interface is protected with a strong password. The utility uses the same service password for all smart meters. The smart meter firmware is proprietary and can be considered as a black box system to the utility. Additionally, the smart meter contains a remote controllable breaker unit.

The data concentrator is the PLC endpoint for the smart meters. Apart from the PLC interface, it has an Ethernet uplink that is connected to the headend system over a fibre optic link secured via VPN. The data concentrators are all situated in physically secure locations such as substations or transformer stations operated by the utility. The headend system is located at the utility and comprises a proprietary manufacturer software implementation that is executed on an off-the-shelf server system. The system is connected to a metering VLAN to communicate with the data concentrators. Over a separate link, the system is connected to the MDM system, which is essentially a large proprietary database system supplied by the smart metering system manufacturer. It is executed on an off-the-shelf server system and has an uplink connection to a stand-alone SAP system used for billing purposes.

From this system description, it is apparent that the smart meter is a critical device: due to its physical location, the smart meter can be easily accessed by attackers and subject to physical attacks which are in general more powerful than typical network attacks. In comparison, physical access to the data concentrator becomes less likely for an external attacker, whilst systems hosted at the utility (i.e. the headend and the MDM system) are very unlikely to be physically accessible to external attackers.

Considering external attacks, the following attack vectors on a smart meter are conceivable:

- *Unauthorised use of the optical communication interface.* The attacker might need to break the configured password first (e.g. by utilising physical attacks, which are much more powerful than typical password brute-force attacks), and might then be able to re-configure the smart meter or exploit a software vulnerability.
- *Physical attacks on the smart meter device.* This would allow an attacker to deconstruct the smart meter device and potentially read out the firmware, the system configuration, as well as system credentials and key material. This information could be used to gain access to remote systems over the PLC network.
- *Unauthorised communication over the PLC network.* As a consequence, an attacker could potentially control remote devices, although additional information on the PLC implementation or credentials and key material might be required first.

For the PLC data concentrator, possible attack vectors could be:

- *Remote attacks over PLC.* If an attacker has figured out how the PLC communication works, remote attacks could be used against the data concentrator.
- *Remote attacks over the uplink connection.* Although more critical systems are available over the uplink connection, an attacker might still consider to attack the data concentrator due to the potential to control large amounts of smart meter devices.
- *Physical attacks on the data concentrator.* This is the most powerful type of attack. Similar to smart meter devices, an attacker could use physical attacks to extract the firmware, key material, credentials, and other critical information from the data concentrator. Using the collected information, the potential to conduct remote attacks on other data concentrators, smart meters, or even headend system rises.

For the headend, MDM and other utility-hosted systems, potential attack vectors are:

- *Remote attacks over the data concentrator uplink.*
- *Remote attacks over the Internet or other public networks* that, due to inadequate security controls, enable access to critical headend systems. For instance, this could be caused by a malware infection through a targeted attack on a utility employee, which spreads over the internal network until it reaches critical headend systems.
- *Physical attacks,* though these are very unlikely due to the secure hosting within the utility's facilities.

By combining the attack vectors of the different devices, potential composite attack vectors that originate from easily accessible devices and propagate to the critical headend systems become apparent. However, these are less likely than stand-alone attacks on devices which are physically easy to access, such as smart meters.

Considering the presented attack vectors from the perspective of smart meter devices and external attackers, viable attack scenarios could be:

- *Exposure of weak encryption in the PLC uplink.* Either by analysing the PLC communication or by disassembling the hard- and software implementation of a smart meter device, the attacker discovers that the encryption protecting the PLC traffic is easy to break, and is thus able to decrypt any communication within the PLC network (cf. NESCOR failure scenario AMI.24, 2013). Similarly, this attack also provides the potential of compromising other devices in the PLC network.
- *Exposure of smart meter vulnerabilities.* By analysing the smart meter hard- and software implementation, an attacker discovers and publicly discloses smart meter vulnerabilities, which can be exploited by the attacker and by other, potentially less experienced individuals to conduct remote attacks over the PLC network (cf. NESCOR failure scenario AMI.25, 2013).
- *Exposure of credentials and key material.* Either by analysing the PLC communication, by utilising the optical configuration interface, or by reverse engineering the hard- and software implementation of the smart meter, an attacker gains access to the configured credentials and key material within the smart meter device. As a result, this information could be publicly disclosed and widely used for remote attacks on the AMI infrastructure (cf. NESCOR failure scenario AMI.23, 2013).
- *Access to headend systems* through malware infection or targeted attacks on publicly available systems of the utility (cf. NESCOR failure scenario AMI.3, 2013).

If internal attackers such as rogue employees are considered as well, the attack potential rises dramatically due to the potential abuse of otherwise benign control actions and procedures. For instance, through a rogue employee or an accidental action of an authorised employee, a mass remote disconnect command could be sent out over the PLC network to the smart meters, resulting in a power cut due to the remote controllable breakers within the smart meters (see NESCOR failure scenario AMI.1, 2013).

3.3.4.2 Wide Area Monitoring, Protection, and Control (WAMPAC)

Due to the criticality of the WAMPAC network, a utility has taken precautions against potential attacks. The redundant SCADA and NTP systems hosted at the utility can only be accessed by a small number of authorised employees. The system is physically separated from other communication networks. Maintenance operations can only be performed by temporarily enabling access to the maintenance functionalities. From the utility to the field, mostly fibre links are employed that are located at the top of high voltage power poles. Directional radio links are used for a small number of devices in rural areas. To secure both the fibre and any other communication media, state-of-the-art VPN tunnelling is employed. Field units such as Phasor Measurement

Units (PMUs), Phasor Data Concentrators (PDCs) or breakers and analogue control systems are typically located in physically protected areas. In addition, the utility has WAMPAC systems located in secondary substations as well as in medium- and low-voltage generation stations. Secondary substations and low-voltage generation stations are typically small and often situated in rural areas. Since these systems can be easily physically accessed by attackers, the utility employs components that have the full VPN functionality built into the devices by the manufacturer. As a result, any communication to or from these devices is VPN-protected.

Due to the strong physical protection of the systems hosted in the utility's premises, the physically more easily accessible systems in the secondary substations and the low-voltage generation stations are more prone to an external attack. Similarly, the accessibility of the communication links needs to be considered. The directional radio links are physically easier to access than the fibre links.

For the physically well-protected systems at the utility's premises, the following attack vectors are conceivable from the perspective of an external attacker:

- *Denial of Service (DoS) attacks on the network, VPN and NTP infrastructure.* To mount this attack, the attacker needs to have access to the WAN. The VPN tunnel effectively protects the inner systems if credentials and key material are not available to the attacker.
- *DoS attacks on the wireless infrastructure.* Due to easy accessibility, an attacker manages to jam or flood wireless links with erroneous messages.
- *Software vulnerabilities.* The systems at the utility contain software vulnerabilities that are exploited by an attacker. However, the VPN tunnel provides protection unless the attacker gains knowledge of credentials and key material.

For the physically less protected systems in secondary substations or low-voltage generation stations, the attack vectors from the perspective of an external attacker are:

- *Physical attacks on WAMPAC devices.* An attacker utilises powerful physical attacks on accessible devices allowing him, for instance, to read out the firmware, configuration, credentials, or key material, potentially providing the attacker with the information necessary to access the VPN network. In addition to the extraction of sensitive information from the devices, the attacker could also leverage physical attacks to change the configuration of a device, or inject malicious code such as malware or backdoors into the system.
- *Injection of bogus measurement data.* An attacker compromises the local authentication at a WAMPAC device and injects bogus measurement data to destabilise the grid.

Considering the presented attack vectors from the perspective of external attackers, viable attack scenarios could be:

- *Physical attacks on WAMPAC devices in secondary substations.* An attacker mounts a physical attack on a less protected WAMPAC device in a secondary substation and manages to extract the device's configuration data, including credentials and key material to access the VPN network. Subsequently, the communication with the control centre can be compromised resulting in the attacker's ability to send arbitrary control messages to other WAMPAC devices and the control centre (cf. NESCOR failure scenario WAMPAC.6, 2013).

- *DoS attack on wireless WAMPAC communication links.* Although all traffic is encrypted by the VPN tunnel, the attacker is able to inject large amounts of wireless signalling traffic that causes the wireless modems to massively slow down the VPN traffic. As this affects also the NTP service, time-critical WAMPAC services become unsynchronised (cf. NESCOR failure scenario WAMPAC.1, 2013). Similar DoS attacks could be targeted on the VPN systems.

3.3.4.3 Distribution Grid Management (DGM)

A utility has a wide-ranging DGM system in place that ranges from primary and secondary substations to plug-in electric vehicles (PEVs), low-voltage generation, or smart buildings. Whilst the Distribution Management System (DMS) and the systems located in primary substations are physically well-secured from external attackers, systems in the field are easier to access. The utility thus leverages the manufacturer's in-device VPN implementation so that any communication outside the embedded devices is cryptographically protected. The configuration is thus comparable to the WAMPAC case study above, with the difference that the number of devices which are more easily accessible to attackers is higher. From the perspective of external attackers, these devices are thus of high interest. Due to the similar system configuration, also the attack vectors are similar.

Specifically, for physically more easily accessible systems, viable attack vectors considering external attackers are:

- *Physical attacks on in-field DGM devices.* An attacker could utilise powerful physical attacks on accessible devices allowing him, for instance, to read out the firmware, the configuration, the credentials or the key material from those devices. These attacks could provide the attacker with the necessary information to access the VPN network. Subsequently, the attacker might leverage this information to compromise the DMS system through the VPN uplink channel. In addition to the extraction of sensitive information from the devices, the attacker could also leverage physical attacks to change the configuration of a device, or inject malicious code such as malware or backdoors into the system.
- *Attacks on the wireless infrastructure.* As wireless links are physically easy to access, an attacker might jam these links, flood the wireless links with messages, or target the implementation of the wireless routers. Access to the DMS traffic is however protected by the VPN.
- *DoS attacks on the DMS uplink.*

By levering these attack vectors, the attacker can potentially impact the physically well-protected DGM systems in the utility's premises (similar to the WAMPAC case study above). Accordingly, viable attack scenarios from the perspective of external attackers are:

- *Malicious (software) modification of field devices* (cf. NESCOR failure scenario DGM.3, 2013).
- *Remote access to the DMS system* by leveraging information gained from physical attacks on field devices (cf. NESCOR failure scenario DGM.5, 2013).

3.4 SMART GRID RISK ASSESSMENT

The primary objective of cybersecurity risk assessment is to gain an understanding of the amount of risk from cybersecurity failures attached to every asset within a given system setting, based on analysis of threats, vulnerabilities, and attack vectors. With this knowledge, stakeholders are able to define security requirements and select the right protection measures, and to focus on the most critical components. This section focuses on the assessment of likelihood and impact as part of the risk assessment, outlines the challenges of risk assessment in smart grids, and explains the approaches which have been suggested to date.

3.4.1 BASIC CONCEPTS

In general, *risk* is the potential for an unwanted negative outcome resulting from an incident, event, or occurrence (NIST, 2014, Vol. 1). Risk is usually determined by estimating the *likelihood* of a certain failure or attack and its *impact*. The likelihood can be measured, for example, by the amount of incidents or successful attacks per year, and depends on various factors such as the system setting and its environment, or adversary capabilities and motivation. The impact often includes power loss, equipment damage, safety issues (e.g. human casualties), potentially leading to revenue loss, legal liability issues, or loss of public confidence (NESCOR, 2013). Obtaining realistic values for both parameters is a challenging task, which usually requires a lot of expertise from different areas. Input may be obtained, for example, from the asset owners or users, from information security and electrical engineering experts, and from legal bodies and national government authorities (ISO/IEC 27005, 2011).

> Risk assessment involves determining the value of the information assets, identifying relevant threats and vulnerabilities, determining and prioritising the risk posed by these, and evaluating the effect of existing controls on this risk (ISO/IEC 27005, 2011). Eventually, additional or alternative controls can be proposed. A total elimination of all risk is not feasible; usually, a certain residual risk is accepted by the organisation conducting the assessment, depending on its risk appetite and available resources.

Table 3.3 Detailed Ranking of Top-ten NESCOR Failure Scenarios (NESCOR, 2013). I: impact, C: cost.

ID	Team 1			Team 2			Team 3			Team 4		
	I	C	I/C	I	C	I/C	I	C	I/C	I	C	I/C
AMI.1	9	3	3	1	0.1	10	9	0.1	90	0	0.1	0
DER.1	9	3	3	9	3	3	3	0.1	30	3	1	3
WAMPAC.1	9	1	9	9	3	3	1	0.1	10	1	3	0.33
WAMPAC.6	9	3	3	9	3	3	1	0.1	10	1	3	0.33
Generic.1	9	3	3	9	3	3	9	0.1	90	3	1	3
Generic.2	9	3	3	9	3	3	9	1	9	3	3	1
Generic.3	9	3	3	9	3	3	9	1	9	9	9	1

Existing risk assessment methods are divided into *quantitative* and *qualitative approaches*. Quantitative methods use metrics that represent the probability and impact of a threat. As this often proves to be a difficult task with highly subjective outcomes due to the shortage of reliable data on incidents, qualitative approaches are widely used instead, which may also be able to take advantage of other sources of information that are not readily quantifiable, such as threat graphs and game-theoretic models. ENISA maintains a repository[3] of risk assessment standards, methods and tools.

As an exemplary risk assessment, Table 3.3 shows the scores for the ten highest ranked NESCOR failure scenarios given by four different teams (NESCOR, 2013). Following a qualitative method, scores of 0, 1, 3 or 9 were used to assess the impact (I) of the failure scenario from minor to significant, whilst scores of 0.1, 1, 3 or 9 were used to assess the cost (C) to the threat agent to carry out the failure scenario successfully. The risk was then calculated by dividing impact by cost (I/C), as the cost can be interpreted as the inverse of the likelihood of a successful attack (the higher the cost, the lower the likelihood). The rows of Table 3.3 show that the assessment given by different teams can vary significantly; for example, the risk posed by failure scenario AMI.1 has both the highest (90) and the lowest possible value (0) given by Teams 3 and 4, respectively.

With the appearance of new threat scenarios and ageing of the system, risk may vary over time, and must therefore be continuously managed to maintain the desired security level. This requirement leads to the risk management cycle depicted in Figure 3.3, which is composed of the phases of risk assessment, risk mitigation, and risk monitoring. In the *risk assessment* phase, threats are identified (e.g. based on historical and empirical data of cyber-attacks, expert knowledge, and known vulnerabilities in the system), and their respective likelihood and impact on the system is assessed. Subsequently, mitigating actions are determined and implemented in the *risk mitigation* phase, until the desired residual risk is reached, i.e. the risk that is

---

[3]Available at http://www.enisa.europa.eu/activities/risk-management/current-risk/risk-management-inventory

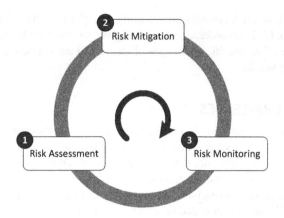

FIGURE 3.3

Diagram of risk management cycle, which shows the iterative stages of risk assessment, mitigation, and monitoring.

accepted by the organisation depending on its risk appetite and available resources. For example, the likelihood of attacks can be decreased by reducing the vulnerability of the system components, for instance, by encrypting the communication channels, using firewalls, and intelligent routing algorithms (preventive action) (Vukovic et al., 2012). Additionally, detective actions (i.e. monitoring) should be applied to allow timely detection of incidents and anomalies caused by threat agents, for example by deploying anti-virus software, network traffic analysis (Garitano et al., 2011), and fault detection algorithms (Ding, 2008). Once an anomaly or attack is detected, mitigation actions may be taken to contain and neutralise the attack, for example by replacing the compromised components or using redundant components. In the *risk monitoring* phase, the effectiveness of the defensive actions and the evolution of risk over time is evaluated by continuously assessing the known and newly discovered system vulnerabilities, as well as the deployment of the threat mitigation actions. For instance, in the case of deception attacks, the attacker may find attack strategies that bypass the current detection mechanisms, remaining undetected (see Chapter 6 for a detailed study of this scenario).

Cybersecurity risk assessment has originally been defined for conventional ICT systems. However, smart grid risk assessment is different, and remains challenging for system stakeholders, utility providers, manufacturers and system developers for several reasons: whilst risks for traditional ICT systems focus on the confidentiality, integrity and availability of information (mostly in that order), in industrial control systems and, more specifically, smart grids, operational reliability is of utmost importance, and the priority therefore is on availability, followed by integrity and confidentiality (IEC62443-2-1, 2010). This means that cybersecurity risk assessment for smart grids must be combined with safety aspects. However, current risk assessment frameworks are mostly focused either on conventional ICT systems, e.g. the Baseline Protection Catalogues developed by the German Federal Office for Information

Security (2013), or on traditional power grids, see (NERC, 2002) or (ANSI/ISA-99.00.01, 2007). Little consideration has been given to smart grids and their characteristic attributes. The specific challenges of smart grid are explained in more detail in the following section.

3.4.2 MAIN CHALLENGES

Risk assessment in smart grids is a challenging task for various reasons. Due to the cyber-physical nature of smart grids, ICT-focused risk assessment methods are not readily applicable. Besides pure cybersecurity threats, safety aspects must be considered as well, including the interrelations between the two, and the potential for cascading effects across several domains or sub-systems. Additionally, the complex combination of legacy systems and new technologies in a smart grid requires novel risk assessment methods that are able to cater for both. These rather technical challenges are aggravated by the growing complexity of the organisational dependencies with unclear boundaries and responsibilities, and lack of transparency. In the following paragraphs, these challenges to smart grid risk assessment are set out in more detail.

3.4.2.1 Managing Safety and Security Risks

Cyber-attacks to an electric power grid have the potential to result in safety-related incidents, i.e. those that could result in a loss of life (cf. Section 3.3.1). For example, data injection attacks may be used to change measurement values of grid devices (Chen et al., 2012), or timestamps of measurement data could be compromised. Further challenges include data integrity attacks (Li et al., 2012), which have the goal of inserting, changing or deleting data in network traffic. These types of attacks can lead to delayed or incorrect control decisions, potentially causing equipment damage, or triggering unsafe use of grid components. A different example, where the relation between security and safety issues is more apparent, is energising lines under maintenance by gaining access to the Distribution Management System, e.g. using a utility worker's laptop, or subverting distribution control communications directly, see (NESCOR failure scenario DGM.15, 2013). Eventually, such attacks could result in safety-related incidents involving injuries of utilities staff members or even death by electrocution.

In the safety domain, a number of analysis techniques have been applied by the community for a number of years. Examples of these include the *Hazard and Operability (HAZOP)* (Tyler et al., 2008) and *Failure Modes and Effect Analysis (FMEA)* (Department of Defense, 1980) techniques, which can be used to identify hazard scenarios and the failure modes and their effect on a system, respectively. The aim is to identify potential weaknesses that could impair the reliability, availability, or safety or a system or process. Similarly, in the security domain, a number of techniques exist for threat and vulnerability analysis, including Microsoft's *STRIDE* method (Hernan et al., 2006) and attack trees (Schneier, 1999); the latter being very closely related to fault tree analysis (Mahar & Wilbur, 1990), which is commonly used for safety analysis. Whilst these two classes of analysis methods are mature, their combined use to understand the safety-related incidents that could emerge from cyber-attacks is still in its infancy. An attempt to integrate both approaches has been presented by Schmittner et al. (2014): the FMEA cause-effect chain approach is applied to examine the effects of cybersecurity threats and vulnerabilities. However, a fully integrated approach which supports safety and security analysis and the interrelations between both is yet to be developed. A particularly challenging fact in this regard is that, from a safety point of view, a stable system is required which does not undergo any changes, whilst cybersecurity postulates frequent adaptations, patches and updates to cope with an evolving threat landscape.

3.4.2.2 Analysing Cyber-physical Risks

In a smart grid, ICT elements and physical elements are closely linked, and automated actions are triggered by sensors, actuators, and control elements. The resulting challenges for risk assessment are closely related to the issue of safety in the smart grid.

The fact that the smart grid is a cyber-physical system has two major implications for risk assessment: (i) in addition to the cyber threats and vulnerabilities that must be considered, physical risks must also be assessed – this both increases the number of scenarios that have to be assessed and introduces the challenge of understanding the relative importance of cyber versus physical risk; and (ii) the physical impact of an attack must be assessed, e.g. in terms of disturbance to energy supply, which can be particularly difficult to determine for cyber-threats. For instance, it is not readily apparent what effect cyber-attacks, such as a DoS attack to a part of a smart grid's ICT infrastructure, could have on the physical operation of a grid. Whilst the impact might be limited currently, as ICT services play an ancillary role, this may change in the future with ICT supporting increasingly critical functions of a grid.

Traditional ICT security provides a number of techniques and tools for assessing the risk from cyber-attacks and securing a system, but these are usually not readily applicable to cyber-physical systems, and not necessarily sufficient to secure those, as safety aspects and reciprocal effects and interdependencies are often not considered. Appropriate tools and strategies are required to understand and mitigate attacks on cyber-physical systems. The modelling and simulation of different attack scenarios can help to understand the potential physical impact of a cyber-attack on the smart grid, for example the effects that tampering with measurement signals have on smart grid control algorithms. To this end, existing tools such as OMNeT++ (http://www.omnetpp.org) and GridLAB-D (http://www.gridlabd.org/) can be combined and / or extended. Engaging in such activities will bring a deeper insight in the threats to be considered, and the specific resources that require (special) protection.

3.4.2.3 Understanding the Risks to Legacy Systems

The future smart grid will contain new ICT components that enable a greater degree of monitoring and control, primarily at the medium and low-voltage levels. This transformation happens as an incremental process rather than a sudden leap, as most components of the electrical grid have a lifecycle of 20 years or more. This means that our power supply will be provided by a combination of legacy systems and new components for the next decades. Consequently, a practical risk management approach for smart grids must be able to deal with a complex combination of legacy systems and new technologies.

In this context, both the risk from legacy systems and the risk to legacy systems by introducing new sub-systems should be considered. In some cases, the different technologies may not interact, e.g. because they use different protocols. When they do interact, there may be unclear security outcomes because of poorly documented legacy systems – such risks may be challenging to evaluate. Therefore, the first step towards addressing this challenge is developing a clear picture of the existing legacy systems, sub-systems and components in the electrical grid. The security risks associated with adding new sub-systems to the grid should then be examined whilst these are at a conceptual level. Such an analysis at design-time can help to identify topological vulnerabilities, and ensure that secure architectural decisions are made.

Alongside these forms of analysis, concrete threat and vulnerability assessment can be undertaken, e.g. via penetration testing, to understand the implementation-based risks that are related to legacy systems. However, it is widely understood that legacy industrial control systems can be fragile when subject to active vulnerability scanning, which can result in the need for manual procedures, thus increasing the complexity of smart grid risk assessment. Similarly, the limited possibilities to perform active security tests may require expensive testing facilities that represent copies of the operational infrastructure, or limited passive tests being realised that are based on eavesdropping communication, for example.

3.4.2.4 Complex Organisational Dependencies

The power grid is a complex system, which in the liberalised European energy market involves a number of different organisations with different roles, including Energy Producers, Transmission System Operators (TSOs), Distribution System Operators (DSOs), and energy suppliers. The smart grid has the potential to add more stakeholders, such as telecommunications providers and cloud service providers, for example to support the implementation of an Advanced Metering Infrastructure (AMI). Energy customers in the smart grid have a potential role as energy producers operating their own equipment, potentially as part of a community of energy producers or a *Virtual Power Plant*. Additionally, a diverse range of equipment suppliers and solutions providers can be drawn upon to implement different sub-systems of the smart grid. This complex web of organisational dependencies and responsibilities has the potential to make risk assessment and management very challenging. For example, assessing the risks associated with third-party services and solutions is difficult, because of a lack of transparency. Additionally, the diversity of suppliers and solutions providers can lead to interoperability issues and different, not readily compatible security provisions.

It is widely understood in the ICT sector that organisational boundaries are breaking down, making risk assessment problematic – the use of third-party cloud services by companies is a good example of this phenomenon. With the widespread use of ICT solutions in the smart grid, these problems become inherent. Also, determining which organisation is responsible for accepting the risk burden and potential liabilities can be difficult. For example, it may not be clear whether the manufacturer, supplier, or operator (DSO) is responsible for potential security issues of a specific device that is deployed in the distribution grid. An important step towards solving this problem is to stipulate minimum security requirements for smart grid components, and require manufacturers to prove that these requirements have been successfully verified for a given component, for example through independent security testing.

3.4.2.5 Understanding Cascading Effects

A cascading effect is an unforeseen chain of events that occurs when an event in a system has a negative impact on other, related systems. Cascading effects can occur in conventional power grids, for example when lines are overloaded and a line trip causes other lines tripping (NESCOR, 2013). However, the issue becomes more complex with the smart grid being a *system of systems*, where incidents in each of the interconnected ICT sub-systems have the potential to cause problems in another. This issue is closely related to the previously discussed challenge of cyber-physical impact analysis, i.e. that a cyber-attack to an ICT sub-system could result in an effect in the power grid. However, here a more general problem applies, in which one attempts to analyse effects across multiple sub-systems that could be both cyber and physical. A particularly pathological case relates to the dependency between ICT systems and a supporting power infrastructure – a cyber-attack could result in a disturbance in its supporting power supply, such as a localised blackout, that could in return result in the ICT systems becoming unavailable when a battery-based uninterruptible power supply expires. To understand such cascading effects, appropriate models of the infrastructure must be developed, along with an understanding of how the impact of an attack could propagate through it.

Understanding cascading effects is closely related to understanding the complexity of secure systems, where the combination of established techniques can still be flawed from a security point of view, and the security properties of individual subsystems are not necessarily preserved in the superordinate system (NIST, 2014, Vol. 3). Both a thorough system design and extensive security testing is of major importance to prevent and detect such vulnerabilities that have the potential to cause cascading failures. A part of secure and resilient system design is to foresee self-diagnostic and self-healing abilities of smart grid components, so that incidents can be contained and recovered from before they affect other, related systems.

Another important aspect is that power grids support other critical infrastructures such as water supply and transportation, which means that the effects of power grid disruptions on other critical infrastructures also need to be considered. Currently, the cascading effects of outages and service interruptions on other infrastructures are not well understood, especially when they have been maliciously planned with the aim to cause major disruptions (NIST, 2014, Vol. 3). Gaining a thorough understanding of such interdependencies is ever more important given the possibility of large-scale remote attacks on smart power grids.

3.4.3 EXISTING RISK ASSESSMENT FRAMEWORKS

So far, only a relatively small number of frameworks addresses risk assessment for critical (energy) infrastructures. This section gives an overview of the state of the art in smart grid risk assessment, relating to the challenges outlined above. The focus is put on recent EU activities and initiatives such as the developments within the framework of the M/490 mandate (CEN-CENELEC-ETSI Smart Grid Coordination Group, 2014).

In its report on *Guidelines for Smart Grid Cyber Security*, the *Smart Grid Interoperability Panel Cyber Security Working Group (SGIP-CSWG)* launched by the *U.S. National Institute of Standards and Technology (NIST)* defines a high-level architecture categorising the interfaces in a smart grid, and presents an approach to identify security requirements for these interface categories by performing a risk assessment (NIST, 2014). Both a top-down and a bottom-up approach is used in implementing the risk assessment: the top-down approach includes defining smart grid components or domains and their logical interfaces, focusing on the six functional priority areas *Electric Transportation, Electric Storage, Wide Area Situational Awareness, Demand Response, Advanced Metering Infrastructure,* and *Distribution Grid Management*. The bottom-up approach focuses on well-understood problems such as user authentication, key management for meters, and intrusion detection for power equipment, taking into account different vulnerability classes. Examples of vulnerability classes considered are procedural vulnerabilities (such as lack of security awareness and training or inadequate incident response), software and firmware vulnerabilities, poor authentication or protocol design, or network-related vulnerabilities such as inadequate segregation or insufficient redundancy (NIST, 2014, Vol. 3). As part of the bottom-up approach, interdependencies among smart grid domains or systems were considered for the impact analysis, thus addressing potential cascading failures. The focus is on cyber-only vulnerabilities, as opposed to the specifics of the smart grid being a cyber-physical system.

NIST-IR 7628 and ISO 27002 have been the basis for a report on smart grid security by ENISA (2012). It provides a set of specific security measures for smart grid service providers, aimed at establishing a minimum level of cybersecurity. The importance of performing a comprehensive risk assessment before selecting appropriate measures is pointed out, but no specific methodology is recommended. The *Reference Security Management Plan for Energy Infrastructure* developed for the European Commission (2010) is intended to provide guidance for operators of energy grids or components thereof, and contains recommendations on performing a risk assessment, based on the *Performance and Risk-based Integrated Security Methodology (PRISM)*.

The European standardisation bodies CEN, CENELEC and ETSI have issued a report on *Smart Grid Information Security (SGIS) (2014)* addressing cybersecurity and risk assessment in smart grids in response to the M/490 Smart Grid Mandate by the European Commission. The aim of the SGIS methodology is to provide concepts and tools to help stakeholders to integrate information security into daily business. It relates to SGAM in the sense that the security requirements differ per SGAM zone and domain, and each SGAM layer has its own security view. SGIS provides a framework to assess the criticality of smart grid components by focusing on power loss caused by ICT systems failures. Five *SGIS Security Levels* (from *low* to *highly critical*) are used to classify inherent risk attached to individual information assets. Highly critical assets are those that could lead to a power loss above 10 GW when disrupted (pan-European incident), whilst the lowest level applies to assets whose disruption could lead to a power loss under 1 MW (town or neighbourhood incident). By determining the Security Level for an information asset, the corresponding essential security requirements for that asset are determined. SGIS also provides high-level guidance in terms of the recommended Security Levels for the cells of the smart grid plane (spanned by SGAM domains and zones), as well as a set of recommendations on appropriate security measures for mitigating the risks, depending on Security Level, and relating to the domains suggested by ENISA (2012) as well as the different SGAM layers.

The SGIS approach starts with identifying the relevant information assets through a use case analysis. Additionally, the *supporting assets* that the primary asset relies on, for instance, hardware, software, network, personnel, site, organisation's structure (see ISO/IEC 27005, 2011) must be identified and considered in the risk assessment as part of a dependency map, as these have vulnerabilities that can be exploited in order to harm the primary asset. In case a particular information asset appears in different use cases, those should be grouped and considered collectively in order to obtain a complete picture; alternatively, the highest risk impact level for that asset across all use cases may be considered (CEN-CENELEC-ETSI Smart Grid Coordination Group, 2014). Next, the Security Level of each information asset is determined. As usual for risk assessment, the Security Level depends on impact and likelihood. The impact is expressed in five *Risk Impact Levels* that use different measurement categories (operational risks relating to availability; legal, human, reputational, and financial risk). To determine the Risk Impact Level for a specific information asset, every category (and subcategory) has to be evaluated for different analysis scenarios, and for each of the C-I-A properties individually. Eventually, every information asset obtains three Risk Impact Levels (one each for confidentiality, integrity, and availability); if different levels are assigned per analysis scenario, then the highest level is considered. The combination of these three values prioritised in the right way determines the Security Level of the asset under analysis. The effective likelihood is determined by considering threat agents with different capabilities, resources, and motivation, taking into account the supporting assets. The resulting effective likelihood for every information asset will be the highest level value of all their supporting assets (CEN-CENELEC-ETSI Smart Grid Coordination Group, 2014).

The SGIS methodology and, in particular, the Risk Impact Level evaluates *inherent risk*, i.e. assets without any security measures in place. The reason for this approach is that, eventually, the outcome should express the importance and significance of the asset for the organisation in itself. Therefore, this approach goes only part of the way, as an important step in an overall risk assessment is to evaluate the effect of existing controls on the risk.

3.5 CONCLUSION

The growing use of ICT to support new functionalities in power grids introduces threats from cyber-attacks. Threat and vulnerability analysis and risk assessment are of paramount inportance for understanding the potential negative impact of cyber-attacks on the grid's underlying ICT infrastructure, as well as their consequences for the power grid and its stakeholders. However, risk assessment in smart grids is challenging due to their cyber-physical nature, which requires an integration of cybersecurity- and safety-focused risk assessment methods. Moreover, the fact that the present power grid undergoes an incremental transformation into a smart grid requires that a practical risk assessment method takes into account this gradual transformation, for example by complementing the theoretical reasoning with a hands-on security analysis to identify vulnerabilities and potential exploits (see also Chapter 4). In any case, risk assessment is not a one-time exercise, but rather a cyclic process of evaluating and managing different risks, which needs to be repeated regularly. Eventually, each organisation operating in the area of smart grids must define and apply its own detailed risk assessment methodology for securing the power grid, depending on its specific requirements and boundaries. However, established methods and best practices should be taken into account. Each actor is responsible for contributing their share towards a secure smart grid. For example, manufacturers of smart grid components could be obliged to demonstrate how protection against certain failure scenarios and cybersecurity attack vectors is accomplished, and which mitigation actions are supported by the product (NESCOR, 2013). Utilities need to be aware of their responsibility to properly assess, manage, and maintain the security of their infrastructure. National authorities and public bodies should collectively drive the establishment an adoption of joint standards, policies, and best practices, and foster further research into cyber-physical systems security and smart grid risk assessment.

ACRONYMS

AMI	Advanced Metering Infrastructure
CEN	European Committee for Standardization
CENELEC	European Committee for Electrotechnical Standardization
DER	Distributed Energy Resources
DGM	Distribution Grid Management
DoS	Denial of Service
DR	Demand Response
DSO	Distribution System Operator

ENISA	European Union Agency for Network and Information Security
ET	Electric Transportation
ETSI	European Telecommunications Standards Institute
FMEA	Failure Modes and Effect Analysis, see (Department of Defense, 1980)
GWAC	GridWise Architecture Council
HAZOP	Hazard and Operability study, see (Tyler, Crawley & Preston, 2008)
IEC	International Electrotechnical Commission
MDM	Meter Data Management
NERC	North American Electric Reliability Corporation
NESCOR	U.S. National Electric Sector Cybersecurity Organization Resource
NIST	U.S. National Institute of Standards and Technology
NTP	Network Time Protocol
PDC	Phasor Data Concentrator
PLC	Power Line Communication
PMU	Phasor Measurement Unit
SCADA	Supervisory Control and Data Acquisition
SGAM	Smart Grid Architecture Model, see (CEN-CENELEC-ETSI Smart Grid Coordination Group, 2014)
SGIS	Smart Grid Information Security, see (CEN-CENELEC-ETSI Smart Grid Coordination Group, 2014)
STRIDE	Spoofing, Tampering, Repudiation, Information Disclosure, Denial of Service, and Elevation of Privilege, see (Hernan, Lambert, Ostwald, & Shostack, 2006)
TOE	Target of Evaluation
VPN	Virtual Private Network
WAMPAC	Wide Area Monitoring, Protection, and Control

REFERENCES

Annex I.2 to Directive 2009/72/EC of the European Parliament and of the Council (2009).

ANSI/ISA-99.00.01 (2007). Security for Industrial Automation and Control Systems: Concepts, Terminology and Models.

CEN-CENELEC-ETSI Smart Grid Coordination Group (2014). Reports in response to Smart Grid Mandate M/490. Available at http://www.cencenelec.eu/standards/Sectors/SustainableEnergy/SmartGrids/Pages/default.aspx.

Chen, P.-Y., Cheng, S.-M., & Chen, K.-C. (2012). Smart attacks in smart grid communication networks. *Communications Magazine, IEEE, 50*(8), 24–29.

Department of Defense (1980). MIL STD 1629A, Procedures for Performing a Failure Mode, Effect and Criticality Analysis.

Ding, S. X. (2008). *Model-based fault diagnosis techniques: Design Schemes*. Springer.

ENISA (2012). Appropriate security measures for smart grids. Available at http://www.enisa.europa.eu/activities/Resilience-and-CIIP/critical-infrastructure-and-services/smart-grids-and-smart-metering/appropriate-security-measures-for-smart-grids.

ENISA (2013). Smart Grid Threat Landscape and Good Practice Guide. Available at https://www.enisa.europa.eu/activities/risk-management/evolving-threat-environment/sgtl/smart-grid-threat-landscape-and-good-practice-guide.

Falliere, N., Murchu, L., & Chien, E. (2011). W32.Stuxnet Dossier, Version 1.4. Available at https://www.symantec.com/content/en/us/enterprise/media/security_response/whitepapers/w32_stuxnet_dossier.pdf.

Federal Office for Information Security (2013a). IT Baseline Protection Catalogs. Available at http://www.bsi.bund.de/gshb.

Federal Office for Information Security (2013b). Protection Profile for the Gateway of a Smart Metering System, BSI-CC-PP-0073. Available at https://www.bsi.bund.de/SharedDocs/Zertifikate/PP/aktuell/PP_0073.html.

Federal Office for Information Security (2013c). Protection Profile for the Security Module of a Smart Metering System (Security Module PP), BSI-CC-PP-0077. Available at https://www.bsi.bund.de/DE/Themen/SmartMeter/Schutzprofil_Security/security_module_node.html.

Garitano, I., Uribeetxeberria, R., & Zurutuza, U. (2011). A review of SCADA anomaly detection systems. In E. Corchado, V. Snasel, J. Sedano, A.E. Hassanien, J.L. Calvo, & D. Slezak (Eds.), *6th International Conference on Soft Computing Models in Industrial and Environmental Applications, volume 87 of Advances in Intelligent and Soft Computing* (pp. 357–366). Berlin, Heidelberg: Springer.

GridWise Architecture Council Interoperability Framework Team (2007). Interoperability Context-Setting Framework. Available at http://www.caba.org/resources/Documents/IS-2008-30.pdf.

Hansman, S., & Hunt, R. (2005). A taxonomy of network and computer attacks. *Computers & Security*, *24*(1), 31–43.

Hernan, S., Lambert, S., Ostwald, T., & Shostack, A. (2006). Uncover Security Design Flaws Using The STRIDE Approach. *MSDN Magazine*, November.

IEC62443-2-1 (2010). Industrial communication networks – Network and system security – Part 2-1: Establishing an industrial automation and control system security program.

IEEE (2014). IEEE Report to DoE QER on Priority Issues, IEEE.

ISO/IEC 27005 (2011). Information technology – Security techniques – Information security risk management.

Li, X., Liang, X., Lu, R., Shen, X., Lin, X., & Zhu, H. (2012). Securing smart grid: cyber attacks, countermeasures, and challenges. *IEEE Communications Magazine*, *50*(8), 38–45.

Mahar, D. J., & Wilbur, J. W. (1990). *Fault tree analysis application guide*. Reliability Analysis Center.

National Electric Sector Cybersecurity Organization Resource (NESCOR) Technical Working Group 2 (TWG2) (2012). Wide Area Monitoring, Protection, and Control Systems (WAMPAC) – Standards for CyberSecurity Requirements.

National Electric Sector Cybersecurity Organization Resource (NESCOR) Technical Working Group 1 (TWG1) (2013). Electric Sector Failure Scenarios and Impact Analyses, v1.0.

National Institute of Standards and Technology (NIST) (2010). Special Publication 1108: NIST Framework and Roadmap for Smart Grid Interoperability Standards, Release 1.0.

National Institute of Standards and Technology (NIST) (2014). NISTIR 7628, Revision 1. Guidelines for Smart Grid Cybersecurity: Volume 1: Smart Grid Cybersecurity Strategy, Architecture, and High Level Requirements, Volume 2: Privacy and the Smart Grid, Volume 3: Supportive Analyses and References. Available at http://nvlpubs.nist.gov/nistpubs/ir/2014/NIST.IR.7628r1.pdf.

North American Electric Reliability Council (NERC) (2002). Security guidelines for the electricity sectors: vulnerability and risk assessment. Available at http://www.iwar.org.uk/cip/resources/nerc/Security%20Guidelines%20for%20the%20Electricity%20Sector%20-%20Version%201.pdf.

Reference Security Management Plan for Energy Infrastructure (2010). Prepared by the Harnser Group for the European Commission under Contract TREN/C1/185/200. Available at http://ec.europa.eu/energy/infrastructure/studies/doc/2010_rsmp.pdf.

Report from the Commission (2014). Benchmarking smart metering deployment in the EU-27 with a focus on electricity (COM/2014/0356 final). Available at http://eur-lex.europa.eu/legal-content/EN/TXT/?uri=COM:2014:356:FIN.

Schmittner, C., Gruber, T., Puschner, P., & Schoitsch, E. (2014). Security Application of Failure Mode and Effect Analysis (FMEA). *SAFECOMP 2014* (pp. 310–325), LNCS 8666, Springer.

Schneier, B. (1999). Attack trees. *Dr. Dobb's Journal*, December.

Symantec (2014a). Dragonfly: Western Energy Companies Under Sabotage Threat. Available at http://www.symantec.com/connect/blogs/dragonfly-western-energy-companies-under-sabotage-threat.

Symantec (2014b). Dragonfly: Cyberespionage Attacks Against Energy Suppliers, Symantec Security Response. Available online at: http://www.symantec.com/content/en/us/enterprise/media/security_response/whitepapers/Dragonfly_Threat_Against_Western_Energy_Suppliers.pdf.

Tyler, B., Crawley, F., & Preston, M. (2008). *HAZOP: Guide to best practice* (2nd ed.). Rugby: IChemE. ISBN 978-0-85295-525-3.

Vukovic, O., Sou, K. C., Dan, G., & Sandberg, H. (2012). Network-aware mitigation of data integrity attacks on power system state estimation. *IEEE Journal on Selected Areas in Communications*, *30*(6), 1108–1118.

Resilience Against Physical Attacks

Martin Hutle* and Markus Kammerstetter†

*Fraunhofer AISEC, Germany; †Automation Systems Group,
Vienna University of Technology, Austria

4.1 INTRODUCTION

Devices for the smart grid are – compared to classic IT systems – special in the sense that they are often located in an area that is physically accessible to attackers even though they are considered to be highly security-critical. Examples (see also Chapter 3 about threats) are smart meters that are located in private households, or intelligent devices that are placed outside the trusted environment of the network operator's premises. Such devices are therefore prone to physical attacks, where the attacker is able to make use of more potent methods to compromise a device in comparison to the techniques that are applicable remotely (i.e. over a network connection; see Chapter 5).

The current chapter describes extensively the different types of physical attacks, briefly shows basic protection mechanisms which are today's state-of-the-art, and finally elaborates to hardware security modules, specifically those using physically uncloneable functions.

4.2 PHYSICAL ATTACKS

Having physical access to devices opens a completely new dimension of attack vectors. Target of such physical attacks can be e.g. smart meters, PLCs, local distribution network transformers, actuators, sensors, PV devices, gateways, and data concentrators.

The embedded nature of such devices often gives a false impression of security: while for a mobile device, like a laptop, it is obvious that an unencrypted hard disc can be read out easily when an attacker gets his hands on the device, it is less obvious that this applies to many other forms of storage that appears in such equipment.

4.2.1 GOALS OF PHYSICAL ATTACKS IN THE CONTEXT OF SMART GRID DEVICES

The goal of an attacker of a smart grid device can be divided into two categories:

4.2.1.1 Information Gathering

Here the attacker gets illegitimate access to information. This attack scenario refers to the violation of the generic security objective "confidentiality". Although much of the data in the smart grid is machine generated (such as sensor values), the impact on privacy of the users may still be high. The most prominent example is here the potential access to smart metering data, which led to significant public concerns against the application of smart metering devices. However, when it comes to physical attacks, the primary impact on privacy is usually limited. This is because the attacker can potentially access only information that is stored in the device, a device he was already able to get physical access to, either because it was in his premises or because he was able to illegally get access to it.

The more significant target for an attacker is the acquisition of information that can be used in further steps for additional attacks: these can be network-based attacks (see Chapter 5) and for manipulating the device under attack (see below). One important type of information here is key material: if a symmetric master key is stored on the device, that is common to a certain class of devices, this key can be used to compromise a huge number of devices remotely. Individual symmetric keys, and private keys of asymmetric cryptography are usually less problematic, but they still allow an attacker to impersonate the device and use e.g. a trusted connection to bypass firewalls, and perform further attacks on the other endpoint of the connection. But not only passwords and keys are interesting for an attacker, by extracting and analysing the firmware and software that is running on a device, an attacker can identify vulnerabilities or hidden device features in the code that can be used for standard attacks such as buffer overflows.

> **EXAMPLE**
>
> During a local attack on a smart metering device, an attacker discovers a proprietary engineering command in the firmware allowing the power switch to be controlled. The attacker transmits this command to other smart meters on the network in order to blackout surrounding households.

Finally, the extraction of software or firmware is relevant with respect to intellectual property (IP) protection. Intelligent field devices in the smart grid often rely on algorithms, parameters, and other form of intellectual property. While these attacks do not impair the stability of the smart grid, they may introduce severe financial harm to those producers that had large development costs for their products.

> **EXAMPLE**
>
> During a local attack on a smart metering device, the attacker gets access to a master password, which allows him to access a restricted part of the smart

meter's web-interface where metering parameters can be configured. With that information, any smart meter can be manipulated to record less consumption without breaking any seal.

4.2.1.2 Manipulating the Device Under Attack

Here the attacker manipulates the functionality of the embedded device in an unauthorized fashion. This refers to the violation of the generic security objectives "integrity" and "authenticity". Manipulation of the mechanical and electrical parts of a smart grid device is always feasible if an attacker gets physical access to the device, and is not a matter of IT security. However, being able to manipulate the programmed functionality of a smart grid device can be a critical threat to the smart grid, since such an attack can be simultaneously applied to a large number of devices by a single attacker.

A manipulated device can also be used by an attacker as a platform to compromise other parts of the system, since network-based security measures usually prevent attacks from outside. A device that is compromised by a physical attack might have privileged access to other components in its network segment, and therefore act as a beachhead to attacking further devices.

EXAMPLE

An intelligent device that is used to control a circuit breaker is part of a control system of the substation it belongs to. The substation is together with other substations connected to a central SCADA system, which is usually a PC-based platform. If an attacker can successfully compromise a single circuit breaker's control system, it could use the field bus system interconnecting the sensors and actuators in the substation to send commands to these sensors. In current technology, there is are usually no authentication and integrity measures implemented at that level, such that doing so does not involve any further weaknesses of the system. In addition, the attacker can use the uplink connection to compromise the SCADA system. Chances are much better here, since the attacker does not have to overcome any firewall and other isolation measures, and the system is probably more vulnerable on this interface, as attacks on this side are mostly not expected.

4.2.2 OVERVIEW OF PHYSICAL ATTACKS

Physical attacks (Weingart, 2000) are very powerful in general, but sophisticated attacks require not only expert knowledge but also increasing resources in terms of time and money. The following table gives a classification of different techniques with respect to their attack potential. It is important to note that especially the classes of attacks with low and medium attack potential are relevant candidates in the context of smart grid security.

Attack Potential	Techniques	Typical Equipment	Typical Equipment Costs (€)
Low	Access to local storage Accessing open interfaces Probing on buses Simple faults	memory chip reader, logic analyser, microcontroller/ FPGA boards	less than 1,000
Medium	Simple side channel attacks Glitching attacks	digital oscilloscope, signal generator, FPGA boards	2,000 – 10,000
Elevated	Enhanced side channel attacks EMA DPA Template attacks Semi-invasive Attacks	high-resolution digital oscilloscope, FPGA boards, chemical depackaging	10.000 – 50,000
High	Invasive attacks Fault attacks	(laser) probing station, chemical depackaging, focussed ion beam	more than 50.000

The techniques with low attack potential in this table are different from the others in the sense that they typically target systems without security functions like encryption and integrity checks. The attacks of the other three classes on the other hand can target weaknesses in already established cryptographic routines as well.

Figure 4.1 shows a typical taxonomy of physical attacks. In general, there are three categories depending on how invasive (i.e. non-invasive, semi-invasive and fully invasive) the attacks are with respect to opening up integrated circuit (IC) microchips inside an embedded system. With non-invasive attacks, the ICs are not opened at all.

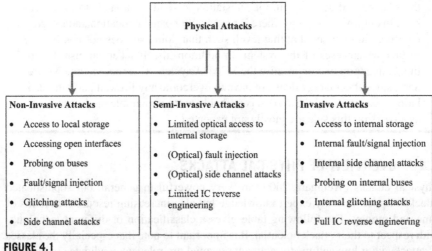

FIGURE 4.1

Taxonomy of physical attacks.

The attacks are thus mostly limited to the electrical signals accessible from the printed circuit board (PCB) within the system as well as possible device emanations that can be used for performing side channel attacks. Non-invasive attacks can be very powerful already as the attacker has full control over the system environment (such as electrical signals, temperature, system clock, etc.). Semi-invasive attacks go further by opening up ICs so that the die within is visible (either from the front or from the backside). The IC stays fully functional as the isolating and protecting passivation layer is not removed. This allows the attacker to see what is inside the microchip and thus also perform optical attacks such optical fault injection or optical emanation analysis. With invasive attacks, the protecting passivation layer is removed as well. If the IC is kept functional, this allows the attacker to observe communication on internal buses or even inject own signals for the attackers advantage. On the other side, invasive attacks also allow full reverse engineering of microchip internals. In the following sections, different attacks within this taxonomy are described in more detail.

4.2.3 ACCESS TO LOCAL STORAGE (NON-INVASIVE)

Accessing the information stored on an embedded device is often very easy, if information on these devices is not encrypted. Some devices are equipped even with removable and/or highly standardized storage such as SD cards, memory cards, hard discs, etc. But also any other form of non-volatile memory is not protected by its embedded nature. Memory chips such as flash or ROM can be unsoldered and read out by memory chip readers. For more complex settings, e.g. when no standard modules are used, the unsoldered memory chip can be integrated on a microcontroller board together with a self-written read-out routine. Bus probing (see below) is hereby helpful to reverse-engineer the protocol between the memory module and the processor.

Figure 4.2 shows how this low-cost attack can be conducted on a typical smart meter device. The flash memory was removed from the smart meter (left) and then resoldered to a breakout board (right). As the breakout board makes all flash memory chip device pins available through its connectors, a microcontroller board can be

FIGURE 4.2

Flash memory chip in a smart meter (left), smart meter memory chip soldered to breakout board for readout.

easily connected to read out the full memory content (i.e. the firmware) of the smart meter by utilizing a self-written routine.

If required by the attack, data and code on the memory modules can be also altered, or the memory module may be replaced at all by the attacker's own memory module in the original device.

4.2.4 ACCESSING OPEN INTERFACES (NON-INVASIVE)

Embedded devices come with plenty of interfaces. Network interfaces are always good attack targets. Smart grid devices, such as PLCs or PV control systems are usually not supposed to be connected directly to the Internet. Therefore one might find weaknesses in the network stack of wired network interfaces that are already patched for most standard IT systems. Ethernet with TCP/IP is used for those network connections, but there are other standards such as power-line communication or serial protocols, including MBUS. Power-line suffers also from the fact that many consider the physical nature of the interface, i.e. being modulated on the power line, as a sufficient barrier for an attacker. In fact, even with simple equipment it is not. In addition, the local attacker can also access wireless network interfaces. Beside communication based on IEEE 802.11, and the well-known weaknesses in WEP and WPA (Wong, 2003), a smart grid device might support other protocols such as GPRS, Wireless M-Bus, or even protocols from the home automation field (ZigBee, 6LoWPAN, etc.).

A very important class of interfaces for local attacks comprises debugging ports, such as JTAG or serial consoles. These debugging interfaces allow an attacker to get intra-chip information during runtime with little effort and without depackaging the chip.

EXAMPLE

The JTAG debugging port can be used to read out any register in a chip in operation. Depending on the chip, the Test Mode Select Input pin has to be activated, and then the registers can be read out bitwise. Any key that is stored at some time in a register – and this is the case if any cryptographic operation is performed by the IC – can be read out by this method. Similarly, the full firmware can be read out from non-volatile memories just the same way. Figure 4.3 shows an exemplary setup how the attack could be carried out on Smart Grid devices. On the left the JTAG and In-Circuit Emulation (ICE) ports within a widely used substation automation system are visible could be used to obtain secret internal device information. On the right it is shown how JTAG is used with a JTAG dongle to debug a smart meter.

4.2.5 BUS PROBING (NON-INVASIVE)

An alternative approach to gather information from embedded devices is to listen to the information that is exchanged on the platforms bus systems. A simple logic

FIGURE 4.3

JTAG and In-Circuit Emulation (ICE) ports inside a substation automation system (left), connected JTAG interface on a smart meter (right).

FIGURE 4.4

Bus probing on the internal bus of a microSD card.

analyser is hereby sufficient. Logic analysers that can be connected with USB to any computer are available already for a few Euros.

Figure 4.4 shows that bus probing attacks are even feasible in case microscopic circuit board traces. On the left side a very thin wire has been soldered to the exposed circuit traces on a microSD card that interconnect the internal card controller with the flash memory chip. To connect the logic probes to those wires, a simple breakout board was used. On the right side the intercepted signals are visible on the logic analyser.

4.2.6 FAULT/SIGNAL INJECTION (NON-INVASIVE)

In contrast to non-invasive bus probing attacks where the attacker passively intercepts the signals on a bus, it is also possible to take an active role by purposely modifying or even injecting own signals. This can be done rather easily by utilising readily available microcontroller or FPGA development boards. Assuming the simple case that inside an embedded system two devices communicate with each other, there is usually a sender and a receiver. Unless more advanced techniques such as bus arbitration are used, these roles between the devices are typically fixed. However, as signal injection is done by a second sender (i.e. an FPGA board) this could lead to issues as both senders would drive the bus in different directions. The solution is to perform a man-in-the-middle (MITM) attack where the connection between the two original devices is cut and the FPGA board is inserted in between. This allows the attacker to selectively forward and arbitrarily modify any communication between the two original devices.

EXAMPLE

A PV smart grid device communicating over an unencrypted but proprietary PLC (power line communication) protocol has a SoC controller chip and a modem chip on its circuit board. By probing the bus between the controller and the modem chip, the attacker was able to identify the messages that report how much power is fed into the utility grid. As the PLC protocol behind the modem is unknown to the attacker, he uses a cheap microcontroller board to modify the power measurement value transmitted on the bus to the modem chip. The modem chip accepts the modified message and sends it over to PLC network to the utility. Ultimately, this allows the attacker to report an arbitrary amount of generated power.

4.2.7 GLITCHING ATTACKS

Most common CPUs, FPGAs or microcontrollers are based on synchronous logic meaning that they require a system clock signal. Each time the clock signal occurs, the internal logic of the device advances to the next state. For instance with a CPU, this could be an instruction that is executed. Besides, the device needs to be powered by supplying a voltage to its power pins.

Figure 4.5 shows a greatly simplified version of how a synchronous system typically works. On the left side, the current computation result is stored inside a register (i.e. a set of Flip-Flops). If the clock signals the system to continue, the register makes its internal state available on the output. Consequently, the data is transferred through the combinational logic block and, after enough time has passed, the result

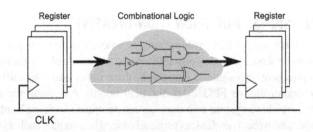

FIGURE 4.5

Synchronous Register-Transfer-Logic (RTL).

of the computation is available at the input of the subsequent register on the right. The time it takes for all signals to go entirely through the combinational logic block typically accounts for the major part of the required delay between two adjacent clock events (i.e. the maximum possible clock frequency of the system). Real-world systems comprise a huge number of such Register Transfer Logic (RTL) blocks ultimately triggered by the system clock.

With glitching attacks (Skorobogatov and Anderson, 2003), several of the physical properties of a system can be exploited to perturb the operation of the system to the attacker's advantage. The two predominant types of glitching are *clock glitching* and *voltage glitching*.

4.2.7.1 Clock Glitching

With clock glitching, the attacker supplies the clock signal to the system just as within a usual system. However, at a time of the attacker's choosing (for instance when a security critical instruction is executed), one or more intentionally too fast clock pulses are supplied. If the delay between those clock cycles is less than the time required for the data to pass through the combinational logic block, the input to the next register does not contain the finished computation result. Instead, some of the signals are still in their previous or in an intermediate state while others might be finished already. Besides, not all RTL blocks have the same time requirements. Considering a CPU logic implementation, the combinational logic within a complex CPU instruction might have a significantly higher logic delay in comparison to comparably simple implementations such as the CPUs program counter. As a result, clock glitching is especially effective against security critical conditional jumps or cryptographic computations in the firmware. Figure 4.6 provides an example of how an idealized clock glitch signal could look like.

While clock glitching attacks can be conducted with lab equipment such as signal or pattern generators, the low-cost approach typically uses FPGA boards for clock and glitch generation (Figure 4.7). In addition to finding the right glitch parameters (i.e. number of glitches or glitch duration), the key question is when to start the glitch attack. While more advanced techniques are available, brute force (i.e. trial and error) based approaches often work well if the test setup is automated. For instance, this can be achieved by automating the FPGA glitch generation and system interaction with custom software or scripts running on a PC.

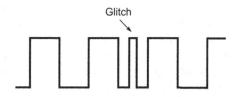

FIGURE 4.6

Glitch in the clock signal.

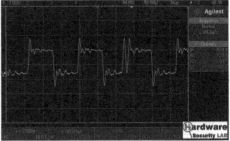

FIGURE 4.7

FPGA development board used for clock glitching (left), generated clock glitch measured at the target device (right).

EXAMPLE

A charging station for electric vehicles at the customer's premises is connected to a secure communication network. The attacker discovers that the device can be switched into a service mode if the utilities service password is entered. Since the attacker doesn't know the service password, clock glitching is applied to transform the execution of the conditional password checking branch instruction in the system's CPU into a non-branch instruction. The result is that although an invalid password was entered, the attacker can 'jump over' the password check and enter the service mode. The attacker discovers that through the service mode, the credentials and encryption keys of the utility's secure communication network can be read out.

4.2.7.2 Voltage Glitching

A change of the supply voltage impacts the device operation in multiple ways. If a lower voltage is used, the overall logic delays increase. Within an integrated circuit, signal traces have a capacitance that is for instance impacted by the length of the trace. Each time the state of the signal changes (i.e. from a logic 1 to a 0 or vice-versa), the driving transistors need to transfer current until the desired new state has been achieved. The less voltage is available for this task, the longer it takes. Hence the maximum operating frequency of the IC is decreased as well which can render the IC more susceptible to clock glitching attacks. Besides combinational logic, different types of memory such as flip-flops, registers and various types of RAM and non-volatile memories are affected through the voltage change as well. Memories often work by comparing a stored charge with a threshold reference voltage. Depending on the memory technology, the memory content could be interpreted as logic 1 if the stored charge is higher than the provided threshold. Otherwise, the state is considered to be a logic 0. However, if an attacker changes the threshold voltage far enough, the stored charge in a memory cell could be interpreted the wrong way.

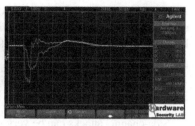

FIGURE 4.8

FPGA based voltage glitching setup (left), voltage glitch waveform and supply voltage measurement (right).

Since the overall device operation is impacted by the voltage change, attackers typically either increase or drop the supply voltage to a device only for a short period of time. The result is a sudden voltage glitch causing memories such as the registers in between combination logic to output an invalid state. Similar to clock glitching attacks, this can be effectively used to bypass security checks or perturb cryptographic computations. Figure 4.8 shows an exemplary voltage glitching setup. The FPGA board on the left as well as the target system under attack is controlled by custom software on a PC. A resulting voltage glitch waveform is depicted on the right.

4.2.8 SIDE-CHANNEL ATTACKS

Side-channel attacks, first introduced by Kocher (1996), exploit the *implementations* of cryptographic algorithms or software. When performing a side-channel attack, some observable behaviour of the (cryptographic) routine implementation is used to obtain additional information that allows the attacker to decode some cipher text, calculate the cryptographic keys or obtain details of the executed instructions and data within the system. This is in contrast to classic cryptanalysis, where weaknesses of the cryptographic primitive itself are exploited. Side-channel attacks can be classified along two axes (Fan et al., 2010):

1. Invasive vs. non-invasive: Invasive attacks require opening the device under attack. This usually refers to the chip level, where depackaging of the chip might be needed. Invasive attacks can be further divided into semi-invasive and fully-invasive attacks. The difference is that with semi-invasive attacks the passivation layer of the chip stays intact whereas with fully invasive attacks, the chip is further deprocessed depending on the requirements of the particular attack. In the context of the smart grid, also another abstraction level is relevant, namely whether the embedded device needs to be opened (and therefore seals are broken). However, for most side-channel attacks this is case.
2. Active vs. passive: While passive attacks restrict themselves to only observe the device's behaviour, an active attack also manipulates the device's operation e.g. by injecting various types of faults (electrical, optical, etc.) or by employing glitching attacks.

Since side-channel attacks base on physical phenomena and not (only) on mathematics, there are numerous attacks and one can be sure that for the future there will be even more. The most common attacks are, in increasing order of complexity:

- Timing attacks
- Power analysis attacks (SPA, DPA, Template attacks)
- EM-attacks

Side-channel attacks can be very sophisticated, and, as shown in the table earlier in this chapter, also very expensive. Except for smart metering, where e.g. by the German BSI the usage of secure processors is enforced (BSI, 2014), field devices in the smart grid usually come with little security functionality. Therefore, side-channel attacks might be considered less relevant compared to the simple attack methods presented above.

4.2.8.1 Timing Attacks

Timing attacks (Kocher, 1996) exploit data-dependent execution time differences. Consider the password check illustrated in Listing 4.1. The password check uses the user-supplied password `passwd` and compares it against a stored one. At the first glance the password checking routine seems to be secure if a long enough password is used to thwart password guessing attacks. However, a close look into the code reveals that the password immediately returns "false" as soon as the first character in the supplied password is different from the stored one. Instead of a conventional brute force password guessing attack, an attacker can thus measure the time between sending the password guess to the system and the response that the supplied password was wrong. However, if the first character was correct, this response will come back to the attacker a short period of time later since the loop in the password check is executed once again. Due to this timing information, the correct password can be easily guessed in comparison to a conventional brute force attack. However, as the approach needs reliable timing measurements averaging steps are often necessary so that over a higher number of measurements potential non-data-dependent timing differences can be filtered. In fact, this approach works so well that vulnerable cache-timing software implementations can be even attacked over multiple hops on the Internet (Brumley & Boney, 2003).

```
bool check_password(char *passwd)
{
    for (int i=0; i<pass_len; i++)
    {
        if (passwd[i] != stored_passwd[i])
            return false;
    }
    return true;
}
```

LISTING 4.1

Password check implementation that is prone to a timing attack.

EXAMPLE

Smart meters typically have an optical port allowing service and configuration settings to be changed. Since many values can neither be read nor written without the utility password, an attacker uses a low-cost optical interface (Figure 4.9) and measures the response timing for password guesses. Using these attacks, s/he discovers that the password check is vulnerable to timing attacks and the password can thus be easily guessed by the attacker.

4.2.8.2 Power Analysis Attacks

Whenever synchronous logic receives a clock signal, the output of a register is sent through combinational logic and finally reaches the next register (register transfer logic). During that time, the transistors in between need to switch so that single signals or a whole bus get switched from one state into the other. This does not only take time, but it also draws current because of the switching and the capacitances of the various structures within the chip. If the power consumption is measured over time, the resulting power trace is different and thus characteristic for each logic block. If for instance the power consumption of a CPU is observed between clock cycles, each executed individual instruction will have a different power trace. The reason is that within the microchip implementation, the logic that implements the CPU instruction is different as well.

Simple Power Analysis (SPA)

The main idea of simple power analysis (Kocher et al., 1999) is to directly analyse the power trace of a microchip during security relevant tasks. As each operation has

FIGURE 4.9

Optical interface connected to a smart meter for optical timing analysis testing.

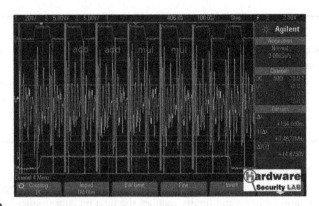

FIGURE 4.10

Exemplary power trace of a microcontroller during the execution of a simple algorithm.

its individual power signature, it is possible to determine which operations are performed within the chip by solely looking at its power consumption between clock cycles. In fact, the power trace of the execution of the same operation looks slightly different if the data supplied to that operation is different as well. The reason is that the more internal states need to be switched, the higher is the power consumption at a specific time. For systems which are not especially hardened against these kinds of attacks, an attacker might thus be able to determine which operations are performed within a microchip by solely looking at the power trace. Even more, the attacker might be able to determine the data that is processed by these operations as well. The impact of these attacks can be especially severe if security critical information such as key material or credentials can be extracted this way.

Figure 4.10 gives an example for a simple power analysis (SPA) attack. In the top of the picture the system clock signal is visible while at the bottom, a custom trigger signal for the measurement has been inserted. The power trace is visible in the centre of the picture (yellow). As visible, the two multiplication instructions executed have a different power trace as the first two addition instructions. With filtering setups and the use of averaging over a high number of equal test runs, the attacker can get a better signal to noise ratio by cancelling out measurement noise. The more precise the power measurements are the better the executed operations and the processed data can be identified.

Mainly depending on the clock frequency the attacker requires a reasonable priced digital oscilloscope to measure power traces and conduct a simple power analysis attack. The power is usually measured over a small shunt resistor between the power supply and the device power pin.

Differential Power Analysis (DPA)

Simple power analysis attacks usually involve significant manual analysis effort and are easy to protect against if the power consumption is internally filtered or randomized (i.e. through the insertion of dummy cycles). Differential power analysis attacks are much more powerful. Here, an attacker takes a high number of power trace measurements first. In the next step, a power model (i.e. hamming weight) is used to compute the theoretic power consumption of a (cryptographic) algorithm with a small number of guessed bits. For instance, in the case of the AES encryption algorithm this could be the first key byte that is used in the first AES round during AES computation. For this first computation, the attacker thus has a high number of measured power traces from the target device as well as the idealized and theoretic power consumption for the key guess using the power model. In order to determine whether the guess was correct, the attacker uses statistical means (i.e. the statistical correlation) to determine "how good" the match between the theoretic power consumption and the real measurements is. This is done for all key guesses (i.e. for 255 key guesses when the first byte of the AES key is targeted). If enough good measurements have been acquired, only one of them will show a strong statistic match. This is continued for the other key bytes as well until the full AES encryption key is recovered.

Due to the high number of measurements and the strong statistical methods, this approach can still lead to results if power analysis attack counter measures have been implemented. To take a high number of measurements with considerable sample length, once again an FPGA board based approach can be utilised (cf. Figure 4.11).

Template and Other Profiling Attacks

Similar to SPA and DPA, template attacks (Chari et al., 2002) use the side-channel information that is leaked through power consumption of cryptographic algorithm implementations. In contrast to the previous two approaches, it assumes that the

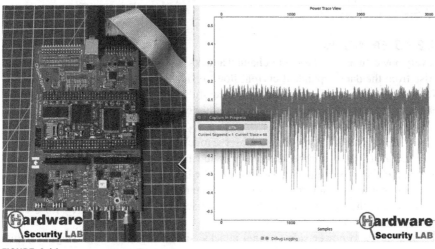

FIGURE 4.11

FPGA based DPA measurement setup.

FIGURE 4.12

Setup for an EM attack (Image: Fraunhofer AISEC / Andreas Heddergott).

adversary has access to an identical device, which is used to build a multivariate stochastical model of the signal and noise of the power trace. This model is the used to iteratively perform a maximum likelihood classification of a prefix of the power sample. Originally shown to be very effective for symmetric cryptographic operations, also asymmetric cryptography has been shown vulnerable to template attacks (Medwed & Oswald, 2008).

The approach can be generalized to any other model-building technique. For instance, machine learning can be used to build a profile of the cryptographic algorithm which is then applied to solve the classification problem in the foresaid iteration (Hospodar et al., 2011).

4.2.8.3 EM Attacks
A very powerful method for side-channel attacks makes use of the EM emissions that arise from the data-dependant current flows inside a device (Agrawal et al., 2002). To obtain sufficient information for a successful side-channel attack, a single probe can be sufficient (see Figure 4.12). With multiple probes, more sophisticated attacks can be performed.

With EM attacks it is possible to observe much faster signals than with e.g. power measurements, since a larger frequency band can be recorded. For power measurements, the signal is often lowpass-filtered. The higher-frequency parts of the signal allows in particular capturing the effects of the combinatorial logic that is between the latches of the circuit. The results of EM attacks can be improved by opening the packaging of the device (see below).

In analogy to power side-channel attacks, simple attacks with a single sample (SEMA), differential attacks with multiple samples (DEMA), and template-based attacks are possible.

FIGURE 4.13

Milling a cavity into the desoldered chip.

4.2.9 IC DECAPSULATION

For semi-invasive and invasive attacks on Integrated Circuits (ICs) it is necessary to open up the IC device and expose the contained silicon die. Depending on the type of attack, the microchip should still be functional after the decapsulation procedure. As a preparation for these kinds of attacks, a common approach is presented. However, other decapsulation and preparation techniques exist as well.

Initially, the microchip to be decapsulated is usually desoldered from the circuit board for easier handling. In the next step a cavity is carefully milled into the centre of the IC package with a Dremel tool (Figure 4.13). The cavity needs to be deep enough to hold a drop of acid in place, but the die below has to stay undamaged from the milling process.

In the next step, the chip is heated up and a drop of acid is carefully applied onto the milled cavity. Usually, nitric acid or sulphuric acid is used for this process (Figure 4.14). After the reaction of the acid with the epoxy package is finished, the chip is rinsed in acetone. The etch steps and rinse steps are repeated until the die is exposed. Depending on the type of attack, it is also possible to completely remove the package this way. For semi-invasive attacks the chip needs to stay functional and just the top epoxy cover of the chip is removed.

 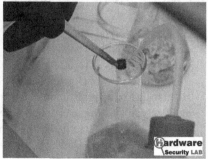

FIGURE 4.14

Chip decapsulation with nitric acid (left), rinsing with acetone (right).

FIGURE 4.15

Chip cleaning in an ultrasonic cleaner (left), still functional chip prepared for semi-invasive attacks.

As soon as enough material from the IC epoxy package has been removed, the chip needs to be cleaned for microscopic analysis (Figure 4.15). This is usually done in an acetone bath inside an ultrasonic cleaner. The result of the decapsulated and cleaned chip is visible on the right side of Figure 4.15. In this state the chip is still functional and the bonding wires are intact.

4.2.10 LIMITED OPTICAL ACCESS TO INTERNAL STORAGE

Depending on the non-volatile memory type in a chip (i.e. mask ROM) it is possible that the content of the memory can be optically read either from the front or from the backside without having to deprocess the chip. However, the approach is limited to memory types that can be optically read without preprocessing the chip.

Figure 4.16 shows a Scanning Electron Microscope (SEM) picture of a via-ROM memory. The memory content is set with tiny via plugs that can be seen optically. An attacker could thus gain access to the internal ROM storage content through a semi-invasive attack.

EXAMPLE

An internetworked smart grid device in a secondary substation uses a proprietary encryption algorithm to secure the protocol exchanged over a wireless transmission link. The attacker was able to intercept the wireless traffic with a low-cost Software Defined Radio (SDR), but is unable to decrypt the traffic. He manages to acquire an outdated similar device through an internet auction and decapsulates the encryption chip in it. He discovers that the chip uses a known CPU architecture and the firmware is stored in an optically readable mask-ROM memory. Using a microscope from a nearby university lab, he manages to dump the memory and reverse engineer the proprietary encryption algorithm. It turns out that the algorithm is weak and, therefore, the attacker manages to wirelessly control the secondary substation devices in his vicinity.

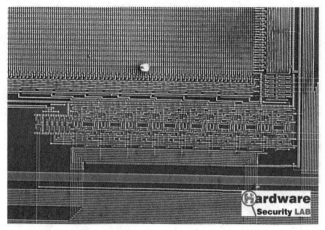

FIGURE 4.16

Lower part of a via-ROM memory and its column driver.

4.2.11 (OPTICAL) FAULT INJECTION (SEMI-INVASIVE)

Introducing faults into cryptographic routines can lead to leakage of information that allows computing secret key material (Boneh et al., 1997). Faults can be injected e.g. with a laser probing station, as shown in Figure 4.17. For this, the package has to be opened, as described in the previous sections. The wavelength of the laser is a limiting factor for the spot size, and therefore the area where the laser energy leads to bit-flips. On the other hand, the optical properties of the silicon have to be taken into consideration. This can be used to attack the chip from the backside with a laser that emanates in the IR range – for these wavelengths, the silicon die is transparent, and the gates are not covered with the metal layer, as it is the case when attacking the chip from the front side.

4.2.12 IC REVERSE ENGINEERING

Similar to the semi-invasive limited access to local storage, it is also possible to perform limited IC reverse engineering with semi-invasive attacks. If through the front- or backside of the IC enough interesting details about the implementation are visible, an attacker might be able to obtain security critical information. Figure 4.18 shows an example about how relevant parts of a logic implementation can be obtained from a cryptographic chip through semi-invasive reverse engineering.

If device secrets are deeply hidden in the silicon, fully invasive IC reverse engineering utilizes IC deprocessing and microscopy techniques to take apart the microchip implementation layer by layer. A typical CMOS IC has a poly-silicon logic layer at the bottom and several metal layers (Cu, Al) at the top which are interconnected with via layers (W) and insulation layers (mostly $SiO2$) in between. The logic layer at the bottom contains the actual circuit implementation with common design elements such as different types of memory, cryptographic cores, a CPU, peripherals or glue logic. A major challenge for deep silicon security analysis is the deprocessing of ICs

FIGURE 4.17

Fault attack with an optical laser (Image: Fraunhofer AISEC / Andreas Heddergott).

with results that are suitable for image analysis. Typical approaches use chemical-mechanical polishing (CMP), wet chemical etching or plasma etching (Figure 4.19).

By using these deprocessing techniques, the attacker can obtain internal information deeply hidden in the chip such as the implementation of proprietary encryption algorithms, the firmware contained within ROM memory (similar to the limited semi-invasive optical access to internal storage but more powerful) or potential counter measures in the chip. An example for the required lab setup to conduct microchip image analysis is visible in Figure 4.20. On the left an analyst uses an automated optical microscope to obtain and analyse microchip pictures. On the right a low-cost Scanning Electron Microscope (SEM) is visible that is used to conduct analyze the internals of newer microchips with smaller feature sizes.

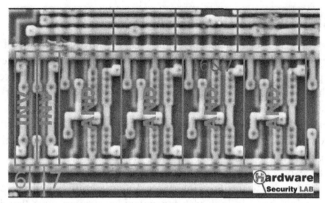

FIGURE 4.18

Obtained logic information from a semi-invasive attack on a cryptographic chip (SEM image).

FIGURE 4.19

Polishing machine (left), chemical deprocessing (middle), plasma etcher (right).

FIGURE 4.20

Microchip image analysis (left), scanning electron microscope (right).

4.3 BASIC PROTECTION MECHANISMS

The simplest threats of local attackers can be countered by being aware of the possibilities a local attacker has, and choosing a system design that mitigates these threats. The first step is to be aware of all open local interfaces, and restrict the access to the system by these interfaces in the same way as one would do for a network interface that is potentially accessible to an attacker.

The interfaces should obviously not allow any unauthorized access, state-of-art authentication mechanisms should be used, and the authentication credentials should be hard to guess. Functionality that is needs not be accessed on those interfaces should not be exposed. The possibility of standard attacks, like buffer overflows should be considered also for those interfaces. Vulnerabilities should be patched by updates. This might be a difficult task for embedded devices once they have been rolled-out. Not needed interfaces should be removed ideally not only from the casing but also from the circuit board.

Probing on busses and signals can be impeded by obfuscating the data that is transmitted over them. Already simple methods, that are not cryptographically secure, can be very effective here, like scrambling the data according to a schema that is given by some shared pseudo-random generator. Of course, using strong cryptography would be even better here, but maybe not feasible e.g. on the lines between a processor and the system's RAM.

Key material should be stored in secure places. Removable storage is the easiest to read out for an attacker, but from any kind of non-volatile memory it is possible to extract data. Secure memory (see Section 6.3) is the preferred choice here. If it is not possible to integrate a secure memory or security processor in the device, sometimes PUFs (see Section 6.5) might be a possibility to securely store a key with which the key material is encrypted before being stored in NV memory.

Furthermore, also non-IT solutions to protect a device are feasible. Sealed cases are effective if breaking the seal can be related to a single person and legally prosecuted. However, one needs to think about potential goals of an attacker: somebody planning a terrorist attack is probably not be scared off by seals.

A rigorous analysis of threats and vulnerabilities can help identifying the right protection measures. Attack trees (Schneier, 1999; Byres et al., 2004) are a good tool to carry out such an analysis. To construct an attack tree, a potential goal of an attacker is placed at the root of the tree. An attacker's goal can be systematically derived by looking at the assets of the device under consideration, and the violation of some security objective (confidentiality, integrity, availability) with respect to this asset. For each goal, a separate tree is generated. In the first step, the attacker's goal is decomposed into sub-goals that allow achieving the goal. These sub-goals can be connected by a logical AND or by an OR. For AND-connected nodes, all sub-goals must be achieved to achieve the goal – this reflects several steps of an attack. For OR-connected nodes, at least one sub-goal has to be achieved to achieve the goal – this reflects attack alternatives. In the next steps, the sub-goals are refined using the same method until a sufficient fine level of granularity is reached. Then the leaves form the set of attacks that need to be considered.

EXAMPLE

Constructing an attack tree for smart meter data manipulation, one starts with identifying potential attack goals. The asset here is the smart meter readings that are transmitted to the service provider. The violation of that asset with respect to integrity gives us the goal that is placed on top of the tree. Then this goal is split into three subtasks – each of these is sufficient to achieve the goal, thus they are connected by an "OR". Further refinement could lead to a tree as follows:

```
MANIPULATION OF TRANSMITTED SMART METER DATA

OR
1  Manipulation of the measurements
        AND
        1.1    Physical access to electrical measurement unit
        1.2    Changing the electrical signal
2  Manipulation of the smart metering device
        OR
        2.1    Physical attack
               OR
               2.1.1 Firmware manipulation
               2.1.2 Malware injection
               2.1.3 Manipulation of signal on internal lines
               2.1.4 ...
        2.2    Network-based attack
               OR
               2.2.1 Network-based manipulation with stolen passwords
                      AND
                      2.2.1.1    Password obtained from physical attack
                      2.2.1.2    Manipulation with password possible
               2.2.2 ...
3  Manipulation during transmission
        3.1    ...
```

The example tree is not complete, as attack trees can become large. Sometimes it might be handy to refer to already existing subtrees, if entries repeat.

4.4 HARDWARE SECURITY MODULES

As we have seen in the previous sections, protecting secrets on a device where an attacker might have physical access can be hard. One solution to this are cryptographic chips that are especially hardened against tampering. Depending on their specific functionality, they are called hardware security modules (HSM)[1], secure

---

[1]Not to be confused with devices from payment domain, which can be directly connected to a network and are standalone systems with e.g. PKI functionality. However, usually these devices contain a secure cryptoprocessor themselves.

crypto-processor, or secure element (SE). A common implementation for normal PCs is the Trusted Platform Module (TPM).

One of the key characteristics of HSMs is that they provide features that make physical attacks as shown before difficult. Countermeasures can include special coating, tampering detection circuitry, and a chip layout that minimizes side-channel effects. In addition, they often provide hardware accelerated cryptographic support.

The two most common form factors for HSMs are (i) smart cards and (ii) integrated circuits. Smart cards are plastic cards with an integrated crypto-processor. Their removable nature allows their usage for user identification and authorization. As such, they can be used to secure the authentication procedure on embedded and programming devices.

For our considerations more relevant are integrated circuits that are integrated onto the hardware board of the smart grid field device. These modules are coupled with low-level serial bus systems such as I2C or SPI to the device's main processor. From a security perspective it is important to note that the communication between the module and the processor is not secured, so that any communication on this bus can be read by a physical attacker with little effort. Therefore, information that has to be kept confidential, such as symmetric keys and private keys for asymmetric cryptography must not leave the security module. Instead, the cryptographic operation is performed by the HSM, that is, the processor sends the information to be signed or encrypted to the HSM, then the HSM performs the cryptographic operation, and returns the result to the main processor.

Typical functionality of a HSM includes:

- Secure storage
- Providing manufacturer keys and root certificates
- Creating asymmetric key pairs
- Random number generators
- Symmetric and asymmetric cryptographic routines
- Application specific secure functions (JavaCard, Applets)
- Lifecycle functions, such as locking, terminating, and erasing a device

EXAMPLE (SMART METER GATEWAY ACCORDING TO THE GERMAN BSI PROTECTION PROFILE (BSI, 2014))

In order to address the public demand for privacy and security in the context of smart metering, the German BSI has issued a protection profile according to common criteria for a smart metering gateway. This device is supposed to bundle security functionality of metering devices (for electricity, gas, water, etc.) and is supposed also to provide a secure gateway platform for future smart home and smart energy systems. The architecture of the smart metering system is shown in Figure 4.21.

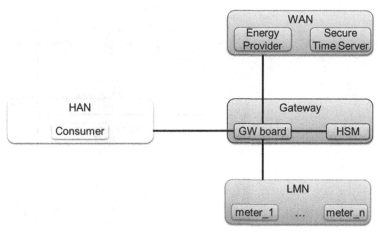

FIGURE 4.21

Smart meter gateway according to the German BSI Protection Profile.

Herein, the gateway board is the interface between the local metering network (LMN), the home automation network (HAN), and the connection to energy providers, metering services, and other entities (WAN). In the protection profile, a rigorous security analysis was performed, that led to a set of security requirements that are mandatory for future smart meters in Germany.

A central part of the architecture according to the BSI is a special hardware security module that is specifically designed for the requirements of the smart meter gateway.

EXAMPLE (ENHANCED SECURITY WITH A JAVACARD 3.0)

In (Angermeier et al., 2012), an alternative architecture for implementing a secure smart metering gateway is proposed. The design (see Figure 4.22) is based on some programmable hardware security module (such as e.g. a Java-Card 3.0) and provides a significantly higher level of security. Similar techniques can not only be applied for smart meters but also for other devices in the smart grid.

The basic idea of the approach is that all security relevant functionality is encapsulated in the hardware security module. In particular, the secure communication channels (in this case with the energy provider and the smart meter) terminate directly in the HSM. The gateway board acts as a firewall, is responsible for the lower communication layers, and provides mass storage. Sensitive data is stored outside the HSM only in encrypted form, i.e. this information is present in an unencrypted fashion only inside the HSM.

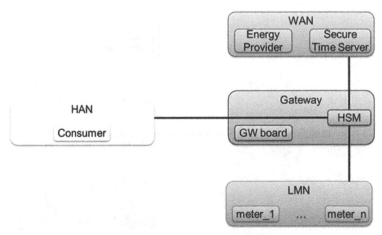

FIGURE 4.22

Enhanced security with a JavaCard 3.0.

> The HSM handles smart meter data aggregation, securely time-stamping this information, and transmitting smart meter data to authorized entities. Due to this design, a physical attacker cannot get access to any sensitive data unless he is able to break the tamper resistant security module.

4.5 INTEGRITY PROTECTION AND ATTESTATION

In addition to the application of hardware security modules mentioned in the previous section, HSMs can serve as root of trust for protecting the integrity of the platform. The trusted platform module (TPM) (Challenger et al., 2008) is a hardware security module specialized for this purpose.

The basic idea is that during a boot process (see Figure 4.23), every part of the system is checking the integrity of its higher level parts by hashing the state and comparing it with a securely stored reference hash. To ensure that this process is not tampered by some malware in the BIOS, the system boot process needs to start in

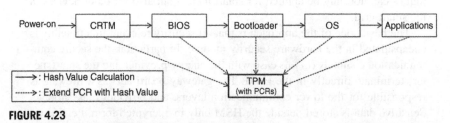

FIGURE 4.23

Secure boot process with a trusted platform module.

some specialized hardware the core root of trust for measurement (CRTM). In PCs, the hardware functionality for the secure boot process involves CPU, north bridge (MCH), south bridge (ICH), and TPM.

From a general point of view one can distinguish between:

- *Secure boot*, where integrity is checked before starting the step in the boot sequence. If the integrity check fails, the boot sequence is stopped. As a consequence, a compromised system is not booted at all.
- *Authenticated boot*, where the system boots completely, independent of the hashed values. However, the information gained during the boot sequence is for communication to prove the integrity to 3rd parties.

For PC systems, secure boot is nowadays somehow standard. But it is also possible to use these techniques for embedded devices (Khalid et al., 2013). Here, due to the constraint resources of the platform, the large variations in system architectures and the sometimes missing hardware support for the CRTM, custom solutions are necessary.

4.6 PHYSICAL UNCLONEABLE FUNCTIONS

Physical Uncloneable Functions (PUFs) Pappu 2002 (Suh, 2007) provide another possibility to add authentication and key storage capabilities in a highly secure way to embedded devices. The research on PUFs is a rather recent branch of research, which offers some intriguing advantages compared to classical approaches, but has not yet proven its applicability for a broader range of products.

4.6.1 MOTIVATION

Storing secrets in NV memory suffers from several shortcomings:

- Normal NV memory can be read out easily
- Active circuitry for anti-tampering needs to be battery-backed, such an approach is not appropriate for field devices in the Smart Grid.
- HSMs have protection measures, but devices that are in the field for a long time are subject to new forms of attacks where these measures might not be sufficient anymore. In any case, additional hardware is necessary.

The basic idea of PUFs and related concepts is to make use of the natural and inherent variances of physical structures, even if they originate from the same production process. A prominent – and practically important – example is the variances in the IC fabrication process, resulting e.g. in observable differences in the speed of electrical signals in digital circuits. The normal effort in chip design would be to mitigate these effects with clocked latches, such that any two chips with the same design behave in the same way. When designing a PUF, exactly the opposite is enforced, i.e. the circuitry is equipped with some measurement capabilities, so that for each individual device a unique "fingerprint" can be derived.

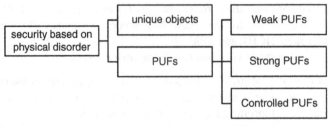

FIGURE 4.24

Classification of techniques using random nature of physical objects.

4.6.2 CLASSIFICATION OF PUFS AND RELATED CONCEPTS

The idea of exploiting the unique nature of physical objects can be extended to many other concepts than just timing in integrated circuits.

Techniques based on the random nature of physical objects can be classified as given in Figure 4.24 (Rührmair et al., 2012).

4.6.2.1 Unique Objects

A unique object is a physical entity that exhibits a small, fixed set of unique analogue properties upon being measured by external equipment.

Unique objects can be useful in product protection, and hereby assist the legal prosecution of copyright infringement (different from product protection measures that prevent copies by technical means). Since unique objects require external measurement equipment and therefore local presence of the verifier, they are less relevant for smart grid applications.

4.6.2.2 Physical Uncloneable Functions (PUFs)

As implied by the name, PUFs in the stricter sense are physical objects that implement a random but stable function. That is, the PUF is challenged with some input sequence (for PUFs implemented in silicon this is usually a bit sequence), and they respond with an output sequence. A specific challenge c with response r is called a challenge-response pair (CRP). Based on the number and nature of CRPs, PUFs can be classified into weak PUFs and strong PUFs:

1. **Weak PUFs** have only a low number of CRPs. Since in this case it is possible for an attacker to learn all CRPs, such a PUF is only useful when the responses never leave the circuitry. Therefore, a weak PUF needs to be observed by internal measurement mechanisms. The response to a specific challenge then acts as a secret, from which other keys can be derived. Examples for weak PUF implementations are the ring oscillator PUF (RO-PUF) and the SRAM PUFs.
2. **Strong PUFs** are characterized by a high number of CRPs and complex challenge-response behaviour. A strong PUF can be naturally used for authentication but a strong PUF can also be used like a weak PUF. Examples for strong PUFs are the arbiter PUF, and PUFs based on bistable rings (BR-PUF, TBR-PUF).

4.6.3 PROPERTIES OF PUFS

When evaluating the quality of PUFs, several metrics are relevant Maiti, Gunreddy, & Schaumont (2013):

1. **Inter-chip variation** is used to characterize the uniqueness of PUFs. It can be measured by taking the average Hamming distance between the responses of two PUFs when supplied with the same challenge.
2. **Intra-chip variation** is used to characterize the robustness of PUFs. It can be measured by taking the average Hamming distance between two responses to the same challenge on a PUF.

A good PUF design tries to achieve a large inter-chip variation and a small intra-chip variation. Randomness of the PUF can be captured by the entropy of the response bit-stream. The bias of a PUF is the deviation from the 0.5 probability of a 0 resp. 1 for a single bit of the PUF response. Obviously, a large bias has also influence on entropy, inter-chip variation and intra-chip variation.

4.6.4 EXAMPLE IMPLEMENTATIONS OF PUFS

4.6.4.1 SRAM PUF

An SRAM PUF employs the start-up behaviour of SRAM cells (Guajardo, 2007). When an SRAM cell is powered without being initialized, its start-up state is undefined. Moreover, due to the inherent variances in the gates of the cell, the uninitialized states are random and device specific. The bit string of such an array can be seen as a weak PUF, and therefore be used for key generation. An SRAM PUF is different from the following ones, as it can be implemented without hardware changes using any already existing SRAM in the system. It is therefore an example for an *intrinsic PUF*.

4.6.4.2 Ring Oscillator PUF

The ring oscillator PUF (Suh, 2007) in Figure 4.25 achieves a unique fingerprint by comparing the relative frequencies of oscillating rings composed of inverters. The output is only a single bit, where the value depends on which ring is faster.

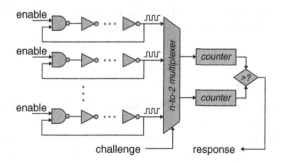

FIGURE 4.25

The ring oscillator PUF (Image from (Merli et al., 2013), permission granted).

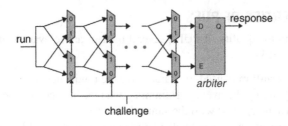

FIGURE 4.26

The arbiter PUF (Image from (Merli et al., 2013), permission granted).

A multiplexer can be used to compare more than one ring, and the selection signal of the multiplexer is then the challenge. Since the number of challenge response pairs is low, this is an example for a weak PUF. By combining the bits for a fixed sequence of challenges, a secret key is generated.

4.6.4.3 Arbiter PUF

The arbiter PUF, as depicted in Figure 4.26, was one the first PUF architectures based on CMOS gates (Gassend et al., 2002, Lee et al., 2004). In this design, the challenge is selecting a sequence of delay elements. Depending on which path is faster, the PUF outputs 0 or 1. Because of the delay elements that are needed, the arbiter PUF cannot be implemented in FPGA. In addition, the arbiter PUF has been shown to be vulnerable to machine learning attacks and is therefore – although initially intended for generating a large number of challenge-response pairs and therefore allowing challenge-response authentication – only useable as a weak PUF.

4.6.4.4 Bistable Ring

The bistable ring PUF was proposed by Chen et al. (2011), Chen et al. (2012), and is depicted in Figure 4.27. After enabling the reset line, the PUF will oscillate until it stabilizes into one of two states. As a result, either 0 or 1 is generated as the PUF response. The bistable ring PUF is able to generate a complex challenge-response behaviour and is therefore a strong PUF.

A variant of the bistable ring PUF was recently proposed under the name twisted bistable ring (Schuster & Hesselbarth, 2014). This design is based on a similar idea, and achieves a smaller bias than the normal bistable ring PUF.

4.7 CONCLUSION

The practicability of a broad usage of PUFs needs still to be explored. However, some properties of PUFs make this concept very attractive for application in smart grid devices (Stumpf & Böttinger 2013). In particular, the possibility to securely store key material without the need for dedicated hardware, such as hardware security modules, might lead to cost-efficient solutions. The number of intelligent field devices is expected to be large in the future, and therefore equipping them with extra hardware

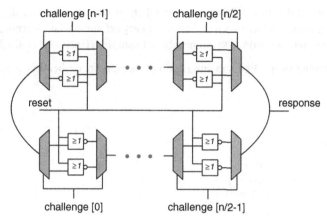

challenge [n-1]   challenge [n/2]

reset   response

challenge [0]   challenge [n/2-1]

FIGURE 4.27

The Bistable Ring PUF (Image from (Merli et al., 2013), permission granted).

might be a significant and limiting cost factor. A second point is the high security level of PUFs. Hardware security modules come with explicit features that counteract invasive attacks. These countermeasures might be overcome one day by an attacker, given that in the smart grid, devices might be in the field for a long time. The security of PUFs comes from the fact that any invasive attempt to manipulate the structure would destroy the information that is stored therein. However, first results show that also PUFs are vulnerable to side-channel attacks (Delvaux and Verbauwhede, 2014).

From a general point of view, a PUF can be used in two basic applications (Suh & Devadas 2007):

- *Key generation.* This is the main application for weak PUFs. From the responses to the limited set of challenges, a secret key is derived. In contrast to the application for authentication, here it is important that the PUF response is stable. Since PUFs naturally come with noise, error-correction methods have to be applied, so that for each query, the PUF generates the same key. These error-correction methods require helper data that needs to be stored in NV memory. Two common methods are the code-offset fuzz extractor (Dodis et al., 2004) and index based syndrome coding (Yu & Devadas, 2010).

  The main attack against this usage of PUFs is the application of side-channel attacks (e.g. EM attacks) to learn the secret key of the PUF.
- *Authentication.* The complex challenge-response behaviour of strong PUFs can be used to directly authenticate a device. To this end, before deploying the device, a large list of challenge-response pairs are generated and stored in a secure database on the verifier's side. If at a later time the device needs to be authenticated, the verifier takes a random challenge from the stored set and sends this to the PUF. After the PUF responds, the verifier is able to compare the PUF response with the one from the database. Of course, every challenge-response pair can be used only once.

It is important that the challenge-response behaviour is not predictable. Machine learning techniques have been shown to be very effective when learning the underlying function from a small number of samples (Hospodar et al., 2012).

By employing strong PUFs in smart grid devices, both application scenarios can be realized.

ACRONYMS

BR-PUF	Bistable ring PUF
CRP	Challenge-response pair
DEMA	Differential EM analysis
DPA	Differential power analysis
EM	Electromagnetic
FPGA	Field-programmable gate array
HAN	Home area network
HSM	Hardware security module
IP	Intellectual property
LMN	Local metering network
MITM	Man-in-the-middle
PCB	Printed circuit board
PLC	Programmable logic controller
PLC	Powerline communication
PUF	Physical uncloneable function
PV	Photovoltaics
RO-PUF	Ring oscillator PUF
RTL	Register-transfer logic
SCADA	Supervisory control and data acquisition
SE	Secure Element
SEMA	Simple EM analysis
SoC	System on a Chip
SPA	Simple power analysis
TBR-PUF	Twisted bistable ring PUF
TPM	Trusted platform module

REFERENCES

Agrawal, D., Archambeault, B., Rao, J., & Rohatgi, P. (2002). The EM side-channel(s). In *Proceedings of CHES 2002, LNCS, Vol. 2523* (pp. 29–45). Redwood City, CA, USA.
Angermeier, D., Böttinger, K., Ibing, A., Schuster, D., Stumpf, F., & Wacker, D. (2012). A secure architecture for smart meter systems. In *IEEE SmartGridComm 2012*.
Boneh, D., DeMillo, R. A., & Lipton, R. J. (1997). On the importance of checking cryptographic protocols for faults. In *Advances in Cryptology — EUROCRYPT '97, LNCS 1233* (pp. 37–51).
Brumley, D., & Boney, D. (2003). Remote timing attacks are practical. In *Proceedings of the 12th Usenix Security Symposium, 2003*.

Bundesamt für Sicherheit in der IT (2014). *Common Criteria Protection Profile BSI-CC-PP-0073-2014*. Retrieved from https://www.bsi.bund.de/SharedDocs/Downloads/DE/BSI/Zertifizierung/ReportePP/pp0073b_pdf

Byres, E. J., Franz, M., & Miller, D. (2004). The use of attack trees in assessing vulnerabilities in SCADA systems. In *Proceedings of the International Infrastructure Survivability Workshop*.

Challener, D., Yoder, K., Catherman, R., Safford, D., & Doorn, L. V. (2008). *A practical guide to trusted computing*. IBM Press.

Chari, S., Rao, J. R., & Rohatgi, P. (2002). Template attacks. In *CHES 2002, LNCS 2523* (pp. 13–28).

Chen, Q., Csaba, G., Lugli, P., Schlichtmann, U., & Rührmair. U. (2011). The bistable ring PUF: A new architecture for strong physical unclonable functions. *HOST 2011*, 134–141.

Chen, Q., Csaba, G., Lugli, P., Schlichtmann, U., & Rührmair. U. (2012). Characterization of the bistable ring PUF. *DATE 2012*, 1459–1462.

Delvaux, J., & Verbauwhede, I. (2014). *Attacking PUF-based pattern matching key generators via helper data manipulation. Topics in Cryptology–CT-RSA 2014* (pp. 106–131). Springer International Publishing.

Dodis, Y., Reyzin, L., & Smith, A. (2004). Fuzzy extractors: How to generate strong keys from biometrics and other noisy data. In C. Cachin, & J. Camenisch (Eds.), *Advances in Cryptology – EUROCRYPT 2004, ser. Lecture Notes in Computer Science, Vol. 3027* (pp. 523–540). Berlin/Heidelberg: Springer.

Fan, J., Guo, X., De Mulder, E., Schaumont, P., Preneel, B., & Verbauwhede, I. (2010). State-of-the-art of secure ECC implementations: a survey on known side-channel attacks and countermeasures. In *IEEE International Symposium on Hardware-Oriented Security and Trust (HOST)*.

Gassend, B., Clarke, D., van Dijk, M., & Devadas S. (2002). Controlled physical random functions. In *Computer Security Applications Conference, Proceedings* (pp. 149–160).

Gassend, B., Clarke, D., van Dijk, M., & Devadas S. (2002). Silicon physical random functions. In *CCS '02: Proceedings of the 9th ACM conference on computer and communications security* (pp. 148–160). New York, NY, USA: ACM.

Hospodar, G., Gierlichs, B., De Mulder, E., Verbauwhede, I., & Vandewalle, J. (2011). Machine learning in side-channel analysis: a first study. *Journal of Cryptographic Engineering*, *1*(4), 293–302.

Hospodar, G., Maes, R., & Verbauwhede, I. (2012, December). Machine learning attacks on 65nm Arbiter PUFs: Accurate modeling poses strict bounds on usability. In *WIFS* (pp. 37–42).

Khalid, O., Rolfes, C., & Ibing, A. (2013). On implementing trusted boot for embedded systems. In *IEEE International Symposium on Hardware-Oriented Security and Trust (HOST)*, *75*(80), 2–3, June 2013.

Kocher, P. (1996). Timing attacks on implementations of Diffie-Hellman, RSA, DSS, and other systems. In *Advances in Cryptology—CRYPTO '96. Lecture Notes in Computer Science 1109* (pp. 104–113). doi:10.1007/3-540-68697-5_9.

Kocher, P., Jaffe, J., & Jun, B. (1999). Differential power analysis. In *Proceedings of Crypto 1999, LNCS, Vol. 1666* (pp. 398–412). Santa-Barbara, CA, USA, August 1999.

Lee, J.W. (2004). A Technique to Build a Secret Key in Integrated Circuits for Identification and Authentication Applications.

Maiti, A., Gunreddy, V., & Schaumont, P. (2013). A systematic method to evaluate and compare the performance of physical unclonable functions. In *Embedded Systems Design with FPGAs* (pp. 245–267).

Medwed, M., & Oswald, M. E. (2008). Template attacks on ECDSA. In *9th International Workshop, WISA 2008, LNCS* (pp. 14–27). Jeju Island, Korea, September 23–25, 2008.

Merli, D., Sigl, G., & Eckert, C. (2013). Identities for embedded systems enabled by physical unclonable functions, number theory and cryptography. *Lecture Notes in Computer Science, Vol. 8260* (pp. 125–138). Springer, 2013.

Pappu, R. (2002). *Physical one-way functions*. PhD thesis.

Rührmair, U., Devadas, S., & Koushanfar, F. (2012). Security based on physical uncloneability and disorder. In *Introduction to Hardware Security and Trust 2012* (pp. 65–102).

Schneier, B. (1999). Attack trees. *In Dr. Dobb's journal, 24*(12), 21–29.

Schuster, D., & Hesselbarth, R. (2014). Dieter Schuster, Robert Hesselbarth: Evaluation of bistable ring PUFs using single layer neural networks. In *Trust and Trustworthy Computing, Lecture Notes in Computer Science, Vol. 8564*, pp. 101–109.

Skorobogatov, S. P., & Anderson, R. J. (2003). Optical fault induction attacks. *Cryptographic Hardware and Embedded Systems-CHES 2002* (pp. 2–12). Berlin/Heidelberg: Springer.

Stumpf, F., & Böttinger, K. (2013). When the lights go out—Attacks and security solutions for smart meter. In *Proceedings of the 23rd SmartCard Workshop*. Fraunhofer Verlag, 2013.

Suh, G. E., & Devadas, S. (2007). Physical unclonable functions for device authentication and secret key generation. In *Proceeding DAC '07 Proceedings of the 44th Annual Design Automation Conference*, 9–14.

Weingart, S. H. (2000). Physical security devices for computer subsystems: A survey of attacks and defenses. *Cryptographic Hardware and Embedded Systems—CHES 2000* (pp. 302–317). Berlin/Heidelberg: Springer.

Wong, S. (2003). The evolution of wireless security in 802.11 networks: WEP, WPA and 802.11 standards. Retrieved from *http://www.sans.org/rr/whitepapers/wireless/1109.php*, *28*(7), 05.

Yu, M. -D. M., & Devadas, S. (2010). Secure and robust error correction for physical unclonable functions. *In IEEE Des. Test, 27*(1), 48–65.

Secure Communications in Smart Grid: Networking and Protocols

5

Kieran McLaughlin*, Ivo Friedberg*,†, BooJoong Kang*, Peter Maynard*, Sakir Sezer*, and Gavin McWilliams*

*Centre for Secure Information Technologies (CSIT), Queen's University Belfast, UK;
†Austrian Institute of Technology, Vienna, Austria

5.1 INTRODUCTION

The term "Smart Grid" is an attractive and convenient phrase. It is a hook on which we are able to hang many related, but essentially different and diverse, technologies. Building a "Smart Grid" really means improving existing power systems by making them "smarter". By integrating modern information and communications technology (ICT) into a power system, we can make it "smarter" by providing enhanced sensor, control and communication capabilities. These enhancements enable us to generate, collect, analyse and react to much more data about the physical condition of the electrical grid than before. Such enhancements can be exemplified in the smallest scale, between devices at a substation level, right up to the national scale, where central operational control centres collect and respond to transmission system data on a national and international scale.

The lifeblood supporting the aforementioned smarter operations is the provision of a significantly enhanced and pervasive IT network infrastructure. The central and crucial role played by Smart Grid communications networks make their reliability and resilience a fundamental priority. In this regard, from a cyber-security perspective, the challenges are twofold:

1. The provision of a new communications platform that penetrates every corner of the power system presents a possible conduit for cyber-attacks against the function of the physical power system, and the ICT systems supporting the power system.
2. The communication platform itself –the networking related devices and the protocols–offer an additional attack surface that can be targeted to affect the operation of new Smart Grid controls.

This chapter will explore the most widely relevant standard Smart Grid communication technologies and the protocols involved. Given the power system itself is a system-of-systems, each with their own particular environmental and performance related requirements, it is no surprise that a variety of different communications media and protocols have emerged to support these differing systems. Therefore another aspect we will explore is how communications protocols that once existed in "closed" systems have evolved to be used with modern TCP/IP based networking standards, and the consequences for cyber-security that have emerged as a result. The latter parts of the chapter will explore cyber-attacks operated via and against the Smart Grid communications network, and finally cyber-security strategies and best practices towards protection, monitoring and attack detection.

5.1.1 AN OVERVIEW OF THE COMMUNICATION NETWORK

Several different views exist regarding what a Smart Grid architecture looks like. A widely accepted viewpoint is the Conceptual Reference Diagram for Smart Grid Information Networks, described by Bryson & Gallagher (2012), which comprises seven domains: markets, operations, service providers, bulk generation, transmission, distribution, and customer. Considering this as an initial viewpoint, Figure 5.1

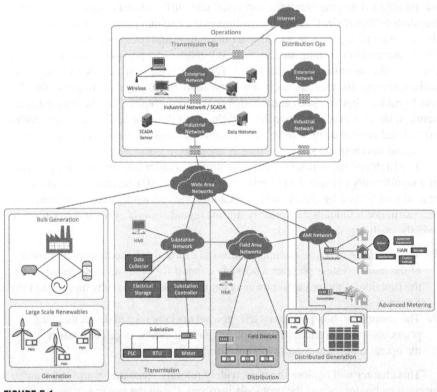

FIGURE 5.1

Smart Grid communication overview.

depicts a view of a generic Smart Grid architecture focused on communications, and comprising those systems with direct cyber-physical communication and control interactions. At the bottom of the figure are the classic power system components of generation, transmission and distribution, as well as the customer side, which includes advanced metering infrastructure (AMI) and localised grid-connected distributed generation at the customer. Notice also that generation includes separate communications groups for bulk generation (which are traditionally geographically centralised) and large scale renewables (which are often more geographically remote and disperse), each of which have different communication requirements. The top of the figure comprises systems and communications interconnections necessary for the operational control of the various power systems domains below. Implicitly embedded within the overall architecture is also the classic industrial control systems (ICS) hierarchical network topology, that comprises the enterprise network, industrial or supervisory control and data acquisition (SCADA) network, field area networks, and substation level or process control networks.

Within each boxed area in the figure, communication groups are formed with regard to functionality. Communications in one functional group are comparable regarding the protocols in use or the enforced quality of service requirements. At the same time communications between the functional groups is required to enable the overall Smart Grid functions. In terms of cyber-security, each functional group introduces different vulnerabilities and attack risks to the Smart Grid, which in total build the attack surface of the communication network.

5.1.2 THE COMMUNICATIONS NETWORK AS AN ATTACK SURFACE

An *attack surface* describes a view on a system that provides the sum of all vulnerabilities in the system that can be used by an unauthorised entity to insert data into, modify or extract data from the system. By exploiting the vulnerabilities immediately visible to them, an attacker can use additional methods to further infiltrate communications and networked systems, and exploit deeper vulnerabilities by infecting systems with malware, propagate malware between different systems, pivot to attack other connected systems, alter the expected behaviour of a system, and so on. In this regard, single acts of intrusion are often not sufficient for an attacker to reach their ultimate goal. This leads to the use of multi-staged attacks where the immediate attack is only one step in a more complex chain of related events (see Chapter 6 discussion on the Stuxnet attack). The possible number of attack steps and different targets is potentially large and complex for a system of systems like the Smart Grid. However, for any multi-stage attack to be successful, the common thread will always be that the attacker is able to utilise the Smart Grid communications infrastructure as an access path that allows them to achieve their goal. Therefore, the preconditions for an attacker to achieve their goal are that the communications network must be vulnerable itself in some way, and/or blind to the communications activities of the attacker. Consequently in order to secure against attacks that exploit the communications network, or use the communications networks as a vehicle for the exploitation of end points, a secure communication network requires, (i) minimal inherent vulner-abilities, (ii) effective visibility of attacker activities, in order to enable countermea-sures to be invoked. We will revisit these requirements later, but first we will look at the format and functions of several widely used communications protocols.

5.2 SMART GRID COMMUNICATION STANDARDS

The history of communication protocols in ICS and SCADA systems, such as those deployed in power systems, reflect an evolution from proprietary point-to-point links towards open and standard protocols used across distributed systems (Ten et al., 2007).

As shown in Figure 5.2, until the 1990s control system communications were generally secure from cyber-attacks because of proprietary hardware, software, com-munications protocols and, importantly, their isolation from the outside world. The additional interoperability and connectivity of modern control systems, including those in the Smart Grid, presents many challenges in order to make the systems se-cure from cyber-attacks. Furthermore, since the lifecycle of equipment in the power system is 15-20 years or more, it is not uncommon that new digital *smart* devices must coexist with older *dumb* analogue devices. This raises integration issues, be-cause both old and new communications protocols frequently coexist, which makes the security of the overall system more difficult to manage due to different require-ments, inherent vulnerabilities and communications characteristics.

Reflecting on what has happened, and what is currently happening as we pass through the "2010s", it is conceivable that this decade may turn out to be a period where previously obscure, specialist knowledge of ICS and Smart Grid communica-tions became common currency among those interested in perpetrating cyber-attacks.

5.2.1 FUNCTIONAL GROUPS OF SMART GRID COMMUNICATIONS

To better understand the challenge of securing the diverse Smart Grid environment, we will introduce and discuss standards and approaches based on the functional groups identified in Figure 5.1, specifically including the AMI, field devices and substations, and control centre related communications (Wei et al., 2010).

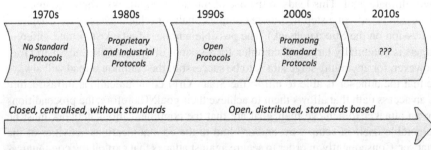

FIGURE 5.2

Evolution of communication protocols in control systems.

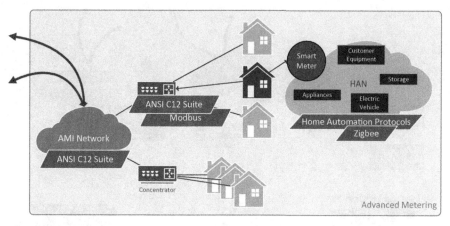

FIGURE 5.3

Detailed view on advanced metering infrastructure communication and available protocols.

5.2.1.1 Advanced Metering Infrastructure

The advanced metering infrastructure (AMI) provides two way communications between distribution substations and smart meters that are installed in homes (see Figure 5.3). Each smart meter is connected to various devices via a home area network (HAN). It can read information from the devices (like current load demands of appliances or charging state of energy storage) but can also issue commands. These commands are used to enforce peak demand management with intelligent charge cycles scheduling of electric vehicles or by shedding heavy loads during peak times. The collected information is transmitted by the meter to an area concentrator where it can get pre-processed before being further transmitted to the next distribution substation. At the same time, substations can send demand managing commands to the concentrators. The collected data can also be used for real-time billing.

The quality of service requirements of the communications in this functional group are not generally critical. Strict real-time communication is not required. Instead, for billing purposes, reliability of the communication is a critical factor. Privacy concerns have also been raised, e.g. (Fan et al., 2013) regarding the data measured by the smart meters.

For the implementation of the HAN various home automation protocols can be used. Zigbee is perhaps the solution with the broadest support between vendors and standardisation bodies in recent years. For the AMI the American National Standards Institute (ANSI) developed a set of standards known as the C12 suite that defines communication protocols, a table structure for utility application data as well as accuracy and performance metrics for smart meters.

5.2.1.2 Field Devices and Substation Communication

A number of different functional groupings are identified in Figure 5.4, related to field devices and substation communications. The first group encompasses the

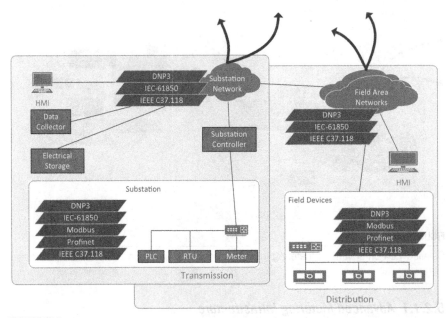

FIGURE 5.4

Communications and protocols in use for the transmission and distribution group.

communication between field devices. This group often has a very low available network bandwidth. At the same time delays have to be kept at a minimum. Typical applications are the collection of measurement data by concentrators, or the command for a circuit breaker to trip. Therefore data integrity and availability are the biggest requirements. Field devices like phasor measurement units (PMUs) might also rely on time-synchronisation to provide their features. Low-level protocols like Modbus or C37.118 are most common in this group.

Field devices are controlled by substations over a field area network. The same network can also be used to communicate between substations. The transmission focuses on the exchange of measurement data or commands to enforce protection schemes (e.g. breaker tripping). The protocols used are similar to field device communication but also more complex protocols like IEC-61850 can be used.

Communications within substations can be split between time-critical communications - which again coordinate protective schemes - and non-time critical communications that are used to update configurations or perform fault processing. Due to the different requirements, various protocols can be used for different communication paths within a substation as illustrated in Figure 5.4.

5.2.1.3 Control Centre Communication
Figure 5.5 gives the final overview of the functional communication groups. It shows a detailed view on control centres. From here two groups can be identified.

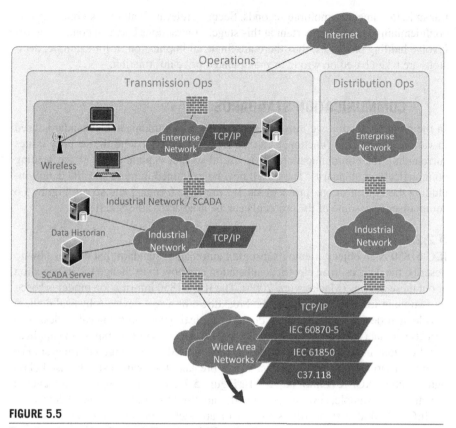

FIGURE 5.5

Functional grouping for control centre communications.

First, communications have to take place between substations and control centres. Second, inter-control-centre communications are used to coordinate between different control centres. The communication between control centres and substations can again be separated in operation-critical and non-operation-critical communications. Typical applications of the operation-critical communications are the control and monitoring of substation automation as well as configuration management or fault processing. Restrictions on transmission time are normally between 100ms and 1s, and there is generally significantly more network bandwidth available than in previous groups (up to 100Mbps). The protocols used can again differ between the different use cases. IEC-61850 can cover most of the applications in place.

Different control centres have to communicate in order to exchange fault or alarm data for contingency analysis or emergency operations. Furthermore, metering data needs to be exchanged over territorial boundaries for optimal operation. High network bandwidth is available on these communication links while common transmission times are multiple seconds. Security relevant features like integrity and confidentiality are very important at this stage. Transactions between control centres involve bidding processes, thus there are financial implication if, for example, decisions are taken based on wrong or manipulated price information.

5.2.2 COMMUNICATION STANDARDS

In the previous section we introduced some of the communications standards used in various Smart Grid functional groups. In order to understand the security issues surrounding the communications, it is useful to first explain some of the leading communications standards. These will now be examined in more specific detail, including the typical usage, protocol stacks, message formats, and so on. Figure 5.6 summarises how some of the protocols can be used across the Smart Grid.

5.2.2.1 IEC 61850

IEC 61850 is an object oriented substation automation standard that defines how to describe the devices in an electrical substation and how to exchange the information about these devices (Mackiewicz, 2006). The IEC 61850 information model is based on two main levels of modelling: the breakdown of a real device (physical device) into logical devices, and the breakdown of logical device into logical nodes, data objects and data attributes. The approach of IEC 61850 is to decompose the application functions into the smallest entities which are used to exchange information. For example a virtual representation of a circuit breaker class, with a standardised class name such as XCBR (Zurawski, 2004). Figure 5.7 gives an example of the layered structure, for example, several logical nodes are used to build up a logical device.

IEC 61850 also standardises the set of abstract communication services (Abstract Communication Service Interface– ACSI, part 7-2) allowing for compatible exchange of information among components of a power system. IEC 61850 offers three types of communication models: client/server type communication services model, a publisher-subscriber model, and sample values model for multicast measurement values. Figure 5.8 shows the communication stack of IEC 61850.

The generic object oriented substation event (GOOSE) message structure supports the exchange of a wide range of possible common data organised by a dataset. The GOOSE message is multicast and is received by the intelligent electronic devices (IED) which have been configured to subscribe to it. GOOSE messages contain information that allows the receiving device to know that a status has changed and the time of the last status change. The message frame consists of the following: destination/source media access control (MAC) addresses (DEST/SRC), tag protocol identifier (TPID), tag control information (TCI), Ethernet type, application identifier (APPID), length, two reserved fields and application protocol data unit (APDU) as shown in Figure 5.9.

Figure 5.10 shows parameters included in the GOOSE APDU. The data and commands carried by the APDU is critical to the underlying physical operations of the devices sending and receiving these messages. The integrity and availability

HAN	• Metering	• Wireless	• Zigbee
	• Load balancing on appliance level	• LAN	• Proprietary HAN protocols
AMI	• Collecting metering information	• Wired	• ANSI C12
		• Cellular	
	• Load balancing	• WiMAX	
		• Power Line Carrier	
Field Device Communication	• Collection of measurement data	• Power Line Carrier	• DNP3
		• Wired	• Modbus
	• Load balancing commands	• Wireless	• C37.118
Substation Communication	• Coordinate protective relays	• Power Line Carrier	• DNP3
			• IEC 61850
	• Configuration and Settings	• Wired	• Modbus
			• C37.118
Substation to Control Centre Communication	• Substation control	• Wired	• DNP3
		• Wireless	• IEC 61850
	• Updating configuration or settings of Substations	• Cellular	• C37.118
		• WiMAX	
	• Alarm/Fault processing		
	• Monitoring		
	• Metering		
Inter Control Centre Communication	• Fault and alarm data exchange	• Wired	• IEC 60870-5
		• WAN	
	• Meter data exchange		

FIGURE 5.6

Functional Communication Groups Overview.

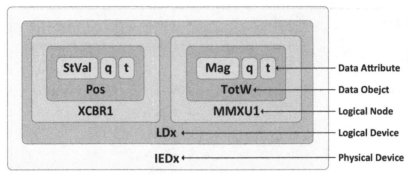

FIGURE 5.7

IEC61850 Object Model.

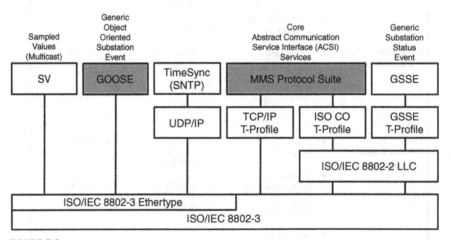

FIGURE 5.8

IEC61850 communications stack.

DEST	SRC	TPID	TCI	Ethertype	APPID	Length	Reserved 1	Reserved 2	APDU
6 Bytes	6 Bytes	2 Bytes	2 Bytes	2 Bytes	2 Bytes	2 Bytes	2 Bytes	2 Bytes	n Bytes

FIGURE 5.9

GOOSE message frame.

of these messages therefore plays a significant role in the security related connected systems. A detailed analysis of the GOOSE message structure is presented by Kriger et al. (2013).

IEC 61850 also defines mappings between the abstract services/objects to a specific protocol such as MMS (Manufacturing Message Specification). For the sake of

DATASET	ObjectReference	Name of the GOOSE data set
APPID	VISIBLE_STRING65	Application identifier
GOCBREF	ObjectReference	Name of the GOOSE control block
T	EntryTime	
STNUM	INT32U	State number
SQNUM	INT32U	Sequence number
TEST	BOOLEAN	(TRUE) test | (FALSE) no-test
CONFREV	INT32U	Configuration revision
NDSCOM	BOOLEAN	Set when the data in the GOOSE message is invalid
GOOSEDATA	(*)	Information of the GOOSE message

FIGURE 5.10

GOOSE application protocol data unit (APDU).

brevity, we will not go into detail of these mappings here, other than to say MMS objects and services can be mapped according to the IEC 61850-8-1 specification.

5.2.2.2 IEC 60870-5

The IEC 60870-5 series is widely used for transmission of SCADA telemetry control and information, particularly in Europe and China. IEC 60870-5-101 is a transmission protocol for basic telecontrol tasks between a central telecontrol station and telecontrol outstations. It was released in 1995 and originally written for serial communications. The release of the IEC 60870-5-104 standard, in 2000, presents a combination of the application layer of IEC 60870-5-101 and the transport functions provided by TCP/IP. IEC 60870-5-104 is widely used in SCADA communications from remote field locations in electrical grids, as well as by water and gas utilities.

Figure 5.11 shows the structure of an IEC 60870-5-104 packet payload, or APDU. The APDU consists of two parts, the application protocol control information (APCI) and application service data unit (ASDU). The APCI is used as a communication

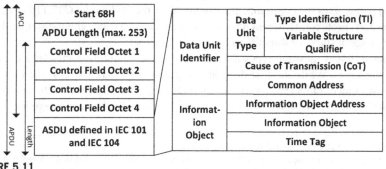

FIGURE 5.11

IEC 60870-5-104 APDU.

```
⊞ Transmission Control Protocol, Src Port: 2404 (2404), Dst Port: 3342 (3342), Seq: 201589628, Ack: 35, Len: 23
⊟ IEC 60870-5-104-Apci: -> I (2,1)
      START
      ApduLen: 21
      .... ...0 = Type: I (0x00)
      Tx: 2
      Rx: 1
⊟ IEC 60870-5-104-Asdu: ASDU=0 M_SP_TB_1 Spont    IOA=0 'single-point information with time tag CP56Time2a'
      TypeId: M_SP_TB_1 (30)
      0... .... = SQ: False
      .000 0001 = NumIx: 1
      ..00 0011 = CauseTx: Spont (3)
      .0.. .... = Negative: False
      0... .... = Test: False
      OA: 0
      Addr: 0
   ⊞ IOA: 0
```

FIGURE 5.12

IEC 60870-5-104 packet in Wireshark.

start and stop mechanism for the ASDU. The APCI typically contains a start character, 68H, a length field (containing the length of the APDU) and a control field. The
ASDU contains the application data, such as the device common address and system
readings, contained in information objects.

Figure 5.12 shows an example of an IEC 61850-5-104 packet displayed by Wireshark[1]. In the figure we can see that the port used is 2404 (the standard TCP port number for this protocol), in this case connecting to a destination port of 3342. The packet
segments in Wireshark show the APCI and ASDU, as introduced in Figure 5.11. In
the ASDU for example we can see that this particular packet has a Cause of Transmission (CoT) value 3, spontaneous. Similar to the previous comments regarding the
APDU in IEC 61850, these fields represent commands and data that are integral to
the underlying operation of the physical power system.

Finally, although not specifically discussed in this chapter, it is worth noting the
companion IEC 60870-5-103 standard defines TCP/IP based communications for
interoperability between protection equipment at a substation level.

5.2.2.3 IEEE C37.118

The IEEE C37.118 standard is defined in two parts and aims to provide an open standard for reporting the measurements of synchrophasors[2] (IEEE Std C37.118.2, 2011).
The first part defines form, format and quality requirements of synchropahsors; the
second part defines the communication protocol. In the OSI model C37.118 is a layer
4 (transport) protocol. Different network protocols can be used with the standard, for
the IP protocol stack, or directly on top of raw Ethernet.

Four different message types are defined: data, configuration, header and command messages. While the first three are only sent from data sources, such as phasor measurement units (PMUs) or phasor data concentrators (PDCs), the command
message is received by data sources. Figure 5.13 shows the basic message format as

---

[1]Wireshark packet analyser: https://www.wireshark.org
[2]A synchrophasor is "a complex equivalent of a sinusoidal wave quantity such that the complex modu-
lus is the cosine wave amplitude and the complex angle (in polar form) is the cosine wave phase angle"
calculated using a standard time signal as reference for measurements.

SYNC	FRAMESIZE	IDCODE	SOC	FRACSEC	DATA 1		DATA n	CHK
2 Bytes	2 Byte	2 Byte	4 Bytes	4 Bytes	1 - 256 Bytes	...	1 - 256 Bytes	2 Bytes

FIGURE 5.13

Standard message format in C37.118.

defined in the standard. The SNYC field encodes the type of the message as well as the version of the protocol used. An IDCODE field is used to identify a device and a specific data stream the device is handling. Since synchrophasors are inherently reliant on timing, each message is time-stamped using the second-of-century (SOC) and the FRACSEC field. Finally, depending on the message type different data fields describe the payload. For a detailed definition of the data fields for every message type the reader is referred to the standard document (IEEE Std C37.118.2, 2011). A checksum builds the final field.

5.2.2.4 DNP3

The Distributed Network Protocol (DNP) first appeared in 1998 and became DNP3 after a number of revisions. It is used in various SCADA applications and mostly for communication between master stations and substation devices, like remote terminal units (RTUs), intelligent electronic devices (IEDs) or PMUs. It was especially designed with reliability in mind while keeping efficient what makes it very suitable for real-time data transfers. It also supports time-stamped data transmission for use with PMUs.

Figure 5.14 shows different communication ways within DNP3. The protocol defines a set of data classes at the slave node. In an initial communication phase, all buffered data points are collected by the master to get up to date. After this initial step, the master can query one or more classes separately making the process more effective. At the same time DNP3 supports two-way communication. That way the slave node can issue unsolicited responses in the case of new high priority events. The consequent use of acknowledge flags by the master is one reliability feature. Unacknowledged responses get retransmitted. An additional acknowledgement layer for each master request is also supported by the protocol (not shown in Figure 5.14).

Figure 5.15 shows the packet layout if DNP3 is transmitted in TCP/IP packets; the protocol is not limited to this transmission protocol. Again reliability is design inherent. CRC checks can be performed for the whole DNP3 packet but also for every data block in the payload in order to prevent corrupted or missing data more reliable.

DNP3 and IEC 60870-5-104 can be traced back to the same development work, and similar cyber-security problems exist. Although checks are made for integrity, DNP3 lacks authentication and encryption (although the Secure DNP3 variation specifies this). Well known DNP3 function codes and data types mean it can be easy to manipulate and compromise a DNP3 communication session.

5.2.2.5 Modbus

Modbus is an application layer messaging protocol that provides master/slave communication between devices. As an application layer protocol Modbus operates

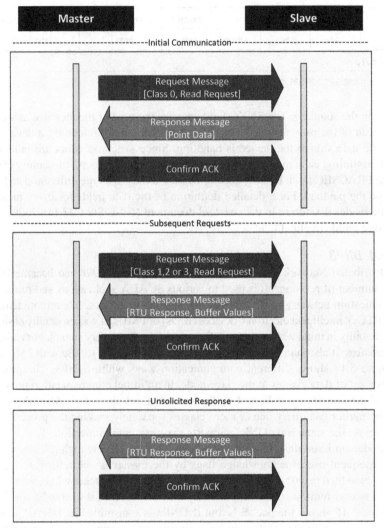

FIGURE 5.14

DNP3 communication protocols.

widely independent of the underlying network protocol. This made it easily adaptable to both, serial and routable protocols, and can be seen as one of the reasons for its success in industry. Another reason is its simplicity. Modbus does not rely on authentication which results in very little overhead when communicating, thus making it very suitable for small devices with little processing power.

The request response model of Modbus can be seen in Figure 5.16. It supports three Protocol Data Units (PDUs) – Modbus Request, Modbus Response and Modbus Exception Response – and a wide range of Function Codes. Function Codes and

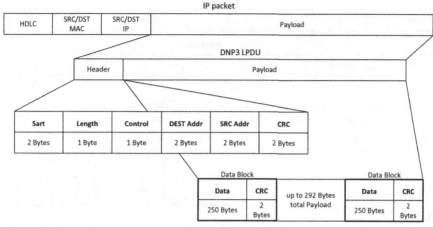

FIGURE 5.15

DNP3 packet description.

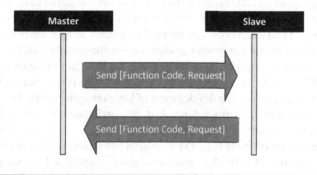

FIGURE 5.16

Request/Response protocol in Modbus.

Data Requests can be used for various commands, the most popular including the control or read of I/O devices or reads and writes on registers.

Several variants of Modbus exist, and make use of different network layer protocols for transmission. Modbus RTU and Modbus ASCII are examples for serial transmission while Modbus TCP relies on TCP/IP for transportation. Figure 5.17 shows an example Modbus TCP packet structure (Knapp, 2011). To address security considerations the IEC 62351 standard can be used on Modbus.

5.2.3 IEC 62351: SECURITY

The IEC 62351 set of standards was developed to address security for communications protocols, including IEC 61850 (GOOSE, SV and MMS), IEC 60870-5-104 and DNP3, and IEC 60870-5-101 and serial DNP3 (Cleveland, 2012). Various

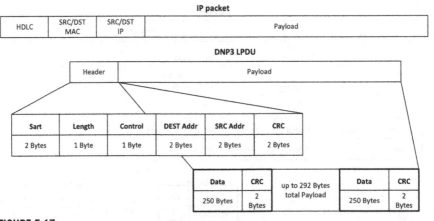

FIGURE 5.17

Modbus TCP packet description.

security objectives are specified for each of the protocols addressed, such as authentication using digital signatures, authorising access, prevention of eavesdropping and spoofing, etc. For example IEC 62351-3 specifies that standard TCP/IP Transport Layer Security (TLS) encryption can be used to protect against eavesdropping, and authentication can be used to protect against man-in-the-middle attacks.

As well as addressing specific security problems in legacy communications protocols, IEC 62351 includes: specifications to address Role-Based Access Control for power system management; the development of key management specifications to allow keys to be generated, distributed, revoked, etc.; and a security architecture to provide guidelines on security related components and functions, and their interaction.

The development of the IEC 62351 standards has influenced the development of more secure versions of individual communications standards. For example Secure DNP3 is essentially a revision of DNP3 that complies with the IEC 62351-5 security specifications. Releases and revisions of the IEC 62351 parts have been ongoing since 2007. However, despite these specifications, the security standards are often not applied in practice. For many systems already in place, retro-fitting these security measures is not an option due to practical constraints such as the inability to take critical systems offline for long periods to make changes, or the inability to update existing devices due to limited functionality. Old systems that have been in place for several years without the IEC 62351 standards in place are likely to be in place for several more years without changes. Indeed, new equipment is being deployed today without IEC 62351 type measure being adopted.

> *With an understanding of the communication protocols that can be applied to enable the smart grid, we can contextualise their use by returning to the example architecture that was introduced in Chapters 1 (and which is further elaborated on in Chapter 6). Figure 5.18 shows the candidate communication protocols and media that could be used between the different components.*

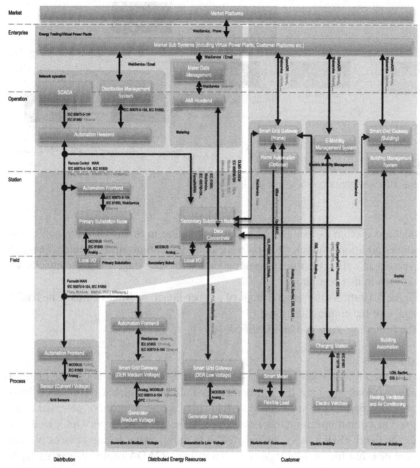

FIGURE 5.18

Detailed view of an exemplary Smart Grid System, including suggested communication protocols and media.

Source: (Kammerstetter et al., 2014)

5.3 ATTACKING SMART GRID NETWORK COMMUNICATIONS

Cyber-attacks on Smart Grid infrastructures are not limited to attacks on communication infrastructures. Different components can be targeted at various stages of the attack. Nonetheless, communication mechanisms are always used in an attack. Therefore communications have to be seen as an enabling factor to every attack; even if they do not provide attack vectors on their own. As seen in the previous section, security

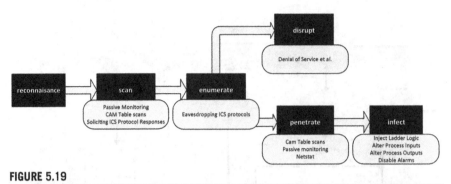

FIGURE 5.19

General attack process on industrial control networks.

considerations often do not get the required attention in Smart Grid protocols. This introduces additional attack vectors in the communication infrastructure. These attack vectors as well as the role of communication in other stages of cyber-attacks will be analysed in this section.

Figure 5.19 shows the general steps of a cyber-attack on Smart Girds, which takes advantage of the communications.

The following steps can be identified:

Reconnaissance

In a first step the attacker tries to gather as much information about the target as possible without engaging the infrastructure. Publicly available information about the company, partners or specialised systems in place are sources of potential attack vectors. On a communication level websites like the Sentient Hyper-Optimized Data Access Network (SHODAN) can be used to search internet facing devices by port, protocol or other filters. Many devices that utilise SCADA protocols can easily be identified using this site. Here communication infrastructure is used as an enabling factor to identify the system architecture, target devices, firmware information and ultimately points for intrusion.

Scan

After identifying the network architecture the scanning phase is used to identify devices and hosts in the network. Additional Internet Control Message Protocol (ICMP) techniques can be further used to gather additional system information. Network masks, open ports and protocols in use (mainly identified by standard ports) are identified in a first stage. Further, protocol specific functions can be used to determine further network information, information on device roles in the communication set-up (masters and slaves) or specific identifiers. At this stage communication specific attack vectors come into play. In particular, the lack of encryption and authentication in most current protocols in use in Smart Grids enables the possibilities for the protocol specific scanning techniques.

Enumeration

The enumeration phase focuses on retrieving user credentials to leverage closed access points and further penetrate the network. Ready-to-go exploit kits like Metasploit[3] can be used to leverage known attack vectors on well-known operating systems or applications. In Smart Grid environments the following credentials are of special interest:

- HMI Users
- Inter-Control Centre Communication Protocol (ICCP) Control Servers
- Historian database credentials
- Master addresses of any master/slave based protocol

At this stage communications again act more often as an enabling factor than a direct point of attack, however, protocol vulnerabilities can also provide a route to retrieve data. For example, unencrypted authentication processes may be targeted for the sniffing of passwords.

During enumeration (and partly also at previous stages) the attacker's options are not limited to technical means. Social engineering techniques such as spear phishing campaigns can be used to gain information about a target system.

Disruption

When we talk about disruption we talk most of the time about disruption of communication services. Denial of Service (DoS) attacks on industrial services can be as easy as performing network scans. For some systems, limits on latency or jitter are very strict and can be violated by the increased traffic introduced by packets from network scanning. Scanning can even be performed through active firewalls (McClure et al., 2009).

The intended effects of system disruption can vary, but are typically to prohibit control commands or measurements from being successfully transmitted. However disruptions might also be used to cause distraction to security operators by triggering a flood of alarms to hide other more subtle intrusive activities within the system.

Penetration

Once applications and devices in the network are identified, various attack vectors can be exploited by malware to penetrate and infect the Smart Grid. An example of penetration in the context of Smart Grid communications are Man-in-the-Middle (MITM) attacks. The attacker tricks communicating nodes into believing they are directly communicating, while the attacker intercepts all the traffic. A successful attack allows the attacker not only to sniff all communication but also to drop packets, insert new packets or manipulate existing packets as required.

---

[3]http://www.metasploit.com/

5.3.1 BASIC ATTACKS ON COMMUNICATIONS

5.3.1.1 Denial of Service (DoS)

DoS attacks are a set of, technically different, attacks that all result in a service being temporarily unavailable. The attacks usually involve exhaustion of a certain resource of a service or its underlying infrastructure making it unreachable for the intended users. These resources might include memory, the number of processes available, or network bandwidth available, and once underway are often very difficult to mitigate. Distributed Denial of Servie (DDoS) attacks usually involve a large number of infected machines (bots) to generate load on the resource that is to be exhausted.

In their simplest form, DoS attacks target a specific system that needs to provide public access to provide its service but they are not limited to this case. DoS attacks can also be launched from within a network after an initial intrusion of a vulnerable node in the network. Furthermore, communication mediums can be targeted as well as protocol flaws or the nodes in the network.

5.3.1.2 DoS on Communication Mediums

An often forgotten attack vector is a physical attack on the communication infrastructure. This is especially feasible for DoS attacks. Physical security of widely dispersed communication infrastructures is often not possible. While wired communication can be effected by "cutting the wire", cellular communication can be jammed to prevent communication (Ricciato et al., 2010).

5.3.1.3 ARP Spoofing and MAC Flooding

The Address Resolution Protocol (ARP) is widely used to provide mapping between the Network Layer and the Data Link Layer (see OSI model). When an IP datagram is sent over the network it needs to be mapped to a corresponding MAC address, which is used to identify the intended receiver on the Data Link Layer. This mapping information is cached in the network nodes. In order to receive this message an ARP Request message is broadcasted in the network which then should be answered by the machine with the requested IP address. As ARP is a stateless protocol, the identity of the sender cannot be authenticated and therefore the mapping can be intentionally altered. This results in packets being transmitted to the wrong host and can be used for eavesdropping, the alteration of data packets or DoS attacks.

Similar to ARP spoofing is MAC flooding. This attack exploits vulnerabilities in network switches that occur if the Content Addressable Memory (CAM) table runs out of space and cannot store any new mappings between IP addresses and MAC addresses anymore. The switch then reverts to a default state where it only broadcasts all received IP datagrams which can then be used to retrieve valuable information.

ARP spoofing and MAC flooding can be used to gather data or as first step towards more sophisticated attacks (Yang et al., 2013), such as Man-In-The-Middle (MITM) attacks, session hijacking or DoS.

5.3.1.4 Man-In-The-Middle (MITM) Attacks

In a Man-In-The-Middle (MITM) attack, the attacker impersonates the two communicating nodes by making them believe they are talking directly to each other. Instead the attacker keeps up an encrypted or unencrypted communication with both communicating parties with the ability to access, alter or drop packets or inject new packets. In order to achieve this, the attacker needs to be able to impersonate each party to an extent where it is accepted by the other party. This attack can only be executed if the initialisation phase does not rely on secure authentication of the communicating parties (node authentication) or if this authentication process is flawed (Samineni et al., 2012).

> *Samineni et al. (2012) discusses ways in which it is possible to perform stealth and semi-stealth MITM attacks using ARP spoofing. This is where the targets are left with no record in their ARP table of the attack. It explains what a MITM attack is and how to prevent such attacks. Gao et al. (2010) shows how command injection is done using ettercap and other techniques.*

The following attacks are possible primarily because of the lack of encryption and authentication implemented for the protocols outlined in section 2.2.

5.3.1.5 Replay

Using MITM attacks an attacker can record communication between nodes and replay this communication in order to hide real system behaviour without detailed knowledge about the system. These replayed packets might result in errors or undefined behaviour at the receiving end. The replayed packets can be altered before the replay or can be left as recorded. Such an attack may be executed by an attacker without detailed knowledge about the underlying system.

5.3.1.6 Session Hijacking

In session hijacking, a valid communication session is taken over by the attacker. The attacker does not have to have the means to establish a valid session, and instead intercepts and takes control over an authorised node that has established a valid connection. This session is then used by the attacker for unauthorised communication with the victim.

5.3.1.7 Injection

Using the MITM attack the attacker can inject or alter readings and commands in the communication stream in real time. While intercepting all packets the packets can be dropped, altered or new packets can be injected with arbitrary outcome. This attack is very problematic if executed by an experienced user, as it is hard to detect and can potentially have a significant effect. An attacker is able to manipulate measurement values from remote sites as well as to suppress or inject control commands between two communicating nodes.

Power grid control centres use meter readings to calculate an estimation of the state of the grid using an underlying grid model. This state estimation can detect bad measurements and substitute them with model based replacements. It was shown by (Liu et al., 2011) that, if an attacker has control over a sufficient number of measurement values, this control mechanism can be circumvented given sufficient knowledge of the underlying system model.

Although control mechanisms are in place to detect false measurements, intercepted commands are not that easy to mitigate especially if they are time constrained.

5.3.1.8 Miscellaneous Attacks

Pietre-Cambacedes et al. (2011) bring to light issues which Smart Grid system administrators might overlook, such as isolating control networks from the internet, exposure due to standard ICT system and software vulnerabilities, and misconfiguration of firewalls. These problems could allow attackers to penetrate the network, and once they have gained access to the network they are much more likely to be able to perform more targeted attacks against specific Smart Grid communications.

5.3.2 ATTACKS ON SMART GRID COMMUNICATION PROTOCOLS

Following on the above description of basic communications attacks on communications, this section examines current research published with regard to the execution of the described attacks on Smart Grid protocols.

5.3.2.1 Modbus and DNP3

Robinson (2013) highlights that with the original focus on efficiency rather than security, protocols like Modbus and DNP3 in use today have little to no security measures. The lack of authentication in Modbus means that remote terminals accept commands from any machine that appears to be a master. The lack of integrity checking or encryption allows messages to be intercepted, altered and forwarded (MITM). For DNP3, messages from an outstation can easily be spoofed, making it appear to be unavailable to a master. It is also common that passwords may be sent across the network in clear text. Robinson further highlights practical hindrances to deploying modernised protocol versions such DNPSecure, where the necessary system downtime is not feasible in critical systems.

Morris & Gao (2013) investigate attacks such as response and measurement injection, and command injection using the MODBUS protocol. The attacks have been performed in a laboratory setting, detailed in Morris & Vaughn et al. (2011). This paper details various levels of injection attacks ranging from naive injection which randomly injects values, to complex injections, or targeting of specific fields and values based on domain knowledge. It also outlines possible consequences, such as sporadic sensor measurements, altered system control schemes and altered actuator states. The results range from partial communication disruptions right up to complete shutdown of devices.

5.3.2.2 IEC 61850

Kush et al. (2014) present a vulnerability within the GOOSE communication service of IEC 61850. This paper describes an exploit of the vulnerability and proposes a number of attack variants. By sending GOOSE frames containing higher status numbers, it prevents legitimate GOOSE frames from being processed and effectively causes a hijacking of the communication. This attack could be used to implement a DoS or manipulate the subscriber.

Hoyos et al. (2012) also demonstrate a practical attack by exploiting weaknesses in GOOSE. This paper describes how to insert spoofed messages with incorrect data between each valid message. How to implement this attack is shown using Scapy, which is a Python program that enables the user to sniff, dissect, forge and send network packets. This attack is possible due to the unencrypted & unauthenticated nature of the GOOSE messages.

5.3.2.3 IEC 60870-5

SCADAStrangeLove (2013) explains how to detect IEC 60870-5 devices on the network, they have also released python scripts which can identify and return the common address of an IEC 60870-5 device. The common address is an address used for all data contained within the IEC 60870-5 packet, used to identify the physical device. Using these existing scripts it would be possible to scan a network for specific IEC 60870-5 hosts. As discussed at the beginning of section 3, network reconnaissance is the first step in a successful attack. This script could be used to detect possible targets for a man-in-the-middle attack, by confirming the end device is using the IEC 60870-5 protocol and obtaining its address.

In Dondossola et al. (2008, 2009) they cover the use of DoS attacks on networks running the IEC 60870-5 protocol and following industry security standards, such as VPN endpoint security.

Maynard et al. (2014) present a MITM attack on industrial control systems relying on the IEC 60870-5-104 protocol for communication in a Smart Grid remote substation environment. It further shows different high level attacks using the MITM attack like replay, modification or injection attacks.

5.3.2.4 IEEE C37.118

IEEE C37.118 is the most widely used protocol for communication with PMUs and PDCs. These devices rely on exact time-synchronisation for operation. This synchronisation is typically provided by GPS. Shepard et al. (2012) analysed the effects of GPS spoofing on power grids that rely on PMUs for stability managements. Their results show that GPS spoofing can be used to force intentional generator tripping as well as equipment damage.

Morris & Pan et al. (2011) evaluated the resilience of PMUs using C37.118 over IP against DoS attacks. They increased the network load by sending floods of ARP requests, PPPOE packets and IPv4 packets, subsequently rendering the tested devices unresponsive. Further, the authors conducted protocol mutation tests to evaluate the resilience against malformed packets.

An extensive vulnerability analysis regarding PMUs and the C37.118 protocol was further performed by Coppolino et al. (2014).

5.4 APPROACHES TO SMART GRID NETWORK COMMUNICATION SECURITY

At the beginning of this chapter, we introduced the idea that a secure communication network requires, (i) minimal inherent vulnerabilities, (ii) effective visibility of attacker activities. The following sections will introduce specific strategies that can be used to address these high-level objectives, while taking into account the Smart Grid-specific communication standards and attacks discussed in the preceding sections. The strategies covered include: best practice in network configurations for security: appropriate use of security appliances in the network to secure the perimeter, segregate the network, and provide network monitoring capabilities; and also the security standards directly related to power systems data communications.

5.4.1 MINIMAL VULNERABILITIES

Establishing and maintaining a network with minimal vulnerabilities requires a network topology that mitigates threats and known vulnerabilities, minimises the impact of successfully exploited vulnerabilities, and is kept up-to-date with security patches.

Mitigating threats can be achieved in some measure by adopting traditional network defence in depth strategies (Stawowski, 2007). The idea of defence in depth itself incorporates several principles, such that multiple overlapping protection approaches, whose functions are not interdependent, are used to protect a system, providing diversity and redundancy of protection. To implement this, the first step is that Smart Grid communications infrastructure should be segregated into security zones with defined boundaries. Each security zone should include a group of assets that share a common security policy. In practice a zone could include assets that communicate to carry out a common control function: for example a localised substation level control network focused around IEC61850 communications that incorporates IEDs, etc.; or a more distributed SCADA communication network comprising RTUs, master and slave devices which is focused around DNP3 or IEC60870 communications, for instance. The security zones that are closest to the physical power grid components and control devices should be behind the deepest layers of defence and operate the highest levels of security policy that allow only essential network communications in and out of the zone. For example, a substation level control network zone should be well segregated from a corporate enterprise network zone, with multiple security appliances and security zones providing separation. Segregation such as this will be investigated in more detail later.

Threats can also be mitigated by disabling unnecessary services in network connected Smart Grid devices, and networking equipment itself. Enabled, but unused, services present an unnecessary attack surface (i.e. open TCP ports can be scanned and probed). Even services that are unlikely to be of intrinsic interest to an attacker may have a vulnerability that can be exploited and used to pivot towards an end goal. Networking devices such as routers and switches can come with services initially enabled which may be unnecessary and present a security risk, for example Finger, IP

Redirects, Proxy ARP, etc. that can operate on Cisco devices could provide a target for exploitation[4].

Keeping the communications up-to-date with security patches can be difficult to manage and problematic due to the characteristics of the devices and protocols that are used for communications in a Smart Grid. The difficulty of patch management in control systems such as Smart Grids is currently an issue of much debate and attention (Pauna & Moulinos, 2013). Patching is sometimes not possible for operational reasons. It may be that other indirect mitigation steps need to be taken to support the security of a device that has known unpatched vulnerabilities, for example through network monitoring via appropriate intrusion detection rules, or by adding new rules to a firewall at the border of a security zone. It is not just end devices and Smart Grid services that can be vulnerable. Vulnerabilities exist in devices and services supporting the function on the network, such as routers, switches, protocol gateways, etc., and consequently Smart Grid operators should also have processes in place to manage patching of such network-specific devices and network services. As this chapter focuses specifically on the security of communications, we will not discuss patching further, but for interested readers the ICS-CERT website is a good starting point for more information[5].

5.4.2 VISIBILITY OF ATTACKER ACTIVITIES

In the last section we talked about *minimal* vulnerabilities because there will always be vulnerabilities in any network. Vulnerabilities will exist because:

- While a network can be designed to provide defence in depth, segregation of functions and assets, etc., these design features will only improve defence and detection capabilities, but never provide 100% security.
- Even if we keep up-to-date with all patches and mitigations, unknown zero-days and unannounced vulnerabilities are widespread.

To improve the security of the Smart Grid communication beyond minimising vulnerabilities requires the addition of processes that allow us to monitor the communications for activities that are indicative of an attack. By continuously monitoring the communications we can attempt to detect attacks that we have been otherwise unable to prevent.

Section 1.3 identified how attacks could exploit the inherent vulnerabilities in the protocols introduced in Section 1.2. Consequently it is necessary that tools and processes are implemented that aim to detect attempted exploits attacking such communications. Network Security Monitoring (NSM) is an approach that adopts the collection, analysis, and escalation of indications and warnings to detect and respond to intrusions (Bejtlich, 2013). The kind of communications data that can be collected

---

[4]Network Security Baseline: Disabling Unnecessary Services, Cisco. http://www.cisco.com/c/en/us/td/docs/solutions/Enterprise/Security/Baseline_Security/securebasebook/sec_chap4.html#wp1056396
[5]https://ics-cert.us-cert.gov/

and analysed for NSM includes; full content, extracted content, session data, statistical data, and alert data. The data ranges all the way from full, unfiltered packet captures, to alerts that are generated for example by an IDS. Collecting the full suite of NSM data is likely to be impractical for most Smart Grid systems, so an effective and manageable NSM approach can be configured to focus on providing the highest granularity of information only at the most important security zones, e.g. the communications closest to the physical components of the power system. By implementing an approach of collecting and assessing NSM type data from security zones in the network that use Smart Grid protocols, such as those in Section 1.2, security operators can attempt to identify and mitigate detected suspicious activities against the key cyber-physical assets in the Smart Grid network.

5.4.3 PROTECTION

Protection can be implemented primarily by using firewalls, which sit at the border between networks, making decisions about what communications should be allowed or denied, based on the addresses, data, and other information associated with the traffic. Firewalls are typically called upon to block communications due to unauthorised access attempts from automated attack tools, port scanning, malware, and so on.

Basic packet filter firewalls allow ingress or egress access based on packet properties such as source/destination address, source/destination port, protocol, and TCP flags. A key weakness of such firewalls is that they cannot detect spoofed information such as fake IP addresses. Stateful inspection at the transport (TCP) layer can be used to improve the capabilities of firewalls. For control networks with specialised protocols, inspection can be carried out at the application layer (in the packet payload data) to analyse protocol and device specific information, including stateful analysis of communications.

A first step towards protecting Smart Grid communications against cyber-attack is to ensure the communications network is configured in a way to give us the best chance to forestall attempted attacks, and minimise the effects of any attack related actions that are initially successful. Segregating different networks into separate security zones is regarded as best practice towards this goal. The objective is to limit the possibility of problems on the corporate network affecting the critical devices accessed and managed via the control network. In the case of cyber-attacks, the corporate network often provide a rich source of vulnerabilities offering an opportunity for attackers to use such systems as a beachhead for further, deeper attacks aimed at the core Smart Grid assets.

Stouffer et al. (2015) provide a number of significant recommendations towards protection of control systems in this regard. It is recommended that the control system should be logically separated from the corporate network on physically separate network devices. Connectivity with the corporate enterprise network should be via minimal access points, and a single point if possible. To protect the control network from unauthorised traffic, a stateful firewall should be configured between the two network zones that denies all unauthorised communications. Stateful firewalls intercept packets at the network layer and inspect them to see if they are permitted by an existing firewall rule, while usually keeping track of each connection in a state table. For example TCP header values can be inspected to monitor the state of each connection. All packets are compared to the firewall's state table to determine whether their state contradicts the expected state. Deep packet inspection can also be used to analyse each packet's content at the application layer to allow the firewall to compare profiles of benign protocol activity against observed events to identify deviations. Stateful analysis at the application layer can be applied to specific Smart Grid protocols, such as those previously introduce in this chapter. For example, Goldenberg & Wool (2013) investigated Modbus, while Yang et al. (2014) investigated IEC 60870-5-104.

At a minimum NIST recommends that the segregating firewall provide source and destination filtering based on MAC addresses, in addition to TCP and UDP port filtering, and Internet Control Message Protocol (ICMP) type and code filtering.

Where there is a practical business need for communications between the corporate and control zones (and many would argue there is *never* a justifiable need) best practise is to provide an intermediate "demilitarized zone" (DMZ) network, connected to the firewall, that facilitates restricted communication between only the corporate network and the DMZ, and the ICS network and the DMZ. In such an arrangement the corporate network zone and the ICS network zone never communicate directly. Figure 5.20, illustrates a security architecture proposed by Slay and Miller, which uses a DMZ to separate a SCADA system from the corporate network. Shared resources are placed in the DMZ, such that corporate network users can obtain plant and control data by querying a DMZ historian.

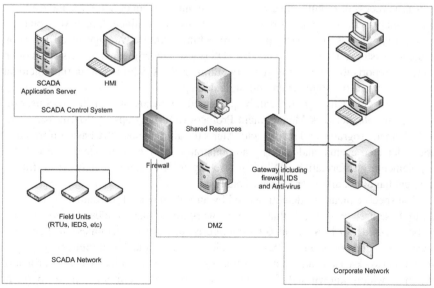

FIGURE 5.20

DMZ architecture for SCADA.

Control networks themselves can be further segmented and protected based on different functions, locations, and security policies. For example a network segment may be created around devices with a common communications protocol, or within a single substation environment. Appropriate policing of segment boundaries makes it more difficult for an attacker to penetrate a specific set of core Smart Grid systems within any given segment. It also helps to contain any breaches that are successful from affecting other protected segments.

When deploying any devices with blocking capabilities in and ICS network, careful consideration must be given to ensure that delays introduced in the communications (due to processing the packets) does not interfere with the underlying functions of the physical system.

As well as actions that block packets (blacklisting), it is possible to take the converse approach (whitelisting) where only network traffic that is deemed acceptable is allowed to pass. A whitelisting approach can be developed based on any underlying protocol, allowing a device like a firewall to enact fine-grained policies based on deep inspection of packets at the application layer to check for permitted functional operations, message formats, and so on. Only application layer data that is specifically allowed by the security policy is allowed to pass the security appliance enforcing the whitelist.

5.4.4 DETECTION

Where a firewall is often a first line of defence, intrusion detection can be considered as providing a second line of defence. Scarfone & Mell (2007) define intrusion detection as a process of monitoring events in a computer system or network, and carrying out an analysis to find signs of possible violations (or imminent threats of violation) of security policies. The basic procedure behind taking advantage of an intrusion detection system (IDS) is that when the IDS (by whatever means) detects signs of an attack, it reports the incident to security administrators, who would initiate incident response actions to minimise any possible damage.

These events, called *alerts*, can be presented via means such as the IDS user interface, Simple Network Management Protocol (SNMP) traps, syslog messages, or user-defined programs and scripts, etc. Alerts usually include only basic information about detected events, and security administrators may need to access the IDS for supplementary information. IDSs can also log information that may be useful for incident handling, and later forensics analysis.

The specific means of detection used by an IDS may be, for example, rules similar to those used by firewalls that allow network traffic that violates security policies to be detected. An IDS can also be configured to identify reconnaissance activity, such as host and port scans, which may indicate that an attack is imminent. The open source network-based intrusion detection system (NIDS) called Snort[6] is probably the most widely known and used IDS in the research community. It can perform

---

[6]https://www.snort.org/

protocol analysis, content searching, and content matching on network traffic in real-time. Other open source IDS tools include Suricata[7] and Bro[8], as well as many proprietary commercial offerings.

This Snort IDS rule detects when an unauthorised DNP3 client attempts to write information to a PLC or other field device (Digital Bond, 2015):

```
alert tcp !$DNP3_CLIENT any -> $DNP3_SERVER $DNP3_PORTS \
(flow:from_client,established; content:"|05 64|"; depth:2; \
pcre:"/[\S\s]{10}(\x02|\x04|\x05|\x06|\x09|\x0A|\x0F|\x12)/iAR"; \
msg:"SCADA_IDS: DNP3 - Unauthorized Write Request to a PLC"; \
reference:url,digitalbond.com/tools/quickdraw/dnp3-rules; \
classtype:bad-unknown; sid:1111207; rev:1; priority:1;)
```

This IEC 60870-5-104 Snort IDS rule detects a possible attempt at a buffer overflow (Yang et al., 2013):

```
alert tcp $104_CLIENT any <> $104_SERVER $104_PORTS \
(flow:established; dsize: >255; \
msg:"SCADA_IDS: IEC 60870-5-104 - Potential Butter Overflow"; \
classtype:bad-unknown; sid:66666010; rev:1; priority:1;)
```

Scarfone & Mell (2007) define three traditional subsets of intrusion detection technologies; signature-based, anomaly-based, and stateful protocol analysis.

- A signature is a pattern, or string, that corresponds to a known threat. Observed events are compared to known signatures to detect threats. This is effective against known threats but ineffective against unknown threats, zero-days, and vulnerable to evasion techniques. However it is simple and usually fast to process, and false positives are often low.
- Anomaly-based detection is a process that compares definitions of what activity is considered normal against observed events to identify significant deviations. The definition of what is normal may be threshold-based or profile-based.
  - A threshold-based process can monitor the frequency of occurrence of certain events and raise an alarm when violation of the threshold occurs. Examples in the communications could be the number of packets per second, the size of certain packets or flows, etc.
  - Profile-based anomaly detection focuses on characterising the past behaviour and detection of any change. This normally requires a training period, and careful selection of meaningful characteristics to observe.

---

[7]http://suricata-ids.org/
[8]https://www.bro.org/

The traditional challenge for anomaly-based detection is to minimise the number of false positives. An additional common problem is inadvertently including malicious activity within a profile.

- Stateful protocol analysis is the process of comparing predetermined profiles or definitions of benign protocol activity for each protocol state against observed events to identify deviations. The principle is similar to stateful firewalls. This can be very effective but there are also challenges:
  - Complexity of the analysis for performing state tracking for many simultaneous sessions.
  - Accurate models of protocols are difficult to develop. Particularly as in practice vendors do not always comply with standard specifications in the same way.
  - Attacks that do not violate the characteristics of generally acceptable protocol behaviour are not detected.

According to Stouffer et al. (2015), network-based IDS are most often deployed between the control network and the corporate network in conjunction with a firewall. This improves security by enhancing the ability to detect attacks entering or leaving the system, i.e. this helps satisfy our previously defined key requirement for visibility of attacker activities.

Current IDS products are effective in detecting and preventing well-known attacks, but until recently they have not addressed attacks against ICS protocols and their specific vulnerabilities as outlined previously in this chapter. IDS vendors are beginning to develop and incorporate attack signatures for various ICS protocols, and there is growing academic research into intrusion detection and anomaly detection, specifically focused on ICS environments such as the Smart Grid. The next section provides a brief summary of some of this emerging research.

5.4.5 CURRENT RESEARCH

Protocol specific research includes Morris & Jones et al. (2013), who investigated a set of Modbus signatures; Yang et al. (2013) who investigated signatures for IEC 60870-5-104; Digital Bond's set of DNP3 signatures[9]; and Goldenberg & Wool (2013) and Yang et al. (2014), who each proposed stateful protocol analysis for Modbus and IEC 60870-5-104 respectively.

Genge et al. (2014) proposed a connection pattern-based approach to detect network traffic anomalies in critical infrastructures. They model the architecture of an ICS with a graph model $G = (V, E)$. V is the set of vertices which are ICS nodes such as programmable logic controllers (PLCs), human–machine interfaces (HMIs) and RTUs. E is the set of pairs of vertices, known as edges, which denote connections between network components. Each edge also has one more tuple k which denotes the protocol. They automatically generate detection rules specific to each IDS based

---

[9]http://www.digitalbond.com/tools/quickdraw/dnp3-rules/

on the ICS model. Snort rules are used as detection rules, which include source/destination IP addresses, source/destination port numbers and the type of protocol. With these Snort rules, the IDS can whitelist allowed traffic.

Saeedi et al. (2014) proposed a network anomaly detection method using machine learning algorithms for intrusion detection in the Smart Grid AMI. A data mining classification algorithm is used to detect known attacks alongside a rule-based IDS is applied in a genetic algorithm to detect unknown attacks.

A network anomaly detection method based on a machine learning algorithm for IEC 61850 automated substations was investigated by Yoo & Shon (2015). Features were selected from the packet fields to allow normal-behaviour profiling using an SVM approach. Fields that were expected to have no value change between packets were excluded. The WEKA tool was used for clustering. The work requires further experiments to focus on attack detection, but the initial results are interesting.

An unsupervised intrusion detection method was investigated by Almalawi et al. (2014). Based on an initial training data set, the method then consists of two phases: an automatic identification of consistent and inconsistent states of SCADA data and an automatic extraction of proximity detection rules from identified states. SCADA data, such as sensor measurements and actuator control data, are data sources for the proposed method. The consistency of such data represents the normal system state, while any inconsistency indicates a malicious action. The identification phase is based on density-based outlier detection and extracting detection rules based on a fixed-width clustering technique. This method performs both phases in an off-line mode.

Koutsandria et al. (2014) proposed a network-based IDS for power grid protection, focusing on protective digital relays. The research is based on a "hybrid" set of specification-based IDS rules, combining common network signatures with physical constraints that focus on the physical expected operation of the physical system. Modbus packets are analysed and classified as acceptable or suspicious by comparing specific packet data fields to the specified system model. The authors highlight the challenge of customising this kind of approach for different and large systems.

Hong et al. (2014) focused on intrusion detection in a substation environment. A network-based anomaly detection system for the IEC 61850 communication services is proposed that samples IEC 61850 SMV and GOOSE messages. A set of predefined rules are used to detect violation of the expected standard format. This forms part of a larger analysis of attack scenarios in the substation environment, and a proposed host-based monitoring approach.

Barbosa (2014) investigates a specification-based detection method based on two characteristics: stable connection and traffic periodicity. Because the connection matrix, the pairs of communicating hosts, of SCADA networks does not change considerably over time, flow-level whitelists are proposed to define an access control list that determines which entities may access which resources. It was found that SCADA traffic exhibits a strong periodic pattern and this characteristic causes cycles, i.e., requests that are sent with the same frequency. An algorithm to find all cycles from a given training set was presented.

Faisal et al. (2014) conducted a performance analysis experiment on seven existing data stream mining algorithms (Accuracy Updated Ensemble, ActiveClassifier, LeveragingBag, LimAttClassifier, OzaBagAdwin, OzaBagASHT, and SingleClassifierDrift) and assessed their suitability to serve as an IDS in different areas of the AMI. They propose some algorithms that require only minimal computing resources, which offer moderate levels of accuracy, can potentially be used as an IDS embedded in a smart meter IDS. Other results showed algorithms, requiring more computing resources may offer higher accuracy levels for intrusion detection in data concentrators and AMI headends. Tabrizi (2014) also investigates IDS for smart meters, specifically targeting host-based intrusion detection.

5.5 CONCLUSION

The Smart Grid is essentially an evolution of the current electrical grid. The current infrastructure will not be unplugged and replaced over a weekend. Indeed a transformation has already been taking place over many years, with various improvements being made in incremental steps. We have already seen how this approach is leaving security vulnerabilities in the communications; for example the low adoption of encryption, authentication, etc. as specified for many common protocols in IEC 62351.It is clear that mistakes have been made where communications infrastructure has been deployed without a comprehensive risk analysis informed by the modern cyber-security threat landscape. It is reasonable to conclude that one danger created by inevitable incremental changes, is that it is difficult to achieve security by design, and also difficult to assess risks and mitigate vulnerabilities across such a broad, complex and evolving communications landscape.

In simple terms, we identified two aspects needed to support a more secure grid: (i) minimal inherent vulnerabilities, (ii) offer effective visibility of attacker activities, in order to enable countermeasures to be invoked. In this chapter we highlighted some of the basic ingredients necessary to improve the cyber-security of Smart Grid communications. The first issue addresses effective segregation of functionally different parts of the communication networks to allow security policy enforcement; for example the use of DMZs, appropriate deployment of protective devices such as firewalls, which may include protocol whitelisting, stateful protocol analysis, etc. These measures support minimising vulnerabilities in the communications, but also help to restrict the effect of any successful attacks so they only affect a particular subnet, or group of devices.

We have also highlighted the use of intrusion detection technologies to enhance the visibility of what is going on in the communications. There will always be gaps in security, and the use of IDS sensors helps to give operators sight of possible attacker behaviour. This is a challenging area of research for Smart Grid, and we have highlighted a number of very recent publications focussing on improving IDS technology and customising it towards the requirements that are specific to the

Smart Grid. Future endeavours are likely to continue towards investigating how to utilise cyber-physical information to detect anomalous behaviour due to cyber-attack. Additional challenges remain in how we can effectively integrate, manage and operate IDS sensors across varied and geographically large underlying physical systems. As we move towards further use of cyber-physical information, a different challenge is whether we can integrate cyber-attack countermeasure actions into the physical control domain in order to add resilience to the physical system itself. Finally, a significant challenge, and opportunity, is how domain experts in both ICT and electrical power systems can collaborate successfully to address those challenges together.

ACRONYMS

ACSI	Abstract Communication Service Interface
AMI	Advanced Metering Infrastructure
ANSI	American National Standards Institute
APCI	Application Protocol Control Information
APDU	Application Protocol Data Unit
ARP	Address Resolution Protocol
ASDU	Application Service Data Unit
CAM	Content Addressable Memory
CoT	Cause of Transmission
DoS	Denial of Service
DMZ	Demilitarized Zone
GOOSE	Generic Object Oriented Substation Event
HAN	Home Area Network
HMI	Human–Machine Interface
ICCP	Inter-Control Centre Communication Protocol
ICMP	Internet Control Message Protocol
ICS	Industrial Control Systems
ICT	Information and Communications Technology
IDS	Intrusion Detection System
IED	Intelligent Electronic Device
MAC	Media Access Control
MITM	Man-In-The-Middle
MMS	Manufacturing Message Specification
NSM	Network Security Monitoring
PDC	Phasor Data Concentrators
PDU	Protocol Data Unit
PLC	Programmable Logic Controller
PMU	Phasor Measurement Unit
RTU	Remote Terminal Units
SCADA	Supervisory Control And Data Acquisition
SHODAN	Sentient Hyper-Optimized Data Access Network
SNMP	Simple Network Management Protocol
TLS	Transport Layer Security

REFERENCES

Almalawi, A., Yu, X., Tari, Z., Fahad, A., & Khalil, I. (2014). An unsupervised anomaly-based detection approach for integrity attacks on SCADA systems. *Computers & Security, 46,* 94–110.

Barbosa, R. (2014). *Anomaly detection in SCADA systems: A network based approach.* Doctoral dissertation. University of Twente.

Bejtlich, R. (2013). *The practice of network security monitoring: Understanding incident detection and response.* No Starch Press.

Bryson, J., & Gallagher, P. D. (2012). *NIST framework and roadmap for smart grid interoperability standards, release 2.0.* National Institute of Standards and Technology (NIST), NIST Special Publication 1108R2.

Cleveland, F. (2012). *IEC 62351 security standards for the power system Information infrastructure.* IEC TC57 WG15 Security Standards, Version 14.

Coppolino, L., DAntonio, S., & Romano, L. (2014). Exposing vulnerabilities in electric power grids: An experimental approach. *International Journal of Critical Infrastructure Protection, 7*(1), 51–60.

Digital Bond. DNP3 rules. Retrieved from http://www.digitalbond.com/tools/quickdraw/dnp3-rules/rule-1111207/

Dondossola, G., Garrone, F., Szanto, J., & Gennaro, F. (2008). A laboratory testbed for the evaluation of cyber attacks to interacting ICT infrastructures of power grid operators. In *Proceedings of CIRED Seminar: SmartGrids for Distribution.*

Dondossola, G., Garrone, G., Szanto, J., Deconinck, G., Loix, T., & Beitollahi, H. (2009). ICT resilience of power control systems: experimental results from the CRUTIAL testbeds. In *Proceedings of the IEEE/IFIP International Conference on Dependable Systems Networks* (pp. 554–559).

Faisal, M. A., Aung, Z., Williams, J. R., & Sanchez, A. (2014). Data-stream-based intrusion detection system for advanced metering infrastructure in smart grid: A feasibility study. *IEEE Systems Journal, 9*(1), 1–14.

Fan, Z., Kulkarni, P., Gormus, S., Efthymiou, C., Kalogridis, G., Sooriyabandara, M., & Chin, W. H. (2013). Smart grid communications: overview of research challenges, solutions, and standardization activities. *IEEE Communications Surveys Tutorials, 15*(1), 21–38.

Genge, B., Rusu, D. A., & Haller, P. (2014). A connection pattern-based approach to detect network traffic anomalies in critical infrastructures. In *Proceedings of the Seventh ACM European Workshop on System Security* (pp. 1–6).

Goldenberg, N., & Wool, A. (2013). Accurate modeling of Modbus/TCP for intrusion detection in SCADA systems. *International Journal of Critical Infrastructure Protection, 6*(2), 63–75.

Hong, J., Liu, C. C., & Govindarasu, M. (2014). Integrated anomaly detection for cyber security of the substations. *IEEE Transactions on Smart Grid, 5*(4), 1643–1653.

Hoyos, J., Dehus, M., & Brown, T. X. (2012). Exploiting the GOOSE protocol: A practical attack on cyber-infrastructure. In *Proceedings of the IEEE Globecom Workshops* (pp. 1508–1513).

IEEE Std C37.118.2. (2011). IEEE standard for synchrophasor data transfer for power systems.

Kammerstetter, M., Langer, L., Skopik, F., Kupzog, F., & Kastner, W. (2014). Practical risk assessment using a cumulative smart grid model. In *Proceedings of the 3rd International Conference on Smart Grids and Green IT Systems.*

Knapp, E. (2011). *Industrial network security: Securing critical infrastructure networks for smart grid, SCADA, and other industrial control systems* (1st ed.). USA: Syngress/Elsevier.

Koutsandria, G., Muthukumar, V., Parvania, M., Peisert, S., McParland, C., & Scaglione, A. (2014). A hybrid network IDS for protective digital relays in the power transmission grid. In *Proceedings of the 5th IEEE International Conference on Smart Grid Communications* (pp. 908–913).

Kriger, C., Behardien, S., Retonda-Modiya, J., Behardien, S., & Retonda-Modiya, J. C. (2013). A detailed analysis of the generic object-oriented substation event message structure in an IEC 61850 standard-based substation automation system. *International Journal of Computers Communications & Control, 8*(5), 708–721.

Kush, N., Ahmed, E., Branagan, M., & Foo, E. (2014). Poisoned GOOSE: Exploiting the GOOSE protocol. In *Proceedings of the Twelfth Australasian Information Security Conference, Vol. 149* (pp. 17–22).

Liu, Y., Ning, P., & Reiter, M. K. (2011). False data injection attacks against state estimation in electric power grids. *ACM Transactions on Information and System Security, 14*(1), 13.

Mackiewicz, R. E. (2006). Overview of IEC 61850 and benefits. In *Proceedings of the IEEE PES Power Systems Conference and Exposition* (pp. 623–630).

Maynard, P., McLaughlin, K., & Haberler, B. (2014). Towards understanding man-in-the-middle attacks on IEC 60870-5-104 SCADA networks. In *Proceedings of the 2nd International Symposium for ICS & SCADA Cyber Security Research*.

McClure, S., Scambray, J., & Kurtz, G. (2009). *Hacking exposed: Network security secrets and solutions*. McGraw-Hill.

Morris, T., Pan, S., Lewis, J., Moorhead, J., Reaves, B., Younan, N., & Madani, V. (2011). Cybersecurity testing of substation phasor measurement units and phasor data concentrators. In *Proceedings of the 7th Annual ACM Cyber Security and Information Intelligence Research Workshop*.

Morris, T., Vaughn, R., & Dandass, Y. S. (2011). A testbed for SCADA control system cybersecurity research and pedagogy. In *Proceedings of the Seventh Annual Workshop on Cyber Security and Information Intelligence Research*.

Morris, T. H., & Gao, W. (2013). Industrial control system cyber attacks. In *Proceedings of the 1st International Symposium for ICS & SCADA Cyber Security Research*.

Morris, T. H., Jones, B. A., Vaughn, R. B., & Dandass, Y. S. (2013). Deterministic intrusion detection rules for MODBUS protocols. In *Proceedings of the 46th Hawaii International Conference on System Sciences* (pp. 1773–1781).

Pauna, A., & Moulinos, K. (2013). *Windows of exposure… a real problem for SCADA systems? Technical report, ENISA*.

Pietre-Cambacedes, L., Tritschler, M., & Ericsson, G. N. (2011). Cybersecurity myths on power control systems: 21 misconceptions and false beliefs. *IEEE Transaction on Power Delivery, 26*(1), 161–172.

Ricciato, F., Coluccia, A., & D'Alconzo, A. (2010). A review of DoS attack models for 3G cellular networks from a system-design perspective. *Computer Communications, 33*(5), 551–558.

Robinson, M. (2013). The SCADA threat landscape. In *Proceedings of the 1st International Symposium for ICS & SCADA Cyber Security Research* (pp. 30–41).

Saeedi, A., Yaghmaee, M. H., & Sagharidooz, N. (2014). Genetic based intrusion detection system in advanced metering infrastructure. In *Proceedings of the CIRED Workshop*.

Samineni, N. R., Barbhuiya, F. A., & Nandi, S. (2012). Stealth and semi-stealth MITM attacks, detection and defense in IPv4 networks. In *Proceedings of the 2nd IEEE International Conference on Parallel Distributed and Grid Computing* (pp. 364–367).

SCADA StrangeLove. (2013). SCADA security deep inside. Retrieved from http://scadastrangelove.blogspot.co.uk/2013/11/scada-security-deep-inside.html.

Scarfone, K., & Mell, P. (2007). *Guide to intrusion detection and prevention systems (IDPS)*. NIST Special Publication, 800.

Shepard, D. P., Humphreys, T. E., & Fansler, A. A. (2012). Evaluation of the vulnerability of phasor measurement units to GPS spoofing attacks. *International Journal of Critical Infrastructure Protection*, 5(3–4), 146–153.

Stawowski, M. (2007). The principles of network security design. *ISSA Journal*, 29–31.

Stouffer, K., Lightmen, S., Pillitteri, V., Abrams, M., & Hahn, A. (2015). *Guide to industrial control systems (ICS) security*. NIST Special Publication, 800-82 R2.

Tabrizi, F. M. (2014). A model-based intrusion detection system for smart meters. In *Proceedings of the IEEE 15th International Symposium on High-Assurance Systems Engineering*.

Ten, C. W., Govindarasu, M., & Liu, C. C. (2007). Cybersecurity for electric power control and automation systems. In *Proceedings of the IEEE International Conference on Systems, Man and Cybernetics* (pp. 29–34).

Wei, D., Lu, Y., Jafari, M., Skare, P., & Rohde, K. (2010). An integrated security system of protecting Smart Grid against cyber attacks. In *Proceedings of the Innovative Smart Grid Technologies* (pp. 1–7).

Yang, Y., McLaughlin, K., Littler, T., Sezer, S., Pranggono, B., & Wang, H. F. (2013). Intrusion detection system for IEC 60870-5-104 based SCADA networks. In *Proceedings of the IEEE Power and Energy Society General Meeting* (pp. 1–5).

Yang, Y., McLaughlin, K., Sezer, S., Yuan, Y. B., & Huang, W. (2014). Stateful intrusion detection for IEC 60870-5-104 SCADA security. In *Proceedings of the IEEE Power and Energy Society General Meeting* (pp. 1–5).

Yoo, H., & Shon, T. (2015). Novel approach for detecting network anomalies for substation automation based on IEC 61850. *Multimedia Tools and Applications*, 74(1), 303–318.

Zurawski, R. (2004). *The industrial information technology handbook*. CRC Press.

Cyber-Secure and Resilient Architectures for Industrial Control Systems

6

André Teixeira*, Friederich Kupzog[†], Henrik Sandberg*, and Karl H. Johansson*

*ACCESS Linnaeus Centre, KTH Royal Institute of Technology, Stockholm, Sweden;
[†]Austrian Institute of Technology, Vienna, Austria

6.1 INTRODUCTION

Feedback control is essential in modern systems, being a core component of electronic devices, vehicles, industrial plants, and large-scale critical infrastructures such as the electric power grid. The ubiquitous use of feedback control loops is very much due to the technological developments in computation, actuation, and sensing, together with a strong theoretical development of the field over the recent decades (Åström & Kumar, 2014). In this chapter, we will highlight the role of control loops for modern Smart Grids, and the challenges in terms of cyber security that come with these type of technology. We further drill down into threats that were discussed in Chapter 3, and show their concrete instantiation in context of industrial control systems. Eventually, we propose a model for risk assessment in case of false-data injection attacks on power systems and discuss its applicability.

6.1.1 CYBER SECURITY CHALLENGES IN INDUSTRIAL CONTROL SYSTEMS

The simplest instance of a feedback control system consists of two blocks, as illustrated in Figure 6.1(a): a physical plant, with sensors measuring its relevant variables and actuators driving its behaviour, and a controller that computes the control signal to be applied to the plant. Such a representation accurately captures the essence of control systems until the 1960s, when feedback controllers were comprised of mechanical or analogue electronic devices with reliable sensor-to-controller and controller-to-actuator links. The technological development during the digital era since the 1960s has led to the increased use of digital controllers and communication networks in many control applications, effectively transforming them into networked control systems, as depicted in Figure 6.1(b) (Samad et al., 2007). The digital revolution led to several opportunities to increase the overall efficiency of control systems, as well as their successful use in many domains (Samad & Annaswamy, 2011). Using information technology (IT) infrastructures, digital controllers, sensors, and

149

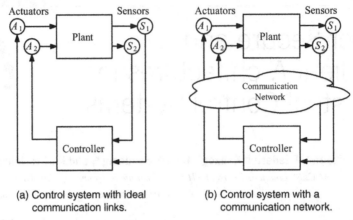

(a) Control system with ideal   (b) Control system with a
    communication links.   communication network.

FIGURE 6.1

Schematic of control systems with ideal and imperfect communication links.

actuators from the low-level control layer could now be integrated with high-level
supervisory layers, giving birth to supervisory control and data acquisition (SCADA)
systems. As illustrated in Figure 6.2, the lower layers of SCADA systems consist of
sensors and actuators interfaced with programmable logic computers (PLC) at local
stations, or with remote terminal units (RTU) imbued with extended communication
capabilities at remote locations. Measurement data are collected by RTUs and PLCs
and transmitted to the higher layers of the SCADA system through heterogeneous
communication networks. Low-level control may be implemented in the PLCs or
RTUs, which receive supervisory commands and set-points from the higher levels.

In addition to facilitating communication between different hierarchical layers, SCADA systems provide also other functionalities, such as human-machine
interfaces (HMI), workstations, historian databases, and integration with corporate IT systems. These components have become an integral part of modern
ICS, enabling an efficient and flexible operation of the physical system. A typical ICS architecture is depicted in Figure 6.2. Here, the corporate IT system is
connected to the supervisory layer of the SCADA system through firewalls. At
the SCADA system's supervisory level, historian databases and software application servers enable the efficient operation of the ICS. The workstation and HMI
are used to configure and monitor the low-level components, respectively. In the
lower layer, local stations have programmable logic controllers (PLC), typically
with wired communication capabilities. The PLC receives measurements from
sensors (S_i) and controls the physical system through actuators (A_i). A similar
description applies to the remote station, where PLCs are replaced with remote
terminal units (RTU) with extended communication capabilities, e.g. wireless
communication or wired Internet access. The layers within the SCADA system
are connected through heterogeneous communication networks, using wired and
wireless communications. The ICS may be connected through firewalls to external

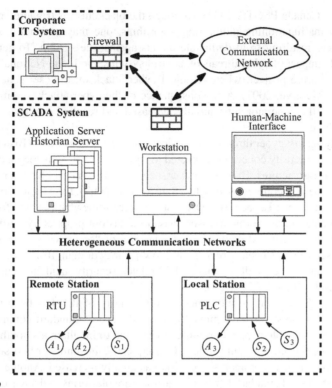

FIGURE 6.2

Schematic of a typical ICS architecture with the SCADA and corporate IT systems.

networks and systems, such as other ICS and remote stations. (The figure is adapted from (U.S. GAO, 2004).)

Novel challenges surface with the tighter integration of IT in control systems and the use of pervasive technologies, such as the Internet and wireless communication. In particular, a new concern has recently come into focus: that of security and resilience of control systems against malicious adversaries (Åström & Kumar, 2014; Rieger et al., 2009; Samad et al., 2007).

6.1.2 THREATS AGAINST INDUSTRIAL CONTROL SYSTEMS

There exist several threats to ICS, both physical and cyber, be they unintentional or malicious. A key feature of a resilient control system is its ability to maintain state awareness and acceptable performance under unexpected events (Rieger et al., 2009). Failing to achieve such properties can have dire consequences, as illustrated by the U.S.-Canada Northeastern blackout in 2003, which resulted in severe economic losses (U.S.-Canada PSOTF, 2004). Although the blackout was triggered by natural events and malfunctioning monitoring algorithms, one may envision comparable consequences resulting from deliberate threats against the system. To demonstrate the possible impact of cyber threats on control systems, the Idaho National Lab conducted the Aurora project, where a staged cyber-attack on a diesel generator was performed (Meserve, 2007). As a consequence of the cyber-attack, the mechanical vibrations of the generator substantially increased and resulted in physical damage to the machine.

Security against cyber threats is a classical concern for IT systems (Bishop, 2002). Therefore, the security concern is expected to carry over to ICS, as they increasingly rely on IT infrastructures. However, cyber security of ICS has not been a major concern during the past couples of decades (Samad et al., 2007), for which (Krutz, 2006) points a few reasons: Legacy SCADA systems were somewhat isolated from external communication networks and were based on custom proprietary hardware and software, which conferred them a reasonable level of "security by obscurity". Additionally, security has been perceived as a low-priority domain from an economical perspective, given the small number of ICS-related security incidents reported over the last decades (U.S. GAO, 2004).

Recently, the awareness and concern over security of ICS has been increased. Modern SCADA systems have moved towards the use of standard communication technologies, to enable access to remote devices and to facilitate a smooth interface between devices from different vendors. Consequently, the number of possible attack points for malicious cyber agents to exploit has greatly increased. Another common practice is the use of standard hardware and software platforms to decrease costs and improve flexibility. New vulnerabilities of these standard platforms may be discovered over their life-cycle, which greatly increases the risk of cyber threats to a large number of SCADA systems. In fact, the number of reported ICS-related security incidents has significantly increased over the recent years, from 39 in 2010 to 257 in 2013 (U.S. DHS, 2013).

The best practices and techniques from IT security are a sound first approach to increase the security and resilience of ICS. However, traditional IT security does not consider the interdependencies between the physical components and the cyber domain. A holistic approach is required to effectively handle the complex coupling between the physical process and the IT infrastructure.

The outline of the chapter is as follows. In Section 6.2, we survey information technology and control-centric security tools that can be used to improve the resilience of industrial control systems. Section 6.3 gives an overview of the envisioned control loops in future Smart Grids, and discusses the potential impact of cyber threats targeting them. A case study of false-data injection attacks on power transmission networks is discussed in Section 6.4, where a control-centric risk assessment methodology is used to assess the resilience to such attacks and to allocate the deployment of more modern and secure equipment. Section 6.5 discusses future research challenges in the area.

MALWARE TAILORED AGAINST ICS

Staged cyber-attacks have succeeded in physically damaging generators in test facilities (Meserve, 2007). Despite being a mock threat staged in a contained environment, it was one of the first "proofs of concept" for cyber-attacks on ICS. Another evidence came from the search engine Shodan, created in 2009, which finds electronic devices connected to the Internet (Matherly, 2009), such as routers, printers, computers, and PLCs. Several ICS devices were found and located using Shodan (Shefte et al., 2012), which raised concerns regarding the exposure of ICS to the Internet and external threats (ICS-CERT, 2010). Since then, several advanced threats targeting ICS were reported. Discovered in 2010, the Stuxnet malware was designed to infiltrate SCADA systems with specific hardware and software components (Falliere et al., 2011). The alleged aim of Stuxnet was to physically damage heavy machinery like steam turbines and gas centrifuges present in process plants by interfering with low-level actuators (Rid, 2011). The malware Duqu and Flame were found in 2011 and 2012, respectively (Symantec, 2011, 2012). Some components of these malware appear to be based on Stuxnet's source code and were aimed at espionage attacks, in an attempt to obtain sensitive information for facilitating future attacks. In 2013, Symantec discovered and monitored the actions of a cyber-espionage group named Dragonfly (Symantec, 2014), which targeted mainly organizations within the energy sector and ICS software producers.

6.1.3 ILLUSTRATIVE ATTACK CASE: STUXNET

Out of all the malware threatening control systems, the one that sparked most amazement and concern was Stuxnet, not only because it was the first publicly known malware targeting ICS, but also due to its great complexity and functionalities. In the following illustrative case, we revisit some of the details regarding Stuxnet.

Stuxnet was discovered in 2010 and has been closely examined since then (Falliere et al., 2011). It is the first known malware tailored to compromise PLC software and it has raised several concerns due to its astonishing capabilities:

- four zero-day exploits (flaws previously unknown to the software developers);
- Windows rootkits (software to grant the malware with privileged rights and hide its existence from intrusion detection software);
- first infection through USB drive;
- infected devices can spread the malware through local networks;
- peer-to-peer communication between infected devices;
- self-update capabilities using the Internet and peer-to-peer communications;
- remains dormant and continues spreading until a specific PLC software is found;
- first known PLC rootkit;
- ability to modify PLC software and hide the modified code.

Further analysis of Stuxnet shed light on its main goal and operation, from which plausible attack scenarios can be constructed. In particular, the attack scenario described in Figure 6.3 has allegedly occurred in reality (Kushner, 2013). This scenario illustrates the complex behaviour of Stuxnet and the potential damage it could have.

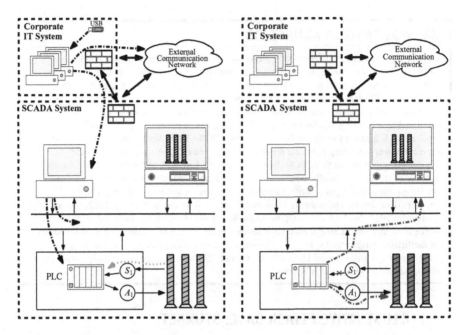

(a) Infection and data recording.   (b) Covert sabotage.

FIGURE 6.3

Three stages of the Stuxnet attack scenario: infection ((a) dash-dotted line), data recording ((a) dotted line), and sabotage ((b) dash-dotted line). (a) Exploiting zero-day flaws, Stuxnet is able to compromise computers through an infected USB drive. Once a device is infected, Stuxnet attempts to update its code from the Internet. Unless the compromised device has the specific platform targeted by Stuxnet, the malware remains dormant and continues spreading infection. Using compromised digital certificates, Stuxnet is able to bypass firewalls and it continues spreading itself through the local communication networks of the SCADA system. Stuxnet's peer-to-peer communication capabilities allow the malware to update itself, even when the compromised device does not have direct access to the Internet. Once the targeted PLC is infected, Stuxnet changes its operation mode. Using the PLC rootkit, the malware modifies the PLC code to perform a disclosure attack and record the received data. (b) After recording data for some time, Stuxnet begins sabotaging the physical system through a disruption attack. While changing the control signal sent to the actuators, Stuxnet hides the damage to the plant by feeding the previously recorded data to the SCADA's monitoring systems.

As concluded by Falliere et al. (2011), after a detailed analysis of the malware's capabilities and behaviour, Stuxnet contains several interesting features: a resourceful and knowledgeable adversary, who aims at covertly disrupting the physical system. Therefore, these features are considered in the attack scenarios discussed throughout this chapter.

6.2 DESIGN OF CYBER-SECURE AND RESILIENT INDUSTRIAL CONTROL SYSTEMS

Given the increasing importance of cyber security in ICS, a relevant and widely-open question is how to increase the overall system's security and resilience to threats. Numerous frameworks and tools have been independently developed in the fields of IT and control systems, which focused on cyber-security and resilience to faults, respectively. This section takes a closer look into IT- and control-centric design patterns and frameworks that may be used to tackle security and resilience challenges in industrial control systems.

6.2.1 IT SECURITY REFERENCE ARCHITECTURE

Information is a ubiquitous key asset in knowledge-driven societies, making information technology the main enabler of numerous technological platforms, e.g. electronic payment, online banking, and stock markets. These information- enabled systems require a reliable and continuous availability of data and services, which motivates the use of redundant and fault-tolerant architectures (Koren & Krishna, 2010).

In addition to reliability, information security is crucial in these applications, given the financial consequences of having external parties accessing and corrupting private data and services. Next we briefly revisit the main concepts behind IT security.

One of the existing standards for security of networked IT systems is the security architecture for Open Systems Interconnection (OSI) (ITU, 1991). The standard provides a systematic framework to describe IT security requirements and characterize approaches to satisfy such requirements. In particular, the security architecture for OSI (ITU, 1991) considers three main concepts: security policy, security services, and security mechanisms. The security policy is a set of requirements and rules stating what behaviours are allowed or not in secure systems. Security services are different functionalities that may be combined to ensure a given security policy. Security mechanisms are tools and procedures designed to prevent, detect, or recover from attacks. Several security mechanisms may be used to achieve a given security service.

As an example, consider a security policy stating that confidentiality violations are not acceptable. This policy may be achieved, for instance, using the following security services: access control and authentication. Access control prevents unauthorized devices from accessing the transmitted data, using mechanisms such as access control lists. Note that the access control service relies on the authentication service, which verifies the identity of devices requesting access to the transmitted data. The authentication service may be implemented using security mechanisms such as digital signatures and encryption.

In addition to the conceptual security framework, the security standard also maps several basic security services to the different layers of the OSI reference model for communication protocols (Krutz, 2006). In fact, several approaches in the literature are aligned with the layered approach of the reference security architecture. For instance, the survey by Chen et al. (2009) discusses several methodologies for security of sensor networks, where security mechanisms and services for different layers were proposed. A similar structure is followed in the other chapters, i.e. Chapter 4 addresses security concerns at the physical component level, while Chapter 5 tackles security challenges at the communication network layer.

6.2.2 CONTROL-CENTRIC APPROACHES

This section focuses on the resilience of control systems, namely the control and monitoring algorithms through which the physical plant is operated. Addressing security and resilience at this conceptual level provides yet another layer of defence against malicious threats.

Performance, reliability, and safety are essential properties of control systems, especially in safety-critical applications such as aircrafts, automotive industry, and industrial robotics. These systems have high hardware redundancy to ensure a reliable operation, possessing sets of redundant actuators and sensors. Managing the redundancy of the system is crucial to achieve safety and reliability. In the 1970s, the proliferation of digital computers reached the aircraft industry, leading the way for fly-by-wire systems (Sutherland, 1968). The use of digital computers in aircrafts also enabled the design of automatic systems to detect hardware failures (Willsky, 1976) and to efficiently manage redundancy and reconfigure the system (Megna & Szalai, 1977). The detection and reconfiguration mechanisms are core components of the fault-tolerant control architecture depicted in Figure 6.4 (Zhang & Jiang, 2008). This fault-tolerant control architecture will be used as a reference architecture in the case study discussed in Section 6.4.

The problem of fault-tolerant control has been extensively addressed since the 1970s, see Patton (1997); Zhang & Jiang (2008) and references therein. The following subsections provide a general overview of model-based fault diagnosis methods (J. Chen & Patton, 1999; Ding, 2008; Hwang et al., 2010) and fault-tolerant control approaches (Zhang & Jiang, 2008; Zhou et al., 1996).

6.2.2.1 Anomaly Detection in Control Systems

The objective of anomaly detection is to assess whether the system is in nominal behaviour (no anomalies), or in an abnormal behaviour (with anomalies). In control systems, anomalies are often caused by physical faults in the systems components, therefore leading to the term "fault detection". In addition to detection the fault, locating its source is also of great relevance, which is known in the literature as "fault isolation". In general, the fault detection and isolation schemes can be classified as either model-based or data-driven methods.

Model-Based Fault Detection and Isolation

In model-based fault detection, the nominal behaviour of the system can be predicted based on plant models and inputs. The basic principle in model-based fault detection is to compare the predicted and real system trajectories, obtaining the so-called

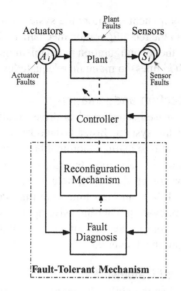

FIGURE 6.4

Fault-tolerant control architecture.

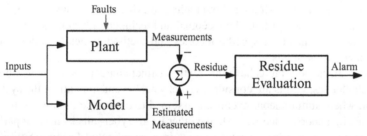

FIGURE 6.5 Model-based Fault Detection Scheme.

The plant model and inputs are used to estimate the output signal. The mismatch between the actual output and its estimate is evaluated to detect faults.

residue, as illustrated in Figure 6.5. The system is declared faulty if there is a significant mismatch indicated by the residue signal. Therefore, one important issue in fault detection is the residue evaluation (Hwang et al., 2010). The objective of this evaluation is to decide whether or not a fault is present, for a given residue signal. In deterministic systems, residue evaluation may be performed by comparing the norm of the residue signal against a threshold chosen to ensure robustness to uncertainties (Ding, 2008). In stochastic systems, the statistical model of the residue signal can be used to design optimal evaluation schemes in the form of hypothesis tests, for instance the generalized likelihood ratio test, sequential probability ratio test, and CUSUM (Basseville & Nikiforov, 1993; Hwang et al., 2010).

The fault diagnosis component monitors the system for faults. The detection of faults triggers actions from the reconfiguration mechanism. Using the fault diagnosis information (dotted line), the reconfiguration mechanism modifies the controller and the plant's structure (dashed lines) to maintain adequate levels of performance.

Data-Driven Fault Detection and Isolation

Complementary to model-based schemes, data-driven fault detection does not rely on (complete) models of the system. Instead, data-driven schemes use previously recorded data from the system to learn its nominal behaviour and to distinguish different faults from one another. Common techniques include multivariate statistical approaches (Vachtsevanos et al., 2006), neural- networks (Ebron et al., 1990; Polycarpou & Helmicki, 1995), and machine learning (Peng et al., 2004). These methods are particularly relevant in data-intensive applications, such as Smart Grid applications. Data mining approaches to anomaly detection and other mechanisms are pursued in further detail in Chapter 9.

6.2.2.2 *Resilient Control Framework*

Resilience may be defined as the ability to maintain acceptable levels of operation in the presence of abnormal conditions. In control systems, abnormal conditions are often caused by physical disturbances and faults. However, due to the cyber physical couplings arising with the use of IT infrastructures in control systems, cyber-attacks are of growing concern. Although both faults and cyber-attacks may lead to abnormal conditions, there are substantial conceptual and technical differences between them that motivate the need for specific theories and methodologies to address security issues in control systems.

Cyber-attacks and faults have inherently distinct characteristics, which pose different challenges. Faults are considered as physical events that affect the system behaviour, where simultaneous events are assumed to be non-colluding, i.e. the events do not act in a coordinated way. On the other hand, cyber-attacks may be performed over a significant number of attack points in a coordinated fashion (Smith, 2011; Teixeira et al., 2011). Moreover, faults do not have an intent or objective to fulfil, as opposed to cyber-attacks that do have a malicious intent. In spite of such differences, fault-tolerant control tools can indeed be used to detect and attenuate the consequences of cyber-attacks on feedback control systems, since these attacks affect the physical behaviour of the system similar to faults.

The different methodologies to achieve fault-tolerant control can be broadly classified as being either passive or active (Zhang & Jiang, 2008). The set of passive methods do not use real-time information regarding the fault. Instead, these methods restrict their attention to a given set of faults that can be characterized and modelled offline. Using these models, the controller is designed so that it mitigates any fault in the considered set. On the other hand, active approaches react to faults by taking advantage of real-time fault information, which may be obtained through the anomaly detection methods previously described.

Robust Control

In the classical control design problem, the main objective is to stabilize the system while attenuating disturbances and noise, under the assumption that the plant and disturbance models are known (Zhou et al., 1996). In practice, there are always discrepancies between the models and the actual system. For this reason, the design of control systems able to handle model uncertainty and unmodeled disturbances has long been a concern. It has been formulated as the robust control design problem. By modelling faults as unmodeled disturbances or model uncertainty, the design of robust controllers to mitigate faults is part of the passive fault-tolerant control approaches (Zhang & Jiang, 2008).

Robust control theory has contributed with several frameworks to handle model uncertainties and disturbances, see Zhou et al. (1996). In all these frameworks, the robust controller is designed to withstand disturbances and uncertainty belonging to a given set of interest. However, there exist drawbacks in using robust control techniques to mitigate faults. One of particular interest is that the performance of the robustly controlled system may be poor under nominal conditions, i.e. without faults. This drawback motivates the use of active fault-tolerant control schemes.

Active Fault-Tolerant Control

Since the 1970s, much research has been conducted in active fault-tolerant control schemes (Lunze & Richter, 2008; Maciejowski, 1997; Zhang & Jiang, 2008). The rationale behind the active approaches is to modify the nominal control system only when faults are present, as to ensure good performance under nominal conditions. Given the large amount of components in power systems, a particularly appealing approach for Smart Grid applications is the online controller reconfiguration (Lunze & Steffen, 2006).

Reconfigurable control proposes methods to reconfigure the control system after a fault has been detected and diagnosed, while avoiding a complete redesign of the control algorithms. The overall objective of control reconfiguration is to minimize the loss in performance inflicted by the fault. This goal may be achieved, for instance, by ensuring the system's stability, maintaining a similar closed-loop behaviour as before the fault (also known as model-matching), or achieving a suitable operating point.

6.2.3 RISK ASSESSMENT FOR CONTROL SYSTEMS

The risk management framework is a common methodology to enhance a system's cyber security (Bishop, 2002; NIST, 2012; U.S. DHS, 2011). As detailed in Chapter 3, the main objective of risk management is to assess and minimize the risk of threats, where the notion of risk is defined as a tuple consisting of a given threat scenario and the corresponding impact and likelihood (Kaplan & Garrick, 1981).

The risk of different threat scenarios may be summarized in a two-dimensional risk matrix (NIST, 2012), where each dimension corresponds to the likelihood and impact of threats, respectively. Additionally, the risk of different threats may be compared through increasing functions of the threat's impact and likelihood.

One of the crucial actions in the risk management framework is risk assessment, which identifies threats and assesses the respective likelihood and impact on the system. A summary of some of the existing approaches to risk assessment in industrial control systems is presented below, while a detailed presentation of risk assessment for Smart Grids may be found in Chapter 3.

Threat scenarios may be identified based on historical and empirical data of cyber-attacks, expert knowledge, and known vulnerabilities in the system (NIST, 2012). The report NESCOR (2014) provides a good example of power system-related threat scenarios identified from expert knowledge. The likelihood of a given threat depends on the components compromised by the adversary in a given attack scenario and their respective vulnerability. Quantitative methods can be used to identify the minimal set of components that need to be compromised for each attack scenario (Sandberg et al., 2010; Sommestad et al., 2013), while the vulnerability of each compromised component is obtained by qualitative means such as expert knowledge and historical and empirical data (Sommestad et al., 2013). The potential impact of a threat may be assessed by qualitative and quantitative methods, for instance, by modelling the system and simulating different attack scenarios (Sridhar et al., 2012). Quantitative approaches to risk assessment for feedback control systems that simultaneously address likelihood and impact are described in Teixeira et al. (2015).

Defining a suitable threat scenario and the respective adversary model is an essential step of risk assessment, since it provides the basis for assessing the corresponding likelihood and impact. Next, we briefly describe an adversary model for feedback control systems (Teixeira et al. 2015), which is later used to illustrate risk assessment in different case studies.

6.2.3.1 Adversary Model

The adversary model considered in this chapter is illustrated in Figure 6.6 and is composed of an attack policy, which is designed to achieve certain goals, and the adversary resources i.e. the system model knowledge, the disclosure resources, and

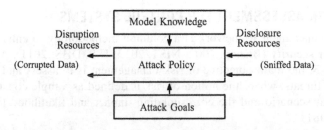

FIGURE 6.6

Adversary model for feedback control systems.

the disruption resources. In particular, the adversary model provides a control-centric abstraction of the potential threat types, threat agents, and attack vectors described in Chapter 3.

The several components of the adversary model can be mapped to the different risk dimensions: impact and likelihood. Specifically, the adversary goals may be stated in terms of the desired impact on the physical system and its operation, while the availability of the adversary resources is inversely related to the likelihood of the attack. That is, the more resources are available to an adversary, the less likely the threat scenario is considered to be. Together with the adversary resources and goals, the attack policy completes the attack scenario, by dictating how the resources are used to achieve the desired goals. In the following, we briefly discuss the different components of the adversary model, which are further detailed and illustrated through several attack scenarios in Teixeira et al. (2014).

Disclosure Resources

The disclosure resources enable the adversary to gather real-time data from the control system through disclosure attacks. Relevant data includes, for instance, the control actions sent to actuators, sensor measurements, set-point commands, and system configuration data such as relay statuses, among others.

As seen in the latter description of disclosure attacks, the physical dynamics of the system are not affected by such a class attacks. Instead, these attacks gather intelligence that may enable more complex attacks, such as the replay attacks used by Stuxnet.

Disruption Resources

Disruption resources correspond to the interfaces between the adversary and the physical system, which may be used to affect the system's behaviour. The way a particular attack disturbs the system's operation depends not only on the respective resources, but also on the nature of the attack. For instance, a physical attack directly perturbs the system dynamics, whereas a cyber-attack disturbs the system through the cyber physical couplings.

One particular instance of cyber-attacks that may use disruption resources are deception attacks. These attacks modify the data exchanged between the different system components, such as control actions and sensor measurements, in order to disrupt the system's operation. Note that deception attacks do not possess any disclosure capabilities.

Model Knowledge

The amount of *a priori* knowledge regarding the control system is a core component of the adversary model, as it may be used, for instance, to render the attack undetectable. In fact, this is a defining feature of the Stuxnet malware described in Section 6.1.1. For the purposes of this chapter, we consider that the adversary has an estimate of the physical models and the algorithms used in the feedback controller and the anomaly detector.

Adversary Goals and Constraints

In addition to the attack resources, the adversary model needs to also include the intent of the adversary, namely the attack goals and constraints its attack policy. The attack goals can be stated in terms of the attack impact on the system operation, while the constraints may be related to the attack detectability.

Several physical systems have tight operation constraints that, if not satisfied, might result in physical damage to the system. Consequently, the physical impact of an attack can be evaluated by assessing whether or not the system's operation constraints have been violated. In addition to the latter constraints, an attack's impact may also be assessed using other performance metrics, according to which the system's operation is optimized. Specifically, in Smart Grid applications, the operation constraints include the requirement that all voltage levels and power flows are kept within acceptable ranges. On the other hand, the performance metrics may be related to economic and environmental goals, such as the total power losses, power generation costs, and use of renewable energy sources.

Highly-valued adversary goals may be treated as constraints that the attack must satisfy. One common highly-valued constraint in several attack scenarios is to remain hidden from anomaly detectors, as to delay triggering protective actions to counter the attack.

6.3 CYBER SECURITY CHALLENGES IN ELECTRIC POWER SYSTEMS

In order to precisely discuss the security relevance in a Smart Grid, it is necessary to relate to an architecture describing the basic components of the system and the way they interact. Here, the term architecture refers to the overview of components in a real Smart Grid system rather than abstract architectural guidelines or design patterns. The architecture of a concrete Smart Grid is described in Chapter 5. The following sections refer to this architecture.

6.3.1 NEW CONTROL LOOPS IN SMART GRIDS

From an IT perspective, the Smart Grid adds a number of communication links to the existing system. However, from a functional point of view, the essential change is that a number of additional control loops are established, that make grid operation more efficient but also more complex. The exact design of these control loops is subject to intensive research (see discussion below); many of them did not yet find their way into industry-scale solutions. Figure 6.7 depicts mentioned new control loops in context of the previously introduced architecture.

CL1. Energy Balancing with Load Flexibility

In a power system with significant amount of volatile renewable generation, the balancing of demand and supply has to be realized with additional storage

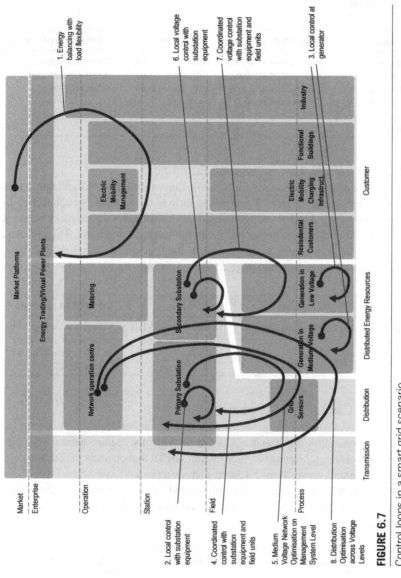

FIGURE 6.7

Control loops in a smart grid scenario.

capacities and/or flexibility on the demand side. The core concept applied here is to aggregate many smaller flexible loads and use the overall flexibility of this pool and trade it on existing energy markets serving this purpose (see e.g. Gantenbein et al. (2012)).

Sensors	Actuators	Controller	Controlled process
Frequency Sensors, dedicated power measurements at interconnection points	Active power set points of generators, configuration of Customer Energy Management Systems	Primary, secondary and tertiary controller on transmission level	Balance of supply and demand in a control zone or balancing group

CL2. Local Control with Substation Equipment

This is a state of the art approach for optimization of voltage band utilization in medium voltage distribution grids. The winding ratio of the transformer connecting high and medium voltage level is changed based on the voltage measurement on the secondary bus bar and the controller stabilizes the secondary voltage. This effectively filters out voltage variations from the high voltage grid and allows the full voltage band to be used by the distribution grid below the transformer.

Sensors	Actuators	Controller	Controlled process
Medium voltage sensors	On-load-tap-changer	In-built On-Load-Tap-Changer Transformer Controller	Voltage level at nodes in medium voltage power grid (limitation to allowed voltage band).

CL3. Local Control at Generator

State of the art power system generators employ a number of different control loops for efficient operation. Inverter-based systems typically require a maximum power point tracker (see e.g. Maranda & Piotrowicz (2013)) that chooses the correct current to drain maximum power from a source such as a photovoltaic array. From the grid side, more and more requirements for voltage and frequency control are developed in order to guarantee stable system operation with a large share of renewable generators (Andren et al., 2015).

Sensors	Actuators	Controller	Controlled process
Internal process sensors in generation unit	Generator set points	In-built generator controller	Active power, reactive power, frequency (before synchronisation and connection with grid), maximum power point tracking

CL4. Coordinated Control with Substation Equipment and Field Units

This is an extension of the previous control loop. New sensor and actuator technology allows advanced methods for optimised operation (and also planning) of medium voltage networks. In order to increase the hosting capacity for distributed generation, voltage control can be performed using field sensors and actuators in addition to local resources at the substation (Stifter et al., 2012). In urban networks, also current monitoring and active limitations can be an application.

Sensors	Actuators	Controller	Controlled process
Medium voltage sensor, measurements from low-voltage side	On-load-tap-changer, feeder configuration (switches), active and reactive power set points of distributed generators, secondary substation controllers	Primary Substation Controller	Voltage level at nodes in medium voltage power grid (limitation to allowed voltage band). Potentially limit line load

CL5. Medium Voltage Network Optimisation on Management System Level

Similar to the substation-level controller, an alternative control architecture is to integrate additional sensors and actuators in existing distribution management systems and process the voltage control functionality together with optimal power flow calculations (Eichler, 2013).

Sensors	Actuators	Controller	Controlled process
Medium voltage sensor, measurements from low-voltage side	On-load-tap-changer, feeder configuration (switches), active and reactive power set points of distributed generators, secondary substation controllers	Network operator SCADA system (Distribution management system)	Voltage level at nodes in medium voltage power grid (limitation to allowed voltage band). Potentially limit line load

CL6. Local Voltage Control with Substation Equipment

With the significant rise of low voltage grid-connected photovoltaics, also active voltage control in low voltage networks becomes a requirement. Recently, a number of dedicated controllers and actuators have been developed for this purposes, especially on load tap changer transformers for medium to low voltage application and similar (see e.g. Clark (2014)). These systems operate on locally available measurements only.

Sensors	Actuators	Controller	Controlled process
Dedicated local voltage and current sensors	On-load-tap-changer or similar, potentially local storage system	Secondary Substation Controller	Voltage level at nodes in low voltage power grid (limitation to allowed voltage band). Potentially limit line load

CL7. Coordinated Voltage Control with Substation Equipment and Field Units

New sensor and actuator technology allows advanced methods for optimised operation (and also planning) of low voltage networks. In order to increase the hosting capacity for distributed generation, voltage control can be per- formed using also sensors and actuators in the field to actively keep voltages in the allowed voltage band and avoid or delay demand for grid reinforcement by a substation-level controller (Kupzog et al., 2014). In urban networks, also current monitoring and active limitations can be an application.

Sensors	Actuators	Controller	Controlled process
Smart Meters, dedicated grid sensors	On-load-tap-changer or similar, feeder configuration (switches), active and reactive power setpoints of distributed generators, storage systems	Secondary Substation Controller	Voltage level at nodes in low voltage power grid (limitation to allowed voltage band). Potentially limit line load

CL8. Distribution Optimisation across Voltage Levels

Emerging control approaches focussing on low or medium voltage level only might negatively interfere with each other without proper design and/or central coordination. The aim of this use case is to maintain system stability, avoid contradictory control actions, as well as to perform reactive power balancing on the basis of sensor data from the field.

Sensors	Actuators	Controller	Controlled process
Smart Meter, dedicated grid sensors	Low Voltage: On-load-tap-changer, feeder configuration (switches), active and reactive power setpoints of distributed generators, storage systems	Substation controllers, Network operator SCADA system (Distribution management system)	Maintain system stability, avoid contradictory control actions, reactive power balancing
	Medium Voltage: On-load-tap-changer, feeder configuration (switches), active and reactive power setpoints of distributed generators, secondary substation controllers		

6.3.2 **VULNERABILITIES IN FEEDBACK-CONTROLLED SMART GRIDS**

As outlined in the previous section, there exists a trend towards the ubiquitous use of IT and control loops in Smart Grids. Therefore, cyber security concerns in industrial control systems naturally carry over to Smart Grids, as detailed in Chapter 3. Moreover, based on the new control loops that are envisioned to exist in Smart Grids, depicted in Figure 6.7, a preliminary set of potential vulnerabilities and their respective impact is readily described below.

Following a bottom-up approach, we focus on the physical infrastructure and describe some of the critical Smart Grid functionalities that must be ensured at all times: **active and reactive power control, supply and demand balance, voltage control,** and **frequency control**. The impact of potential cyber threats to the Smart Grid functionalities is directly related to their importance in maintaining stability and safety of the grid. On the other hand, the vulnerability of such functionalities depends on the possible attack entry points that may be used by cyber adversaries. To better understand the impact of such threats, next we briefly discuss the main objectives of these functionalities and the consequences that could occur if they fail. A mapping between these functionalities and the new control loops is also provided, which indicates the possible attack entry points: the **actuators, controllers,** and **sensors**.

F1. Local Active and Reactive Power Control

Power control consists of the ability of correctly adjusting the local power generation and consumption to match the corresponding set-points that are provided by higher-level control loops. The active and reactive power control is mainly supported by the control loop 3, where advanced control schemes enable micro-generators and inverter-based distributed energy resources (DERs) to provide the desired power injections. This functionality is an essential feature to support voltage stability, compensate for the volatility of renewable energy sources, and ensure that transmission lines are not overloaded. Therefore, failing to maintain such functionality may lead to undesirable events, such as load shedding, voltage brownout, and even blackouts. Furthermore, as the Smart Grid's dependence on renewable energy sources increases, so does the criticality of active and reactive power control, to meet the required high levels of flexibility to volatile power generation.

F2. Supply and Demand Balance

Balancing supply and demand is an essential task within power systems, particularly in the presence of volatile renewable generation. The supply and demand balance is partially supported by the control loops 1 and 3, as well as the **active and reactive power control** functionality. With the use of IT infrastructures, it became possible to coordinate spatially-distributed generators and DERs, which allows an efficient allocation of power generation across the Smart Grid. One of the benefits of such coordinated allocation of power generation is the reduced need for costly ancillary services and spinning reserves to tackle unexpected demand and supply variations. On the other hand, the failure of such functionality, combined with the reduction of ancillary services, may lead to load shedding in the presence of abrupt load variations.

F3. Voltage Control

A critical functionality of power distribution grids is to maintain the voltage levels within acceptable ranges, typically within 95% to 105% of the nominal value. In legacy distribution grids, voltage control is enforced through suitable controllers that remotely operate a reduced number of actuators, such as tap-changer transformers and switched capacitor banks, which are placed at the feeder substation and throughout the distribution grid, respectively. The controllers' decisions are made based on a handful of voltage measurements, typically taken at some of the end buses of the distribution lines, which are often insufficient to ensure complete observability of the voltage levels at all buses (Teixeira et al., 2014). Distribution grids with a high penetration of renewable energy sources may experience localised voltage fluctuations, whose mitigation requires a higher degree of voltage controllability. Therefore, legacy voltage control schemes with reduced observability and controllability require wider safety margins and operational constraints to prevent voltage collapse, which leads to a less efficient use of the distribution grid.

In Smart Grids, the voltage control is partially supported by the control loops 2 through 8, as well as the **reactive power control** functionality. The envisioned increase of intelligent IT-enabled DERs in Smart-Grids yields higher degrees of voltage controllability and observability, which may be used to enhance the voltage control functionality, and thus improve the grid's hosting capabilities and ancillary services (Andren et al., 2015). However, the large amount of micro-generation at the distribution grid also raises numerous challenges. For instance, the unsupervised operation of DERs may lead to undesired behaviours, such as voltage rise in the presence of high reactive power generation. Additionally, the control of several spatially-distributed DERs requires a suitable coordination of the different control loops through the IT infrastructure, as to prevent contradictory actions from multiple devices. As such, loss of communication capabilities may threaten the proper coordination of multiple DERs, or even leave these devices uncontrolled, and result in voltage collapse.

F4. Frequency Control

Another crucial feature is Smart Grids is the ability to maintain the grid's frequency close to the nominal value, e.g. 50 Hz in the European grid. Failing to keep the frequency within acceptable ranges may result in generators being disconnected by over- or under-frequency protection relays – which, in turn, may further reduce the ability to control the grid's frequency and lead to cascading failures.

The frequency control is supported by the **active power control functionality** and the control of generators and inverters through the control loop 3. In legacy power grids, frequency control is mainly implemented at the transmission level, since little or no power generation is available at the distribution level. However, given the large amount of micro-generation and DERs present in Smart Grids, there exist several new challenges requiring frequency control at the distribution level. A prime example of such needs is the so-called "50.2 Hz frequency problem" in Germany, where regulations impose that photovoltaic (PV) energy generators be disconnected when the frequency rises to 50.2 Hz. Having all PV generators disconnected by such over-frequency protection may result in the loss of a large amount of generation capability, which poses a dire threat to the supply and demand balance.

6.3.3 EXISTING CONTROL LOOPS IN MODERN POWER TRANSMISSION NETWORKS

As previously stated, most of the tools and control schemes at the distribution layer are yet to be fully developed and put into practice. However, the same does not apply to the transmission layer, where SCADA systems have been employed since the 1960s. Therefore, to better illustrate cyber security concerns on a concrete feedback-controlled system, we refer to power transmission networks in the remainder of this chapter.

SCADA systems in power transmission networks have evolved substantially since they were introduced in the 1960s (Wu et al., 2005). While the early systems were mainly used for logging data, today, modern SCADA systems are enhanced with Energy Management Systems (EMS) that provide system-wide monitoring and control capabilities to meet performance, safety, and reliability requirements (Balu et al., 1992; Shahidehpour et al., 2005).

Modern SCADA/EMS systems collect large amounts of measurement data and, using the State Estimator (SE) with detailed models of the network, provide the human operator with estimates of the real-time network state. The estimated state information is then used by optimization tools, such as the Optimal Power Flow algorithm, to compute optimal supervisory control actions that minimize the transmission network operation costs while ensuring that safety and reliability requirements are met.

6.3.3.1 Vulnerabilities in Power Transmission Networks

As discussed by Giani et al. (2009), there are several potential vulnerabilities in the SCADA system architecture, see Figure 6.8. They include RTUs (A1 and A5), communication networks between the RTUs and the control centre (A2 and A6), and the IT software and databases in the control centre (A3). In fact, there are several reports regarding cyber-attacks on SCADA systems operating power networks (CBSNews, 2009; Gorman, 2009).

The supervisory operation of some power networks is market-driven, meaning that the prices paid to power producers vary according to the current estimated state of the system and the available resources. The California electricity crisis in 2000–2001 (FERC, 2003), a consequence of both a flawed market design and covert market manipulations, shows that there may exist economic incentive to tamper with the power system operation.

Since legacy equipment with limited cyber-security capabilities is ubiquitous in power networks, the design of secure power systems faces numerous challenges.

For instance, given the large cost of securing legacy devices, the question of where to deploy modern equipment with enhanced cyber-security features is highly relevant. The answer to such question enables the cost-efficient deployment of limited protection resources to increase the system's security. One suitable approach is to assess the risk of threats to the system, namely to quantify the likelihood and impact of a given device being compromised by malicious adversaries. This problem is discussed in further detail in the remainder of this chapter.

6.4 CASE STUDIES: RISK ASSESSMENT FOR FALSE-DATA INJECTION ATTACKS ON POWER SYSTEMS

Consider the power system structure depicted in Figure 6.8, which for the moment is simplified by neglecting the feedback control. The simplification is made because it can lead to a more streamlined presentation of the main concept of risk assessment. In addition, in its own right the simplified structure is relevant in analysing the cyber security of state estimation in large-scale systems, such as electric power systems, and gas and water distribution networks.

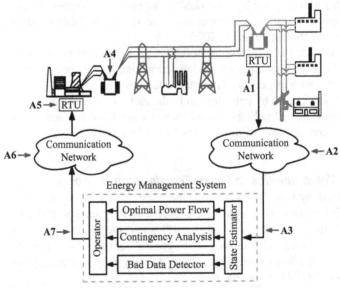

FIGURE 6.8

Schematic diagram of the electric power transmission network and its SCADA system with possible IT vulnerabilities. Measurements taken from the RTUs are sent through the SCADA system to the control centre. The received measurements are used by several EMS applications, which provide state-awareness and control recommendations to human operators. The human operators decide the appropriate control actions and apply them through the SCADA system.

(The figure is adapted from U.S.-Canada PSOTF (2004).)

The present case study focuses on the risk assessment of a given threat scenario. Following the methodology described before in this chapter, the threat scenario considers a cyber adversary with full knowledge of the power grid's model and control algorithms, who aims at injecting false-data in some of the measurements while remaining undetected. The adversary possesses limited disruption resources, corresponding to a limited set of measurements that can be corrupted.

The risk assessment in this section focuses on analysing the threat's likelihood, indicated by the minimum number of sensors that need to be compromised by the adversary for a given attack scenario. The minimum number of compromised sensors is a relevant indicator of the threat's likelihood because the sensors are often geographically distributed in networked control systems. As a result, coordinated attacks compromising multiple sensors need to be carried out simultaneously in different locations and they are difficult to implement.

The model for risk assessment is the relationship between the static plant states $x \in \mathbb{R}^{n_x}$ and the measurements $\tilde{y} \in \mathbb{R}^{n_y}$ received at the control centre. This is described by the expression

$$\tilde{y} = Cx + \Delta y, \tag{6.1}$$

where C is the measurement matrix, and $\Delta y \in \mathbb{R}^{n_y}$ is the measurement data attack. In a typical static state estimation problem such as the power network case, there are more measurements than states and hence the measurement matrix is assumed to have full column rank (Abur & Exposito, 2004; Monticelli, 1999). The least squares estimate of the states is $\hat{x} = L\tilde{y}$, with $L = (C^T C)^{-1} C^T$, and the estimate of measurements can be expressed as $\tilde{y} = C \tilde{x}$. Thus, the measurement residual used by the anomaly detector can be described by

$$r = y - \tilde{y} = (I - CL)\tilde{y}. \tag{6.2}$$

Such a residual is, in general, sufficient to detect the data corruption Δy in the form of a single error involving only one faulty measurement (Abur & Exposito, 2004; Monticelli, 1999). However, in face of a coordinated malicious attack on multiple measurements the anomaly detector can fail. In particular, Liu et al. (2009) reported that an attack of the form

$$\Delta y = C \Delta x, \tag{6.3}$$

for an arbitrary bias Δx, would not result in any residual in (6.2), in addition to the residual caused by other factors, such as measurement noise. In fact, the set of stealthy deception attacks with respect to the anomaly detector (6.2) and a zero detection threshold is characterized by (6.3). Although stealthy attacks may be obtained from (6.3), distinct choices of Δx may yield data corruptions Δy requiring significantly different amount of adversary resources, in terms of the number of measurements that need to be corrupted. This number is also an indicator of the likelihood of the success of stealthy attack, as discussed earlier in this subsection.

Next we characterize the stealthy attack vectors with the minimum number of nonzero entries, as a concrete example of the quantitative method for risk assessment.

6.4.1 MINIMUM-RESOURCE ADVERSARY POLICIES

There is a significant amount of literature studying the stealthy attack in (6.3) and its consequences to state estimation data integrity (Giani et al., 2013; Kim & Poor, 2011; Kosut et al., 2010; Liu et al., 2009; Sou et al. 2013b). Liu et al. (2009) numerically showed that stealthy attacks (6.3) are often sparse. To analyse the stealthy attacks with the minimum number of nonzero entries, in Sandberg et al. (2010) the notion of security index ρ_j for the j-th measurement was introduced as the optimal objective value of the following cardinality minimization problem:

$$\min_{\Delta x} \|C\Delta x\|_0$$
$$s.t. \ e_j^T C\Delta x = 1 \tag{6.4}$$

where $\|C\Delta x\|_0$ denotes the cardinality (i.e. the number of nonzero entries) of the vector $C\Delta x$, j is the label of the measurement for which the security index ρ_j is computed, and e_j denotes the j-th column of the identity matrix. The security index ρ_j is the minimum number of measurements an attacker needs to compromise in order to attack the j-th measurement without being detected by the anomaly detector. In particular, a small security index implies that the corresponding measurement is relatively easy to compromise in a stealthy attack, therefore indicating the likelihood of such a threat.

Because of the cardinality minimization, computing the security indices can sometimes be hard. In fact, it can be established that problem (6.4) is NP-hard using techniques from McCormick (1983); Tillmann & Pfetsch (2012). As a result, known exact solution algorithms for (6.4) are enumerative by nature. Three different typical exact algorithms include (a) enumeration on the support of $C\Delta x$, (b) finding the maximum feasible subsystem for an appropriately constructed system of infeasible inequalities (Jokar & Pfetsch, 2008), and (c) the big M method (Tsitsiklis & Bertsimas, 1997), which leads to an optimization problem that can be modelled as a mixed integer linear programming problem and solved using available software such as CPLEX (IBM, 2014).

6.4.1.1 Case Study: The IEEE 14-bus Benchmark

As a numerical case-study, the security index problem for all measurements in the IEEE 14-bus benchmark system is considered. This and other benchmark systems are provided with the software toolbox MATPOWER (Zimmerman et al., 2009). In this case study, all line power flows and bus power injections of the benchmark systems are measured. In other words, the full measurement assumption holds when the security index problems are solved using the techniques developed by Sou et al. (2013b).

The security indices for all measurements are depicted in Figure 6.9. For a better interpretation of the security indices with respect to the power network, Figure 6.10 shows the IEEE 14-bus system with measurements color-coded to indicate which ones are more vulnerable to stealthy data attack and which ones are resilient. The

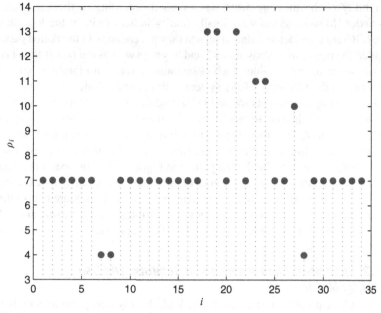

FIGURE 6.9

Security index for the IEEE 14 bus test case.

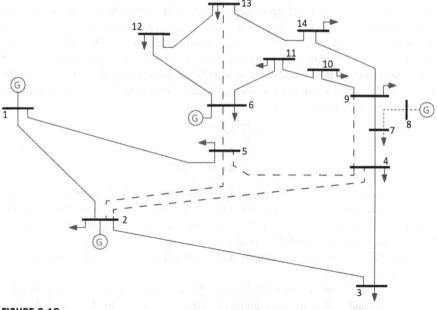

FIGURE 6.10

The IEEE 14-bus power network with measurements color-coded according to their security index: less than 7 (dotted pattern), equal to 7 (solid pattern), and greater than 7 (dashed pattern).

vulnerability of the measurements was assessed according to their respective security index. Measurements with small security indices (with value less than 7 in Figure 6.10) are considered vulnerable, and they are coded with the dotted pattern. In particular, the power injections at bus 7 and bus 8, as well as the power flow between these two buses are vulnerable. Such observation agrees with intuition, since buses 7 and 8 are on the boundary of the system with relatively little redundancy. On the other hand, the measurements located in the middle of the system (e.g. all the flows from bus 5, except the one to bus 3) are considered resilient, with security indices much greater than 7. This also agrees with intuition: the measurements in the middle of the network are highly connected and have great redundancy. The resilient measurements are coded with the dashed pattern in Figure 6.10. The rest of the measurements are coded with the solid pattern in Figure 6.10, with security index being 7.

As illustrated in this example, the security indices for all measurements allow the network operator to pinpoint the security vulnerabilities of the network, and to better protect the network with limited resources. Several approaches to increase security are briefly revisited next.

6.4.1.2 Incremental Improvements in Security: The Use of Security Metrics

One possible approach to decrease the risk of stealthy deception attacks is to encrypt the data and communication channels. Since a large part of today's power grid equipment is old, data encryption can be costly to implement because of the corresponding update of the equipment. Therefore, the following question is of great importance to measurement data integrity: given limited protection resources (the number of devices for data encryption), which measurements should be encrypted in order to maximize the benefits of the protection resources? The risk assessment outcome from computing the measurements' security indices may be used to sort the measurements in terms of their vulnerability and identify those that should be protected. In fact, a variant of the security index problem (6.4) can help provide an answer to the previous question:

$$
\begin{aligned}
&\min_{\Delta x} \|C\Delta x\|_0 \\
&s.t.\ e_j^T C\Delta x = 1 \\
&\quad\ e_k^T C\Delta x = 0\ \forall i \in C_p
\end{aligned}
\tag{6.5}
$$

where C_p is the index set of the encrypted measurements which cannot be attacked. By comparing the security indices for different sets of protected measurements, it is possible to evaluate the effect of different protection strategies, and determine the best one to be implemented. For example, Vukovic et al. (2012) consider a lexicographic optimization of some security metrics which are based on the security index computation related to (6.5).

In the case where it is impractical to encrypt all measurements, it becomes critical to detect and isolate the measurements which are under attack. Effective attack isolation enables the damage control (e.g. removing attacked measurements for state estimation) to be performed in a timely fashion before the attack can lead to any incident with significant consequences. Sou et al. (2013a) present a distributed procedure for isolating the data attacks on power system transmission line power flow measurements, based on secure bus voltage magnitude measurements. The work by Kosut et al. (2011) develops a generalized likelihood ratio test to detect the presence of data attacks, based on the assumption that the normal measurements follow a known Gaussian distribution. Mechanisms to detect data attacks based on known-secure PMU measurements and known pattern of system states are presented in Giani et al. (2013).

6.4.2 MAXIMUM-IMPACT RESOURCE-CONSTRAINED ADVERSARY POLICIES

The problem of stealthy false-data injection attacks was discussed in the previous section, for which security indices that quantify the adversary's effort were described. However, the role of feedback control was neglected and, thus, the potential impact of such attacks on the overall system was not considered. In future IT-enabled power systems, many new control loops are envisioned to be closed over communication infrastructures. Therefore, considering the impact of false-data injection attacks through the feedback loop is of significant interest.

Recall the power system depicted in Figure 6.8 and note that the measurement data are used by the EMS software to recommend suitable control actions to the operator. These control actions are computed to ensure a safe and efficient operation of the system in the presence of unknown disturbances. In the case of power systems, this relates to, for instance, satisfying power flow limits along transmission lines and minimizing power losses in the presence of unknown power loads. In such closed-loop systems, the false-data injected in the measurements may affect the control actions applied to the system and, consequently, they may disrupt the system operation and compromise its safety. In this section, we analyse scenarios of false-data injection attacks on closed-loop systems and discuss security indices that consider both the adversary's effort and the attack impact.

Motivated by the closed-loop system depicted in Figure 6.8, consider a two-stage control problem where the system in the first stage is at an unknown initial state x, while a given control action u is applied to the system in the second stage in order to drive it to a new state x_{new}. In particular, we suppose the physical system is described by the static model

$$\tilde{y} = Cx$$
$$x_{new} = x + Bu \tag{6.6}$$

where the initial state is unknown, and the model parameters B and C are known. The output $\tilde{y}$ is available to the controller in the first stage, which is used to compute the input $\mu \in \mathbb{R}^{n_u}$ to control the state of the system at the second stage. Using the model parameters, the unknown state x is estimated using the measurements $\tilde{y}$, which is used to compute a suitable input u. Given this scheme, the state at the final stage, x_{new}, is described as

$$\hat{x} = L\tilde{y},$$
$$u = K\hat{x}, \qquad (6.7)$$
$$x_{new} = x + Bu$$

The parameter K in the control algorithm $u = K\hat{x}$ is computed so that the system's performance is optimised. In particular, to measure the system's performance, we consider the convex cost function

$$J(x_{new}) = x_{new}^T P x_{new} \qquad (6.8)$$

where the controller's objective is to minimize the cost function.

Now consider that the measurements are corrupted by a malicious adversary, as described in the previous section, i.e.

$$\tilde{y} = Cx + \Delta y. \qquad (6.9)$$

Supposing the adversary aims at remaining stealthy with respect to the residue (6.2), the attack is constrained to be of the form $\Delta y = C \Delta x$. As seen in Section 6.4, the latter attack policy yields a zero residue. Moreover, the state estimate computed from the corrupted measurements is given by

$$\hat{x} = x + \Delta x. \qquad (6.10)$$

Recalling the model description in (6.7), the final state is described by

$$x_{new} = (I + BK)x + BK \Delta x, \qquad (6.11)$$

from which one observes that the false-data may affect the final state of the physical system. Next we characterize the stealthy attack vectors with a constrained number of nonzero entries that maximize the cost $J(x_{new})$, which leads to a risk index that accounts for likelihood and impact of attacks.

Recalling that the system's performance is measured by $J(x_{new})$, consider the scenario where the attacker aims at stealthily injecting false-data to maximize the impact on the system with respect to the cost function. Similarly to the security index in Section 6.4, the risk index μ_j (N, x) for a measurement j is introduced as the optimal objective value of the following optimization problem

$$
\begin{aligned}
&\max_{\Delta x} \ J(x_{new}) \\
&\text{s.t. } x_{new} = (I + BK)x + BK \Delta x \\
&\qquad \|C\Delta x\|_0 \leq N \\
&\qquad |e_j^T C\Delta x| = 1
\end{aligned}
\qquad (6.12)
$$

for some initial state x and maximum number of resources $N > 1$. The risk index μ_j (N, x) assesses the maximum impact achieved by a stealthy attack, while corrupting the j-th measurement with one unit and corrupting at most N measurements.

6.4.2.1 Case Study: The IEEE 14-bus Benchmark

In the following, we revisit the scenario considered in Section 4.3.1 and compute the risk index for each measurement. For simplicity, the risk indices are computed for a zero initial state, for which we define $\mu_j (N) = \mu_j (N, 0)$ as the risk index.

The system's operation performance is measured according to the total resistive losses in the power network, which are captured by the quadratic cost function (6.8). The risk indices for all measurements, normalized between 0 and 1, are depicted in Figure 6.11 for different limits on the number of compromised measurements. Interestingly, note that the attacks on the power injections of buses 7 and 8 (measurement indices 7 and 8, respectively) have no impact on the system operation. These same measurements were deemed vulnerable with respect to the security index, since they only required 3 measurements to be corrupted. This observation motivates the need to assess not only the threat's likelihood, but also its impact on the physical systems operation. On the other hand, the power injection measurements for buses 2, 4, and 5 (measurement indices 2, 4, and 5, respectively) have the highest impact, due to which they are considered to have the highest risk. A closer look also reveals that these measurements belong to relatively well-connected buses.

6.5 **CONCLUSION**

This chapter discussed some of the potential vulnerabilities of IT-enabled industrial control systems. As possible solutions to ensure the security of modern industrial control systems, specifically the Smart Grid, IT security architectures and control-centric approaches were described. Additionally, some of the new control loops envisioned for Smart Grids were described, followed by a discussion on the potential impact and vulnerability of critical functionalities within Smart Grids.

As a case study, the attack scenario of false-data injection attacks on power transmission networks were analysed, where trade-offs between impact and required resources for stealthy adversaries were considered. In particular, risk indices quantifying the likelihood and impact of such attacks were discussed and illustrated.

The security and risk metrics were of combinatorial nature and may be hard to compute for large systems. Hence, developing efficient algorithms to compute or approximate such metrics is a relevant direction. In particular, application- specific models may provide structural properties that can be leveraged to develop efficient algorithms, as was recently shown for electric power systems (Sou et al., 2013b).

Although the case of stealthy adversaries is interesting, analysing the performance of resilient control systems with detectable adversaries is also relevant. In particular, resilience metrics for the case when threats are detected and mitigated have been proposed (Wei & Ji, 2010).

The attack scenarios discussed in the chapter were only comprised of false-data injection attacks. In these scenarios, the adversary aimed at disrupting the system by tampering with the sensor data. In addition to such scenarios, disclosure attacks gathering private information from the plant and control algorithms are also relevant.

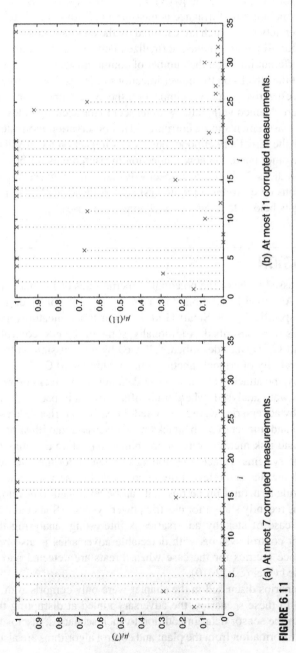

(a) At most 7 corrupted measurements.

(b) At most 11 corrupted measurements.

FIGURE 6.11

Normalized risk indices for the IEEE 14 bus benchmark with at most 7 and 11 corrupted measurements.

Methodologies to address privacy while ensuring adequate levels of control and estimation performance are required to handle disclosure attacks.

ACRONYMS

DER   Distributed Energy Resource
EMS   Energy Management Centre
HMI   Human-Machine Interface
ICS   Industrial Control System
IT   Information Technology
OSI   Open Systems Interconnection
PLC   Programmable Logic Controller
SCADA   Supervisory Control and Data Acquisition
RTU   Remote Terminal Unit

REFERENCES

Abur, A., & Exposito, A. (2004). *Power system state estimation: Theory and implementation.* Marcel-Dekker.

Andren, F., Bletterie, B., Kadam, S., Kotsampopoulos, P., & Bucher, C. (2015). On the Stability of local Voltage Control in Distribution Networks with a High Penetration of Inverter-Based Generation. *IEEE Transactions on Industrial Electronics, 62*(4), 2519–2529.

Åström, K. J., & Kumar, P. R. (2014). Control: A perspective. *Automatica, 50*(1), 3–43.

Balu, N., Bertram, T., Bose, A., Brandwajn, V., Cauley, G., Curtice, D., & Wrubel, J. (1992). On-line power system security analysis. *Proceedings of the IEEE, 80*(2), 262–282.

Basseville, M., & Nikiforov, I. V. (1993). *Detection of abrupt changes: Theory and application.* Upper Saddle River, NJ, USA: Prentice-Hall, Inc.

Bishop, M. (2002). *Computer security: Art and science.* Addison-Wesley Professional.

CBSNews. (2009, November 8). Cyber war: Sabotaging the system. CBSNews. Retrieved from http://www.cbsnews.com/news/cyber-war-sabotaging-the-system-06-11-2009/.

Chen, J., & Patton, R. J. (1999). *Robust model-based fault diagnosis for dynamic systems.* Kluwer Academic Publishers.

Chen, X., Makki, K., Yen, K., & Pissinou, N. (2009). Sensor network security: A survey. *IEEE Communications Surveys & Tutorials, 11*(2), 52–73.

Clark, S. W. (2014). Improvement of step-voltage regulating transformer efficiency through tap changer control modification. In *IEEE PES T&D Conference and Exposition.*

Ding, S. X. (2008). *Model-based fault diagnosis techniques: Design schemes.* Springer Verlag.

Ebron, S., Lubkeman, D., & White, M. (1990). A neural network approach to the detection of incipient faults on power distribution feeders. *IEEE Transactions on Power Delivery, 5*(2), 905–914.

Eichler, R. (2013). Next generation network analysis applications for secure and economic integration of distributed renewable generation in distribution grids. In *Proceedings of the 22nd International Conference and Exhibition on Electricity Distribution (CIRED).*

Falliere, N., Murchu, L., & Chien, E. (2011, February). W32.Stuxnet dossier. Retrieved from www.symantec.com/content/en/us/enterprise/media/security_response/whitepapers/w32_stuxnet_dossier.pdf.

FERC (2003). Final report on price manipulation in western markets. Retrieved from www. ferc.gov/industries/electric/indus-act/wec.asp.

Gantenbein, D., Binding, C., Jansen, B., Mishra, A., & Sundstrom, O. (2012). EcoGrid EU: An efficient IT approach for a sustainable power system. In *Sustainable Internet and ICT for Sustainability (SustainIT)*.

Giani, A., Bitar, E., Garcia, M., McQueen, M., Khargonekar, P., & Poolla, K. (2013). Smart grid data integrity attacks. *IEEE Transactions on Smart Grid, 4*(3), 1244–1253.

Sastry, S., Johansson, K. H., & Sandberg, H. (2009). The VIKING project: An initiative on resilient control of power networks. In *Proceedings of the 2nd International Symposium on Resilient Control Systems*.

Gorman, S. (2009, April 8). Electricity grid in U. S. penetrated by spies. *The Wall Street Journal*, Retrieved from http://online.wsj.com/articles/SB123914805204099085.

Hwang, I., Kim, S., Kim, Y., & Seah, C. E. (2010). A survey of fault detection, isolation, and reconfiguration methods. *IEEE Transactions on Control Systems Technology, 18*(3), 636–653.

IBM (2014). IBM ILOG CPLEX Optimizer. Retrieved from http://www-01.ibm.com/software/integration/optimization/cplex-optimizer/.

ICS-CERT (2010, October). ICS-ALERT-10-301-01: Control system internet accessibility. Retrieved from https://ics-cert.us-cert.gov/alerts/ICS-ALERT-10-301-01.

ITU (1991). ITU-T X.800: Security architecture for open systems interconnection for CCITT applications. Retrieved from http://handle.itu.int/11.1002/1000/3102.

Jokar, S., & Pfetsch, M. E. (2008). Exact and approximate sparse solutions of underdetermined linear equations. *SIAM Journal on Scientific Computing, 31*(1), 23–44.

Kaplan, S., & Garrick, B. J. (1981). On the quantitative definition of risk. *Risk Analysis, 1*(1), 11–27.

Kim, T., & Poor, H., 2011. Strategic protection against data injection attacks on power grids. *IEEE Transactions on Smart Grid, 2*(2), 326–333.

Koren, I., & Krishna, C. M. (2010). *Fault-tolerant systems*. Morgan Kaufmann.

Kosut, O., Jia, L., Thomas, R., & Tong, L. (2010). Malicious data attacks on smart grid state estimation: Attack strategies and countermeasures. In *Proceedings of the First IEEE international conference on smart grid communications*.

Kosut, O., Jia, L., Thomas, R. J., & Tong, L. (2011). Malicious data attacks on the smart grid. *IEEE Transactions on Smart Grid, 2*(4), 645–658.

Krutz, R. (2006). *Securing SCADA systems*. Wiley Publishing, Inc.

Kupzog, F., Schwalbe, R., Prüggler, W., Bletterie, B., Kadam, S., Abart, A., & Radauer, M. (2014). Maximising low voltage grid hosting capacity for PV and electric mobility by distributed voltage control. *Elektrotechnik & Informationstechnik, 131*(6), 188–192.

Kushner, D. (2013, February 26). The real story of stuxnet. IEEE Spectrum. Retrieved from http://spectrum.ieee.org/telecom/security/the-real-story-of-stuxnet.

Liu, Y., Reiter, M. K., & Ning, P. (2009). False data injection attacks against state estimation in electric power grids. In *Proceedings of the 16th ACM Conference on Computer and Communications Security*.

Lunze, J., & Richter, J. H. (2008). Reconfigurable fault-tolerant control: a tutorial introduction. *European Journal of Control, 14*(5), 359–386.

Lunze, J., & Steffen, T. (2006). Control reconfiguration after actuator failures using disturbance decoupling methods. *IEEE Transactions on Automatic Control, 51*(10), 1590–1601.

Maciejowski, J. (1997). Reconfigurable control using constrained optimization. In *Proceedings of the European control conference*.

Maranda, W., & Piotrowicz, M. (2013). Calculation of dynamic MPP-tracking efficiency of PV-inverter using recorded irradiance. In *Proceedings of the 20th International Conference on Mixed Design of Integrated Circuits and Systems (MIXDES)*.

Matherly, J. C. (2009, January). Shodan: the computer search engine. Retrieved from http://www.shodanhq.com/help.

McCormick, S. (1983). *A combinatorial approach to some sparse matrix problems* (Unpublished doctoral dissertation). Stanford University.

Megna, V., & Szalai, K. (1977). Multi-flight computer redundancy management for digital fly-by-wire aircraft control. In *Proceedings of Compcon*.

Meserve, J. (2007, September 27). Staged cyber attack reveals vulnerability in power grid. *CNN*, Retrieved from http://edition.cnn.com/2007/US/09/26/power.at.risk/index.html.

Monticelli, A. (1999). *State estimation in electric power systems: A generalized approach.* Kluwer Academic Publishers.

National Electric Sector Cybersecurity Organization Resource (NESCOR). (2014). Electric sector failure scenarios and impact analyses. Retrieved from www.smartgrid.epri.com/doc/NESCOR%20failure%20scenarios%2006-30-14a.pdf.

National Institute of Standards and Technology (NIST) (2012, September). Special publication 800-30: Guide for conducting risk assessments. Retrieved from http://csrc.nist.gov/publications/nistpubs/800-30-rev1/sp800_30_r1.pdf.

Patton, R. J. (1997). Fault-tolerant control systems: The 1997 situation. In *IFAC Symposium on Fault Detection Supervision and Safety for Technical Processes*.

Peng, J. -T., Chien, C., & Tseng, T. (2004). Rough set theory for data mining for fault diagnosis on distribution feeder. *IEE Proceedings-Generation, Transmission and Distribution*, *151*(6), 689–697.

Polycarpou, M., & Helmicki, A. (1995). Automated fault detection and accommodation: A learning systems approach. *IEEE Transactions on Systems, Man and Cybernetics*, *25*(11), 1447–1458.

Rid, T. (2011). Cyber war will not take place. *Journal of Strategic Studies*, *35*(1), 5–32.

Rieger, C., Gertman, D., & McQueen, M. (2009). Resilient control systems: Next generation design research. In *Proceedings of the 2nd Conference on Human System Interactions*.

Samad, T., & Annaswamy, A. (Eds.) (2011). The impact of control technology. *IEEE Control Systems Society*. Retrieved from http://www.ieeecss.org/general/impact-control-technology.

Samad, T., McLaughlin, P., & Lu, J. (2007). System architecture for process automation: Review and trends. *Journal of Process Control, 17*(3), 191–201.

Sandberg, H., Teixeira, A., & Johansson, K. H. (2010). On security indices for state estimators in power networks. In *First Workshop on Secure Control Systems*, CPSWEEK. Stockholm, Sweden.

Shahidehpour, M., Tinney, F., & Fu, Y. (2005). Impact of security on power systems operation. *Proceedings of the IEEE*, *93*(11), 2013–2025.

Shefte, W., Al-Jamea, S., & O'Harrow, R. (2012, June 12). Cyber search engine shodan exposes industrial control systems to new risks. *The Washington Post*. Retrieved from http://www.washingtonpost.com/investigations/cyber-search-engine-exposes-vulnerabilities/2012/06/03/gJQAIK9KCV_story.html.

Smith, R. (2011). A decoupled feedback structure for covertly appropriating networked control systems. In *Proceedings of the 18th IFAC World Congress*.

Sommestad, T., Ekstedt, M., & Holm, H. (2013). The cyber security modeling language: A tool for assessing the vulnerability of enterprise system architectures. *IEEE Systems Journal*, *7*(3), 363–373.

Sou, K. C., Sandberg, H., & Johansson, K. (2013b). On the exact solution to a smart grid cyber-security analysis problem. *IEEE Transactions on Smart Grid, 4*(2), 856–865.

Sou, K. C., Sandberg, H., & Johansson, K. H. (2013a). Data attack isolation in power networks using secure voltage magnitude measurements. *IEEE Transactions on Smart Grid, 5*(1), 14–28.

Sridhar, S., Hahn, A., & Govindarasu, M. (2012). Cyber-physical system security for the electric power grid. *Proceedings of the IEEE, 100*(1), 210–224.

Stifter, M., Schwalbe, R., Tremmel, W., Henein, S., Brunner, H., Bletterie, B., & Pointner, R. (2012). DG DemoNet: Experiences from volt/var control field trials and control algorithm advancements. In *Proceedings of the 3rd IEEE PES International Conference and Exhibition on Innovative Smart Grid Technologies (ISGT Europe)*.

Sutherland, J. P. (1968). Fly-by-wire flight control systems. In Joint meeting of flight mechanics and guidance and control panels of AGARD.

Symantec (2011, November). W32.Duqu: The precursor to the next stuxnet

Symantec (2012, May). Flamer: Highly sophisticated and discreet threat targets the middle east. Retrieved from www.symantec.com/connect/blogs/flamer-highly-sophisticated-and-discreet-threat-targets-middle-east.

Symantec (2014, July). Dragonfly: Cyberespionage attacks against energy suppliers. Retrieved from http://www.symantec.com/content/en/us/enterprise/media/security_response/whitepapers/Dragonfly_Threat_Against_Western_Energy_Suppliers.pdf.

Teixeira, A., Dán, G., Sandberg, H., Berthier, R. Bobba, R., & Valdes, A. (2014). Security of Smart Distribution Grids: Data Integrity Attacks on Integrated Volt/VAR Control and Countermeasures. In *Proceedings of the American Control Conference*.

Teixeira, A., Dán, G., Sandberg, H., & Johansson, K. H. (2011). Cyber security study of a SCADA energy management system: stealthy deception attacks on the state estimator. In *Proceedings of the 18th IFAC World Congress*.

Teixeira, A., Shames, I., Sandberg, H., & Johansson, K. H. (2015). A secure control framework for resource-limited adversaries. *Automatica, 51*(1), 135–148.

Teixeira, A., Sou, K., Sandberg, H., & Johansson, K. (2015). Secure control systems: A quantitative risk management approach. *IEEE Control Systems, 35*(1), 24–45.

Tillmann, A. M., & Pfetsch, M. E. (2014). The computational complexity of the restricted isometry property, the nullspace property, and related concepts in compressed sensing. *IEEE Transactions on Information Theory, 60(2)*, 1248–1259.

Tsitsiklis, J., & Bertsimas, D. (1997). *Introduction to linear optimization*. Athena Scientific.

U.S.-Canada Power System Outage Task Force (PSOTF). (2004, April). Final report on the August 14th blackout in the United States and Canada. Retrieved from http://energy.gov/sites/prod/files/oeprod/DocumentsandMedia/BlackoutFinal-Web.pdf.

U.S. Department of Homeland Security (U.S. DHS). (2011). Risk management fundamentals. Retrieved from www.dhs.gov/xlibrary/assets/rma-risk-management-fundamentals.pdf.

U.S. Department of Homeland Security (U.S. DHS). (2013). ICS-CERT year in review. Retrieved from http://ics-cert.us-cert.gov/sites/default/files/documents/Year_In_Review_FY2013_Final.pdf.

U.S. Government Accountability Office (U.S. GAO). (2004, March 15). Critical infrastructure protection: Challenges and efforts to secure control systems (No. GAO-04-354). Retrieved from http://www.gao.gov/assets/250/241726.pdf.

Vachtsevanos, G., Lewis, F. L., Roemer, M., Hess, A., & Wu, B. (2006). *Intelligent fault diagnosis and prognosis for engineering systems*. John Wiley & Sons, Inc.

Vukovic, O., Sou, K. C., Dán, G., & Sandberg, H. (2012). Network-aware mitigation of data integrity attacks on power system state estimation. *IEEE Journal on Selected Areas in Communications*, *30*(6), 1108–1118.

Wei, D., & Ji, K. (2010). Resilient industrial control system (RICS): Concepts, formulation, metrics, and insights. In *Proceedings of the 3rd international symposium on resilient control systems*.

Willsky, A. S. (1976). A survey of design methods for failure detection in dynamic systems. *Automatica*, *12*(6), 601–611.

Wu, F., Moslehi, K., & Bose, A. (2005). Power system control centers: Past, present, and future. *Proceedings of the IEEE*, *93*(11), 1890–1908.

Zhang, Y., & Jiang, J. (2008). Bibliographical review on reconfigurable fault-tolerant control systems. *Annual Reviews in Control*, *32*(2), 229–252.

Zhou, K., Doyle, J. C., & Glover, K. (1996). *Robust and optimal control*. Upper Saddle River, NJ, USA: Prentice-Hall, Inc.

Zimmerman, R. D., Murillo-S'anchez, C. E., & Thomas, R. J. (2009). MATPOWER's extensible optimal power flow architecture. In *IEEE power and energy society general meeting*.

Establishing a Smart Grid Security Architecture

7

Robert W. Griffin* and Lucie Langer†

*RSA – the Security Division of EMC, Ireland; †Austrian Institute of Technology, Vienna, Austria

7.1 INTRODUCTION

As mentioned already in Chapter 1, in systems as complex as Smart Grid, it is extremely valuable, before beginning detailed design and implementation, to establish an architecture that provides a longer-term and more durable understanding of the system, its components and their interrelationship. For Smart Grid, a good example of this is the California Independent System Operator (ISO) "Smart Grid Roadmap and Architecture" first published in December 2010. That document describes a 10-year plan for implementing Smart Grid at California ISO, mapping that plan to an architectural model that describes the essential components of the system and the interaction between them. This includes defining the roadmap for instrumenting security within their Smart Grid solution, shown in Figure 7.1.

In this roadmap, implementation of various aspects of security for their solution, including authentication, situational awareness and audit processes, is preceded by an evaluation of existing standards and strategies, identification of gaps and then development of architectural strategies that enable changes to existing systems while building and deploying enhancements to or replacements for those existing capabilities. The constraint of adapting or replacing existing systems is one that confronts most organizations responsible for implementing Smart Grid solutions. Establishing the architecture for the solution can help significantly in managing that transition, both for the solution as a whole and for the security-related aspects of that solution in particular.

Among the most valuable resources available to organizations implementing Smart Grid solutions are the various reference architectures for Smart Grid. We have touched on several of these resources already in earlier chapters, particularly in the discussion of Gridwise™, NISTIR 7628 and SGAM in Chapter 4 and if IT security reference architectures in Chapter 5. But there are so many resources available in this area that it is difficult to know which ones are the most valuable and how best to apply them.

Across the extensive and rapidly expanding materials that relate to cyber-physical security for the Smart Grid, there is considerable variation in the use of terms such as "security reference architecture", "security architectural model", "security

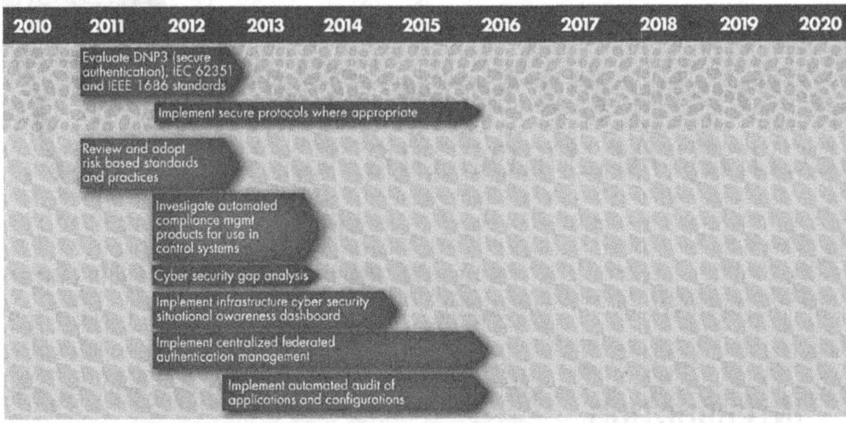

FIGURE 7.1 California ISO Smart Grid Security Roadmap

architectural framework", "security control framework", "security guidance", "security taxonomy" and many other related terms. For example, the Smart Energy Reference Architecture (SERA) by Microsoft (2013) and the Smart Grid Reference Architecture (SGRA) by IBM, Cisco and Southern California Edison (2011) are both called reference architectures and are provided by industry. However, they differ substantially in what they include and how they are organized. Similarly, the first volume of NISTIR 7628 defines a "logical reference model" for the Smart Grid that, though referenced by the Smart Grid Architecture Model (SGAM) defined by the CEN-CENELEC-ETSI Smart Grid Coordination Group, is conceptually different from SGAM. Both the "E-Energy Referenz-Architektur" and the DISCERN project "Identification of Current System Architecture" provide approaches to applying SGAM, but the approaches are different from each other and even more so from the "design process" defined in the IEEE "Foundation for Intelligent Physical Agents" (FIPA).

There are various studies and standards that provide structure, taxonomies, ontologies and other ways of organizing this broad set of materials. For example, ISO 42010, referenced in the CEN-CENELEC-ETSI "Smart Grid Reference Architecture", provides a valuable perspective on the purposes, contents and organization of reference architectures. Papers such as "Towards a Bottom-up Development of Reference Architectures for Smart Energy Systems" Irlbeck et al., 2013 propose approaches to address both the need for references architectures for the Smart Grid and the discrepancies between and gaps within existing reference architectures.

Reference architectures can take different views, depending on the specific aspects of a Smart Grid they relate to, for example security, communication, functionality and technology. While there is no such thing as "the" Smart Grid reference architecture, the issue is not just one of terminology and approach. Rather, the breadth and diversity of the resources that are termed reference architectures, architectural models, architectural frameworks, architectural methodologies and so on indicates that there are in fact several different purposes that these resources attempt to address. Rather than adopting or developing a definition of the term "reference architecture" and mapping the diverse resources to it, a more useful approach is therefore to identify the high-level purposes that these resources address and then assist organizations in understanding the effectiveness of the resources in meeting those purposes.

We see four major purposes that are served by the range of resources that are called or associated with the term "reference architecture", focused on helping organizations to:

1. Understand and adopt effective **methodologies** for establishing an effective and durable long-term approach to securing their Smart Grid environment. This is the purpose of such resources as the "Smart Grid Information Security" (SGIS) resource (part of the family of resources created under the EU M/490 mandate).
2. Define durable **architectures** (including technology-, process- and people-related components) that will secure an organization's Smart Grid environment over the long-term. This is the purpose behind the NISTIR 7628, SGAM and Sandia "Microgrid Security Reference Architecture" families of resources.
3. Develop particular **designs** based on those architectures. This is the area addressed by resources such as the Microsoft "Smart Energy Reference Architecture" (SERA).
4. Create mathematical and algorithmic **models,** simulations and analyses of those designs in order to evaluate its performance, predict failures and so on. This is the purpose of resources such as the "Cybersecurity on SCADA" resource from the EU FP7 Cockpit CI project.

These purposes are complementary and mutually supporting for an organization looking to achieve the over-arching goal of implementing resilient, dynamic and responsive capabilities, related not only to technology but also to processes and people, to secure their Smart Grid environment. We found that across the extensive range of resources related to Smart Grid reference architectures, there are three resources, or rather resource families, that are most directly and comprehensively helpful to an organization needing to achieve this goal. These resources are:

- NISTIR 7628 and related resources
- Resources created under the M/490 mandate as well as related resources not directly created under that mandate
- Sandia "Microgrid Security Reference Architecture" and related resources

The first two of these families of resources, in particular, are the essential tools for defining the architecture for a specific Smart Grid environment. They provide comprehensive and complementary methodologies, organizing principles and detailed information on technology, process- and people-related capabilities that an organization should consider when addressing the security of their particular Smart Grid environment.

The "Microgrid Security Reference Architecture", though less comprehensive in itself and in terms of related resources, nonetheless is also an important resource to consider. In particular, it explores security issues that have special implications both within an individual microgrid and in the interconnection of a particular microgrid both with another microgrid and with a larger Smart Grid environment. These issues have not yet been explored in NISTIR 7628 and M/490 to the same level, and this resource is therefore important.

In the discussion of developing a Smart Grid security architecture in Section 7.3 below, therefore, we will focus on NISIR 7628, SGAM and the Microgrid Security Reference Architecture. However, there are also other valuable resources that are related to the Smart Grid that do not directly address the needs of an organization focused on the goal of securing their real-world Smart Grid environment. For example, the family of IEC standards related to the Smart Grid, including 61850, 62351 and other standards, are generally addressed to technology vendors, rather than Smart Grid organizations, and focus on the secure and interoperable implementation and integration of technological capabilities from those vendors. The same is true of the family of IEEE standards for Smart Grid. These standards are referenced by NISTIR 7628 and the M/490 resources because they are essential to ensuring Smart Grid interoperability, resilience and security. But precisely because of the extensive references to the IEC and IEEE standards in the M/490 resources, an organization implementing security in a real-world Smart Grid implementation should not have to master the IEC and IEEE standards in the way that it should master NISTIR 7628 and the M/490 resources. Rather, we will discuss the IEC and IEEE standards in terms of their relevance during the design process.

7.2 ADOPTING A SMART GRID SECURITY ARCHITECTURE METHODOLOGY

In Section 7.3 below, in discussing the development of a Smart Grid security architecture, we touch on resources that are useful in using these three core resource families that we recommend. For example, we discuss the ENISA "Smart Grid Security Recommendations", which document a number of important key findings that serve as input for understanding NISTIR 7628 and SGAM. We also touch on resources such as the security profiles developed by the "Advanced Security Acceleration Project for Smart Grid (ASAP-SG)" that are helpful in developing a detailed design for Smart Grid security, and on other resources, such as the EU FP7 Cockpit project, that are useful for modeling Smart Grid security.

Among the most important of these additional resources are those that focus on helping organizations adopt a Smart Grid security methodology – that is, a process or approach to architecting and developing a secure Smart Grid environment. Some of these resources, such as ISO 42010 and the Irlbeck paper are most useful for standards organizations and similar groups that are focused on developing guidance for other organizations. But a number of other resources are focused on providing more direct guidance for electric utilities and other organizations that have to deploy, manage or assess security capabilities in an actual Smart Grid environment. This latter purpose is addressed most comprehensively by two methodological resources:

- The "NISTIR 7628 User's Guide" (2014) and related resources (such as NIST 1180R3 "Framework and Roadmap for Smart Grid Interoperability Standards"). These resources provide an approach, based on defined activities, to assist organizations in using NISTIR to define and implement the security strategy and capabilities for their Smart Grid.
- The resources created under the European Union M/490 Mandate, including the "Smart Grid Information Security (SGIS)" (2012) and related resources intended to show how to integrate security into Smart Grid implementations through the use of the Smart Grid Architecture Model (SGAM).

These two resources reference each other, explaining how NISTIR 7628 and SGAM/SGIS can be used together by organizations. They provide complementary guidance that any organization working on security capabilities for their Smart Grid should take advantage of. The resources are discussed in more detail below in the parts of Section 7.3 that focus on NISTIR 7628 and M/490, respectively.

There are two additional resources that are particularly valuable in terms of using SGAM.

- The BSI "E-Energy Referenz-Architektur" (available only in German).
- The "Identification of Current System Architecture" document from the EU FP7 DISCERN project (2013).

These documents derive technical models for a particular Smart Grid implementation (including security capabilities) from the Smart Grid Architecture Model (SGAM). The "E-Energy Referenz-Architektur" in particular elaborates a number of use cases for Smart Grid in terms of these technical models.

Before moving on to applying these methodologies in defining a specific Smart Grid architecture, it is worth noting that there are Smart Grid reference architectures that are intended to provide a methodology for or assist in the standards development process, rather than in developing a specific real-world Smart Grid architecture, design and models. This is the case with the IEC 62357 "Reference Architecture for Power System Exchange", for example, which maps the family of IEC standards related to the Smart Grid in order to show their inter-relationships, identify gaps and provide a future vision. As mentioned above, the family of IEC Smart Grid standards, like IEEE 2030 and related standards, also has an important role in terms of achieving interoperable and secure Smart Grid implementations. But we believe that this role, for an organization that is developing and deploying a Smart Grid environment, fits most importantly in the context of design decisions.

As in the California ISO roadmap, it is important not only to take advantage of the guidance provided in these methodological documents, but also to identify gaps in the methodologies that need to be addressed. Tools such as the threats and attack scenarios that are identified in the NESCOR cybersecurity failure scenarios are very helpful in reviewing the architectures to ensure that significant risks have been addressed. These scenarios can be complemented by analysis of particular real-world attacks, such as Stuxnet, and attacks on the oil and gas infrastructure in the United States and Saudi Arabia.

One critical gap is in architectural considerations is related to the use of microgrids. As discussed in the Sandia "Microgrid Security Reference Architecture" referenced above, microgrids can play an extremely valuable role in isolation of Smart Grid capabilities in the event of cyber-attacks, minimizing the cascade of impact from one segment of a Smart Grid to another. It can also provide important benefits in terms of the iterative adoption of new capabilities, including security capabilities, by reducing the risk of adverse impact across the whole of a grid solution in the case of installation or upgrade issues. Architectural models such as a federation of microgrids, as opposed to integration of microgrids in a heterogeneous grid/microgrid architecture, represent significant opportunities and decisions that are not yet explored in the methodological materials for NISTIR 7628 and SGAM. It is important to look for gaps such as these not only in the reference architectures you may work from, but also in the methodologies that you may adopt or adapt.

7.3 DEFINING YOUR SMART GRID SECURITY ARCHITECTURE

As discussed in the previous sections, existing Smart Grid reference architectures provide an indispensable resource for developing a Smart Grid Security Architecture applicable to the particular requirements, constraints and opportunities of your own Smart Grid environment. This section, therefore, focuses on how to apply NISTIR 7628, SGAM and the Microgrid Security Reference Architecture (MSRA) in the specific architecture for a given Smart Grid environment.

For each reference architecture, we present a summary of its key features and intended applications. We then discuss gaps and limitations in that reference architecture that need to be considered when applying it to establish security capabilities for a Smart Grid implementation. Finally, we provide guidance on how to use the reference architecture and point to resources that define a methodology for that reference architecture as comprehensively as possible.

Following this discussion of NISTIR 7628, SGAM and MSRA, we discuss several of the gaps and limitations in more detail, in terms of their significance for and how they can be addressed in a specific Smart Grid security architecture.

7.3.1 NISTIR 7628

7.3.1.1 Summary of NISTIR 7628 Approach
As described in the NIST Smart Grid Framework (SP 1108R3), NISTIR 7628 Guidelines for Smart Grid Security is:

- An overview of the cybersecurity strategy used by the Cyber Security Working Group (CSWG) to develop the high-level cybersecurity Smart Grid requirements;

- A tool for organizations that are researching, designing, developing, implementing, and integrating Smart Grid technologies, both established and emerging;
- An evaluative framework for assessing risks to Smart Grid components and systems during design, implementation, operation, and maintenance; and
- A guide to assist organizations as they craft a Smart Grid cybersecurity strategy that includes requirements to mitigate risks and privacy issues pertaining to Smart Grid customers and uses of their data.

The guidelines in NISTIR 7628 are neither prescriptive nor mandatory. Rather they are advisory and are intended to facilitate each organization's efforts to develop a cybersecurity strategy effectively focused on prevention, detection, response, and recovery.

Originally published by NIST in 2010, NISTIR 7628 consists of three parts:

- Volume 1: Smart Grid Security Strategy, Architecture and High-level Requirements. A revised version of Volume 1 was released by NIST in 2013.
- Volume 2: Privacy and the Smart Grid.
- Volume 3: Supportive Analyses and References.

The NISTIR 7628 standard itself, particularly Volume 1, focuses on defining detailed technical requirements across all Smart Grid domains (generation, distribution, operations etc.). The intended scope is broad and encompasses an extensive set of sub-systems in each domain (for example, nineteen sub-systems in the operations domain, including AMI, customer data management and so on).

Additional materials have been created to assist organizations interested in using NISTIR 7628:

- Introduction to NISTIR 7628 Guidelines for Smart Grid Cyber Security (published 2010 by SGIP). This document provides an overview of NISTIR 7628.
- Guide for Assessing the High-level Security Requirements in NISTIR 7628 Guidelines for Smart Grid Cyber Security (published 2012 by SGIP). This document provides guidance on establishing a security assessment process for Smart Grid security, using NISTIR 7628.
- NISTIR 7628 User's Guide (published 2014 by SGIP). This document defines a process for identifying and maintaining Smart Grid security requirements, using NISTIR 7628.

NISTIR 7628 is closely related to a number of other U.S. government documents, including the following:

- U.S. Department of Homeland Security (DHS), National Cyber Security Division. Catalog of Control Systems Security: Recommendations for Standards Developers. The catalog presents a compilation of practices that various industry bodies have recommended to increase the security of control systems from both physical and cyber-attacks. It was a source document for the NIST Interagency Report NISTIR 7628.

- U.S. Executive Order (EO) 13636: Improving Critical Infrastructure Cybersecurity and the related "Presidential Policy Directive on Critical Infrastructure Security and Resilience". Both reflect and provide justification for the security requirements defined in NISTIR 7628.
- NIST 1108R3 Framework for Smart Grid includes NISTIR 7628 in the list of recommended standards.
- NIST 7823 Smart Metering Infrastructure Smart Meter Upgradeability Test Framework, though it does not reference NISTIR 7628, provides a complementary test approach for AMI.
- The Cyber Security Capability Maturity Model (C2M2) also references NISTIR 7628.

NISTIR 7628 is referenced widely in government, industry and academic publications and standards, including the following:

- Detailed analysis of 7628 in terms of Distribution Energy Resources (DER) in EPRI Cybersecurity for DER Systems;
- The NERC_CIPv5_Mapping_v2.xls document provides mapping of NISTIR 7628 to NERC CIP standards; and
- The CEN-CENELEC-ETSI Smart Grid Coordination Group Smart Grid Information Security, which defines the Smart Grid Information Security (SGIS) model, includes an appendix mapping NISTIR 7628 to SGIS security levels.

As noted in the introduction to NISTIR 7628, this multi-part standard "is intended primarily for individuals and organizations responsible for addressing cyber security for Smart Grid systems and the constituent subsystems of hardware and software components. These individuals and organizations compose a large and diverse group that includes vendors of energy information and management services, equipment manufacturers, utilities, system operators, regulators, researchers, and network specialists. In addition, the guidelines have been drafted to incorporate the perspectives of three primary industries converging on opportunities enabled by the emerging Smart Grid: utilities and other businesses in the electric power sector, the information technology industry, and the telecommunications sector". The guidelines address multiple domains in the Smart Grid, as shown in Figure 7.2.

> NISTIR 7628 is not an architecture, but rather "an analytical framework that organizations can use to develop effective cyber security strategies tailored to their particular combinations of Smart Grid-related characteristics, risks, and vulnerabilities" (NISTIR 7628, Vol. 1, p. viii). It can also be used as a tool for cyber security assessments, as described in the "SGIP Guide for Assessing the High-level Security Requirements in NISTIR 7628".

7.3.1.2 NISTIR 7628 Gaps and Limitations with Respect to Smart Grid Security

NISTIR 7628, along with the associated Introduction, Assessment guide and User's Guide, provide a valuable resource for organizations defining, designing or deploying

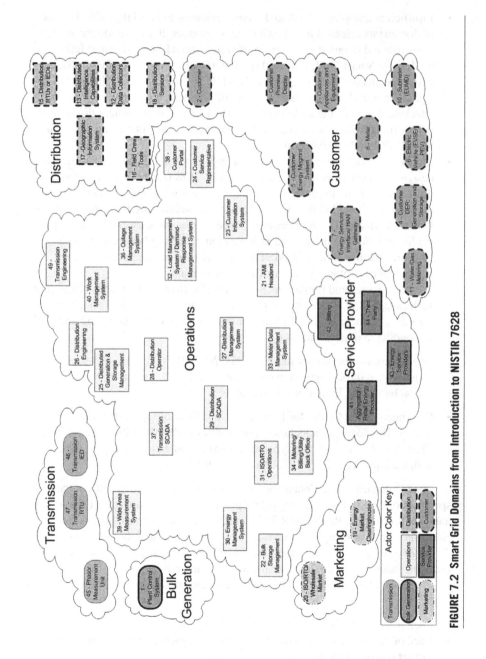

FIGURE 7.2 Smart Grid Domains from Introduction to NISTIR 7628

a Smart Grid system. We see three issues, however, in terms of the application of NISTIR 7628:

- Insufficient mapping of risk and attack scenarios to NISTIR 7628. The set of documents released by NESCOR in September 2013 provide the most extensive and detailed exploration of various attack scenarios and failure models for Smart Grid. One of those documents, "Analysis of High Risk Failure Scenarios", does reference NISTIR 7628. However, neither in that document nor elsewhere that we know of is there a thorough mapping of attack scenarios to the architecture. In the Chan et al. document discussed below, this problem is cited as one of the reasons for limitations and issues in the NISTIR 7628 architecture.
- The lack of a detailed methodology for applying NISTIR 7628 to Smart Grid design and deployment. Though the NISTIR 7628 User's Guide is helpful in this regard, it is focused on requirements definition and management, rather than on adapting NISTIR 7628 into a detailed architecture for a specific Smart Grid deployment. The significant variances across industry architectures for the Smart Grid (see below) are an indication of the gap between the high-level architecture defined in NISTIR 7628 and the detailed decisions that organizations deploying a Smart Grid have to make.
- Technical issues and limitations in the NISTIR 7628 strategy and architecture, such as lack of consideration of physical security issues, lack of specification regarding privacy, and insufficient strategies for detecting, analyzing and responding to targeted attacks.

Of the various documents that reference NISTIR 7628, only two provide a detailed analysis of the strengths and limitations of NISTIR, focusing on this third issue (technical issues and limitations) listed above:

- Comments of the Center for Democracy and Technology Draft NISTIR 7628 (2009). This focuses on technical limitations in NISTIR 7628 related to privacy.
- Chan et al, On Smart Grid Cybersecurity Standardization: Issues of Designing with the NISTIR 7628 (2010) Chan et al., 2010.

The Comments of the Center for Democracy and Technology call out the lack of specification in NISTIR 7628 regarding privacy, including in terms of the use cases and data flows under the NISTIR 7628 architecture that are necessary to understand risk of and provisions against exposure of personally identifiable information (PII). To our knowledge, these use cases and data flows have not yet been defined by government, industry or academic publications or standards.

The Chan et al. paper identifies two significant issues for the NISTIR 7628 architecture:

- Lack of consideration of physical security issues, and
- Lack of consideration of privileged user issues, particularly in terms of utility impact on consumer privacy.

We see both these issues as significant. One critical implication of these issues is the need to have comprehensive and integrated security analytics capabilities, for example to address attack scenarios in which the defensive security mechanisms are subverted or bypassed, such as by social engineering in order to steal credentials of privileged users.

The gap with regard to security analytics is a symptom of a more fundamental issue with regard to NISTIR 7628. While providing a valuable overview of the range of security capabilities that should be considered by any organization designing, deploying, evaluating or auditing Smart Grids, NISTIR 7628 is based on assumptions about security strategy that, while best practice at the time NISTIR 7628 was written, are no longer adequate to the transformations that have occurred in the threat landscape, business models, and in infrastructure technology in the past several years. In particular, security strategies have to include responding to targeted attacks by aggressive and well-funded adversaries who will succeed in bypassing defensive mechanisms. These strategies therefore have to include detection, analysis and response strategies that are not adequately developed in NISTIR 7628. The strategies should also consider application of federated microgrid models that would facilitate responding to such attacks by dynamic reconfiguration of the larger grid to avoid seriously compromised portions of the larger grid.

7.3.1.3 Applying NISTIR 7628 to Smart Grid Security Architecture

NISTIR 7628 and the related documents listed above represent the most detailed set of materials available to organizations that are architecting Smart Grid deployments. The logical model described in NISTIR 7628 (often called the "spaghetti model") provides the most comprehensive diagram of the interrelationships of security-related aspects of Smart Grid architecture.

NISTIR 7628 is therefore a valuable resource for achieving effective cybersecurity for the Smart Grid. There does not appear to be authoritative research regarding the use and adoption of NISTIR 7628, although the NIST Smart Grid website says that NISTIR 7628 has "achieved wide recognition and use". The number of citations of NISTIR 7628 in government, industry and academic publications is a strong indication of likely consideration of NISTIR 7628 in development of individual Smart Grid deployments. We did not find specific references to the use of NISTIR 7628 in case studies of Smart Grid deployments, but it was mentioned as having been consulted in interviews with a number of electric utilities in the European Union.

However, the technical gaps identified above are significant and need to be addressed. NISTIR 7628 needs to be complemented by new materials related to understanding risk and attack scenarios, defining use cases for privacy, and to designing effective Smart Grid security solutions based not only on NISTIR 7628 but also taking material from other resources such as the Sandia Microgrid Reference Architecture, as discussed in the introduction to this document.

7.3.2 RESPONSE TO EU MANDATE M/490

7.3.2.1 Summary of M/490 Approach

The M/490 Smart Grid framework, including the Smart Grid Architecture Model (SGAM) and related resources, aims to integrate different state-of-the-art approaches in a European setting. The purposes of SGAM include mapping different Smart Grid use cases to a common architecture model, establishing a framework for analyzing different implementations of a Smart Grid architecture, providing a common view and language for different stakeholders, and identifying standardization and interoperability gaps.

In 2012, the Smart Grid Coordination Group (SG-CG) Reference Architecture Working Group (SG-CG/RA) formed by the European standardization institutions CEN, CENELEC and ETSI presented a Smart Grid Reference Architecture for Europe as part of their response to the EU Smart Grid Mandate M/490. This is the European equivalent to the U.S. NIST Smart Grid Framework (NIST SP 1108). The major contributions of the M/490 work on reference architectures are twofold: first, a European Conceptual Model has been defined by adapting the NIST Conceptual Model to the European market, mainly by adding a dedicated DER domain. Second, a three-dimensional Smart Grid Architecture Model (SGAM) has been introduced to facilitate the analysis of Smart Grid use cases. Another important part of the M/490 framework is the report on Smart Grid Information Security (SGIS), which provides an approach for assessing inherent risk of Smart Grid assets. These contributions are discussed in more detail below.

As shown in Figure 7.3, the EU Conceptual Model defined as part of the M/490 framework consists of four main domains (operations, grid users, markets, and energy services), each of which contains one or more subdomains and system actors reflecting the different roles within the European electricity market. The operations and grid users' domain reflect the physical processes of the power system, such as generation, transport, distribution, and consumption, and include (embedded) ICT-enabled system actors. The markets and energy services domains refer to the trade of electricity products and services, and the participation in the processes of trade and system operations representing grid users (energy services). The grid users' domain is defined by roles and actors involved in power generation, consumption, and storage, and reflects the flexibility concept which has been introduced by the M/490 working groups to support future demand-response use-cases.

In addition to the European Conceptual Model, the CEN-CENELEC-ETSI Smart Grid Reference Architecture framework defines the Smart Grid Architecture Model (SGAM). SGAM aims to

- Provide a common view and language to support different stakeholders in discussing a given system context;
- Integrate different state-of-the-art approaches in a European setting;
- Provide a technology- and solution-independent framework for analyzing different implementations of a Smart Grid architecture;

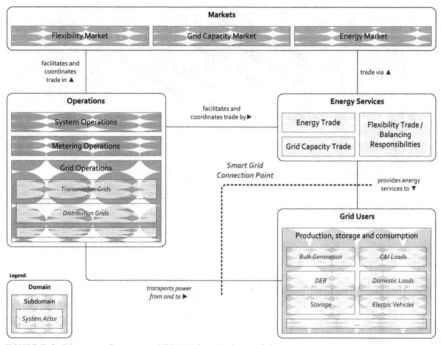

FIGURE 7.3 European Conceptual Model for the Smart Grid

- Facilitate the planning of migration activities from legacy systems to future Smart Grid architectures; and
- Provide criteria for identifying standardization and interoperability gaps.

SGAM is defined by zones, domains, and interoperability layers (see Figure 7.4). While the zones are derived from the hierarchical levels of information management in power systems (from field via process, station towards operation and enterprise level), the domains reflect the different stages of power generation, transmission, distribution, and consumption within the electrical energy conversion chain. Electrical domains and information management zones span the Smart Grid plane. In the third dimension, SGAM features five interoperability layers which are an abstracted and condensed version of the originally eight GridWise interoperability layers, and represent different stakeholders' views. The base layer is the component layer, where physical and software components are situated. On top of that, communication links and protocols between these components are located in the communication layer. The information layer holds the data models of the information exchanged. The function layer holds the actual functionalities and the uppermost business layer describes the business goals of the system.

The main objective of SGAM is to facilitate an abstract representation of Smart Grid architectures and related stakeholders' views (represented by different

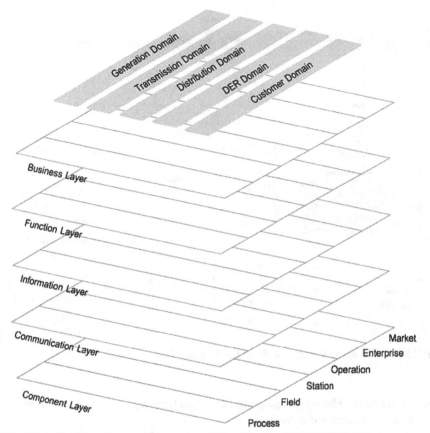

FIGURE 7.4 The Smart Grid Architecture Model developed by CEN-CENELEC-ETSI

architecture viewpoints or interoperability layers, respectively), and to provide a framework for analyzing and comparing different implementation scenarios. By placing entities such as processes, functions, data objects, protocols and components in the appropriate location within the SGAM cube, the relation between this entity and related entities can be depicted and subsequently analyzed: "A consistent mapping of a given use case or function means that all SGAM layers are covered with an appropriate entity. If a layer remains open, this implies that there is no specification (data model, protocol) or component available to support the use case or function. This inconsistency shows that there is the need for specification or standard in order to realize the given use case or function. When all five layers are consistently covered, the use case or function can be implemented with the given specifications / standards and components".

The SGAM framework can be applied to map different use cases to a common architecture model and analyze the use cases from different points of view, thus identifying standardization gaps related to the implementation of the individual use cases. As such, SGAM provides guidance to standardization bodies and technical committees. Security and privacy are cross-cutting issues that need to be considered on each individual layer. By defining Smart Grid assets and their interconnections for each of the SGAM cells, threat and vulnerability analysis and risk assessment for Smart Grids is supported. The risk assessment approach suggested by CEN-CENEL-EC-ETSI is laid down in the report on Smart Grid Information Security (SGIS) as part of their response to the M/490 mandate.

The SGIS methodology provides a framework to assess the criticality of Smart Grid components by focusing on power loss caused by ICT systems failures. Five SGIS Security Levels (from low to highly critical) are used to classify inherent risk attached to individual information assets. Highly critical assets are those that could lead to a power loss above 10 GW when disrupted (pan-European incident), while the lowest level applies to assets whose disruption could lead to a power loss under 1 MW (town or neighborhood incident). By determining the security level for an information asset, the corresponding essential security requirements for that asset are determined. SGIS also provides high-level guidance in terms of the recommended security levels for the cells of the Smart Grid plane (spanned by SGAM domains and zones), as well as a set of recommendations on appropriate security measures for mitigating the risks, depending on security level, and relating to the domains suggested by ENISA as well as the different SGAM layers. The SGAM Toolbox supports use-case modeling and related cybersecurity risk analysis according to the proposed SGAM and SGIS methodologies.

SGAM postulates that, when developing ICT interoperability standards, the relation to markets, products, services and (business) processes must be well understood to ensure that ICT systems really support the business. This is reflected by the business architecture view (top SGAM interoperability layer), which requires the definition of (market) roles, e.g. drawing upon the Harmonized Electricity Market Role Model by ENTSO-E, EFET and ebIX. According to SGAM, there is currently no evidence on gaps requiring new communication standards for Smart Grids. However, guidance regarding the options provided in the different standards is required – that is, communication profiles that take into account interoperability requirements need to be developed. This is viewed as a task for standardization bodies. SGAM recommends the Internet Protocol (IP), as the technology most probably capable of ensuring that communications are future-proof as well as for avoiding unnecessary gateways in different parts of the Smart Grid communication network. Recommendations regarding the applicability of available communication technologies to different Smart Grid sub-networks are also provided.

7.3.2.2 M/490 Gaps and Limitations with Respect to Smart Grid Security

Similarly to NISTIR 7628, SGAM follows a centralized view on power generation, distribution and demand response. Therefore, alternatives would have to be found when seeking a model that supports decentralized scenarios, such as in a microgrid-based architecture.

The purpose of reference architectures in general, and SGAM more specifically, is to facilitate the representation and analysis of Smart Grid architectures. As such, they remain neutral regarding the use of specific Smart Grid technologies, as opposed to a specific instance of a Smart Grid architecture. Such an instantiation is required for depicting the different demonstrators and to perform a security analysis and risk assessment in a specific deployment context. This also requires considering the migration process from legacy systems to novel, "smart" components, for example. In this regard, the SGAM and SGIS methodologies support a rather static approach. For example, the SGIS methodology foresees determining the *inherent risk* posed by a certain Smart Grid asset and requires considering the asset without any security measures whatsoever in place. While a static approach is beneficial for considering a snapshot of the current system characteristics, it is not sufficient for a thorough and flexible security analysis that pays tribute to the evolving nature of the power grid and must therefore be complemented with a dynamic assessment which considers evolving threats and security controls.

As opposed to SGAM, the SGIS methodology seems not to be very well-known among Smart Grid stakeholders yet. When speaking to stakeholders, we have experienced that some of those who do know SGIS and have tried to use it for carrying out a Smart Grid risk assessment have encountered a number of obstacles, such as the lack of guidance regarding the tool support. Most importantly, the SGIS approach requires an extensive assessment of all information assets across all relevant use cases. Depending on the outcome of this assessment, each asset is assigned an SGIS Security Level which relates to the potential power loss associated with a loss or compromise with that specific asset. This result is very broad and does not reflect other categories of impact (for example, safety implications or legal liability issues). While these impacts are considered part of the assessment, the associated conclusions get lost along the way, leaving the organization conducting the assessment with a vague expression of the asset value in terms of a Security Level between one and five.

7.3.2.3 *Applying M/490 in EU Smart Grid Security Projects*

The M/490 framework and SGAM in particular has been used as a reference model in many EU Smart Grid projects. Strictly speaking, although it is not a reference architecture in the sense of providing boundaries within which certain architecture decisions may be taken, SGAM is a powerful tool for establishing a common language between different experts and stakeholders in the Smart Grid. It thus facilitates the architecture development process and supporting a common representation of Smart Grids use-cases and interoperability viewpoints both for current and future energy grid implementations.

In the EU FP7 project DISCERN, SGAM has been used to depict the present system architectures of participating DSOs by having them individually answer questions relating to each SGAM interoperability layer. The German E-Energy project has been closely collaborating with the M/490 working groups and has provided valuable insights in terms of use case modeling based on SGAM.

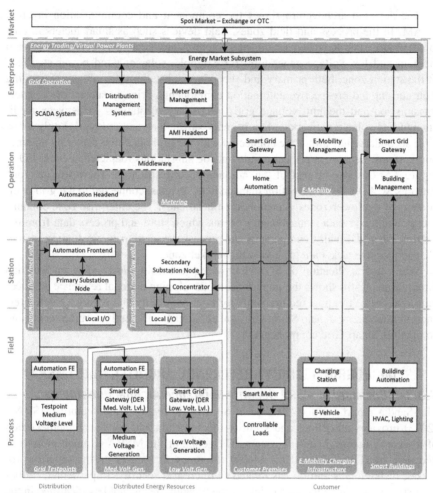

FIGURE 7.5 (SG)2 Architecture Model

To provide a more concrete example of the use of the M/490 reference model, we describe here an SGAM-based architecture model for Austrian Smart Grids Kammerstetter et al., 2014 (see Figure 7.5). It was developed in a national research project on Smart Grid security named Smart Grid Security Guidance (SG)[2], to provide a common basis for a risk assessment complemented by practical security tests and was jointly aimed at establishing security controls for national distribution system operators. The architecture model includes specific Smart Grid devices and protocols that are typically deployed in the Austrian distribution grid, or that at least will be deployed in the near future, and focuses on the customer, DER, and distribution domains.

The depicted architecture shows the component and communication layer of SGAM. In the process and field zones, field devices such as smart meters in customer premises or dedicated sensors and actuators are located, as well as distributed medium and low-voltage generators (for example, solar or wind power stations). In the station zone, both primary and secondary substations are situated, including their current and prospective automation components. Primary substations connect transmission and medium voltage grids, secondary substations sit between medium and low voltage networks. Most primary substations and (currently) only a few large secondary substations are connected with the grid operation center by automation systems. Sensors at critical points outside substations (depicted as local I/O in Figure 7.5) can also be part of this automation infrastructure. The operation zone contains SCADA and distribution management systems, connected to the grid components of the lower zones via automation head ends. The enterprise zone contains energy and meter data management systems which store and process data from the distribution grid. Finally, components and processes related to energy trading such as the energy spot market are located in the market zone.

While this application of SGAM provides just a high-level view on Austrian Smart Grids, it still shows the importance of developing national reference architectures that define minimal requirements for interoperability and security. Such reference architectures can help Smart Grid stakeholders to efficiently develop secure and compatible Smart Grid components.

7.3.3 MICROGRID SECURITY REFERENCE ARCHITECTURE (MSRA)

7.3.3.1 Summary of MSRA Security Reference Architecture Approach

The Sandia report entitled "Microgrid Security Reference Architecture (MSRA)" (2013) provides guidelines and security recommendations for the implementation of a secure microgrid control system. The scope of the MSRA is much more limited than NISTIR 7628 and the M/490 resources. It focuses on the security processes, technologies and threats related to microgrid security. In particular, it does not explicitly examine the viewpoints of the breadth of stakeholders identified in the SGAM framework, nor the range of subsystems in NISTIR 7628.

It starts by presenting a high-level concept of operations for a microgrid, including operational modes, necessary power actors, and the communication protocols that are typically employed. The document then describes general network and industrial control system-specific vulnerabilities, a threat model, information assurance compliance concerns and design criteria for a microgrid control system network and shows how the MSRA design approach addresses these concerns by segmenting the microgrid control system network into what the MSRA calls "enclaves" and grouping enclaves into functional domains. Finally, the report discusses cyber actors that can help mitigate potential vulnerabilities, in addition to performance benefits and vulnerability mitigation that may be realized using this reference architecture.

This conceptual discussion provides an example of a microgrid control system network implementation. The example describes the types of communication occurring on that network, example data exchange attributes for actors in the network, an example of how the network can be segmented to create enclaves and functional domains as well as how cyber actors can be used to enforce network segmentation and provide the necessary security.

Unlike NISTIR 7628 and the M/490 mandate resources, the Sandia report largely stands by itself, with little external elaboration in terms of methodology, detailed implementation guidance and so on. However, the architecture was applied in the Smart Power Infrastructure Demonstration for Energy Reliability and Security (SPIDERS) project during 2014. Figure 7.6 shows the architecture that was used in the demonstration.

This includes both static and dynamic analysis of the deployment architecture using several tools, such as the DHS Cyber Security Evaluation Tool (CSET). There are also a number of important resources that complement the Sandia report, even though they may not explicitly reference the report. The most important of these is the FINSENY FP7 project "Microgrid Functional Architecture Description", which provides valuable insights on microgrid architecture when using the Sandia Microgrid Reference Architecture both for microgrids within a centralized grid architecture and also in a distributed, federated microgrid architecture. FINSENY provides detailed guidance on the application of security technologies in microgrid architectures such as the table provided in the project report.

The FINSENY project does not reference the Microgrid Security Reference Architecture. But the information provided in the project report is in general consistent with the MSRA and a valuable complement to it. Similarly, the report by Glover and Guttromson on the SPIDERS project showed several interesting techniques for analysis of microgrid load simulation and adaptable communications networks that can be valuable in using data analytics to detect anomalous behavior indicators of possible cybersecurity attacks in microgrids.

7.3.3.2 MSRA Gaps and Limitations with Respect to Security Architecture

In a presentation given at the 2014 IEEE Power and Energy Society general meeting, Jason Stamp discussed the results to date of the SPIDERS project. In the summary of those results, the first conclusion is that "the proposed microgrid design requirements and recommendations analysis is effective". That conclusion seems more than justified; SPIDERS provides a cogent demonstration of the value of a Smart Grid architecture that uses federations of microgrids as a means of achieving resiliency and flexibility.

However, there are a number of gaps and limitations in the development of microgrid reference architectures in general and in the Microgrid Security Reference Architecture in particular.

- **Methodological gaps**. As discussed above, though the MSRA can certainly be applied as a complementary concept within the M/490 methodology, including in combination with NISTIR 7628, there is no detailed exploration yet (to our knowledge) of what such an integration would mean. Most importantly, a

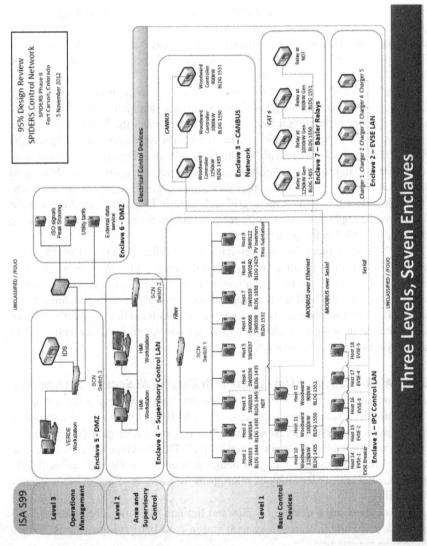

FIGURE 7.6 Microgrid Reference Architecture for SPIDERS Demonstration

microgrid-based architecture such as SPIDERS would need to be considered as an alternative to, or at least new subsystem within, the centralized models for power generation, distribution and demand response that are the assumption of both NISTIR 7628 and SGAM.

- **Cybersecurity gaps**. There are several critical gaps in terms of the security-related discussions that exist to date for the MSRA. Some of these gaps relate to the threat landscape, such as the relatively little discussion of social engineering attacks that bypass the technical vulnerabilities explored in MSRA and FINSENY documents. Those gaps also relate to critical technologies that can address these issues, such the application of analytics not just to operational issues, such as load management, but also to detection, analysis and response to cyber-attacks.

As discussed in the Glover and Guttromson presentation, there are also numerous areas in which standards would be of considerable benefit in achieving greater interoperability both within and between microgrids. Some of these gaps are being addressed by efforts such as the OASIS Energy Interoperation Technical Committee. But there is still considerable work to do to identify what standards are needed, particularly in terms of standards related to security for microgrid architectures.

7.3.3.3 Applying MSRA in Smart Grid Security Projects

The SPIDERS project, though still underway, has shown that microgrid-based architectures for the Smart Grid are feasible and valuable. It has shown the possibilities for the application of various modeling approaches in that architectural model that, though currently focused on operational issues, have significant application within the cybersecurity domain as well. And though the immediate driver for the SPIDERS project and for MSRA came from military and national defense organizations, the insights from these resources are of significant value in any consideration of microgrids as part of a Smart Grid architecture, design and deployment.

An organization taking advantage of MSRA in a real-world Smart Grid environment is likely to have to do considerable work to investigate and address the limitations discussed above. Nonetheless, we believe that microgrid approaches, including the enclave model used in the SPIDERS project, should be seriously considered at least for subsystems within a larger grid architecture.

7.3.4 ADDRESSING GAPS IN THE SMART GRID REFERENCE ARCHITECTURES

The discussions in the preceding sections have identified several gaps or limitations in each of the three Smart Grid reference architectures that an organization should be aware of, as it applies the resources to their needs. Some of these limitations in one architecture, such as the absence of microgrid architectural considerations in NISTIR 7628 and SGAM, are addressed in another of the resources (in this case, the Microgrid Security Reference Architecture). But there are several limitations that exist across all three architectures:

- Defining the role of monitoring and analytics in the security architecture
- Addressing the integration of legacy and new components
- Improving resistance to social engineering attacks

There are also emerging considerations that are related to transformations in IT, particularly in terms of the integration of enterprise virtualization and cloud computing architectures with Smart Grid that, although not discussed above, are relevant to development of a specific Smart Grid security architecture.

The importance of monitoring and analytics has been touched on in several previous chapters and will be discussed in the context of operational considerations in Chapter 9. Although included in the California ISO architecture and roadmap, monitoring and analytics does not receive a great deal of attention in any of the reference architectures discussed in this chapter. The emergence of targeted attacks, however, has greatly increased the importance of monitoring and analytics as a tool for the rapid detection of attacks that have succeeded in penetrating the defensive capabilities of a Smart Grid implementation. For example, Chapter 5 describes how monitoring can be used to detect attempted exploits that target the communications infrastructure of a Smart Grid implementation. Chapter 6 discusses the enhancement of SCADA systems in power transmission networks by Energy Management Systems (EMS) that provide system-wide monitoring capabilities that can be leveraged in detecting anomalies due to a cyber-attack, rather than to a component failure or malfunction.

> In the California ISO architecture, monitoring and analytics is included as a specific component in which these capabilities are focused. Such a component could be incorporated into the Energy Management System component in the NISTIR 7628 architecture, but having it separated at the architectural level encourages consideration of a broad range of monitoring and analytics capabilities during the design process. For example, monitoring and analysis has been used not only to identify attacks within IT infrastructure, but also fraudulent use of electric power, as discussed by engineers from a Canadian utility at a 2014 Smart Grid conference.

The integration of legacy and new components is also an issue that is discussed to a limited extent in the reference architectures. As discussed in Chapter 5, the relationship of legacy and new components has important implications not only in terms of the roll out of a solution over time, but also in terms of understanding and responding to threats. In particular, understanding the integration of legacy and new components can affect decisions such as where to install sensors within the legacy environment that would enable a greater degree of accuracy in identifying anomalies that could be attacks.

The increased incidence of social engineering attacks has put emphasis on helping users to detect and resist these attacks. On-going user education is invaluable. But unfortunately it's not sufficient, as is shown by the continuing growth in phishing, drive-by, water-hole and other attacks, especially used as part of a larger cyber-attack campaign. Social engineering attacks are included in the NESCOR scenarios, but the Smart Grid reference architectures generally have technological support for users to help them in detecting these kinds of attacks. At the architectural level, these capabilities include risk-based monitoring and analysis technologies that evaluate a broad range of factors to identify potentially fraudulent access to customer information systems, compromised administrator accounts and insider attacks for disruption or information theft. The role of risk-based monitoring and analytics is discussed in Chapter 9.

7.4 **MOVING FROM ARCHITECTURE TO DESIGN**

A Smart Grid security architecture, invaluable as it is, represents only a step towards the implementation and deployment of a Smart Grid solution. In order to take maximum advantage of the architecture, there are several important considerations as you move to design, including how you reference industry standards and vendor standards in that design.

Both IEC and IEEE have developed extensive and valuable families of standards that are related to the Smart Grid. The relevant IEC standards identified in the "IEC Smart Grid Standardization Roadmap" include the following:

- IEC 60870 "Telecontrol equipment and systems protocols" series;
- IEC 61334 "Distribution automation using distribution line carrier systems" series;
- IEC 61850 "Communication networks and systems in substations " series;
- IEC 61968 "Application integration at electric utilities" series;
- IEC 61970 "Energy management system application programming interface" series;
- IEC 62235 "Common Information Model" series;
- IEC 62351 "Power systems management and associated data exchange " series; and
- IEC 62357 "TC57 Architecture" series, especially IEC 62357-1 "Reference Architecture for Power System Information Exchange".

The "IEC Smart Grid Standardization Roadmap" provides a very useful introduction to understanding these IEC standards related to the Smart Grid. The roadmap uses the NISTIR 7628 conceptual model as the context for these standards, then shows the IEC standards in terms of their role in ensuring "a fast, efficient and dependable communications infrastructure". This architecture, shown in Figure 7.7 below, is intended to "identify the boundaries between standards where harmonization is required" and "places existing standards into layers in order to define interfaces between them".

The IEC 62357 and IEC 62351 series of standards span all levels of this reference architecture and are most useful for organizations that are architecting, designing and deploying a Smart Grid solution. IEC 62357-1 "Reference architecture for power system exchange", for example, is helpful during detailed design in order to understand what standards an organization should expect to be supported in equipment that

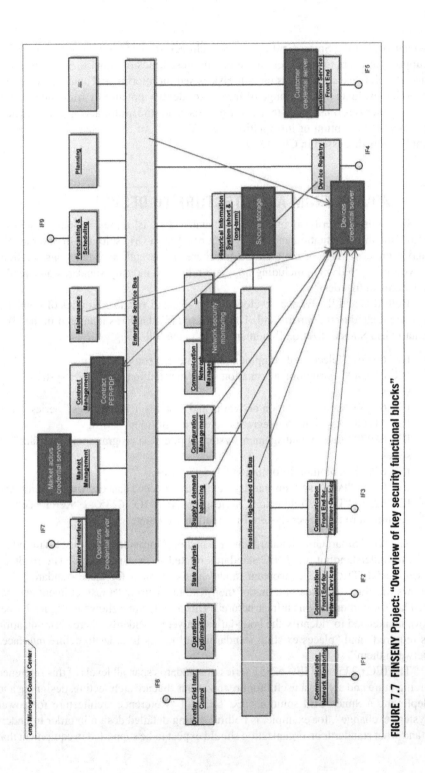

FIGURE 7.7 FINSENY Project: "Overview of key security functional blocks"

they include in their Smart Grid environment. One of the IEC 62351 series, the technical report IEC TR 62351-10 "Security Architecture Guidelines", provides useful guidance related to security controls relevant to Smart Grid. The report also discusses where the various controls are applicable in terms of different Smart Grid domains.

As shown in Figure 7.8, the other IEC Smart Grid standards focus on one or two levels of this architecture:

- The IEC CIM (Common Information model), IEC 69170 and IEC 61968 focus on application interfaces;
- The IEC 61850 and IEC 61334 standards focus on communication services; and
- The IEC 61850 and IEC 60870 standards focus on device interfaces.

Like 62351 and IEC 62357, these standards can also be helpful for organizations that are architecting, designing and deploying Smart Grid environments. In general, however, all the IEC standards are at too low a level to be directly helpful to such an organization. Rather, such organizations should determine whether particular equipment they are considering has implemented these standards and whether that implementation has been tested for interoperability. If the equipment supports these standards, the Smart Grid environment will benefit from the resultant interoperability, proven design, and fit within a durable Smart Grid architecture that these standards afford. For this reason, it is valuable for an organization to have some knowledge of these IEC standards, but it need not have mastery of those standards to the same degree as we recommend for NISTIR 7628 and the M490 resources.

The IEEE has also created an important series of technical standards for Smart Grid, including the following:

- IEEE 2030 series. This set of standards provides guidance about IEEE standards relevant to the Smart Grid, as well as providing a high-level model for Smart Grid into which these standards fit.
- IEEE 1547 series. This set of standards provides Smart Grid interconnection technical specifications and requirements, as well as interconnection test specifications and requirements.

As shown in Figure 7.9 below from IEEE 2030 Basso et al., 2011, the IEEE standards do not address the conceptual level of reference architectures, pointing instead to NISTIR 7628 for that architectural level.

That is, like the IEC standards discussed above, both the IEEE 2030 and IEEE 1547 series are technical standards that complement the NISTIR 7628 and M/490 families of standards. Similarly, the IEEE standards (especially IEEE 2547) are primarily of importance to equipment manufacturers who should implement these standards, as well as the IEC ones, in their products.

Therefore, we believe the IEEE and the IEC standards share the same role. That is, it is valuable for an organization architecting, designing and developing a Smart Grid environment to have some knowledge of the IEEE standards. But it need not have mastery of those standards to the same degree as we recommend for NISTIR 7628 and the M490 resources.

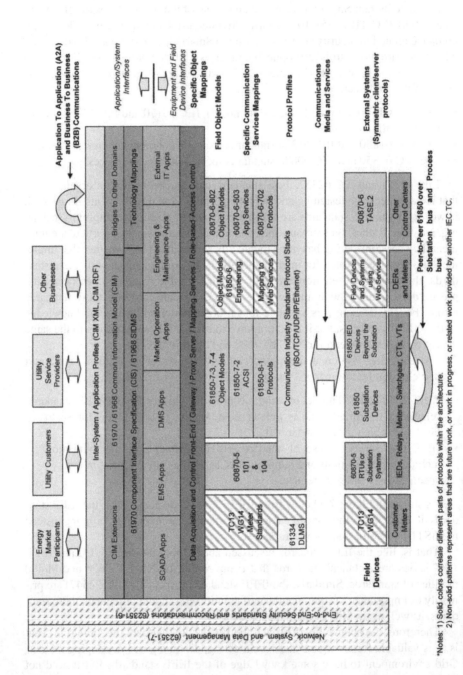

FIGURE 7.8 TC 57 Smart Grid Reference Architecture

*Notes: 1) Solid colors correlate different parts of protocols within the architecture.
2) Non-solid patterns represent areas that are future work, or work in progress, or related work provided by another IEC TC.

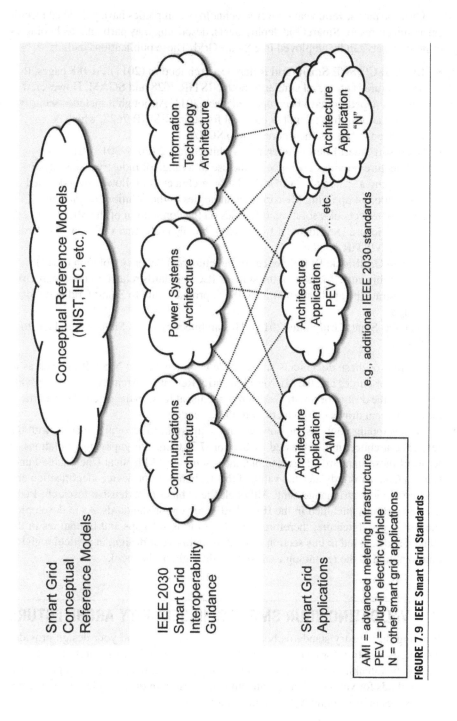

AMI = advanced metering infrastructure
PEV = plug-in electric vehicle
N = other smart grid applications

FIGURE 7.9 IEEE Smart Grid Standards

Over the past several years, several technology companies have published technical architectures for Smart Grid deployments, describing how particular technologies or product sets can be employed in a Smart Grid. These publications include:

- IBM/CISCO/SCE Smart Grid Reference Architecture (2011). At 188 pages, this architecture is at a level similar to both NISTIR 7628 and SGAM. However, it does not appear to have been updated since 2011. Although it includes security considerations, they are not at the level found in NISTIR 7628, which is referenced in but not incorporated into SGRA.
- Microsoft Smart Energy Reference Architecture V2 (2009-2013). This architecture provides guidance on the use of a range of industry standards in developing a specific Smart Grid solution architecture, followed by a detailed explication of applying Microsoft technologies in the solution. Regarding security aspects of a solution, it focuses on the application of the Microsoft SDLC (Secure Development Life Cycle), but also references relevant standards such as NISTIR 7628.
- CISCO GridBlocks™ Reference Architecture and Security Solution (2013). This architecture focuses on the suite of IEC standards related to the Smart Grid to illustrate the application of the CISCO product suite to Smart Grid network design.
- Siemens Smart Grid Suite (2013). This architecture maps Siemens products to SGAM.

All four of these documents are valuable complements to NISTIR (as well as to the M/490 resources and the Microgrid Security Reference Architecture) and provide input to in the design of Smart Grid deployments, at least to the extent that a particular deployment draws on products from these vendors.

In developing your design, however, it is important to recognize that, as with the reference architectures discussed in Section 7.2, there are gaps and limitations in terms of these standards. For example, the discussion of Physical Unclonable Functions in Chapter 4 indicates the value of this technology for device identification and cryptographic key management. Although the subject of extensive research, PUFs are not currently included in the IEC, IEEE and vendor standards. As in developing the security architecture, therefore, you should look for gaps and limitations in the standards discussed in this section when developing your design, in particular giving consideration to the technologies discussed throughout this book.

7.5 VALIDATING YOUR SMART GRID SECURITY ARCHITECTURE

Building on industry standards both for your architecture and your design provides a strong foundation for an effective and stable Smart Grid security architecture. It is extremely valuable, nonetheless, also to subject the architecture and design to various methods for validating the architecture and design in order to identify and remediate issues before beginning implementation.

One approach to this validation, modeling of attack scenarios relative to a particular architecture, has already been discussed in Chapter 6 in terms of risk assessment for false data injection attacks. This modeling can be extremely valuable in identifying segments within a given grid that result in highest impact in the case of the attack, and therefore should be given highest priority in terms both of defensive security capabilities and of monitoring capabilities that can rapidly detect and respond to attacks.

Similarly in Chapter 4, modeling of attacks against physical components provides insight into effective mechanisms in preventing or reducing the impact of such attacks. These insights can have a significant impact on the security architecture, such as in the recommendations regarding key management (in particular the storage of key material) in Section 4.2 and the discussion of using Physical Unclonable Functions for device authentication and key storage. The use of PUFs may be primarily a design decision, but may also become an architectural issue to the extent that it changes how and where a public key infrastructure is used for device identification.

Simulation can provide very different insights into the security architecture, particularly in terms of such issues as resiliency and performance. For example, simulation of specific attack scenarios such as those described in Chapters 4, 5 and 6 against a Smart Grid security architecture and design can reveal unexpected interactions in the case of an attack: tampering with measurement signals, for example, may not only mask attack manipulation of devices from operators, but also affect how the control systems for the affected devices respond, resulting in cascading impact across multiple components not directly manipulated by the attacker. The instrumentation of monitoring and analysis designed to improve the detection and response to attacks, as discussed in Chapter 9, can have negative impacts on the performance of the system; simulation of the monitoring and analysis can uncover these impacts and enable architectural and design choices that mitigate that impact. The simulation of microgrids in the SPIDER project discussed in Section 7.2.3 is an excellent example of the use of simulation to validate a Smart Grid architecture.

7.6 CONCLUSION

Our goal in this chapter has not been to establish a single, canonical security architecture for Smart Grid. Rather, we have shown how the most important of the resources available related to Smart Grid security architecture, particularly NISTIR 7628 and the resources related to the EU M/490 Mandate, can be effectively applied in developing a specific security architecture. In taking advantage of those resources, however, it is also vitally important to recognize their gaps and limitations, as well as to take into consideration the special requirements, constraints and opportunities of your particular Smart Grid environment. These considerations can have a dramatic effect in terms of the opportunity to take advantage of alternatives in your high-level architecture (such as in the use of microgrids), in your detailed architecture (such as in the instrumentation of extensive security data collection and analytics) and in your design (such as in the use of alternatives to PKI for device identification).

ACRONYMS

ASAP-SG	Advanced Security Acceleration Project for Smart Grid
CEN	European Committee for Standardization
CENELEC	European Committee for Electrotechnical Standardization
CSWG	Cyber Security Working Group
DER	Distribution Energy Resources
DHS	Department of Homeland Security
EMS	Energy Management System
ENISA	European Network and Information Security Agency
EPRI	Electric Power Research Institute
ETSI	European Telecommunications Standards Institute
FIPA	Foundation for Intelligent Physical Agents
IEC	International Electrotechnical Commission
IEEE	Institute of Electrical and Electronics Engineers
ISO	Independent System Operator / International Organization for Standardization
IT	Information Technology
MSRA	Microgrid Security Reference Architecture
NESCOR	National Electric Sector Cybersecurity Organization Resource
NISTIR	National Institute of Standards and Technology Interagency Report
PII	Personally Identifiable Information
SCADA	Supervisory Control and Data Acquisition
SDLC	Secure Development Life Cycle
SERA	Smart Energy Reference Architecture
SGAM	Smart Grid Architecture Model
SG-CG	Smart Grid Coordination Group
SGIP	Smart Grid Interoperability Panel
SGIS	Smart Grid Information Security
SGRA	Smart Grid Reference Architecture

REFERENCES

Basso, T., et al. (2011). IEEE Smart Grid Sires of Standards IEEE 2030 (Interoperability) and IEEE 1547. (Interconnection) Status (p. 6). http://www.nrel.gov/docs/fy12osti/53028.pdf

BSI. (2013). E-Energy Referenz-Architektur. https://www.bsi.bund.de/DE/Publikationen/publikationen_node.html

California ISO. (2010). Smart Grid Architecture and Roadmap. http://www.caiso.com/2860/2860b3d3db00.pdf

Chan et al. (2010). On Smart Grid Cybersecurity Standardization: Issues of Designing with the NISTIR 7628. http://ieeexplore.ieee.org/xpl/articleDetails.jsp?arnumber=6400439

Cockpit CI project. (2015). Cybersecurity on SCADA. http://www.cockpitci.eu/

DISCERN. (2013). Identification of Current System Architecture. http://www.discern.eu/datas/DISCERN_WP4_D4_1_Identification_of_present_system_architecture.pdf

DISCERN. (2015). The Project. http://www.discern.eu/project.html

Electric Power Research Institue (EPRI). (2013). Cybersecurity for DER Systems. http://smartgrid.epri.com/doc/der%20rpt%2007-30-13.pdf

Electric Power Research Institute (EPRI). (2015). National Electric Sector Cybersecurity Organization Resource (NESCOR). http://smartgrid.epri.com/NESCOR.aspx

European Union Agency for Network and Information Security (ENISA). (2012). ENISA Smart Grid Security Recommendations. https://www.enisa.europa.eu/activities/Resilience-and-CIIP/critical-infrastructure-and-services/smart-grids-and-smart-metering/ENISA-smart-grid-security-recommendations

Foundation for Intelligent Physical Agents (FIPA). (2015). Wlecome to FIPA. http://www.fipa.org

Greeley Tribune. (2014). Energy Pipeline: Cyber attacks oil and gas. http://www.greeleytribune.com/news/feature2/10355602-113/cyber-oil-attacks-security

IBM et al. (2011). Smart Grid Reference Architecture. http://www.pointview.com/data/files/1/636/2181.pdf

IEC. (2003). IEC TR 62357-1 Reference Architecture for Power System Exchange. http://webstore.iec.ch/p-preview/info_iec62357%7Bed1.0%7Den.pdf

Irlbeck, M. et al. (2013). Towards a Bottom-up Development of Reference Architectures for Smart Energy Systems. http://ieeexplore.ieee.org/xpl/abstractAuthors.jsp?arnumber=6596106

ISO. (2011). ISO/IEC/IEEE 42010:2011. http://www.iso.org/iso/catalogue_detail.htm?csnumber=50508

Kammerstetter, M., et al. (2014). Practical Risk Assessment Using a Cumulative Smart Grid Model. In *3rd International Conference on Smart Grids and Green IT Systems (SMART-GREENS)* (pp. 31–42).

Microsoft. (2012). Smart Energy Reference Architecture. https://www.google.com/?gws_rd=ssl#q=Smart+Energy+Reference+Architecture

National Electric Reliability Corporation (NERC). (2012). Mapping the National Institute of Standards and Technology Interagency Report 7628 Security Requirements to the North American Electric Reliability Corporation Critical Infrastructure Protection Standards. http://www.epri.com/abstracts/Pages/ProductAbstract.aspx?ProductId=000000000001025673

New York Times. (2012). In cyberattack on Saudi Firm, U.S. Sees Iran Firing Back. http://www.nytimes.com/2012/10/24/business/global/cyberattack-on-saudi-oil-firm-disquiets-us.html?pagewanted=all&_r=0

The Advanced Security Acceleration Project for Smart Grid (ASAP-SG). (2015). http://www.enernex.com/projects/advanced-security-acceleration-project-for-the-smart-grid-asap-sg/

Wikipedia. (2015). Stuxnet. http://en.wikipedia.org/wiki/Stuxnet

FURTHER READINGS

British Columbia Utilities Commission. (2013). ICBC 2013 Revenue Requirements: Exhibit C 10-5. http://www.bcuc.com/Documents/Proceedings/2013/DOC_38446_C10-5_BCP-SO_IR2.pdf

California ISO, p. 14.

CEN-CENELEC-ETSI Smart Grid Coordination Group. Smart Grid Information Security (SGIS). Document for the M/490 Mandate. Nov 2012 (first phase), Dec 2014 (second phase). http://www.cencenelec.eu/standards/Sectors/SustainableEnergy/SmartGrids/Pages/default.aspx

Center for Democracy and Technology. (2009). Comments of the Center for Democracy and Technology on Draft NISTIR 7628. https://www.cdt.org/files/pdfs/CDT%20Comment%20NISTIR%207628%20Draft%2012-02-09%20FINAL%20-%20updated.pdf

CEN-CENELEC-ETSI Smart Grid Coordination Group. (2012). Smart Grid Reference Architecture.

CISCO. (2013). GridBlocks™ Reference Architecture and Security Solution. http://www.cisco.com/web/strategy/docs/energy/overview_gba.pdf

Comments to phase 1 of SGIS. (N.D.).

Cork Institute of Technology. (2015). TEC @ Nimbus. http://nimbus.cit.ie/tec/

DHS Cyber Security Evaluation Tool (CSET). (N.D.).

ENISA. (2012). Appropriate Security Measures for Smart Grids. https://www.enisa.europa.eu/activities/Resilience-and-CIIP/critical-infrastructure-and-services/smart-grids-and-smart-metering/appropriate-security-measures-for-smart-grids

ENISA. "Smart Grid Threat Landscape and Good Practice Guide". 09-12-2013.

ENTSO-E. (2011). The Harmonized Electricity Market Role Model. https://www.entsoe.eu/fileadmin/user_upload/edi/library/role/role-model-v2011-01.pdf

EPRI, p. 6.

EU Conceptual Model defined as part of the M/490 framework. (2014).

European Conceptual Model for the Smart Grid, Figure 45 from "Smart Grid Reference Architecture", p. 89. (2014).

Figure from IEC 62357 Part 1: "Reference Architecture for Power System Information Exchange", p. 44 (Figure 4 "Current TC 7 Reference Architecture"). http://webstore.iec.ch/webstore/webstore.nsf/artnum/047066!opendocument

FINSENY FP7 project. (2013). Microgrid Functional Architecture Description. http://www.fi-ppp-finseny.eu/wp-content/uploads/2013/04/FINSENY_D3-3_Microgrid_Functional_Architecture_v1_0_March_2013.pdf

FINSENY Project. Overview of key security functional blocks (p. 163).

Glover, S., & Guttromson, R. (2012). Secure scalable microgrid project at Sandia National Laboratories. http://e2rg.com/microgrid-2012/Sandia_Guttromson_Glover.pdf

Gover and Guttromson, p. 25.

IEC 60870. (2004–2014). "Telecontrol equipment and systems protocols" series. http://www.iec.ch/smartgrid/standards/

IEC 61334. (2001–2011). "Distribution automation using distribution line carrier systems" series. http://www.iec.ch/smartgrid/standards/

IEC 61850. (1995–2014) "Communication networks and systems in substations" series. http://www.iec.ch/smartgrid/standards/

IEC 61968. (2003–2015). "Application integration at electric utilities" series. http://www.iec.ch/smartgrid/standards/

IEC 61970. (2003–2008). "Energy management system application programming interface" series. http://www.iec.ch/smartgrid/standards/

IEC 62235. (2003–2005). "Common Information Model" series. http://www.iec.ch/smartgrid/standards/

IEC 62351. (2007–2014). "Power systems management and associated data exchange" series. http://www.iec.ch/smartgrid/standards/

IEC 62357. (2002–2011). "TC57 Architecture" series, especially IEC 62357-1 "Reference Architecture for Power System Information Exchange". http://www.iec.ch/smartgrid/standards/

IEC TR 62351-10 "Security Architecture Guidelines". 2012. http://webstore.iec.ch/preview/info_iec62351-10%7Bed1.0%7Den.pdf

IEC Smart Grid Standardization Roadmap, p. 18.

IEEE 1547 series. "Standard for Interconnecting Distributed Resources with Electric Power Systems". 2014. http://grouper.ieee.org/groups/scc21/1547_series/1547_series_index.html

IEEE 2030 series. Draft Guide for Smart Grid Interoperability of Energy Technology and Information Technology Operation with the Electric Power System (EPS) and End-Use Applications and Loads". 2011. http://grouper.ieee.org/groups/scc21/2030/2030_index.html

The Smart Grid Interoperability Panel. (2010). Introduction to NISTIR 7628 Guidelines for Smart Grid Cyber Security. https://www.smartgrid.gov/sites/default/files/doc/files/nistir_7628%20.pdf

Introduction to NISTIR 7628, p. 5.

Introduction to NISTIR7628, p. 13.

National Institute of Standards and Technology (NIST). (2013). NISTIR 7823 Smart Metering Infrastructure Smart Meter Upgradeability Test Framework. http://csrc.nist.gov/publications/drafts/nistir-7823/draft_nistir-7823.pdf

National Institute of Standards and Technology (NIST). (2014). NIST Special Publication 1180R3: Framework and Roadmap for Smart Grid Interoperability Standards, Release 3.0. http://www.nist.gov/smartgrid/upload/NIST-SP-1108r3.pdf

NIST smart grid website. www.nist.gov/el/smartgrid/cybersg.cfm

NIST SP 1180R3, p. 3.

NISTIR 7628, p. 16.

Office of Energy Security and Energy Reliability. (2015). Cyber Security Capability Maturity Model (C2M2). http://energy.gov/oe/services/cybersecurity/cybersecurity-capability-maturity-model-c2m2-program/cybersecurity

Sandia MSRA, p. 7.

SGAM, p. 14.

Siemens. (2013). The Smart Grid Suite. http://w3.siemens.com/smartgrid/global/en/products-systems-solutions/smart-grid-4uite/pages/default.aspx

Smart Grid Coordination Group (SG-CG). (2012). Reference Architecture Working Group (SG-CG/RA).

The Smart Grid Architecture Model developed by CEN-CENELEC-ETSI, cf. Figure 8 on p. 30 of "Smart Grid Reference Architecture".

"Smart Grid Reference Architecture", p. 33.

"Smart Grid Reference Architecture", Recommendation 2 and 7 on p. 51.

"Smart Grid Reference Architecture", Recommendation 5 on p. 51.

"Smart Grid Reference Architecture", table on p. 55.

Smart Power Infrastructure Demonstration for Energy Reliability and Security (SPIDERS) during 2014. http://energy.gov/sites/prod/files/2014/01/f7/fupwg_winter2014_Waugaman.pdf

SMB Smart Grid Strategy Group (SG3). (2010). IEC Smart Grid Standardization Roadmap. http://www.iec.ch/smartgrid/downloads/sg3_roadmap.pdf. Also useful is the IEC online standards map available at http://smartgridstandardsmap.com/

SPARKS Smart Grids Week Stakeholder Workshop. (2014). Smart meter (gateway) authentitication and key management using PUFs (Physically Unclonable Functions). https://project-sparks.eu/wp-content/uploads/2014/04/sparks-smart-meter-gateway-puf.pdf

SPARKS. (2015). Microgrid and Smart Grid Resilience. https://project-sparks.eu/blog/ SPIDERS, p. 14.

Stamp, J. (2014). Experiences and Lessons Learned From SPIDERS Microgrids Rollout and Demonstrations. http://www.ieee-pes.org/presentations/gm2014/PESGM2014P-002516.pdf

Stamp, p. 26.

SWW Wunsiedel GmbH. (2015). https://project-sparks.eu/consortium/sww-wunsiedel-gmbh/

The Smart Grid Interoperability Panel. (2012). Guide for Assessing the High-level Security Requirements in NISTIR 7628 Guidelines for Smart Grid Cyber Security. http://www.energycollection.us/Energy-Security/Guide-Assessing-High-Level.pdf

The Smart Grid Interoperability Panel. (2014). NISTIR 7628 User's Guide. http://members.sgip.org/apps/group_public/download.php/3456/NISTIR%207628%20Users%20 Guide%20FINAL-2014-02-27c.pdf

The Smart Grid Mandate M/490 has been issued in March 2011 to be finalised by the end of 2012. The need for another iteration was decided upon in 2012, initiating a second phase of the Mandate, which has been finalized by the end of 2014. http://www.cencenelec.eu/standards/Sectors/SustainableEnergy/SmartGrids/Pages/default.aspx

U.S. Department of Homeland Security (DHS), National Cyber Security Division. (2011). Catalog of Control Systems Security: Recommendations for Standards Developers. https://ics-cert.us-cert.gov/sites/default/files/documents/CatalogofRecommendationsVer7.pdf

U.S. Executive Order (EO) 13636. (2013). Improving Critical Infrastructure Cybersecurity. http://www.gsa.gov/portal/content/176547

U.S: Office of the Press Secretary. (2013). Presidential Policy Directive – Critical Infrastructure Security and Resilience. http://www.whitehouse.gov/the-press-office/2013/02/12/presidential-policy-directive-critical-infrastructure-security-and-resil

www.oasis-open.org/committees/energyinterop

Secure Development Life Cycle

8

Zhendong Ma*, Friederich Kupzog*, and Paul Murdock[†]

*Austrian Institute of Technology, Vienna, Austria; [†]Landis+Gyr, Switzerland

8.1 INTRODUCTION

Since the Smart Grid is basically defined as an addition to the existing power grid infrastructure with an extended information and communication technology layer, there will be virtually no Smart Grid component that does not include software. In order to gain an overview of where security lifecycle assessments can be most complex, it makes sense to distinguish components according to their functionality, rather than their exact position in the overall technical system. Taking this perspective, the Smart Grid is an example of a classical automation system with a field layer (sensors and actuators), an automation layer (communication systems and controllers) and a management layer (centralised systems). One of the ongoing discussions in this context is how much computation actually will take place in a distributed form in substations, customer gateways, etc. and how much of it will be centrally located in different data centres of different stakeholders (distribution grid operator, aggregator, electric mobility provider, etc.). In different countries, there might be different answers to this question. The following discussion takes a Central European view.

A comprehensive overview of functional components in a Smart Grid can be found in (SGCG, 2012). In order to gain insight into the specific tasks accomplished by software-implemented functionality, only three prominent examples shall be discussed in the following, rather than covering all potential components in a Smart Grid. These examples are selected from the power distribution domain and focus on the components in which the introduction of Smart Grid concepts leads to significant changes and extensions of the components from the pre-Smart Grid era.

EXAMPLE 1: THE CUSTOMER GATEWAY

The question of how to interface the energy end users with the management and coordination systems in a Smart Grid is one of the central discussion points in the Smart Grid community, and it can be said that this question is not yet fully solved. Certain appliances, such as heating systems, photovoltaic inverters or charging stations for electric cars will have to be managed in the future and require IT interfaces for this purpose. These can be either be realised on a per-appliance basis, with individual solutions for heat pumps, inverters etc. Alternatively, a central Smart Grid interface for all appliances at a customer's site can be instantiated that handles all Smart Grid-related coordination. From a security perspective, the latter solution may be preferred because a single interface offers a smaller attack surface, which can be secured in a much simpler manner than a large variety of different interfaces with slightly different purposes.

The German Bundesamt für Sicherheit in der Informationstechnik (BSI) has coordinated a large exercise to define the security measures that are required for such a central interface (BSI, 2012). This interface is a software-heavy component, comparable to a firewall, managing security and privacy for the management of grid-relevant generators and loads on the customer's site. This can be a private household, but also a larger site of a small enterprise or even an industrial installation. The main tasks of this interface are billing, generation shedding in case of grid congestion and management of load and generation flexibility in combination with aggregators or virtual power plants.

EXAMPLE 2: SECONDARY SUBSTATION AUTOMATION

Another point in the system where changes are taking place is the secondary substation, which is the last transformer station down the line feeding the low voltage network in which most end customers are connected. It can be seen as a counterpart on the power grid side to the customer interface discussed above. While these secondary substations in the past were mostly mere passive installations with a transformer, fuses as well as hand-operated breakers and re-connectors, IT equipment is finding its way into these substations.

This is primarily motivated by the ongoing smart metering rollout. The majority of European smart meter installations use power line communication for the last mile from secondary substation to the customer, which means that a power line communication endpoint (called the data concentrator) has to be installed in most secondary substations. For collecting metering data from these concentrators, technologies like direct RF links, GPRS or fibre optics in urban areas are used. This results in a large number of secondary substations becoming "online".

Many grid operators have taken this opportunity to add substation automation equipment to secondary substations for monitoring and remote control purposes, since this comes with marginal additional costs when combined with the data concentrator installation. Functionalities realised here include meter data collection, monitoring and local grid control systems (e.g. for optimal tap position of the transformer), access control and others. This includes a number of communication stacks such as DLMS-COSEM for metering, IEC 60870-5-104 or even IEC 61850 for automation, Modbus for local sensors and actuators. See Chapter 5 for a description of these communication protocols. Again, these functions are mostly implemented in software.

EXAMPLE 3: DISTRIBUTION MANAGEMENT SYSTEMS

Distribution Management Systems (essentially SCADA systems for distribution power grids) are not new and existed before the advent of the Smart Grid concept. Distribution grids were originally designed for supplying loads rather than carrying away power generated from distributed generators. With the significant rise of generation capacities in power distribution systems, the functionality required from the management systems has changed. Today's Distribution Management Systems typically contain online details of the medium voltage level. A central functionality is to depict the system status on form of typically large visualisations (screens, projections) and to allow operators to interact with all the active components in the system (switches, on-load-tap-changer transformers, compensation circuits, etc.) The low voltage level is usually not included here, because there is no remote monitoring and control system in place and the level of detail required to depict these systems could not be managed by the low number of operators being in charge of system operation.

The rising number of generators in the low voltage network (mainly photovoltaics) has resulted in two different trends on how to handle this situation in distribution management: the first is a straight-forward extension of existing Distribution SCADA systems to parts of the low voltage systems, usually combined with an advanced alarming solution that allows to draw the attention of the operators to the low voltage only in case of special events. The second trend is to develop low voltage management systems out of the geographical information systems (GIS) that most grid operators maintain for their complete distribution systems. The state of manually operated components such as switches can be, e.g. reported by field operators using an on-line version of the software on a handheld device.

8.1.1 THE DEVELOPMENT OF SOFTWARE FOR THE SMART GRID

Current trends show that a large amount of resource is and will continue to be invested in software development for the Smart Grid. According to Groom Energy (Energy, 2013), there are over 300 companies that are active in the area of Smart Grid software solutions in the market, offering a broad range of products for energy mangers and operators to monitor and optimising energy consumptions based on business rules, intelligence, and user behaviour. The Smart Grid software vendor landscape includes companies for building management systems, utility bill payment, carbon management, energy management, demand response, industrial control, and sub-meters. The nature of the companies developing Smart Grid software include engineering companies, computer and enterprise software companies, network and communication equipment companies, and companies specialised in embed systems.

Depending on the organization, different system development lifecycle methodologies can be used, for example, waterfall, V-model, Rapid Application Development (RAD), prototype, and the spiral model. The waterfall model is probably the most common development lifecycle method. It is a linear and sequential process, including requirements, design, implementation, verification, and a maintenance phase. Equally popular is the V-model, which extends the waterfall model by associating each of the development phases with verification and validation. The RAD model is an alternative to the waterfall model, which aims at reducing effort for planning, and emphasizes development that results in using more prototypes instead of design specifications. The prototype model focuses on creating prototypes, which involve steps to identify basic requirements and to iteratively develop, review, and revise prototypes. The spiral model is a combination of the waterfall and prototype model, which uses a risk-driven process to guide multiple parties in large and complex development projects. It involves a cyclic approach for defining requirements and incrementally developing and refining prototypes.

It can be seen from this discussion that software is playing an increasingly important role in Smart Grid. Consequently, secure development practices, which are integrated into existing development lifecycles, are mandatory.

8.2 THE SECURE SYSTEM DEVELOPMENT LIFECYCLE

Building security into software and implementing it correctly is hard. In his book "Code Complete" (McConnell, 2004), Steve McConnell expects that the industry average is about 1 to 25 errors per 1000 lines of code for delivered software, and 10 to 20 defects per 1000 lines of code for Microsoft during in-house testing. Some of these errors will lead to serious security vulnerabilities. These estimates mainly focus on enterprise PC software. The situation with the software in embedded systems, "where computing is embedded into the hardware itself" (Schneier, Security Risks of Embedded Systems 2014), is by no means better, as "these embedded computers are riddled with vulnerabilities, and there's no good way to patch them". Since many of these embedded systems are used in safety and mission-critical parts of the Smart Grid, it is very challenging to ensure system security in the development lifecycle, and avoid safety incidents and failure caused by cyber-attack.

Insecure software, from operating systems, device drivers, firmware, to applications, will introduce vulnerabilities that make hacking Smart Grid systems easier. Securely developed software is one of the foundations of securing the Smart Grid. Building security into software right from the start is much less expensive than retrofitting security architecture and refactoring insecure code. All these factors call for methodologies and techniques for secure software development.

A viable way to achieve security in the software development lifecycle is to use a well-defined process and methodology. The Secure Development Lifecycle (SDL) refers to the concept and practice of integrating security considerations and activities into the system development lifecycle. The goal of SDL is to design and build secure and dependable systems that are free from vulnerabilities and resilient against security attacks. To ensure wide adoption, SDL is usually integrated into existing development lifecycles that are used by the development team in an organisation. In the context of the Smart Grid, SDL aims to produce secure applications and services and products (e.g. smart meters, communication networks, and information and control systems) that can withstand cyber-attacks throughout the system life time. The following describes the most common SDL methodologies and their applications to the Smart Grid. It provides an overview on secure development best practices.

8.2.1 NIST 800-64

NIST 800-64 defines a process for a secure system development lifecycle (R. Kissel October 2008). The system development lifecycle follows the waterfall model, which consists of five phases: initiation, development and acquisition, implementation and assessment, operations and maintenance, and disposal. Each phase is associated with a set of security activities. Control gates are defined within each phase to verify that security considerations are adequately addressed.

Figure 8.1 gives an overview of the security activities and control gates that are defined in NIST 800-64. Integrating security into the system development lifecycle means that security components addressing specific security risks are included in a project or system as an integral part. These security components include "milestones, deliverables, control gates, and interdependencies".

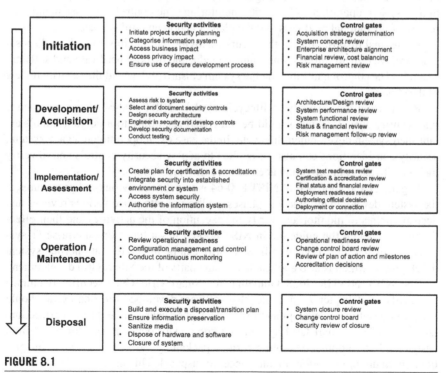

FIGURE 8.1

Overview of NIST 800-64 secure system development lifecycle.

In an initial phase, security considerations related to business risks are identified. The security activities are to identify information security and privacy requirements, and information assets and their way of handling, and the planning of risk management for the whole development. Control gates in the initial phase include reviews of the system and the corresponding security requirements, as well as the plan for acquisition.

In the development/acquisition phase, security activities include risk assessment, security requirements analysis, functional and security testing, security architecture design, and the preparation for system certification and accreditations. The corresponding control gates include reviews of system architecture, design, performance, functionality, and risk management.

In the implementation/assessment phase, the system is installed and evaluated in an operational environment. The main security activities include system and security integration into its environment, system testing, and certification and accreditation. The control gates focus on reviews on system test, certification and accreditation, deployment readiness.

In the operation/maintenance phase, the system is monitored during its operation. Enhancements and modifications to the system are conducted in order to achieve higher performance, efficiency and security. The security activities include operational readiness review, configuration and change management, and the definition of system operation and security monitoring. The control gates are mainly the review of operational readiness and the plan of action and milestones.

In the final disposal phase, the security activities are mainly to make a disposal plan, archive critical information, sanitise media and dispose hardware and software securely. The control gates include the system closure review and the security review of the closure.

Recognising the diversity in lifecycle models, NIST 800-64 also recommends that security considerations should be integrated according to an organisation's established system development lifecycle. In the case of an operational legacy system, security considerations can also be applied to deploy security controls and to verify their effectiveness in providing adequate security protections.

In general, the approach of NIST 800-64 is to define activities and procedures in the system development lifecycle phases, and to put into place various reviews and decision points to monitor and verify the execution of the activities and their effectiveness. Although the guideline in NIST 800-64 has a focus on enterprise IT systems, it provides an overview of how security can be integrated into normal system development, which is also applicable to many parts of the Smart Grid development.

The NIST NISTIR 7628 Guideline for Smart Grid Cybersecurity (Committee, 2014), see Chapter 7, advocates that software developed for Smart Grid should use a secure software development life cycle. Cybersecuriy should be integrated into all phases of the Smart Grid system and component development lifecycle, from design and development, manufacturing, packaging, assembly, system integration, distribution, operation, maintenance, to disposal. This approach should eliminate and minimise software and firmware vulnerabilities that are introduced in the

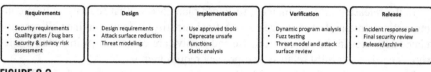

FIGURE 8.2

Microsoft security development lifecycle.

development lifecycle. The vulnerabilities to be considered are manifold and relate to code quality, authentication and authorization, environmental issues, logging and auditing, and the introduction of third-party software among others. As for third-party software, an organisation needs to conduct a due diligence review of a supplier prior to acquiring any system software, firmware, or services. The organization should also employ independent analysis and penetration testing against delivered Smart Grid components.

8.2.2 MICROSOFT SECURITY DEVELOPMENT LIFECYCLE

The Microsoft Security Development Lifecycle (MSDL) (Howard, 2006) is arguably the best known security development lifecycle specification. In essence, MSDL is a software development security assurance process that aims to integrate security and privacy practices into all phases of software development lifecycles. Originally introduced to improve the security of Microsoft software products, it has gained a wide recognition, eventually being adopted by software developers outside Microsoft.

Shown in Figure 8.2, the main part of MSDL includes five phases: requirements, design, implementation, verification, and release. In the requirements phase, security and privacy requirements analysis produces a preliminary requirement specification. Quality gates and bug bars are used to define the criteria for acceptable security and privacy levels to be met in the development lifecycle. Risk assessment is used to identify areas of focus of a software project that needs special attention and hence security and privacy measures. Such a risk-driven approach ensures cost-effectiveness in the planning and distribution of project efforts.

In the design phase, design requirements generate design specifications for security and privacy and security features. The activity of attack surface reduction minimises risks related to potential vulnerabilities and exploits. Threat modelling is used to analyse and identify security risks of software architecture in a structured way.

In the implementation phase, a development toolset with approved security properties, e.g. a toolset without known security flaws, is defined by the developers. Deprecating old and potentially unsafe APIs will minimise the risk of security holes in the software. Static analysis of source code is used as a part of the code review process for the implementation.

In the verification phase, dynamic program analysis and fuzz testing verifies the software in a run-time environment. The verification is completed with a re-review of the threat models and the attack surface to ensure that implementations follow the design specifications.

In the release phase, an incident response plan ensures that security will be continuously maintained after the release. A final security review examines all security related activities in the project. Release and archive are control steps in which a software is certified to fulfil security and privacy requirements.

Threat modelling (Swiderski, 2004) is proposed as a recurring procedure in MSDL in order to identify threats and their impact on a system design. In general, threat modelling specifies system in data flow diagrams and enumerates all possible threats, estimate their impacts on the system, and optionally list their possible mitigations.

Originally, threat modelling was demonstrated as an approach for developing web applications. It is divided into six steps: (1) identify assets, (2) create an architecture overview, (3) decompose the application, (4) identify the threats, (5) document the threats, and (6) rate the threats. The output of threat modelling is a document with a definition of the architecture of the application and a list of threats for the application scenario.

In the first step, information assets that need to be protected are identified. The second step is to find out the function, architecture, configuration, and the technologies of the system. Three tasks are suggested, which are to identify the function of the application by use cases, create a high-level architecture diagram, and identify the technologies and their implementation details. For complex systems, several diagrams for subsystems might be needed for describing the whole system.

In the third step, the main tasks are to identify trust boundaries, data flow, entry points, and privileged code. The findings are documented in a so-called "security profile". A trust boundary can be the boundary of an organization's IT infrastructure, in which all units follow and implement the same security policies. Trust boundaries can also be the boundaries in which all subsystems are mutually authenticated and authorized. Threat modelling proposes to analyse an application's data flow at a high level and decompose it iteratively down to subsystems or sub-subsystems. Entry points are the attack surface where attacks might happen. Analysing and looking for privileged code in a system can help to identify code that runs privileged operations or accesses restricted resources.

A Data flow diagram (DFD) is a modelling method to make this analysis easier and more intuitive. A DFD uses designated symbols to represent external entities, processes and multi-processes, data stores, data flows, and trust boundaries. A process is any software component involved in data processing. Figure 8.3 shows an example of a DFD that is used in threat modelling for a Web application. In the figure, a double circle represents a "multiple process", a collection of applications to process data or perform a certain action. A single circle represents a single process. A square represents an external entity, e.g. a user or a third-party Web application. The parallel lines represent a data store. In this example, the data stores are two databases and one image of the database. A dotted curve is used to annotate the trust boundary. An arrow represents data flow in the system.

In the fourth step, threats are identified and enumerated for each of the component in the DFD. The red lines in the example in Figure 8.3 indicate the identified potential threats in the Web application. The Microsoft STRIDE method is used

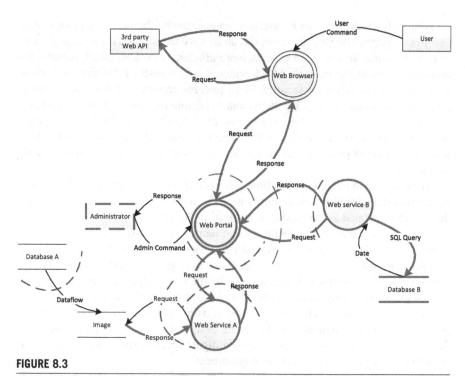

FIGURE 8.3

An example DFD for web application threat modelling.

to help software developers identify threats. The mnemonic STRIDE stands for Spoofing, Tampering, Repudiation, Information disclosure, Denial of service, and Elevation of privilege. This six-letter acronym is used as a guideword for identifying network, host-based, and application threats. Alternatively, if a categorized threat list is available, it can also be used for threat identification. With the help of the STRIDE method or threat taxonomy, the process for threat identification can leverage existing threat knowledge and make the process systematic and efficient with reduced error and uncertainty.

Other approaches such as attack tree or attack patterns are also suggested to facilitate threat identification. Attack trees (Schneier, Attack Trees, December 1999) are a structured way to identify potential threats to an information security asset. An attack tree is literally a tree structure, usually represented graphically, to identify possible attacks and establish their relationships. They consist of nodes and edges. Nodes in an attack tree represent an attacker's actions. Attack trees use a root node to specify an attacker's goal and systematically expand the tree with leaf nodes to enumerate possible attacks that contribute to reach the goal. The leaf nodes are grouped by logical AND and OR relations. Attack trees provide a structured way of security analysis and have the potential to identify hidden threats. For each attack goal, a new tree needs to be constructed.

Although attack trees can be useful to enumerate the threats related to a system design in a systematic way, the analysis can be very tedious and does not scale well to large systems. To make the process more efficient, re-usable attack patterns are proposed to assist the process. Attack patterns are an abstract description of common attacks to information security. Since patterns capture and describe recurring problems and solutions, attack patterns aim to capture the core of methods and procedures associated with exploiting a computer system (Moore, 2001). At the same time, since attack patterns do not include specific details about actual exploits, they avoid the danger of providing full details to a malicious user, who may directly apply the attacks.

The fifth step in the threat modelling process requires documentation of the list of the identified threats and their description. In the sixth step, risks associated with the threats are calculated as the product of probability and damage potential. The results are rated. The estimation of probability and damage (i.e. impact) can be expressed numerically, or be converted from quantitative measurements, e.g. use High, Medium, and Low and then convert them to 3, 2, and 1, respectively. Although the ratings can be subjective and imprecise, influenced by the knowledge and experience of the one conducted the analysis, they provide a viable way to rank and prioritize threats.

In general, threat modelling is designed as a "lightweight" software security approach for system designers to make secure design choices about technologies and functions, for developers to write code to mitigate security risks, and for testers to write better test cases to test security requirements.

Microsoft SDL is endorsed and followed by many individuals and organisations in the industry. It has been shown that strong encryption, authentication, and authorisation were often poorly implemented in smart meters (Pennell, 2010). Therefore, besides adding layered defences, the use of SDL will proactively support the implementation of security and privacy measures during a Smart Grid product's development, third-party auditing, and final software review.

The adoption of the Microsoft SDL for secure development of smart meters has been demonstrated in a case study (Microsoft, 2012). As it is shown, SDL deployment requires a dramatic change in the way of thinking, in which the engineers and developers learned to find ways to stop things from working instead of the conventional mind set of making things work. During the development lifecycle, security risks at all layers of the smart meter functionality are identified in brainstorming sessions. The identified threats are analysed and mitigations are deployed. The threats are then tested to provide evidence of mitigation. The subsystems of the meter, as well as their integration are considered to provide end-to-end security. During the development phase, layers of mitigations are added iteratively until the threats and vulnerabilities are reduced to the point of marginal concern.

8.2.3 OTHER INDUSTRY BEST PRACTICES

In addition to Microsoft, many companies in the IT industry also define their own security development lifecycle. Below are some examples.

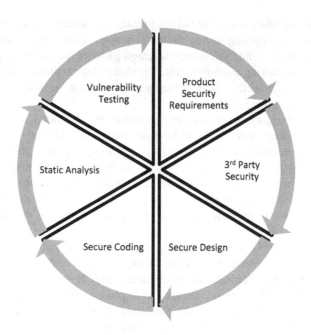

FIGURE 8.4

Cisco secure development lifecycle.

Cisco is an active contributor that provides Smart Grid solutions for networks, computing platform, operations, business applications and services for energy generation, distribution, storage, and consumption. Cisco claims to employ a secure development lifecycle in software development. For example, the Smart Grid router is developed using a secure development lifecycle, in which threat modelling is used for security threat identification and mitigation during the design phase. As a part of secure development, safe Java and C libraries as well as the Federal Information Processing Standards (FIPS) security library are used for secure coding. Static analysis tools are applied for code check. The system is validated through security and penetration testing (CISCO, 2012).

The Cisco Secure Development Lifecycle (Cisco Secure Development Lifecycle) is based on industrial best practices, adaptable to the agile and waterfall development methodologies. As shown in Figure 8.4, the Cisco SDL consists of six parts: product security requirements, third-party security, secure design, secure coding, secure analysis, and vulnerability testing.

The product security requirements include internal product security baseline requirements and market-specific security requirements, which might exceed the baseline This also includes the required certification of the product.

In third-party security, two integral tools are used to identify vulnerabilities in the third-party software. This includes a central repository that tracks the use of third-party software, and automatic alert of threats and vulnerabilities to product owners.

Secure design takes several measures to integrate security in the design phase, including training, applying secure design principles, considering common attack methods and corresponding safeguards, leveraging known secure design patterns and libraries, and considering all entry points. The secure design also adopts the STRIDE analysis and threat modelling for reducing security flaws in the design phase. Secure coding aims to minimize coding errors.

Under secure coding, developers are required to attend training, use safe libraries, follow secure coding guidelines, and use code review and static analysis for security checks. In secure analysis, the development team uses security checkers on their code. In the final vulnerability testing step, test cases are generated for testing vulnerabilities in the protocols, ports, and services. In addition, a product is tested against a variety of security tools from multiple sources. The loose order of the Cisco SDL makes it applicable to the sequential waterfall model, as well as the agile development model.

SAP offers Smart Grid data management software which performs data analytics on data from smart meters, SCADA and other systems in real time. It is developed based on SAP HANA relational database management system. The SAP HANA development is required to integrate security in all phases of the development lifecycle. Various security considerations such as authentication, data access, SQL script etc. are provided either as utility tools or development guide.

SAP applies a security development lifecycle in its software product (SAP, 2013). The approach follows the requirement, design, implantation, testing paradigm. The security and privacy requirements are updated based on public software vulnerabilities databases such as Common Weakness Enumeration (CWE), Common Vulnerabilities and Exposures (CVE), SANS Institute, and Open Web Application Security Project (OWASP). Quality gates are set in the development lifecycle to assess and verify functionality and security of a product. In the testing phase, code review, architecture audit, penetration testing, and static analysis are employed. Furthermore, threat modelling, security assessment, security consulting for development teams, and training are included in the development lifecycle.

Juniper is targeting the Smart Grid market with wireline and wireless LAN and WAN networks, cloud-based data centres, and security solutions. The secure development lifecycle for network products at Juniper Networks (Networks, n.d.) are defined in six practices: secure coding training, security consideration in design, threat modelling, penetration testing, release security review, and incident response plan, as illustrated in Figure 8.5.

Secure coding training is on the top of all activities. The training covers secure coding, secure design, privacy, and secure testing. Security consideration in design requires developers to evaluate vulnerabilities, assess the possibility of threats, and mitigate vulnerability in the design phase.

In threat modelling, a product is evaluated to identify potential threats. The threats are enumerated using CVE identifiers. Based on the result of the threat model, penetration testing uses manual and automated tests to exploit the vulnerabilities in a product. Release Security Review examines a product's security posture before the

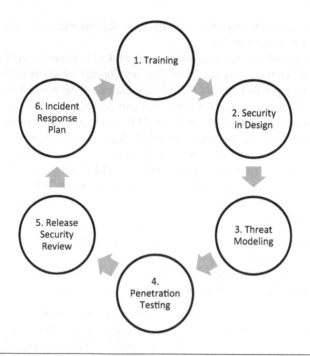

FIGURE 8.5

Juniper networks secure development lifecycle.

release, based on the information of functional specification, threat modelling, and a penetration test.

The Juniper Networks SDL includes an incident response plan that specifies how to respond to new product vulnerabilities and communicate the corresponding threats and mitigations to customers after the release. These threats and vulnerabilities are fed back to Release Security Review.

A wide range of Smart Grid applications and automation systems can be run in virtualised environments for scalability, flexibility, and cost-efficiency. Therefore secure development is equally important for software in virtualised environments. A very similar approach is adopted in VMware's secure development lifecycle, which includes security training in the planning phase, security assessment, threat modelling, static and dynamic analysis, penetration testing in development (including design, implementation, and validation), and security teams monitoring production.

8.3 SECURITY ASSURANCE STANDARDS

Closely related to secure development lifecycles are security assurance standards. Perhaps the most widely-known standard is ISO/IEC 15408 (15408 2009), commonly known as Common Criteria (CC), which specifies the process of specification, implementation, and evaluation of security-critical, high-assurance systems in a rigorous and standardized manner.

In the context of secure system development, CC is mainly used for the evaluation of information security products. The key concept of CC is quite simple. By testing a security product against the security claims of the product, a user can determine with high confidence if the product can actually meet its claims. In a CC evaluation process, a Target Of Evaluation (TOE) is defined as the product or system under evaluation. A user or a user community identifies common security requirements on a class of devices or systems, such as access control devices and systems or key management systems in a Protection Profile (PP) document. A Security Target (ST) document contains the IT security requirements of the TOE and specifies the functional and assurance measures offered by the TOE to meet these requirements. The ST also includes

- Security Functional Requirements (SFRs) that specify the security functionality provided by the TOE,
- Security Assurance Requirements (SARs) that describe the measures taken to assure compliance with the claimed security functionality.

An ST may contain references to the requirements defined in one or more PPs. In general, an ST consists of descriptions of: (1) TOE and its operational environment, (2) the TOE's security objectives, (3) SFRs and SARs, (4) security functions and assurance measures that meet the requirements, (5) claims on the conformance of one or more PPs, and (6) rationale and evidence supporting the security claims. The effort of the evaluation process is ranked numerically from one to seven in Evaluation Assurance Levels (EAL). In this sense, CC provides not only a benchmark for security "due diligence" checking, but also assurance on the design, development, deployment, and lifecycle handling of security-critical systems.

The seven assurance level of EAL are defined as:

- EAL1: functionally tested
- EAL2: structurally tested
- EAL3: Methodically tested and checked
- EAL4: Methodically designed, tested and reviewed
- EAL5: Semi-formally designed and tested
- EAL6: Semi-formally verified design and tested
- EAL7: Formally verified design and tested

According to CC, EAL4 is the highest level at which it is likely to be economically feasible to retrofit to an existing product line. This means that additional cost and effort for security engineering will be needed for anything above EAL4. Such effort usually depends on a high degree of modelling and formal verification, which are time-consuming, difficult, and requires specialized skills (Irvine & Rao, 2011). Karger et al. (Karger, 2011) shows that when building a secure smart-card operating system with EAL5+, the cost for formal verification, testing, and documentation as mandated in CC exceeds the cost for developing the system itself. However, the authors also note that with the availability of security-related tools for development, testing, and analysis, the cost can be reduced.

The ISO/IEC 15408 standard is divided into three parts. Part 1 presents the general model for the evaluation of IT security, Part 2 describes a set of security components for common functional security requirements, and Part 3 defines assurance categories and levels and matches them to the EALs.

CC can significantly increase the security of a system, as well as the confidence of the end-user in the system, by emphasizing good and comprehensive documentation during the system design and development phase. By doing so, the system development team has security as its main objective from the very beginning. It also raises awareness of the security problems throughout the system's design and development phases. Also, it forces the system development team to write and maintain documentations that include system specification, system internals, system tests, and development tools. Such an intensive practice can lead to the project team identifying ambiguities early on and solve the identified problems accordingly.

CC can be applied to the secure development of Smart Grid components. For example, the German Federal Office for Information Security (Bundersamt für Sicherheit in der Informationstechnik, BSI) has released a protection profile for smart meters (BSI, March 2014). The TOE is the Gateway in a Smart Metering System, defined as "an electronic unit comprising hardware and software/firmware used for collection, storage and provision of meter data from one or more meters of one of multiple commodities." The EAL of the PP is set at EAL4, which means the Gateway must be methodically designed, tested and reviewed. It is implementation-independent, meaning that different manufacturers or system developers can use it for the security assurance of their products. The SFRs include security requirements for security audit, communication, cryptographic support, user data protection, identification and authentication, security management, privacy, protection of the TOE security functionality (TSF), and trusted path/channels. The SARs contains a list of applicable assurance components, which include assurance for development, guidance documents, life-cycle support, security target evaluation, tests, and vulnerability assessment. The assurance components are specified in CC Part 3: Security assurance components.

8.4 SAFETY-CRITICAL SYSTEM DEVELOPMENT AND BEST PRACTICES

Many of the devices and systems at the automation and field layer, such as sensors and actuators, control systems that are safety-critical – i.e. their failure could result in injury or loss of human life. Stringent safety and assurance requirements mean that parts of the software and firmware that is developed for the Smart Grid needs to comply with certain safety standards. In the following, several safety-critical system development methodologies and standards are described.

8.4.1 THE DO-178B DOCUMENT

The DO-178B document, entitled "Software Considerations in Airborne Systems and Equipment Certification", is a software assurance and certification standard for safety critical airborne software systems (RTCA, 1992). It provides guidance for developing and determining whether an embedded software system complies with airworthiness requirements for commercial aircrafts.

The main concept of DO-178B is to achieve safety assurance in software development through clearly defined software life cycle processes with associated objectives, activities, and artefacts. DO-178B describes abstract processes, which are aligned with the software development lifecycle and allows for a certain level of flexibility, depending on the actual project. The processes include development and test processes such as planning, requirements, design, coding, integration, and testing, as well as integral processes such as verification, configuration management, quality assurance, and certification liaison. Objectives and activities are an integral part of these processes. The artefacts, such as source code and documentation that are produced in the context of the process, are used for providing evidence for certification.

DO-178B defines five types of Software Level or Design Assurance Level (DAL):

The DAL of a software component is mandatorily determined by its safety criticality from a safety assessment process and hazard analysis. The number of objectives for each DAL ranges from 0 for level E to 66 for level A. In other words, a software vendor for an avionics system must meet and be certified at a certain DAL that is required by the customer.

Implementing and certifying a software product against DO-178B can be quite complex and expensive. However, it is a mature industrial standard, providing very high levels of safety assurance for software development (see Table 8.1). The basics of DO-178B can be applied to other safety-critical software system beyond the avionics domain. Although at the time of writing, there is no direct application of DO-178B to Smart Grid applications. However, it is still beneficiary if critical software in the Smart Grid can adopt some of the features of DO-178B for both safety and security assurance. There is already a proposal (Overman, 2011) to apply the same principle from the aviation industry for the definition of a high assurance Smart Grid architecture that determines the trust model of individual devices within the complex Smart Grid system. The motivation for this is that the aviation industry has addressed

Table 8.1 DO-178B Design Assurance Level (RTCA, 1992)

DAL	Failure Condition	Failure Explanation	No. of Objectives
Level A	Catastrophic	Failure may cause a crash	66
Level B	Hazardous	Failure is safety-significant	65
Level C	Major	Failure is safety-related	57
Level D	Minor	Failure is noticeable	28
Level E	No Effect	Failure has no impact on safety	0

the issue of reliability and security of integrating different components from different vendors into a single system for a long time. In the aviation industry, DO-178B and other standards can be used to categorise control subsystems by their criticalities through to the whole complex system. Therefore, in the Smart Grid domain, the same categorisation can be applied for components of Smart Grid, like meters and actuators. In addition, the fail-safe concept from aviation can also be applied to Smart Grid, in which systems should be designed with expectation that compromised adjacent systems can cause system failures, user error, or cyber-attacks.

8.4.2 THE IEC 61508 STANDARD

The IEC 61508 standard is a basic functional safety standard. It covers the entire safety lifecycle, as well as the software development lifecycle. As defined in IEC 61508, a safety lifecycle includes three main phases: analysis, realization, and operation. In the analysis phase, hazards and risks, and existing layers of protection are identified. Risks are evaluated to decide whether they are tolerable according to the industrial standard. A Safety Instrumented System (SIS) with an assigned Safety Integrity Level (SIL) is used on risk exceeding the tolerable level. The activities are documented in the Safety Requirement Specification (SRS). In the realization phase, a conceptual design of the SIS is made based on the SRS. The next step is to evaluate the conceptual design and to confirm it meets the SRS. The system is then installed and executed. Verification is followed to confirm the SIS is functional at the specified SIL, and reaches a tolerable level of risks. The operation phase starts with validation planning, followed by a start-up review, and operation and maintenance planning. After that, the SIS is in operation. Maintenance and periodic testing are carried out, accompanied by necessary change management, until the SIS is decommissioned. IEC 61508 is been adapted in many domains, such as automotive, railway, manufacturing process, and nuclear power plants. Certification of IEC 61508 includes the audit of the system development process.

8.4.3 THE PHASE PRINCIPLES

In their book, Kleidermacher and Kleidermacher (Kleidermacher, 2012) propose an integrated approach, called PHASE – Principles of High Assurance Software Engineering, as a methodology for developing secure embedded system software and systems. The five principles highlighted in PHASE include:

1. Minimal implementation
2. Component architecture
3. Least privilege
4. Secure development process
5. Independent expert validation

Minimal implementation requires a developer to write the absolutely minimal amount of code possible to implement a function, instead of complex spaghetti code that is prone to vulnerabilities and flaws. Meanwhile, *component architecture* means to compose large software systems from small components that are easier to maintain, test, and limit the impact in case of failure. Safety and security functionalities should be separated into different components to protect critical operations from non-critical operations. *Least privilege* mandates that components are only given access to the resources that are absolutely necessary. The resources can be CPU time, I/O devices, and memory, etc. *Secure development process* means that safety and security critical components must meet high assurance requirements. Change management must be put in place to maintain secure software over the product life time. Code reviews and other controls need to be included in the development process. It requires that ancillary items during the production, e.g. the tool chain that builds the software, are also covered by security controls. Secure coding and comprehensive testing and verification are a part of the secure development process. Finally, high security assurance can only be achieved by independent expert review.

Although the PHASE principles do not define a secure development lifecycle, they can be flexibly integrated into software development for security in Smart Grid.

8.5 SECURE DEVELOPMENT ACTIVITIES

The methodologies that we have thus far described define the overarching principles, concepts, and processes for secure software development. Secure development activities and techniques realise actual actions in the lifecycle.

8.5.1 SECURE PROGRAMMING

Adhering to certain programming standards can significantly improve code quality in terms of security vulnerabilities and flaws. This is especially important when dealing with "troublesome" programming language, such as the C programming language, which are not strongly typed and require careful memory management.

8.5.1.1 The MISRA C Standard

C is the *de facto* programming language for embedded systems, due to its efficient run-time performance. C is a very flexible language, which also makes it more prone to introduce vulnerabilities. For example, a programmer can misunderstand the language or make typing mistakes, which leads to valid but insecure code. The MISRA C (MISRA) is a UK standard, originated by the Motor Industry Software Reliability Association, for coding C for safety-critical embedded systems.

The MISRA C standard achieves the development of reliable C code though the definition of a set of best practices guidelines in the form of coding rules. The latest MISRA C standard from 2012 defines 143 rules and 16 directives. A rule is a short text description of coding requirements. As an example, a rule can specify to not to mix increment (++) and decrement (--) operators in an expression, because doing so can decrease the readability of the code and introduce potential undefined behaviour.

A directive is a rule that is subject to interpretation. Each rule or directive is classified as Mandatory, Required, or Advisory. Each rule is also classified as either a Single translation unit rule or a System rule.

MISRA C further proposes to incorporate other development best practices in addition to following the coding rules, including documented development process, quality system, project management, configuration management, hazard analysis, requirements, design, coding, verification, and validation. Specifically, a safety hazard analysis is needed in order to determine the exact development process.

The standard is supported by many commercial static analysis tools, which are created to check C source code and warn the programmer of the presence of problematic code. Dynamic analysis tools can also be used to check and minimize runtime failures.

MISRA C has been accepted for developing safety-critical embedded systems in many domains, such as telecom and railway. Although developers of software for Smart Grid are not officially mandated to adhere to security and safety standards, it is considered prudent to build software that is eligible for certification. In this case, MISRA C, with standard constructs and practices, will help developers to write safe code (Pitchford, 2013). As of 2014, the market has seen Smart Grid components developed under the MISRA C standard, e.g. file system for smart meters.

8.5.1.2 The ISO/IEC 25010 Standard Series

Sometimes security can be considered as a subset of a much broader software quality issue. The ISO/IEC 25000 series provides a set of standards for system and software quality requirements and evaluation. Among them, ISO/IEC 25010:2011 defines system and software quality models, which provide detailed, consistent terminology for specifying, measuring and evaluating system and software product quality. It defines a quality in use model with five characteristics and a product quality model with eight characteristics. Security is one of the main quality characteristics, with sub-characteristics of confidentiality, integrity, non-repudiation, and accountability. In this way, security considerations can be treated as a part of quality assurance, according to many ISO/IEC quality standards.

8.5.2 SECURE CODE REVIEW

A secure code review is an examination of the source code, either manually and potentially automatically – the aim is to identify and fix security issues in the code before it is subjected to testing. Howard (M. Howard, 2006) defines secure code review as a three step process: identify the secure code review objectives, perform a preliminary scan and prioritize code review effort, and finally review the code.

However, in order to find security flaws, one must first know what to look for. A deep understanding of the core security issues and vulnerabilities is required. According to (J.D. Meier), security issues can be a subset of the following items: SQL injection, cross-site scripting, input/data validation, authentication, authorization, sensitive data, code access security, exception management, data access, cryptography, unsafe and unmanaged code use, configuration, threading, and undocumented public interfaces.

A preliminary scan can help to identify security issues which can then be investigated in full details. The scan can be a combination of tool-based automatic scan or a manual scan. Tools such that perform a static code analysis can be used to identify security issues. The goal is to prioritise the effort to focus more on the code with a higher attack surface or bug density. Howard (M. Howard, 2006) suggests the following heuristics: old code, code run by default, code run in elevated context, anonymously accessible code, code listening on a globally accessible network interface, code written in C/C++/assembly language, code with a history of vulnerabilities, code that handles sensitive data, complex code, code that changes frequently.

Furthermore, Howard states that the actual work of code review should include three steps (M. Howard, 2006): rerun all available code-analysis tools, look for common vulnerability patterns, and look deep into risky code. The re-run of all source-code analysis tools can indicate potential security problems in the code. The warnings and errors from the tools help to locate area of code that needs more in-depth review. When looking for common vulnerability patterns, the reviewer searches a trace for a list of known vulnerabilities, such as integer arithmetic issues, buffer overruns, cryptographic issues, SQL injection, and cross-site scripting. Several techniques can be used to make the process more effective. These techniques include control flow analysis and dataflow analysis (J.D. Meier). In a control flow analysis, functions and branch conditions are examined, in order to step though logical conditions and block executions in the code. A dataflow analysis traces data from input to output. Each input will be evaluated to determine whether it is trustworthy. Control and dataflow analysis also provide contextual information for examining relevant vulnerabilities. A slow but necessary process is to carefully review highly risky code by a small development team. Risky code can be on the hotspot list, such as code that is responsible for data access, input data validation, authentication, authorization, and sensitive data, as well as the ones listed in the common vulnerabilities.

Best practices for secure code review (MITRE) include the following: understand the developer's approach, use multiple techniques, do not assess level of risk, focus on the big picture, follow up on review points, and stick to the intent of the review.

8.5.3 STATIC CODE ANALYSIS

Code review can be assisted by static code analysis. Static code analysis uses automated tools to analyse source code for security flaws. A tool scans through a file for syntactic matches based on "rules" that might indicate possible security vulnerabilities (Chess, 2004). Static code analysis tools are often integrated into a complier frontend to reduce the complexity of the tool chain. A static code analyser must understand the semantics of a program. Developers occasionally make mistakes. Static code analysis is able to detect common security bugs, such as NULL pointer dereferences, buffer overflows, writing to read-only memory, reads of uninitialized objects, resource leads, use of de-allocated memory, and out-of-scope memory usage, for example (Kleidermacher, 2012). However, static code analysis tools have their limitations, as shown in the incident of Heartbleed Bug. In this case, a vulnerability was introduced in the OpenSSL cryptographic software library in the programming phase. In this case, static code analysis tools failed to detect the vulnerability due to the fact that most software programs are not written to allow static analysis (Wheeler).

8.5.4 DYNAMIC CODE ANALYSIS

In contrast to static code analysis, dynamic code analysis examines a program by executing it in a real or virtual environment. Similar to static analysis tools, dynamic code analysis tools can be included into compilers, enabled at different stages of development, testing, and system integration. Dynamic analysis uses instrumentation to examine certain aspects of a program's run-time state. It also establishes program dependencies by relating inputs and outputs to program behaviour (Ball, 1999). Dynamic code analysis is usually combined with static code analysis to maximise the probability of finding security bugs.

8.5.5 CODE COVERAGE ANALYSIS

Since testing is an important element to assure software security and reliability, the quality of the testing itself needs a certain level of assurance. Code coverage analysis is a process to measure the quality of the tests. Specifically, code coverage analysis focuses on the identification of areas of code that are not covered by test cases, and to increase the coverage by additional test cases (Cornett). The measurement of the code coverage can be used as an indirect metric for code quality.

There are many code coverage metrics. For example, in DO-178B, code coverage is defined corresponding to each design assurance level. For level E and D, no coverage is required. Level C requires statement coverage, meaning that all statements (i.e. control flow statements such as *if*, *for*, and *switch*, as well as code contained in these statements on true or false condition) have to be executed at least once by test cases. Level B requires decision coverage, meaning that all decision points (i.e. the Boolean expressions in control structure) in the code must be executed with all possible outcomes. Finally, level A requires modified condition/decision coverage (MC/DC). MC/DC is an enhancement of decision coverage and condition coverage, in which all entry and exit points in a program must be invoked, all decision are executed with every possible outcomes, all conditions in a decision are considered with every possible outcomes, and a condition in a decision is shown to independently affect the outcome of the decision.

There are more metrics for code coverage analysis. A decision on the use of code coverage techniques will affect the scale and complexity of the test cases. As a structured testing technique, code coverage analysis is effective to identify security flaws in the testing phase and increase assurance level.

8.5.6 PENETRATION TESTING

Penetration testing, or "pentesting", is a *clearly defined, full-scale test of the security controls of a system or network in order to identify security risks and vulnerabilities* (Walker, 2011). The purpose of a pentest is to find security holes before the real attackers do. There are three types of tests: black box, white box, and grey box. The black box tests simulate attackers from outside, who do not have any information about the targeted system. In white box tests, the penetration testers assume the role of an insider that has full knowledge of the targeted system. Grey box test simulates an inside attacker, but with only partial knowledge of the targeted system.

Despite the difference that a pentest is "authorised" by the system owner, the steps involved in pentests and actual unauthorised attacks are quite similar. A test usually starts with a reconnaissance phase whose aim is to learn as much as possible about the the targeted system and to gather evidence. In networked-based pentests, the steps involve identifying publically accessible services, and determining operating system versions, patch levels, and modules that have been enabled. Additionally, information to a network, such as server names or IP addresses will be identified (Northcutt, 2006). Based on the findings, the next step is to exploit any identified vulnerabilities.

A number of open source and commercial tools are available for pentesting, such as reconnaissance tools like Nmap (Nmap) for performing network port scans, OpenVAS (OpenVAS) for vulnerability scanning, and exploitation tools like the Metasploit framework (Metasploit) and Kali Linux (Kali Linux), as an "all-in-one" Linux distribution. The result of the pentest is then reported to the development team. The result will not only provide evidence on the hypothetical security risks, but also identify unknown security issues in the development lifecycle.

However, pentesting has limitations when identifying all security issues. In a black box test, since the pen tester does not have full knowledge of the system, it might not be possible to detect a seemingly obvious vulnerability if insider information was available to the attacker. A pentest is not likely to identify all vulnerabilities, due to the fact that it is difficult to set up a system and its services for all possible usage environments and scenarios for pentest. Since a pentest is as good as the person conducting it, the results can vary, depending on the pen tester's experiences and skills.

Despite these limitations, pentesting is still a valuable approach for identifying security issues in order to address them in the testing phase of the development lifecycle. The National Electric Sector Cybersecurity Organization Resource (NESCOR) created guidance on performing pentests on the Smart Grid (NESCOR). The guidance divides the Smart Grid into six product domains: Advanced Metering Infrastructure (AMI), Demand Response (DR) systems, Distributed Energy Resources (DER) systems, Distribution Grid Management (DGM), Electric Transportation (ET) systems, and Wide Area Monitoring, Protection, and Control (WAMPAC) systems. The focuses of each of the product domains include:

- AMI: cryptographic keys used in communications, device passwords, firmware on smart meter, relay, and aggregator
- RD: cryptographic keys used in communications, firmware on field devices
- DER: cryptographic keys and firmware used in networked devices
- ET: cryptographic keys used in communications, firmware on field devices
- WAMPAC: cryptographic keys used in communications, configuration files, protocol passwords, firmware on field devices

Each of the product domains consists of various software and hardware components, and various protocols, requiring different skillsets. Hence the pentests are defined in four tasks: embedded device penetration tasks, network communications penetration tasks, server operating system penetration tasks, and sever application penetration tasks. A salient approach is to define the scope of the pentest of the Smart Grid based on the criticality of the systems.

8.6 CONCLUSION

Secure software is essential for the Smart Grid security. It not only underpins any security architecture and technology designed and deployed in Smart Grid, but also contributes to system reliability and resilience against cyber-attacks.

This chapter describes methodologies, standards, and techniques for building secure software for the Smart Grid. It begins by looking at the Smart Grid from a software point of view. Due to the importance of software in many devices, components, and systems in the Smart Grid, secure software development is a challenging and mandatory issue.

Secure system development lifecycles, such as NIST 800-64 and Microsoft Secure Development Lifecycle (SDL) are proven methodologies for secure IT system development. During all phases of the development lifecycle, security considerations, activities, and evaluation and decision points are integrated into software development. Although there are variations as how and what aspects of security are integrated, security development lifecycle as a general concept and principle is proven to be viable to improve software security.

As many IT system vendors are also active players in the Smart Grid market, the market has seen Smart Grid components developed using secure development lifecycle approaches. As a security assurance standard, Common Criteria represents a rigorous approach to developing security-critical system. In spite of the effort to comply and certify under Common Criteria, this approach has been used for components of Smart Grid, such as the smart metering gateway.

The Smart Grid consists of safety-critical systems. The security of such systems means that software development standards and best practices for safety-critical systems, especially embedded systems are also relevant in the context of Smart Grid. DO-178B is a software assurance standard for aviation industry. Smart Grid development can benefit from applying some of the concepts from DO-178B. In the same way, the functional safety standard IEC 61508 and the PHASE principles, created for dependable software in embedded systems, are readily applicable to many components in the Smart Grid.

This chapter also describes activities and techniques for secure software development. Secure coding standards such as MISRA C and ISO/IEC 25010 series are two examples that help to improve code quality and to minimise security bugs during implementation. Security coding is best complemented by secure code review, in which tools for static and dynamic code analysis can be used to help developers to detect insecure code. Code coverage analysis and penetration testing are two proven approaches in security testing that can be applied to Smart Grid subsystems. Code coverage analysis measures the quality of the test, and z penetration test is an effective method to find security problems before an actual attacker does.

In general, many proven methods and techniques exist for implementing a secure development lifecycle in the Smart Grid. However, in reality, the main force in software development is the team of developers, instead of security professionals. Therefore, the mind-set, as well as the security culture of the development team, is equally important as the expertise and capability of the security team participated in the development lifecycle. In this sense, security training should be included in any secure development lifecycle as one of the core principles.

In the software production environment, secure development often has physical implications, in terms of buildings, access controls, hardware and software development environment and networks. Depending on standards and contracts, auditors may require that secure development processes be executed within secure areas on secure networks and machines.

Just as there is no silver bullet to software security, no secure development lifecycles can guarantee to produce 100% secure software. Nevertheless, by integrating security considerations and complementary activities such as threat modelling, code analysis, and penetration testing, as well as sticking to one or more software development standards, many security issues and human errors can be avoided or detected, and fixed in the development lifecycle. In the long run, the additional investment, in terms of effort and financial cost, is very likely to pay-off because fixing security bugs or retrofitting security into existing systems in the Smart Grid will be more expensive, if it is at all possible.

ACRONYMS

BSI	Bundesamt für Sicherheit in der Informationstechnik
SCADA	Supervisory Control and Data Acquisition
GIS	Geographical Information Systems
RF	Radio Frequency
GPRS	General Packet Radio Service
IEC	International Electrotechnical Commission
RAD	Rapid Application Development

SDL	Secure Development Lifecycle
NIST	National Institute of Standards and Technology
MSDL	Microsoft Security Development Lifecycle
DFD	Data Flow Diagram
FIPS	Federal Information Processing standards
CWE	Common Weakness Enumeration
CVE	Common Vulnerabilities and Exposures
OWASP	Open Web Application Security Project
CC	Common Criteria
TOE	Target Of Evaluation
PP	Protection Profile
ST	Security Target
SFR	Security Functional Requirements
SAR	Security Assurance Requirements
EAL	Evaluation Assurance Levels
TSF	TOE security functionality
DAL	Design Assurance Level
SIS	Safety Instrumented System
SIL	Safety Integrity Level
SRS	Safety Requirement Specification
PHASE	Principles of High Assurance Software Engineering
MISRA	Motor Industry Software Reliability Association
MC/DC	Modified Condition/Decision Coverage
NESCOR	National Electric Sector Cybersecurity Organization Resource
AMI	Advanced Metering Infrastructure
DR	Demand Response
DER	Distributed Energy Resources
DGM	Distribution Grid Management
ET	Electric Transportation
WAMPAC	Wired Area Monitoring, Protection, And Control

REFERENCES

15408, ISO/IEC. (2009). Information technology—Security techniques—Evaluation criteria for IT security.

BSI, German Federal Office for Information Security (2012). Protection Profile for the Gateway of a Smart Metering System.

Ball, T. (1999). The concept of dynamic analysis. *Software Engineering—ESEC/FSE'99*. Berlin/Heidelberg: Springer (pp. 216–234).

BSI (2014). Protection Profile for the Gateway of a Smart Metering System v 1.3.

Chess, B., & McGraw, G. (2004). Static analysis for security, *Security & Privacy, IEEE*, 2(6), 76–79.

CISCO (2012). Cisco Connected Grid Security for Field Area Network. White Paper.

Cisco Secure Development Lifecycle. (n.d.). http://www.cisco.com/web/about/security/cspo/csdl/index.html.

Committee (2014). The Smart Grid Interoperability Panel—Smart Grid Cybersecurity. *Guidelines for Smart Grid Cybersecurity*. NISTIR 7628 Revision 1.

Cornett, S. (n.d.). *Code Coverage Analysis*. http://www.bullseye.com/coverage.html.

Groom Energy. (2013). *Enterprise Smart Grid*. http://www.groomenergy.com/enterprise_ smart_grid_research.html.

Howard, M. (2006). A process for performing security code reviews. *IEEE Security & Privacy*, *4*(4), 74–79.

Irvine, C., Rao, J. R. (2011). Guest Editors' Introduction: Engineering Secure Systems. *Security & Privacy, IEEE*, *9*(1), 18–21.

Meier, J. D., Mackman, A., Wastell, B., Bansode, P., Taylor, J., & Araujo R. (n.d.). *How To: Perform a Security Code Review for Managed Code*. http://msdn.microsoft.com/en-us/ library/ff649315.as.

Kali Linux. (n.d.) https://www.kali.org/.

Karger, P. A., et al. (2011). Lessons learned: Building the caernarvon high-assurance operating system. *Security & Privacy, IEEE*, *9*(1), 22–30.

Kleidermacher, D., & Kleidermacher, M. (2012). *Embedded systems security: practical methods for safe and secure software and systems development*. Elsevier.

McConnell, S. (2004). *Code complete*. Microsoft press.

Metasploit. (n.d.) http://www.metasploit.com/.

Microsoft. (2012). Itron, Inc. SDL Chronicles.

MISRA. (n.d.). http://www.misra.org.uk/.

MITRE. (n.d.). *Secure code review*. http://www.mitre.org/publications/systems-engineering-guide/enterprise-engineering/systems-engineering-for-mission-assurance/secure-code-review.

Moore, A. P., Ellison, R. J., & Linger, R. C. (2001). *Attack modeling for information security and survivability*. Tech. Rep. CMU/SEI-2001-TN-001, Carnegie Mellon University Software Engineering Institute.

NESCOR. (n.d.). NESCOR Guide to Penetration Testing for Electric Utilities v.3.

Juniper Networks (n.d.). *Secure Development Life Cycle*. https://www.juniper.net/us/en/ security/sdl/.

Nmap. (n.d.). http://nmap.org/.

Northcutt, S., Shenk, J., Shackleford, D., Rosenberg, T., Siles, R., & Mancini, S. (2006). Penetration Testing: Assessing your overall security before attackers do. SANS Analyst Programme.

OpenVAS. (n.d.). http://www.openvas.org/.

Overman, T. M., Sackman, R. W., Davis, T. L., Cohen, B. S. (2011). High-assurance smart grid: A three-part model for smart grid control systems. *Proceedings of the IEEE*, *99*(6), 1046–1062.

Pennell, J. (2010). Securing the Smart Grid: The Road Ahead. *ICT Review*. http://ictreview. blogspot.de/2010/02/securing-smart-grid-road-ahead.html.

Pitchford, M. (2013). Security: Key to Smart Energy Software Development. http://rtcmagazine. com/articles/view/103263.

Kissel, R., Stine, K., Scholl, M., Rossman, H., Fahlsing, J., & Gulick, J. (2008). Security Considerations in the System Development Life Cycle, NIST SP 800-64 revision 2.

RTCA (1992). DO-178B Software Considerations in Airborne Systems and Equipment Certification.

SAP (2013). The Security Development Lifecycle at SAP.

Schneier, B. (1999). Attack Trees. *Dr Dobb's Journal*, *24*(12).

Schneier, B. (2014). Security Risks of Embedded Systems. https://www.schneier.com/blog/ archives/2014/01/security_risks_9.html.

SGCG, Smart Grid Coordination Group (2012). First Set of Standards, CEN, CENELEC, and ETSI.

Swiderski, F., & Snyder, W. (2004). *Threat modeling*. Microsoft Press.

Walker, M. (2011). *CEH certified ethical hacker all-in-one exam guide*. McGraw-Hill Osborne Media.

Wheeler, D. A. (n.d.). *How to prevent the next Heartbleed*. http://www.dwheeler.com/essays/heartbleed.html.

Operational Smart Grid Security

Robert W. Griffin* and Silvio La Porta†

*RSA – the Security Division of EMC, Ireland; †EMC Research Europe

9.1 INTRODUCTION TO THE OPERATIONAL SMART GRID SECURITY MODEL

Even after having put in place the most resilient and attack-resistant architecture possible, it is still essential to put in place an operational model that can respond effectively to attacks, intrusions and data exfiltration. This comprehensive approach to data analytics for Smart Grid security is shown in Figure 9.1. The operational infrastructure includes a number of systems:

- Enterprise Geographic Information System (GIS) is the platform that creates and collects information about utility assets (cables, transformers, customers, etc.) and makes that information available to enterprise for monitoring and analysis (ESRI, 2011).
- SCADA systems that control and monitor devices used in power generation, management and distribution.
- Customer information systems that monitor usage, perform billing, handle customer relationships and so on.
- Interfaces with external systems such as weather information, traffic information, satellite imagery, threat intelligence and so on.

Utilities use this combined information for a broad range of applications, including managing a comprehensive picture of the operating environment, detecting and analyzing faults, planning and analyzing the network, and managing security operations. For all these purposes, the utility must understand the relationship of its assets to each other. Since the smart grid is composed of two networks – the electric distribution network and the communications network – utilities must understand the physical, spatial and electronic relationships both within each of these networks and between these networks. For example, the communications network not only enables the collection and consolidation of information from the electricity distribution network, but also provides the means of distributing control information to substations,

External Data Sources

FIGURE 9.1

Comprehensive approach to data analytics.

smart meters and other components in the electricity distribution network. Understanding these interconnections is essential not only in effective operational management but also in security management.

The GIS is particularly important in enabling the utility to understand the electric and communication networks and the relationship between them. It provides a means to monitor the operational and security health of the system, answering such questions as "what sensors have reported anomalous values for the past hour", where the anomaly may be in terms of the historical record for a particular sensor for a particular time period (day, week, month) or in terms of an abstracted pattern of values for sensors providing that particular function. This operational model of the system as a whole takes advantage of device information provided by the SCADA system. But it needs to go beyond that device-specific information to present both a comprehensive perspective on the grid and insight into specific operational and security issues that could affect the availability and safety of the grid.

This visibility into the health of both the electric and the communication networks, as well as components within those networks, enables the smart grid to adapt quickly to prevent outages, whether those are the result of equipment failure, weather conditions, accidents, physical attacks or cyber security events. For example, there have been a number of instances in the United States of substation failures, including the explosion of Ives Dairy substation in Miami, Florida in 1993 (Ragan, 2010). That explosion was caused by the coincidental failures in several control and monitoring system, including the emergency response system that would have notified the grid dispatcher of a serious problem. The more comprehensive monitoring and control systems enabled by smart grid, particularly through the instrumentation of a larger number of more diverse sensors within the substation, can reduce the risk of such events. The instance of physical attacks on the grid, such as the attack on the PG&E (Pacific Gas and Electric) transmission station in Metcalf CA in April 2013, also demonstrates the importance of these more comprehensive operational systems that can detect and respond more quickly to damage to a particular facility in order to limit the impact to the grid as a whole (Tweed, 2014).

Malware like Havex recently appeared, with capabilities to target control systems: Additionally some crimeware trojans, that is, malware like BlackEnergy used to automatic cybercriminal activity, were readapted and extended with modules to operate in industrial control systems (ICS). Havex malware was used between 2011 and early 2013 during the "DragonFly" campaign which targeted energy, gas and oil companies (Symantec, 2014a). In this campaign one of the infection vectors used to spread the malware was the water hole technique, which consisted of compromising SCADA software companies' websites by repacking the malware with the software company's legitimate software. BlackEnergy has a module that scans and targets machines in an IP block searching for well-known open ports used by SCADA control systems. Additionally, the Sandworm crew used a zero-day exploit (CVE-2014-0751) to spread their malware and target HMI servers (Symantec, 2014b). All the above malwares is able to capture screenshots and record operators' activities in the compromised machines.

Another challenge is the state of the ICS machine involved in these architectures as these legacy control systems were usually designed with no security features due the fact that these systems were typically isolated from the Internet. These control systems often run in old OS versions with archaic software and are not updated to support new OS's or new libraries as these would potentially expose them to old unpatched vulnerabilities.

The incidents above show that cyber criminals are increasingly targeting critical IT infrastructures and how they are using the information gained to reduce their knowledge gap on how to use and interact with those systems. They are extreme examples of the kinds of risk that the operational model for the smart grid should consider, but they point to an important principle that should be generally instrumented in the smart grid operational model: that is, the smart grid must have the information, the analytics and the control capabilities to enable it to prevent outages as much as possible, to detect outages quickly when the occur, and to be able to respond to those outages quickly to minimize their impact on the larger grid. To accomplish this, the operational model certainly must be able to detect and respond to failures in equipment, sensors and communications, such as those failures that resulted in the Miami substation explosion. For example, the operational systems (and the GIS in particular) should be able to detect and monitor power surges that might reduce the expected life of a particular transformer; the systems can then institute remedial action as appropriate, and also perform a spatial analysis to define alternative power distribution, load allocation and usage scenarios that would mitigate the impact of failure in that component. Furthermore, the operational model must be flexible and able to quickly adapt as new threats emerge.

> *A major challenge in achieving this operational model is ensuring the quality of the data within the various systems. The grid is transitioning from a relative static topology, in which changes to the physical infrastructure were relatively infrequent, into a more dynamic model in which power sources, power consumers, information sources and information consumers will change much more frequently. Both the sources and consumers will also vary much more widely in terms of reliability and complexity than has been true in the past. For example, power sources will range of very large commercial power stations to small household renewable energy capabilities. Information sources will range from comprehensive sensor capabilities installed by the utility within the distribution network to highly variable information sources in connected cars and home area networks. The utility must be able to maintain an up-to-date operational model that reflects this dynamism in both the communication and the electricity networks so that accurate analysis can be performed and appropriate decisions taken when anomalies are detected that could indicate equipment failure, cyber attacks or other issues.*

As discussed in the PSERC research paper by Govindasaru et al. (2012), the operational model for smart grid must go beyond the conventional focus on distribution and generation infrastructure for fault isolation, remediation and recovery to a focus on information and control across three levels:

- Internal data sources, including event logs, configuration databases, vulnerability scans, etc.
- Applications, including generation control, transmission control, distribution control, customer relationship etc.
- Systems data sources, including SCADA, distribution management, customer information management, etc.
- Network data sources, including communications network (outers, firewalls, packet analysis, etc.) and distribution network (generators, transformers, wires, etc.)
- External data sources, such as threat intelligence, vulnerability reports and other resources that complement the organization's own data.

This more comprehensive approach to information and control both enables and requires a new understanding of data analysis. As discussed by Cardenas (2013), it requires the ability to handle huge amounts of data, to process that data using new analytics and visualization techniques, and to integrate the results of that analysis with governance processes that make those results readily actionable.

These three essential areas of information analysis have been discussed extensively in a recent study by ESG analyst Jon Oltsik (2014). Although not focused on Smart Grid, the study is very relevant to the Smart Grid operational model.

The **data sources** that utilities must use in order to gain visibility include four major areas. The first area is data sources providing information about risk, including sources within the organization and external sources. Second is visibility into the physical and cyber infrastructure. Third is identity information from both the physical and cyber environments. Fourth is application information that provides insight into applications. These sources represent a much greater volume of data than utilities have dealt with in the past, requiring new models for the effective storage and use of this information. Equally importantly, this set of sources represents a much broader diversity of inputs than utilities have dealt with in the past, particularly in terms of such areas as external sources of risk information such as threat intelligence. Utilities will have used comparable operational information, such as MTBF (Mean Time Between Failures) information provided by equipment manufacturers. But they rarely, if ever, will have integrated that operational information with information regarding cyber threats that might target that same equipment. But this correlation of operational and security information is essential in order to understand what the anomalies in equipment behavior might mean.

The **data analytics capabilities** must be able to work with this larger and more disparate set of information, requiring not only a new approaches such as massively parallel processing but also new algorithms. Current security analytics, for example, can spot obvious policy violations through applying a priori rules that look for correlations across events. But most tools cannot look across multiple disparate data sources to identify a possible cyber attack revealed by several independent actions when considered in combination, but invisible from the perspective of any one or these actions. The data analytics systems in the Smart Grid operational model must be able to model "normal" behavior and detect anomalies against those derived patterns, regardless of whether those anomalies reflect equipment failure or cyber attack. The systems will need to draw on a broader range of analytics algorithms than rules based on correlation, including "nested-algorithms" that analyze anomalies across multiple algorithms in order to eliminate false positives, pinpoint problems, and provide security analysts with the right details so they can prioritize and expedite remediation processes. The analytics must enable the utility to understand normal state behavior and look for anomalies that result from malicious activity, performing more detailed contextual analysis to determine the appropriate response.

Moreover, the analytics must support a continuum in terms of the depth the analysis and speed of response. The analytics capabilities must include real-time analytics used for fast incident detection/response and based upon events, logs, NetFlow, network packets, and activity on endpoints. But they must also support asymmetric data analysis of security anomalies and the associated investigations that may span several months or years. This type of asymmetric investigation may require analysts to sift through massive quantities of historical data to piece together patterns, detect malicious behavior, and trace the root of these activities. With asymmetric big data security analytics, security analysts will use an assortment of analytics methods to discover and investigate "low-and-slow" attack patterns.

Improved visualization and query technologies must provide easy-to-use GUIs, comprehensive reports, and intuitive navigation. They must provide visual analytics with 3-D images and simple pivoting across dimensions rather than just spreadsheets and charts. The visualization capabilities, like the analysis capabilities, must support both real-time response and longer-term investigation, including through integration with workflow and data sharing to align incident detection/response with operations. Analysts must be able to work hand in hand with IT and security operations teams once incident detection processes transition to incident response, leveraging effective communication capabilities, investigation tools and end-to-end oversight. This will require workflow tools to manage the incident detection/response process independently but also in interoperation with IT operations and security tools.

Integrating analytics with effective governance processes, including policy management, compliance, risk management, vulnerability management and incident management, is also an essential to an effective Smart Grid operational model. For example, the best strategy for dealing with both operational and security vulnerabilities is to manage them within the context of the overall risk management process for the organization. Managing security vulnerabilities has to start with understanding the potential for exploiting the vulnerability, the interest of attackers this taking advantage of that potential and the impact that such an attack could have. In the context of that more robust understanding and management of risk often termed "risk intelligence", the organization can make the necessary business decisions regarding how to prioritize remediation of the vulnerability, in each of the places where it occurs, against the numerous other competing and complementary security actions that the organization is considering.

Similarly, security analytics must integrate with IT and security incident detection processes. This requires effective workflow tools to manage the incident detection process and to achieve smooth hand-off to incident response processes. The integration requires interoperation with existing security and IT operations tools that facilitate incident analysis and response planning by providing context and insight regarding the source, scope and impact of the incident in order to understand both its immediate level of risk and the potential for risk related to similar incidents that may have occurred but were not detected or remediated.

As noted in a recent IDC report (Feblowitz et al., 2013), the smart grid has also put focus on the privacy of information. Many consumers are concerned that their consumption data collected through the utilities' meters will be shared with third parties or will be accessible to hackers. Privacy of customer data extends to competition as well. Vertically organized utilities are required to keep customer consumption data collected by their distribution subsidiaries separate from their competitive retail subsidiaries. The visibility, analytics and action required for an effective Smart Grid operational model must respect and support these requirements for the privacy of information not only in order to conform to regulatory requirements, but also to engage the human community in effective security.

9.2 VISIBILITY: CYBER INTELLIGENCE AND INFORMATION SHARING

As discussed above, an effective Smart Grid operational model requires visibility into risk, infrastructure, identities and applications. This sections discusses each of these areas in turn.

9.2.1 **VISIBILITY INTO RISK**

Power and utility companies are facing a wide range of new and emerging risks. For example, they are seeing a rise in operational compliance requirements amid a climate of transformations in national and international energy policy. They must address issues regarding public acceptance of initiatives such as AMI (Automated Metering Infrastructure) and the development of new renewable energy capabilities such as wind farms.

Operational risks continue to change as new technologies are employed and as existing relationships with suppliers and consumers change. Smart Grid enhances the traditional electrical grid with communications capabilities that converge utility operations with IT. There are many benefits to this convergence, including increased data for real-time situational awareness, historical analysis and improved customer service. But as noted by Vermesan et al. (2013), in gaining the benefits that come with automated meter reading, demand response management and interactive home networks, utilities also open themselves up to new security risks, shown in Figure 9.2.

These risks can be understood in terms of changes in attackers, attack methods, and exploitable vulnerabilities.

*   New kinds of attacks. Electric utilities become susceptible to sophisticated electronic attacks as power grids integrate communications and distribution systems, employing implementations built on widely-accepted standards. The integration of systems may attract criminal, competitive and nation-state attacks related to stealing customers' payment account information, disrupting electric services and damaging electric infrastructure.
*   New attack points. The integration of new technologies into delivering smart grid services – from electronic metering systems to demand response companies – means there are far more potential points of entry for attackers into Smart Grid than into the closed-grid systems of the past. In addition, the integration of new partners and the establishment of new relationships with existing partners in the Smart Grid supply chain, including cloud services, demand response, equipment suppliers and power resources, increases the number and kinds of attack points. As has been demonstrated by attacks in other industries, electric utilities have become only as secure as the most vulnerable partner in their supply chain.
*   New vulnerabilities. For example, meter readings in the Smart Grid that are transmitted electronically could be tampered with to report lower-than-actual energy use (Searle, 2012). Fraud has always been a possibility with mechanical meters. But the use of smart meters increases the likelihood of vulnerabilities that can be exploited by attacks, such as vulnerabilities in the transmission protocol standards. The disclosure of long-standing vulnerabilities in fundamental security standards such as Secure Sockets Layer (SSL) shows that even well-established technologies can be sources of vulnerabilities that attackers can exploit. The rapid development of new technologies for Smart Grid increases the risk that the technologies capabilities used by utilities and their supply chain will have exploitable vulnerabilities.

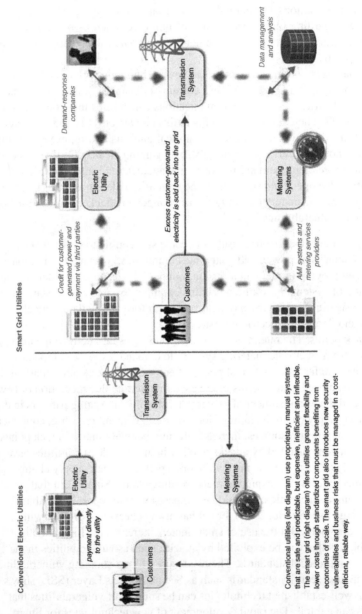

The Smart Grid: More Players, More Risks

Conventional Electric Utilities

Smart Grid Utilities

Demand-response companies

Electric Utility

Transmission System

Metering Systems

Customers

Data management and analysis

Credit for customer-generated power and payment via third parties

AMI systems and metering services providers

Excess customer-generated electricity is sold back into the grid

payment directly to the utility

Conventional utilities (left diagram) use proprietary, manual systems that are safe and predictable, but expensive, inefficient and inflexible. The smart grid (right diagram) offers utilities greater flexibility and lower costs through standardized components benefiting from economies of scale. The smart grid also introduces new security vulnerabilities and business risks that must be managed in a cost-efficient, reliable way.

FIGURE 9.2

More players, more risks.

The Smart Grid industry will need to have much greater understanding of and visibility into these risks. A utility will need to participate in security communities that share information about attackers and attacker strategies in order to benefit from the experiences and research of industry, government and academia. The benefit of this insight into attackers has been demonstrated by information sharing models for the financial services industry, for example, in which each institution can share experiences with new phishing attacks with other financial institutions to share insight into new attackers and new attack methods. The VERIS Community Database Project (VCDB), a community data initiative to catalog security incidents in the public domain using the VERIS framework, provides another such information-sharing community. (www. http://vcdb.org/) Threat reports from government, industry and academic sources also provide important insights into changes in the attacker community, as well as into existing and emerging attack methods.

Reports such as the annual Verizon Breach Reports (Verizon, 2014), the Common Vulnerabilities and Exposures (CVE) list and the Industrial Control Systems Cyber Emergency Response Team (ICS-CERT) continue to demonstrate the importance of visibility into vulnerabilities and processes for addressing those vulnerabilities. Visibility into vulnerabilities continues to be critical in order to understand, prioritize and mitigate the risks related to vulnerabilities. But as a report by Enterprise Management Associates has shown (Oltsik, 2013), enterprises are already overwhelmed by the volume of information they are collecting and analyzing. Visibility into vulnerabilities, therefore, while being as comprehensive as possible, such also leverage analytics capabilities and integration into the larger risk governance processes to enable insight into what vulnerabilities should be addressed, within what time frame. Visibility – not only into risk, but into all the areas explored in this section – means not just the collection of data, but the transformation of that data into information that can be acted on effectively.

9.2.2 VISIBILITY INTO INFRASTRUCTURE

As discussed in detail by Musser (2009), Smart Grid enables the collection and integration of both operational and non-operational data on an unprecedented scale across the grid infrastructure.

Transmission systems for Smart Grid provide much more extensive accurate, timely and extensive information than earlier systems that relied on analog devices for monitoring and control. This includes the ability to detect and record transient disturbances, to isolate the location of disturbances and to provide more precise measurement of disturbances. Phase measurement units (PMUs) and dynamic line rating units are particularly important in terms of providing this monitoring not only for operational purposes, but also as part of the security monitoring and response. For example, physical attacks on critical power lines could result in a cascade of impacts that disrupt service across a broad geographic area. Research on fault isolation, such as the paper by Zhang et al. (2009) has shown the effective use of multivariate analysis of PMU information in order to identify faulty components and faulty sections, then using that information to, accomplish fault isolation. Such faults can be the result not only of mechanical failure or weather conditions, but also of both physical and cyber-attacks. For example, cyber manipulation of the distribution system could result in surges that damage transformers as effectively as natural events such as lightning strikes. Visibility into these faults and into conditions that might trigger such faults is as vital in the identification and remediation of cyber attacks on the transmission system as in the identification and remediation of such faults from other causes.

As noted above, visibility into **substations** is also critical to an effective Smart Grid operational model. Substation sensors enable the monitoring of power flow conditions and equipment performance. They enable monitoring across the substation component, such as transformers, transformer cooling, circuit breakers, switches, relays, batteries, surveillance equipment and meters. They also enable the monitoring of environmental conditions, including temperatures in the substation and meteorological situations that might impact the substation. These monitoring capabilities can identify individual situations that could indicate a cyber attack, such as fluctuations in transformer cooling, unusual behavior in circuit breakers and disabled sensor or control mechanisms. In combinations, the capabilities provide a rich set of data to which analytics can be applied both to detect potential cyber physical attacks and to investigate those potential attacks to disregard false indicators of compromise and to understand actual attacks more fully.

Distribution monitoring has already been impacted significantly by the deployment of smart meters, providing a much more extensive and varied set of information than was available through manual reading of mechanical meters. For example, distribution applications can use field data to establish baseline patterns of real-time power flow conditions. Variations in actual power flow can then be identified quickly and analyzed to determine whether manual or automated changes should be made to line regulators, capacitor banks and other distribution components to address operational requirements. These same variations, however, can also be indications of cyber or physical attacks. Information regarding the variations can be combined other sources to identify potential attacks and appropriate response.

Automated Meter Infrastructure (AMI) information, particularly in combination with other sets of information such as home area network configuration and household information, is already being used to identify potential fraudulent use of electric power (Tweed, 2012). In this case, normal patterns of usage abstracted for the aggregate information from the AMI can be compared against the usage of a particular household, industrial user or other consumer. Anomalies between the abstracted pattern and power consumption by a particular consumer can indicate not only faults in the meter but also meter tampering for purposes of power theft.

Home Area Network (HAN) and Energy Management Control (EMC) Systems have developed in response to consumer interest in optimal control of discretionary power usage and utility interest in optimal control of load conditions. Monitoring information from the HAN can be valuable to the consumer in quickly identifying ways to optimize their power consumption. But here too, patterns of usage can be derived that provide opportunities to detect such issues as attacker compromise of an EMC that could result in significant damage within the consumer environment, such as in the case of an industrial consumer.

Work management systems are increasingly mobile, subject to attacks both in the reception of service instructions and in the transmission of service and operational data. Widespread disruption of a work management system could be part of an attack strategy focused on disruption of service by delaying response to emergency conditions. Monitoring to ensure the health of the work management system is valuable in rapidly identifying and responding to such disruptions.

With Smart Grid, **customer information systems** contain substantially more data than previously. This can contain customer financial information that, if not well-protected, could be of interest to cyber attackers looking for financial gain or doing reconnaissance in preparation for fraudulent activity. The recent cyber attacks against retail enterprises for the purposes of stealing credit card information and user financial account information indicate that such attacks could increasingly be targeted at Smart Grid customer information systems as well as the data in those environments become more extensive.

Generation resources typically already have extensive monitoring capabilities for operational purposes such as automated fault detection and capacity management. Resilience against cyber attacks require enhancements to these capabilities, such as protocol inspection to detect spurious or malformed control commands that could result in disruption of service or damage to the generation resources. The cascading effect of unexpected control outages in the 2006 power disruption in Europe, as analyzed in the UCTE 2006 report (2006, p. 20) resulted in "a significant amount of generation units tripped due to the frequency drop in the Western area of the UCTE system." This situation can be caused by a cyber-physical attack, rather than by a change such as the switching-off that initiated the cascade of failures. The report also noted that "most of the TSOs do not have access to the real-time data of the power units connected to the distribution grids. This did not allow them to perform a better evaluation of the system conditions" (UCTE, 2006, p. 20). Visibility into the relationship of power generation to generator capacity will be critical in identification of and automated response to prevent cascading failure triggered by a cyber event.

Enabling **distributed energy resources,** a major goal of Smart Grid, creates significant challenges with regard to managing grid capacity and resilience due to the complexity of bi-directional energy flows and communications. Disruption of or error in the communication flow as the result of a cyber attack could result in the propagation of inappropriate load commands that could result in disruption of service or damage to components. Fraudulent claims regarding energy production by distributed energy resources could also be introduced into the system if there is inadequate visibility of generation, distribution and consumption data.

Enterprise Information Management (EIM) systems, including the **Geographical Information** Systems (GIS) discussed earlier in this chapter, are an important source of visibility within Smart Grid. Financial management of the utility may be disrupted by attacks on the EIM. Emergency response may be disrupted by attacks on the GIS.

Finally, **Data management and analytics systems** provide the opportunity for integration of data across all of the sources of visibility discussed in this section. This integration has great benefits for operational control, customer satisfaction and realization of business opportunity. But there also needs to be visibility into these analytics systems themselves in order to detect and respond to cyber attacks against these systems. The rise of targeted attacks, particularly those that have been characterized as Advanced Persistent Threats employing extensive reconnaissance, multiple attack vectors and detection-evading tactics (SBIC, 2011), have made security analytics increasingly important in cyber defense, as much for data management and analytics systems as for the other systems discussed above.

As discussed by Popovic et al. (2013), visibility across all these systems has created the opportunity for better observability of power systems, redundancy in measurements and improvement decision-making process wen operating the system. Equally importantly, this visibility into infrastructure creates the opportunity for the application of security analytics to detect and investigate cyber physical attacks, particular in combination with the visibility into risk already discussed and the visibility into identity, information and applications that we discuss in the remaining sections of this chapter.

9.2.3 VISIBILITY INTO IDENTITIES

Effective cyber physical security for Smart Grid, as for any other environment, requires clear and comprehensive visibility into who has access to which resources (including infrastructure, applications and information), who approved that access and whether that access is appropriate based on the individual's business relationship with the organization.

Visibility into identities starts with collecting identity information and entitlements both from structured and unstructured data resources, including cloud and mobile apps. This information should relate to the full spectrum of both internal and external users (employees, partners, customers) across the full range of devices (laptops, tablets, mobile devices) and applications that they use. It should include as comprehensive as possible understanding of the attributes of each user; who they are, what they do and the policies that apply to them. These information sources for identity are shown in Figure 9.3.

This visibility must be balanced against requirements for privacy that come both from the external regulatory environment and internal policies. Both consumers and government agencies are concerned that personal information may be visible within the Smart Grid enterprise in situations where the information is not needed and to individuals who should not have access to it. For example, supply chain relationships may encourage the utility to share customer information with third parties and across national boundaries. It is very important for Smart Grid enterprises, therefore, to be circumspect in what identity information they collect, where and how they store it, and when and with whom they share it.

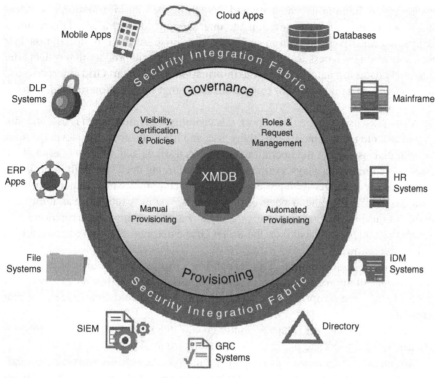

Mobile Apps

Cloud Apps

Databases

DLP
Systems

Security Integration Fabric

Governance

Mainframe

Visibility,
Certification
& Policies

Roles &
Request
Management

ERP
Apps

XMDB

HR
Systems

Manual
Provisioning

Automated
Provisioning

File
Systems

IDM
Systems

Provisioning

Security Integration Fabric

SIEM

Directory

GRC
Systems

FIGURE 9.3

Visibility into identities.

> *Identity intelligence provides essential context that can dramatically improve the effectiveness of security investigations. A security analyst can use identity context to see if the user's access is appropriate, and how the user relates to the application in question. This intelligence is especially important for such issues as detecting Segregation of Duties (SoD) violations, finding orphaned accounts and identifying inappropriate assignment of access privileges for particular users.*

9.2.4 VISIBILITY INTO INFORMATION

The concern about ensuring the protection of identity information raised in the previous section applies in more general terms to all information that is collected, stored and used by a Smart Grid enterprise. As is already apparent in the discussions of visibility into risk, infrastructure and identity, the Smart Grid depends on the collection and use of a broad range of information.

As noted by IDC, the enterprise needs to develop a data and information strategy that ensures that information is available as needed for both current and future requirements. (Feblowitz et al., 2013) At the same time, the strategy must also ensure the confidentiality, integrity and availability of that information in conformance with both external regulation and internal policy and strategy. This requires identifying sensitive information across the enterprise: where it is stored, how is it used and who has access to it. This needs to be a dynamic process that reflects the constantly evolving nature of both the information in the Smart Grid enterprise and in the attackers who may want to gain access to that information to steal, corrupt or destroy it.

Also as discussed in the IDC report, this visibility into information is essential not only in order to understand its sensitivity, use, and lifecycle, but also to leverage it for collaborative aspects of the operational model as a whole and security operations in particular. Information plays a critical role in the driving decisions both in on-going operations and in longer-term projects, in meeting compliance requirements, in evaluating risk and many other aspects of the business. Visibility into the availability and quality of this information empowers the organization to address these requirements. In order to achieve this visibility, the Smart Grid enterprise should have capabilities such as the following:

Knowledge management. This capability ensures that information is captured across all appropriate sources, managed effectively across its lifecycle and disseminated as appropriate to all participants who should have access to that information.

Collaboration support. This capability enables the secure exchange of information across all appropriate participants, including external partners.

Information integration. This capability employs analysis, taxonomies, ontological frameworks and other processes and technologies to enhance the value of managed information and to incorporate it into the business processes.

Many Smart Grid enterprise have seen an increase in collaboration between operations and information technology, particularly for sets of data such as automated meter data that is valuable for outage management and for security analytics. There are still major opportunities in this area and in integration, particularly in areas such as transmission data such as synchro-phasor measurements that are already employed in operations but only rarely for purposes of security analytics.

The IDC paper "Making Good on the Promise of Smart Grid" discusses the importance of data archiving strategy as part of this opportunity for convergence of operational technology (OT) and information technology (IT) (Feblowitz, 2010). Utilities typically archive meter data for a minimum of three years and often for seven years. This reflects regulatory requirements for archived data retention. But there is significant value in archived data that is not realized unless it is readily visible for longitudinal analytics, including for security purposes. Storage tiering represents an important strategy for addressing visibility requirements while minimizing data storage costs. While flash storage may be used for near-real-time analysis of operational safety, reliability and performance, or real-time-analysis related to security, less expensive disk-based technologies can be used for a mid- and long-term data storage, making the information visible even though at a slower access rate.

9.2.5 VISIBILITY INTO APPLICATIONS

The Electric Power Research Institute (EPRI) has suggested that that the goal of the smart grid is to enable a broad range of advanced grid applications, including outage management, real-time contingency management, AMI management, SCADA management, and so on (EPRI, 2010).

Visibility into applications is essential to assessing risks comprehensively and to making informed enterprise-level decisions.

The transformation taking place with advanced metering is a good example. In conventional metering systems, meters were read once a month, totaling 12 reads a year per customer. With advanced metering infrastructure (AMI) meters will be read every 15 minutes, increasing the number of reads per customer by 3,000 times per year. We have touched on the importance of visibility into AMI as an infrastructure and on the importance of visibility into this information from AMI. But equally important is visibility into the AMI applications from both operational and security perspectives. Is the application for receiving and processing information from smart meters encountering connectivity issues that result in lost information? Is it participating in a patch management strategy to ensure it is fully operational and secure? This visibility into the application is critical in ensuring their effective operation and security.

9.3 ANALYTICS: DERIVING PATTERNS AND UNDERSTANDING ANOMALIES

Most Smart Grid enterprises already monitor and analyze at least some of the sources of information discussed above for signs of unusual behavior of people, applications, infrastructure, and communication. But often this analysis is focused on explicit indicators such as previously identified malware signatures or blacklisted IP addresses or domains. Sophisticated attackers can circumvent such telltale, static monitoring approaches by modifying lines of code, by provisioning a new virtual machine in a public cloud, or by registering a new Internet domain as a command-and control or drop site.

Attackers typically operate by collecting information on the security systems and software installed on the target network. This allows them to test their malicious code and also to verify they will evade detection by the target network systems before launching an attack. It's much harder, though for attackers to circumvent monitoring and analysis systems that are watching for unusual patterns and behaviors. Sooner or later, hostile malware or users must do something unusual that breaks with system norms, and that is when Intelligence Driven these kinds of analytic systems, often called "Intelligence-Driven Security", will find them (RSA, 2013).

For example, when it comes to detecting malware, endpoint threat detection solutions don't look for "known bad" files; look for suspicious behaviors. By comparing what's actually running in memory with what should be running based on the files

FIGURE 9.4

Deriving patterns of normal behavior for substations.

residing on the local disk, malware detection tools are better able to identify discrepancies and get a direct, more reliable view of whether illicit code is present.

9.3.1 ANALYTICS: ESTABLISHING PATTERNS OF WHAT IS NORMAL

Intelligence Driven Security systems establish what "good" behavior looks like within an IT environment by monitoring and learning a variety of machine and human activities, from what ports on servers are typically used for outside communications to employees' individual log-in locations and habits. Analytics solutions often rely on logs and configuration information as data sources. But they achieve far greater visibility by also incorporating other sources. The Figure 9.4 shows an example of data integration and information exchange for operational and security analytics for a substation, adapted from Figure 9.1 to include the broad range of input sources described in Popovic's (2013) discussion of Smart Grid data analytics. These input sources input digital protective relays (DPR), digital fault recorders (DFR), digital disturbance recorders (DDR), sequence event recorders (SER), remote terminal unites (RTU) and phase measurement units (PMU), as well as a number of other sources.

Similarly, capabilities such as network packet-capture are important in establishing normal behavior in the IT infrastructure. Full network packet-capture means recording, parsing, normalizing, analyzing, and reassembling all data traffic at every layer of the network stack. As network traffic is captured, it's analyzed and tagged to facilitate subsequent threat analysis and investigation. Capturing and tagging network data enables security analysts to reconstruct users' sessions and activities to understand not just basic details such as what time or to which IP address specific data packets were transmitted, but exactly what information was sent in and out and the resulting damage. These techniques help organizations learn what is "typical" within an IT environment so that future deviations from normal—which often indicate problems—can be identified and investigated as they arise.

9.3.2 ANALYTICS: DETECTING ANOMALIES WITHIN THE OPERATIONAL ENVIRONMENT

With patterns of normal behavior in hand, activities outside the norm can be detected, analyzed and appropriately acted upon. For example, if an anomaly is flagged as a potential security issue, it can be passed to an analyst for further investigation. If the analyst determines that the event is a false positive, the analytics tools can "learn" from that experience so that it is less likely to flag future recurrences of that event as potential security violations.

Analysis systems capture and analyze massive amounts of rapidly changing data from multiple sources, pivoting on terabytes of data in real time, organized into various levels to enable different types of detection. For example, data can be captured and analyzed for potential security issues as it traverses the network. This **capture time analysis** identifies suspicious activities by looking for the tools, services, communications and techniques often used by attackers without depending on logs, events, or signatures from other security systems. Examples of this capture time analysis includes the detection of non-browser software programs running HTTP, protocols over non-traditional ports, and executables embedded in PDF files. Additionally, these sophisticated tools can detect subtle signs of attack by correlating events that seem innocuous in isolation but that are problematic when strung together. Analytical techniques fuse internal inputs from various sources using metadata. These advanced detection mechanisms also act as trip-wires that can provide early warning of potential infiltration. Processing of these information flows happens as they occur, meaning suspicious activities are spotted while there's still time for security teams to stop attacks in progress.

This is comparable to the real-time operational response that is a fundamental capability in Smart Grid systems. Papers such as the California ISO Smart Grid Roadmap and Architecture (30) describe the application of synchro-phasor technology in real-time fault isolation and remediation: "Phasor units measure voltage and electric current physical characteristics. This data can be used to assess and maintain system stability following a destabilizing event within and outside the ISO footprint, which includes alerting system operators to take action within seconds of a system event. This capability reduces the likelihood of an event causing widespread grid instability." Such "capture time analysis" is shown in Figure 9.4 of the Popovic paper (2013), illustrating the extraction of phase current features to determine if a fault has occurred.

This kind of capture analysis and response is important in terms of real-time faults caused by cyber attacks rather than natural disasters or equipment failure. The Aurora attack, in this case referring to the demonstration by Department of Homeland Security conducted at the Idaho National Laboratory (INL) in 2007, showed the creation of an out-of-phase condition that could damage alternating current (AC) equipment (Swearingen, 2013). The attack forced the repeated opening and closing a circuit breaker or breakers to rapidly disconnect and reconnect a generator to the grid, but out of phase. Many circuits of utilities carry varying load profiles, from resistive to inductive loads. These circuits may include rotating equipment. This load profile allows for the real-time failure demonstrated in AURORA to occur. Analytics that detect the anomalous behavior in circuit breakers can enable automated responses that prevent equipment damage or worse.

Analysis systems can also perform **batch analysis** on large volumes of historical security data. In the case of security analytics, such data are needed not only to fulfill most companies' data retention and audit requirements but they are also invaluable in uncovering adversarial tactics that may have taken many months to execute and may even be ongoing. For instance, batch analysis of security data archives can help uncover previously overlooked cyber-attacks in which illicit data was transmitted only sporadically in small, stealthy streams over weeks or months. These types of "low and slow" attack techniques are hard to spot when they are occurring, because they are designed to seem innocuous by taking cover under existing processes and communication streams. These techniques usually become suspicious only when executed in a particular pattern over a specific window of time. Detailed, automated analyses of security data archives can discover attackers in the midst of establishing a foothold, as well as reveal information losses those organizations may not even realize they sustained.

An example of batch analysis is the identification of compromised hosts through the use of large volumes of historical information to establish a pattern of normal behavior for hosts in an enterprise, then the review of that information to identify hosts that diverge from that pattern.

In this first example, HTTPS packet data is used as input. The security analytics tool looks for anomalous HTTP access, DNS lookups, accessed domains, traffic, users, IP addresses, beaconing activities, event timestamps and other network information. Using this information, the tool can create a ranked list of likely malicious IP addresses that require further investigation. Further, the tool can create reports containing additional information regarding the IP addresses that can help in forensics and threat detection. The tool can then also search connections to IP addresses belonging to the same malicious IP subnet to identify other machines that require further investigation.

Batch analysis can also use rapid transitions in DNS addresses to identify potentially compromised hosts, In this case, DNS packet data is used as the input. The security analytics tool looks for anomalous subdomains, users, IP addresses, ISP domains another network information. Using this information, the tool can create a ranked list of likely fast-fluxing domains that are strong candidates for further investigation. Further, the tool can create reports containing historical visibility for about each domain (for example, 30-day history) and additional information regarding the domain that can help in forensics and threat detection.

In summary, batch analyses of can uncover attacker techniques and indicators of compromise that security teams can use in the future to detect similar attacks. More generally, batch analysis enables organizations to detect operational and security anomalies and reconstruct incidents with certainty and detail so they can investigate their losses and remediate problems faster and more effectively.

9.3.3 ANALYTICS: DETECTING ANOMALIES WITHIN THE ADMINISTRATOR ENVIRONMENT

Among the most difficult attacks to detect are those in which the attacker exercises legitimate use cases and capabilities in order to accomplish malicious goals. The attacker hides in plain sight, making it difficult for security personnel to distinguish between legitimate activity and attacker reconnaissance, infection of target systems and other attacks.

This technique is especially dangerous in attacks against administrative environments that may have been compromised as a first step in subversion or destruction of operational systems. Advanced attacks often use social engineering approaches to steal user credentials, trick the user into opening an attachment containing malware or to open URLs that would exploit the user's web browser, leading to potential malware infection. Having established a foothold in the administrator environment through such a technique, the attacker can then leverage any of a number of legitimate system capabilities in order to move laterally across the organization, increasing both the scope and kinds of infection of the Smart Grid environment. This lateral movement can be accomplished by manipulating task scheduling, by creating or modifying services, and by remote reconnaissance or image execution. After the system infection phase, the next steps are 1) to make the attacker presence persistent on the user machine and 2) to start privilege escalation, using a range of techniques that are well-documented in the literature.

In the Windows environment, for example, one of the primary methods by which APT actors utilize existing architecture is by using Windows interconnectivity to increase their foothold into the network. Most commonly, allowed interaction between systems allows attackers to conduct lateral movement. This allows attackers to navigate from the initial compromised hosts to the more high-value targets in the environment.

Before starting with lateral movement, the attacker needs to identify the Windows environment, for example, if it is running in an Active Directory domain or not. In the Active Directory case, the attacker can use different techniques to get an administrator account credential, for example, getting a credential from the NTLM (Windows Challenge/Response authentication protocol) that is stored in the machine memory inside MSV1_0.dll or if the administrator login to the machine was remote, the attacker could find the credential in Kerberos.dll, wdigest.dll or tspkg.dll.

It is important to highlight that the attacker does not need to brute force the credential because they can use the "Pass the hash" technique. This enables the attacker to authenticate in a target server/service using directly the dumped password hash string. This is possible due to a Windows vulnerability which incorrectly uses a *salt* value in the authentication implementation. *Mimikatz.exe*, an open source tool, is often used to accomplish this type of attack.

There are a number of Windows administration tools that are frequently used by attackers in order to move laterally within an organization, infecting more and different kinds of systems. We'll look at four such tools. The first of these is the "at" command (at.exe).

The *at* command was implemented in Windows 2000 as a method of manually scheduling tasks from the command. It was designed to allow administrators to schedule tasks on host or remote systems. However, the command still exists, and is operable, up to Windows 7 and Server 2008 systems. Attackers can use this command to create immediate or longer-term tasks that allow them to execute commands on remote systems. The *at* command works by:

1. Connecting to the IPC$ share on the remote system over TCP/445
2. Creating a named pipe named "atsvc"
3. Sending a JobAdd request with the command to be run.

Once the remote system receives the request, it creates a .job file in the Tasks folder under:\WINDOWS\System32\ with a file name of At < *job number* >.job.

Analyzing the JobAdd request enables the security environment to detect malicious use of the *at* comment. Since the *at* command will submit a known UUID in the bind request to port TCP/445, this value can be detected, and parsed through the stream to the JobAdd. In order to detect malicious use of the at comment, a security analytics environment that has captured the command can parse the command location and length fields and job file name to detect discrepancies from normal use of this command, notifying security personnel of the anomaly.

The second tool frequently used by attackers in the administrative environment is the *schtasks* command. The *schtasks* command was introduced with Windows XP/Server 2003 as a replacement method for the *at* command to allow administrators to schedule jobs from the command line. Adversaries can utilize this functionality to exploit the same attack vector as with the *at* command. While the *at* command uses a well-known endpoint in the form of the named pipe "atsvc", the *schtasks* command uses dynamic RPC endpoint mapping to determine its communication port. As such, it submits the *ITaskSchedulerService* UUID to the RPC endpoint mapping port (TCP/135) and receives a port assignment with which to begin communication. As the UUID for this service is known, a security analytics tool can detect when this UUID is seen passed with the appropriate protocol payload. Once the job is scheduled with the Task Scheduler, security analytics can recognize it as the command being executed by the job, identify it as an anomalous use of *schtasks* and notify security personnel of the potential attack, including displaying the binary that is scheduled to be run.

A third tool frequently used by attackers in the administrative environment is the *sc* command, or *service control*. The *sc* command was introduced with Windows NT 3.51 and included on endpoints as of Windows XP. The *sc* command uses the Service Control Manager Remote Protocol to interact with the Service Control Manger on the local, or remote, system. This command was designed to allow administrator to create, control, or remove services from the command line. It is commonly used by attackers to create new malicious services, disable services that may prove problematic, or remove services as necessary. While there are other command line binaries that allow for control of services remotely (namely *netsvc* and *instsvc*), these do not allow for the creation of new services remotely and as such, the *sc* command is more commonly preferred by attackers. Microsoft has allocated both an RPC interface UUID to present to the RPC endpoint mapping port, as well as a named pipe named "svcctl". As the UUID for this service is known, a security analytics tool can identify when this UUID is seen passed with the appropriate protocol payload. As the purpose of this command is to interact with the database of installed services, the security analytics tool can then scan this database to allow the review of host artifacts resultant from the command's execution. The security analytics tool can then notify security personnel of the potential attack, including displaying the artifacts related to the *sc* command.

A fourth tool frequently used by attackers in the administrative environment is the windows management interface. Windows Management Instrumentation (WMI) is described by Microsoft as "the infrastructure for management data and operations on Windows-based operating systems." (Microsoft, n.d.) It is the latest method provided by Microsoft to conduct administrative tasks on host and remote systems via C + +, Visual Basic, or the *wmic* command-line utility. In order to connect to remote systems, one of two primary methods is used. The first is to specify the connection information in an *SWbemServices* object using a moniker string. This allows the script to communicate with a remote system using the user's current credentials. However, this approach is limited as alternate credentials cannot be supplied and this method is unable to connect to systems across domains. The second method is more flexible, as it allows for specification of target computer, domain, username, and password. As the first method doesn't allow for on-the-fly use of stolen credentials, this second method is more attractive to adversaries. This method involves using the *ConnectServer* method from *SWbemLocator* (*IWbemLocator* for C + + applications) to specify and conduct connection operations.

Both of these methods use the *IWbemLevel1Login* interface to connect to the management services interface within the requested namespace. This is useful in detecting this traffic as the interface must use the pre-designated UUID from Microsoft. As the UUID for this service is known, a security analytics tool can identify the UUID being passed with the appropriate protocol payload. In addition to passing the UUID to the RPC endpoint mapper, the UUID is also sent in remote requests along with parameters containing queries and commands to be executed on the remote system. In the case that *pktPrivacy* is not set, these parameters are sent to the remote system in the clear with a leading value of "__PARAMETERS". This value is resultant from the use of the "_PARAMETERS" class to set input parameters for the aforementioned WMI methods. By detecting the "__PARAMETERS" values and removing the "abstract" values ("__PARAMETERS" is an abstract class), the security analytics tool is able to retrieve and register the parameters given to the *WMI* remote command, including queries and commands to be executed on the remote system. The security analytics tool can once again notify security personnel of the potential attack, including displaying the detected artifacts.

This is just a brief overview of the most popular tools used to accomplish lateral movement. Other tools like *psexec.exe*, *wevtutil.exe*, *winrs.exe* and *net.exe* are also used by attackers to expand their network foothold.

> *Within Windows management, the use of the ExecQuery method is also interesting, as it allows adversaries to conduct actions and reconnaissance on remote systems by conducting WQL (WMI Query Language) queries against the remote system. The strQueryLanguage parameter defines the query language to be used. This parameter must be defined with the value "WQL". The strQuery parameter is required, as it contains the value of the query to be executed. Without pktPrivacy, this value is sent to the remote system in the clear. Knowing that the value of strQueryLanguage must be "WQL", and that the following parameter is the query to be executed, the query itself can be parsed and analyzed for any session that contains the WbemLevel1Login UUID.*

In all four of these examples of attacks within a Windows environment, the difficulty with combatting attackers using these methods is that all four of the capabilities have legitimate use cases within the administrator environment. This serves to increase the utility of these methods to attackers, since the valid use of these capabilities is not detected by most security tools that look for static indicators of compromise, rather than doing dynamic analysis of the use of these kinds of capabilities. Given this exploitation of legitimate communication between systems, it is extremely important for the success of analytical approaches to security that the normal use of these capabilities is well understood and incorporated into the analysis being done, in order to minimize false positives in the detection process. It is even more important to understand the environment in which this activity is seen if response personnel are to combat these threats. Understanding the known methods within the protocols used by these capabilities and determining their typical use and legitimate use cases within the organization's actual environment is essential to applying security analytics in the detection of possible malicious use of these capabilities.

9.3.4 ANALYTICS: INVESTIGATION AND PRIORITIZATION

Advanced analytics tools examine the behavior of machines, networks, and processes to determine whether they are evidencing operational problems, have been compromised by malware and so on. But such tools do more than detect incidents; they assess risk and prioritize alerts for remediation.

For example, files determined to be malicious may warrant a lower prioritization score if they're determined to be malware that causes more of a nuisance than a true threat. Conversely, files that bear no outward signs of tampering may contain a custom-compiled executable designed to run only when it reaches certain systems or when a covert command is given. To uncover this type of dangerous, customized malware, advanced threat detection systems use a series of analytical techniques to rate the risk levels of suspicious files.

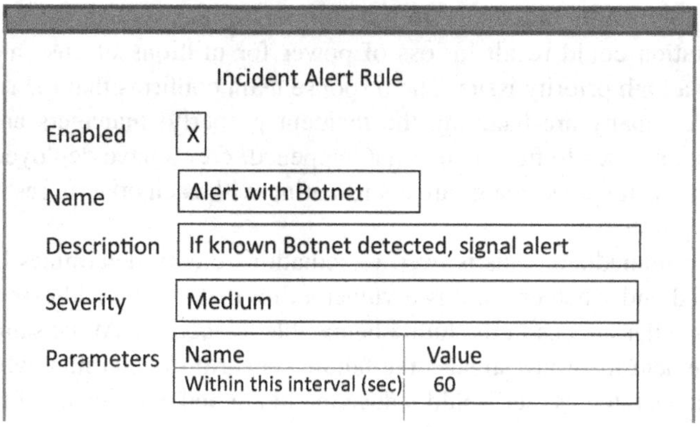

Incident Alert Rule		
Enabled	X	
Name	Alert with Botnet	
Description	If known Botnet detected, signal alert	
Severity	Medium	
Parameters	Name	Value
	Within this interval (sec)	60

FIGURE 9.5

Responding to detected security anomalies.

For example, an organization may set a rule requiring the security system to analyze every new executable coming into its networks. The malware detection system would then "sandbox" new executables, running them in a quarantined environment, recording everything they do, and elevating their risk score if suspicious behaviors are observed, such as changing registry settings or replacing operating system DLLs. Of course, legitimate software could also perform these actions: to integrate functions with existing software or to install a patch, for instance. But if the new executable demonstrates one of these behaviors along with initiating unusual network connections, then its overall risk score skyrockets. In that case, the analytics system should send an alert to an incident management system that could notify the security team of the issue, automatically prevent further introduction of the suspicious file and quarantine it in any systems where it's found. Such an Incident Alert Rule is shown in Figure 9.5.

Similarly, anomalies that indicate operational issues (not necessarily security issues) can be assessed and prioritized in terms of risk. As discussed in the California ISO paper (Cal ISO, 2010) such analysis enables responses that can have a substantial effect on stability of the Smart Grid: "Phasor data is also useful in calibrating the models of generation resources, energy storage resources and system loads for use in transmission planning programs and operations analysis, such as dynamic stability and voltage stability assessment. The technology may have a role in determining dynamic system ratings and allow for more reliable deliveries of energy, especially from remote renewable generation locations to load centers." (p. 8)

9.4 ACTION: MITIGATION, REMEDIATION AND RECOVERY

Visibility and analytics enable effective action for recovery from incidents, remediation of vulnerabilities and mitigation of risk. For example, a cyber attack launched via a compromised communication network against the circuit breakers in a substation results in damage to transformers in the station. Because the disabled substation could result in loss of power for millions of customers, this is assessed as a high priority issue. The response team confirms that the right people within the company are handling the incident properly: managers are conducting forensic analyses to figure out what happened, crews have deployed to fix the problem and the response teams are coordinating with each other to restart systems and restore power.

Once the immediate crisis is over, remediation activity determines how the attack occurred and whether there is a vulnerability that can be addressed to reduce the risk of similar attacks in the future being able to succeed. At the same time, the risk management team investigates the failure scenario to determine whether there are mitigation strategies that would reduce the likelihood and impact of transformer failure, for whatever reason.

9.4.1 ACTION: RECOVERING FROM AND MANAGING INCIDENTS

Even in the best instrumented and most secure operational model, incidents have to be expected. In fact, the number of incidents queued up for handling may be extremely large. It is essential for the incident response system not only to prioritize the incidents in the queue, but also to eliminate false positives and other clutter from the queue. To do this, incidents should be automatically checked against a global repository of items that analysts have previously investigated and resolved, before the new incidents are put on the queue. The incident response system should continually learn from these previous incidents, updated threat information, changes to operational configurations and other data sources in order to simplify the analyst's job as much as possible.

The incident response system should, as much as possible, prioritize the incidents in terms of known or potential impact on the business. The "Security Engineering Report on Smart Grids" by Hwang et al. (2012) explores this impact from two perspectives. The first is technical impact factors:

- Loss of confidentiality. How much data may have been disclosed and how sensitive is it?
- Loss of integrity: How much data could have been corrupted and how damaged is it?
- Loss of availability: How much service may have been lost and how vital is it?
- Loss of accountability: Is the incident traceable to one or more individuals?

The second is business impact factors:

- Financial damage: how much financial damage may result from the incident?
- Reputation damage: How much reputation damage that would harm the business may result from the incident?
- Non-compliance: How much exposure to and risk of non-compliance does the incident introduce?

- Privacy violation: How much personally identifiable information may have been disclosed?

A full understanding of the impact may not be reachable until after the investigation is complete, or even for some length of time after that. But the incident response system should provide what prioritization it can, while ensuring that information related to the periodization decision is available to the response team so that they can ensure that the most important incidents are addressed as quickly as possible.

Incident response system should provide a rich set of context about prospective problems. For instance, for an incident related to a suspicious file that may represent malware, the system should correlate suspicious behaviors about the file (e.g. a driver, a process, a DLL), capture what's known about the file (e.g. file size, file attributes, MD5 file hash) through static and heuristic analysis, provide context on the file owner or user, and so on. Security analysts can then use this information to investigate if the file is malicious, and should be blacklisted, or non-malicious, and should be whitelisted. If an item is deemed malicious, all occurrences of the problem across the entire IT environment can be instantly identified. Then, once a remedy is determined, the security operations team can perform any necessary forensics investigations and/or clean all the affected endpoints.

Incident response systems should also ingest information from external sources to enrich the organization's internal data sources for purposes of incident investigation and response. For example, the security analytics platform and management dashboard should aggregate and operationalize the best and most relevant intelligence and context from inside and outside the organization to accelerate the analysts' decision making and workflows.

Remediation after malware infection is a complicated task. If the compromised machine is vital for the system availability, it is usually not always possible to use previously saved safe machine images. The incident response team should check all the machine environments to remove all potential access points that attackers could utilize. Cyber criminals tend to use different entrench techniques in a victims' network. The term entrenchment is used to describe a technique used by the attackers that allows them to maintain unauthorized access into an enterprise network despite attempted remediation efforts by the victim. The victims' machine can be compromised in a variety of ways; for example the attackers could install web shells, they can add malicious or modified DLL to running web servers, they can utilize RDP backdoors, hide malware that will commence malicious activity after a fixed period of time, etc…

It is always good practice before starting to clean infected machines, to monitor network traffic and search for similar traffic patterns or similar IP connections as well as checking for all the possible lateral movements analyzing forensically the victim's machine. The aim is to perform this in a stealth way so the attacker is unaware they are under surveillance thereby avoiding the possibility that the attacker will lunch countermeasures to cover their evidence or start to deploy other entrenchment techniques to remain in the network. Forensics analysts should search not only for malicious software but also for legitimate software that could be installed on the machine for malicious purposes as well for misconfigurations created by the attackers.

An effective incident response team should be composed of malware experts, IT forensics analysts and network experts thereby giving the organization a wide competency and skills blend to enable successful detection, protection and investigation. Operations teams may be confronted with potential evidence of an infiltration or breach, but find themselves exploring potential causes without success for weeks or even months. When that happens, it helps to bring in people with specialized expertise and tools in incident response (IR). IR specialists can deploy technologies that capture activity on networks and endpoints in key segments of the IT environment. Based on the scans, analyses and supplemental information these technologies generate, experienced IR professionals can usually pinpoint where and how security breaches are occurring and shut down ongoing cyber attacks much faster than organizations can do on their own.

9.4.2 ACTION: REMEDIATING VULNERABILITIES AND ANOMALIES

Responding to the incident itself is essential. But equally important is determining whether there were vulnerabilities that contributed to the incident's occurrence or impact. These vulnerabilities may have been technological, such as software vulnerabilities that provided access for an attacker or that caused unexpected behavior in operation of a component. They may have been process issues that prevented an issue from being recognized until it had reached a critical level or that resulted in the initiation of a failure condition. Or they may be organizational, educational or other issues related to the structure and people of the organization, such as in individual vulnerability to social engineering attacks that resulted in malware infections.

The incident management system should support the determination of such vulnerabilities and assist in the remediation of those vulnerabilities, such as through the remediation planning shown in the Figure 9.6.

Remediation Tasks

Date Created	Priority	ID	Name	Assigned to	Status	Last Updated	Days Open	Incident ID	Created by	Escalation
2014-11-05	Medium	R1411051	Mal host	Smith	New	2014-11-05	0	I1411031	Parsons	No
2014-11-04	High	R1411053	Inf server	Harrison	Act	2014-11-05	2	I1411031	Parsons	No
2014-11-04	Medium	R1411052	Inf server	Harrison	Act	2014-11-05	2	I1411031	Parsons	No
2014-11-04	Medium	R1411051	Inf PC	Taylor	Closed	2014-11-04	1	I1411031	Parsons	No
2014-11-03	Low	R1411053	No sigmal	Smith	Act	2014-11-04	4	I1411031	Parsons	No
2014-11-03	Medium	R1411052	Inf PC	Taylor	Closed	2014-11-04	2	I1411031	Parsons	No
2014-11-03	Medium	R1411051	Inf PC	Taylor	Closed	2014-11-03	1	I1411031	Parsons	No

FIGURE 9.6

Remediation planning.

On a more comprehensive level, an incident may indicate a more fundamental issue in the operational model, such as in terms of missing or improperly instrumented controls. For example, the 2009 paper by the US Department of Energy calls out the vulnerabilities inherent in the older control systems that are currently deployed throughout the United States and that may have to be replaced: "The electric power industry relies heavily on control systems to manage and control the generation, transmission, and distribution of electric power. Many of the control systems in service today were designed for operability and reliability during a time when security was a low priority. Smart Grid implementation is going to require the installation of numerous advanced control system technologies along with greatly enhanced communication networks." (p. 4) This book has disused many of these advanced technologies that may need to be considered as part not only in the initial development of the operational model but also in addressing incidents that occur.

9.4.3 ACTION: MITIGATING RISK

The Smart Grid operational model includes the effective risk management discipline discussed earlier, employing a broad range of factors to make probabilistic decisions about risk and take prioritized actions, including alerts to response teams, to recover from incidents and remediate vulnerabilities. But an incident may also indicate the opportunity to take actions to mitigate the risk associated with that incident.

For example, a well-prepared security teams will know what the organization's valuable information assets are and which systems, applications and users have access to them. Awareness of these parameters help security analysts narrow their field of investigation during a breach so they can address problems faster and with greater confidence. But a given incident may indicate that the security operations teams should conduct a breach readiness assessment or institute

Practice drills to improve the speed and efficacy of their reactions to cyber attacks. They may need to revise their inventory of high-value assets that must be protected based on their new knowledge of what is attractive to an attacker. They may need to review their security policies again business priorities and regulatory requirements.

The Figure 9.7, expanding on a similar diagram in the Popovik paper (2013), provides an example of a process for mitigating risk in response to incidents such as detected intrusions.

Such a process can take advantage of operational incidents, regardless of whether they result from a security incident, equipment failure, natural disaster or any other cause, to enable organizations to take new actions to progressively improve their processes, optimize staffing and skills, modify their technology platforms, change their supplier relationships or take any other of the multiple of actions that could help them better address the risk of such an incident.

These improvements can be assisted by the technology advancements in big data and security analytics systems that deliver "imagine if" capabilities. The bounds of what's imaginable are now being explored by operations professionals

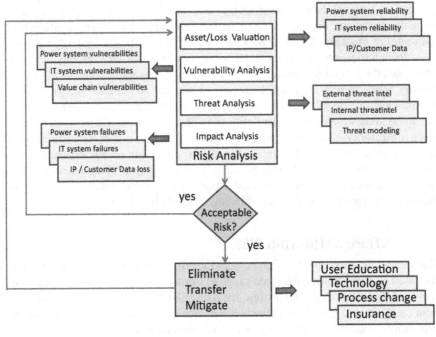

FIGURE 9.7

Risk mitigation.

and business leaders together. For organizations concerned about an effective operational model, these "imagine if" scenarios often focus on injecting better intelligence and context into both operational and security practices. For example, if we apply new analytic approaches to historical data, what could we learn? What do the cyber attacks we've encountered tell us about our business and operational risks? If we add new log sources or external intelligence feeds to our data warehouse, what patterns could we look for that we couldn't even imagine seeing before? What types of intelligence might help us hunt down threats or respond to operational incidents more quickly, including through automated capabilities that do not require human intervention?

An effective operational model for Smart Grid should ensure that this connection between incident response and the risk management process is established and effective.

9.5 THE HUMAN FACTOR AS ASSET

The complex interplay among people, process and technology in security operations makes it challenging to adjust any one element without also adjusting the others.

9.5.1 ENGAGING THE EMPLOYEE COMMUNITY

Harmonizing tools, skills and methodology in operations is essential to providing defense-in-depth and to protecting the organization's critical information assets by enabling the employee community to be more effective. Additionally, perfecting the people-process-technology triad can unlock operational efficiencies by automating routine tasks and streamlining workflows.

If this harmonization is achieved, the result is that operations administrators, security analysts and other staff will spend far less time tracking down information for an investigation or researching the status of an incident. Instead, they can focus their time on enriching intelligence sources, uncovering subtle irregularities in their IT environments that point to serious problems, or hunting down covert threats faster.

Process integration is an important aspect of improving the impact and contributions of the employee community. It eliminates many routine steps, such as copying-and-pasting incident information, that go along with manually joining disparate security operations workflows. Integration also reduces opportunities for error, because activities for complex processes such as incident response can be programmed to follow a deterministic sequence of actions based on best practices. Finally, process integration can facilitate cooperation among different parts of the business—among audit, information security and compliance, for example—and help organizations create a unified view of conditions and risks throughout the organization.

This collaboration across the enterprise is essential in creating a culture of engagement that enables effective operations. Such a culture can have a dramatic impact on security as well, by making encouraging a personal commitment to security by every employee. While social engineering attacks continue to remain a significant threat, the awareness of individual responsibility for security can be a powerful force in helping each employee recognize and avoid responding to such phishing, pharming and vishing attacks.

9.5.2 ENGAGING THE USER COMMUNITY

The importance of engaging the user community is a significant focus in the 2010 "Smarter Energy and Utilities" paper by IBM. It calls out the importance of educating the consumer, for example, pointing to the Mobile Experience Center created by Oncor: "The Center is essentially a "smart home" on wheels that travels throughout the state, allowing customers to experience first-hand how they are now able to make more informed choices about their energy consumption and expenditures than ever before." (p. 4)

Approaches to engaging the user community have been explored in detail in "A 15-Minute Guide to Smart Grid Correspondence with Utility Customers" (EMC, 2010). The paper recommends an integrated communications strategy that includes the following five components in order to engage the customer in a positive attitude toward Smart Grid.

- **Integrated content.** Regardless of the content, information shared with the customer must accurately and consistently represent product and service capabilities. Managing the content centrally helps to ensure that this is true of all contact with the customer.
- **Effective design tools.** Communications should be personalized with specific customer information and content, but should also follow business rules governing design variables, customization parameters and the use of customer data.
- **Multichannel content generation.** Composition and formatting capabilities must support a broad set of electronic and print formats, while meeting scalable production demands.
- **Content archiving.** Legal and regulatory constraints demand the archiving of every piece of utility correspondence. A comprehensive achieve also supports an effective customer relationship.
- **Enterprise integration.** Utilities must be able to integrate document personalization and generation services into existing enterprise applications in order to support per

Engaging the user community has significant benefits in terms of their confidence in the value and effectiveness of Smart Grid. As with the employee community, it also has significant benefits in terms of their confidence and participation in Smart Grid security, as essential for the user as it is for the utility.

9.6 CONCLUSION: SECURITY SHARED IS SECURITY STRENGTHENED

This chapter has touched a number of times on the importance of collaboration as part of the Smart Grid operational model. For example, if security analytics platforms integrate threat intelligence from outside sources, organizations can see the threat landscape as a panorama, not just from the narrow aperture of their own internal IT environments. Enhanced visibility will lead to enhanced security capabilities, vastly expanding options for how security operations centers (SOCs) act and respond to prospective threats.

Most utilities have seen an increase in cooperative efforts between engineering – owners of the operational technology – and IT – owners of information and communications technology. Utilities have not yet crafted a formal organizational structure to handle ownership of OT and IT. At this point, "convergence" is taking place for selected sets of data (e.g. meter signals fed to outage management). Convergence is also occurring from a data security perspective to ensure CIP compliance and adherence to applicable privacy laws. To a lesser extent, utilities are also seeing convergence when it comes to grid asset management. In other cases, data convergence between OT and IT is still future oriented, unfolding, and less transparent, especially for transmission (e.g. synchro-phasor sensor/apps, renewables), engineering/system performance, and marketing.

The "Smarter Energy and Utilities" paper calls out the importance of extending this "collaboration mindset" (IBM, 2010, p. 3) to collaboration across the industry. A number of collaborative forums already exist that are facilitating this collaboration, such as the European Atomic Forum (FORATOM), the Electric Power Research institute (EPRI), the Global Intelligent Utility Network Coalition, and the Global Smart Grid Federation. Participation in forums such as these is part of an effective Smart Grid operational model, as should participation in academic and industry research and collaborative engagement with both existing and new partners in risk management, operational effectiveness and cyber security.

ACRONYMS

3-D	Three-dimensional
AC	Alternating Current
AMI	Automated Metering Infrastructure
APT	Advanced Persistent Threat
CIP	Critical Infrastructure Protection
CVE	Common Vulnerabilities and Exposures
DDR	Digital Disturbance Recorder
DFR	Digital Fault Recorder
DLL	Dynamic Link Library
DLP	Data Loss Prevention
DNS	Domain Name System
DPR	Digital Protective Relay
EIM	Enterprise Information Management
EMC	Energy Management Control
EMC	Company name
EPRI	Electric Power Research Institute
ERP	Enterprise Resource Planning
ESG	Enterprise Strategy Groups
ESRI	Environmental Systems Research Institute
FORATOM	European Atomic Forum
GIS	Geographic Information System
GRC	Governance, Risk and Compliance
GUI	Graphical User Interface
HAN	Home Area Network
HMI	Human Machine Interface
HR	Human Resources
HTTP	Hypertext Transfer Protocol
HTTPS	Hypertext Transfer Protocol Secure
IBM	International Business Machines (company name)
ICS	Industrial Control Systems
ICS-CERT	Industrial Control Systems Cyber Emergency Response Team
IDC	International Data Corporation (company name)
IDM	Identity Management
INL	Idaho National Laboratory

IP	Internet Protocol
IR	Incident Response
ISO	Independent System Operator
ISP	Internet Service Provider
IT	Information Technology
MD5	Message-Digest Algorithm 5
MTBF	Mean Time Between Failures
NTLM	NT Lan Manager
ONCOR	Company name
OS	Operating System
OT	Operational Technology
PDF	Portable Document Format
PG&E	Pacific Gas and Electric
PMU	Phase Measurement Unit
PSERC	Power Systems Engineering Research Center
RPC	Remote Procedure Call
RSA	Company name
RTU	Remote Terminal Unit
SBIC	Security for Business Innovation Council
SCADA	Supervisory Control and Data Acquisition
SER	Sequence Event Recorder
SIEM	Security Information and Event Management
SoD	Segregation of Duties
SSL	Secure Sockets Layer
TCP	Transmision Control Protocol
TSO	Transmission System Operator
UCTE	Union for the Coordination of Transmission of Electricity
URL	Universal Resource Locator
UUID	Universal Unique Identifier
VCDB	VERIS Community Database Project
VERIS	Vocabulary for Event Recording and Information Sharing
WMI	Windows Management Instrumentation
WQL	WMI Query Language
XMDB	Configuation Management Data Base

REFERENCES

Cal ISO. (2010). Smart Grid Roadmap and Architecture. http://www.caiso. com/green/greensmartgrid.html

Cardenas, A. (2013). Big Data Analytics (and Security Intelligence) in Smart Grid Applications. In *IEEE ISGT Conference*. http://sites.ieee.org/isgt/files/2013/03/Cardenas3C.pdf

EMC. (2010). A 14-Minute Guide to Smarter Correspondence with Utility Customers. http://www.emc.com/collateral/software/15-min-guide/h5108-15-min-smart-gridcorrespondence-gd.pdf

EPRI. (2010). Smart Grid Roadmap and Architecture. http://www.smartgrid.epri.com/doc/cal%20iso%20roadmap_public.pdf

ESRI. (2011). Enterprise GIS and the Smart Electric Grid. http://www.esri.com/library/white-papers/pdfs/enterprise-gis-smart-electric-grid.pdf

Feblowitz, J. (2010) Making Good on the Promise of Smart Grid: Information Management is Critical. In IDC. https://www.emc.com/collateral/software/white-papers/utilities-whitepaper-emc-idc-ei224742.pdf

Feblowitz, J., et al. (2013). Using Information Intelligence to Improve Projects in the Energy Sector. In *IDC*. http://www.emc.com/collateral/analyst-reports/idc-usinginfo-intelligence-to-improve-projects.pdf

Govindasaru, M., et al. (2012). Cyber-Physical Systems Security for Smart Grid. http://www.pserc.wisc.edu/documents/publications/papers/fgwhitepapers/Govindarasu_Future_Grid_White_Paper_CPS_Feb2012.pdf

Hwang, H. K., et al. (2012). Security Engineering Report on Smart Grids. https://www.academia.edu/2908216/Security_Risk_Analysis_for_Smart_Grid

IBM. (2010). The State of Smarter Energy and Utilities. Smart Industries Symposium, Barcelona. http://de.slideshare.net/j3juliano/state-of-smarter-utilities

Musser, P. (2009). Smart Grid Data Management and Analytics: What Data to Collect, Integrate, Analyze, Act on and Report. http://www.burnsmcd.com/Resource_/PressRelease/1386/FileUpload/WhitePaper-SmartGrid-Musser.pdf

Oltsik, J. (2013). The Big Data Security Analytics Era is Here. In *ESG*. http://www.emc.com/collateral/analyst-reports/security-analytics-esg-ar.pdf

Oltsik, J. (2014). Information-Driven Security and RSA Security Analytics and RSA ECAT. In *Enterprise Strategy Group*. http://i.crn.com/custom/ESGWhitepaperIntelligenceDrivenSecuritywithRSASecurityAnalyticsandRSAECAT.pdf

Popovic, T., et al. (2013). Smart Grid Data Analytics for Digital Protective Relay Event Recordings. https://www.academia.edu/7691468/Smart_grid_data_analytics_for_digital_protective_relay_event_recordings

Ragan, S. M. (2010). Total System Failure Completely Annihilates Power Station. In *Makezine*. http://makezine.com/2010/12/10/total-system-failurecompletely-ann/

RSA, the Security Division of EMC. (2013). Big Data Fuels Intelligence-Driven Security. http://www.emc.com/collateral/industry-overview/big-data-fuels-intelligence-driven-security-io.pdf

Searle, J. (2012). AMI Penetraion Plan. https://media.blackhat.com/bheu-12/Searle/bh-eu-12-Searle-Smart_Meters-WP.pdf

Swearingen, M., et al. (2013). What You Need to Know (and Don't) About the AURORA Vulnerability. http://www.powermag.com/what-you-need-to-know-and-dontabout-the-aurora-vulnerability/

Symantec. (2014a). Dragonfly: Western Energy Companies Under Sabotage Threat. http://www.symantec.com/connect/blogs/dragonfl y-western-energy-companies-under-sabotage-threat

Symantec. (2014b) Sandworm Windows Zero-Day Vulnerability Being Actively Exploited in Targeted Attacks. http://www.symantec.com/connect/blogs/sandworm-windows-zero-day-vulnerability-being-actively-exploited-targeted-attacks

Tweed, K. (2012). Fraud Should be First Priority for Smart Meter Security. http://www.greentechmedia.com/articles/read/fraud-should-be-fi rst-priority-forsmart-meter-security

Tweed, K. (2014). Attack on California Substation Fuels Grid Security Debate. In *IEEE Spectrum*. http://spectrum.ieee.org/energywise/energy/thesmarter-grid/attack-on-california-substation-fuels-grid-security-debate

UCTE. (2006). Final Report System Disturbance on 4 November 2006. https://www.entsoe.eu/fileadmin/user_upload/_library/publications/ce/otherreports/Final-Report-20070130.pdf

Verizon. (2014). 2014 Data Breach Report. http://www.verizonenterprise.com/DBIR/2014/reports/rp_Verizon-DBIR-2014_en_xg.pdf

Vermesan, O., et al. (2013). Internet of Things: Converging Technologies for Smart Environments and Integrated Ecosystems. http://www.internet-of-things-research.eu/pdf/Converging_Technologies_for_Smart_Environments_and_Integrated_Ecosystems_IERC_Book_Open_Access_2013.pdf

Zhang, Y., et al. (2009). Fault Detection Based on Discriminant Analysis Theory in Electric Power System. In *IEEE*. http://ieeexplore.ieee.org/xpl/login.jsp?tp(&arnumber(5347972&url(http%3A%2F%2Fieeexplore.ieee.org%2Fxpls%2Fabs_all.jsp%3Farnumber%3D5347972

FURTHER READINGS

Al Shaer, E. (2014). Data-Driven Analytics and Automation for Next-Generation Secure and Resilient Systems. http://www.temple.edu/cis/research/documents/20140421EhabAl-Shaer.pdf

Bejtlich, R. (2013). The Practice of Network Security Monitoring; Understanding Incident Detection and Response (Kindle DX version). Amazon.com.

Budka, K., et al. (2014). Communication Networks for Smart Grid (Kindle DX version). Amazon.com.

Cardenas, A., & Moreno, R. (n.d.). Securiing Cyberphysical Systems. http://csrc.nist.gov/news_events/cps-workshop/slides/presentation-8_cardenasmoreno.pdf

Cloud Security Alliance. (2013). Big Data Analytics for Security Intelligence. https://downloads.cloudsecurityalliance.org/initiatives/bdwg/Big_Data_Analytics_for_Security_Intelligence.pdf

Electrical Engineering Portal. (2010). Substation Fire Protection. http://electrical-engineering-portal.com/substation-fire-protection

Engerati. (2014). Smart Metering in Europe: The Challenges are Greater. http://www.engerati.com/article/smart-metering-europe-challenges-are-greater

GTM Research. (2012a). High Performance Analytics for the Smart Grid. http://assets.fierce-markets.com/public/sites/energy/reports/highperformanceanalytics.pdf

GTM Research. (2012b). Understanding the Potential of Smart Grid Data Analytics. http://www.emeter.com/documents/anylst-papers/Understanding-the-Potential-of-Smart-Grid-Data-Analytics.pdf

He, M. (2011). A Data Analytics Framework for Smart Grids: Spatio-Temporal Wind Power Analysis and Synchronphasor Data Mining. http://informationnet.asu.edu/pub/Dissertation_MiaoHe.pdf

Jacobs, J., et al. (2014). *Data-driven security: analysis, visualization and dashboards*. Wiley.

Johnon, M. (2013). Cyber Crime, Security and Digital Intelligence (Kindle DX version). Amazon.com.

Lu, R., et al. (2012). EPPA: An Efficient and Privacy-Preserving Aggregation Scheme for Secure Smart Grid Communications. http://bbcr.uwaterloo.ca/∼rxlu/paper/TPDS-SI-2011-09-0635.pdf

Maheshwari, K., et al. (2012). Toward a Reliable, Secure and Fault-Tolerant Smart Grid State Estimation in the Cloud. http://www.cs.cornell.edu/projects/quicksilver/public_pdfs/isgt_2013.pdf

McCormick, J. (2011). Cyber Security Concepts Demonstration. http://www.smartgrid-live. com/wp-content/uploads/2012/12/Secure-Microgrid-Operations-Cyber-Security-for-Critical-Infrastructure.pdf

Microsoft Corporation. (n.d.). Windows Management Instrumentation. http://msdn.microsoft. com/en-us/library/aa394582%28v(vs.85%29.aspx

Rashman, M. A. (2012). SmartAnalyzer: A Non-Invasive Security Threat Analyzer for AMI Smart Grid. In *IEEE Infocom 2012*. http://ieeexplore.ieee.org/xpl/login.jsp?tp(&arnumber(6195611&url(http%3A%2F%2Fieeexplore.ieee.org%2Fxpls%2Fabs_all. jsp%3Farnumber%3D6195611

Sauer, P. (2012). Cyber-Physical Systems Security for the Smart Grid. http://www.pserc.wisc. edu/documents/publications/papers/fgwhitepapers/Govindarasu_Future_Grid_White_ Paper_CPS_May_2012.pdf

SCE-CISCO-IBM SGRA Team. (2011). Smart Grid Reference Architecture: Using Information and Communication Services to Support a Smarter Grid. http://www.pointview.com/ data/fi les/1/636/2181.pdf

Security for Innovation Council. (2011). When Advanced Persistent Threats Go Mainstream. http://www.emc.com/collateral/industry-overview/sbic-rpt.pdf

Shimeall, T., et al. (2013). Introduction to Information Security. A Strategic-Based Approach (Kindle DX version). Amazon.com.

Shostack, A. (2014). Threat Modeling: Designing for Security (Kindle DX version). Amazon. com.

Software Engineering Institute. (2010). Smart Grid Maturity Model. http://www.sei.cmu.edu/ library/assets/brochures/sgmm-1010.pdf

Sou, K. C., et al. (2012). On the Exact Solution to a Smart Grid Cyber-Security Data Analysis Problem. http://www.burnsmcd.com/Resource_/PressRelease/1386/FileUpload/WhitePaper-SmartGrid-Musser.pdf

Stimmel, C. (2014). Big Data Analytics Strategies for the Smart Grid (Kindle DX version). Amazon.com.

United States Department of Energy (DOE). (2009). Study of Security Attributes of Smart Grid - Current Cyber Security Issues. http://www.inl.gov/scada/publications/d/securing_ the_smart_grid_current_issues.pdf

United States Department of Homeland Security (DHS). (2007). Department of Homeland Security Control Systems Security Program. https://www.muckrock.com/foi/united-statesof-america-10/operation-aurora-11765/#1212530-14f00304-documents

Implementation Experiences from Smart Grid Security Applications and Outlook on Future Research

10

Stylianos Basagiannis*, Rohan Chabukswar*, Yi Yang[†], Kieran McLaughlin[†], and Menouer Boubekeur*

*United Technologies Research Centre, 4th floor Penrose Wharf, Cork, Ireland;
[†]Centre for Secure Information Technologies (CSIT), Queen's University Belfast, UK

10.1 SMART GRID EVOLUTION

The evolution of smart grids nowadays has raised important security concerns around the globe. Automation and control for optimized power distribution on building or district levels opens up new attack vectors to control and manipulate critical infrastructures. Evidence that the smart grid tends to surround us all can be found in the rapid deployment of electrical smart meters, considering that only in the US, approximately 36 million meters are already in use from 2007 (Institute of Electric Efficiency, 2012). In the same line across the European domain, smart grid deployment has been in the front lines of electrical architectural plans. To this end, grid modernization by utilizing ICT tools and interconnectivity services can offer a variety of benefits from accurate monitoring to remote supervision, enabling a more intelligent, resilient and interactive electrical network. Its successful operation though does not depend only on the energy savings; it is considered to be a prerequisite that strong security mechanisms and defences will be engaged while communication grid services and control is enabled. But how can we be certain that evolving smart grids will be secure?

10.1.1 DOCUMENTED INCIDENTS

Real world experiences and reports (Kroposki et al., 2008; Institute of Electric Efficiency, 2012; Tweed, 2011) on documented cyber-security incidents in the grid, show that smart grids controlling sensitive assets and components are an attractive target for attackers. One of the best known security incidents with a massive impact on industrial control systems is Stuxnet (Karnouskos, 2011). The Stuxnet worm, detected in June 2010, was a highly sophisticated malware targeting specific control software developed by Siemens

Corporation. Its core functionality enabled attackers to infect Siemens Programmable Logic Controller units (PLCs) modifying the decision of the control executed by the device while erasing any trace created in the log files. Using a valid digital certificate and exploiting zero-day vulnerabilities, Stuxnet manages to fully control the well-known Siemens WinCC SCADA software, which on its side, allows to manipulate process automation of industrial controllers and even allow access control and user authorization on the controlled components. Until its discovery, Stuxnet was a powerful cyber-weapon that allowed the remote control of safety critical industrial systems for years without being detected. According to Symantec's report approximately 45,000 networks have been infected with Stuxnet, 60% of them being hosted in Iran.

Close to the Stuxnet case, cyber-security incidents have been discovered in September 2011, reported as the Duqu (Duqu, 2011) virus. Believed to be originated from Stuxnet authors, its purpose was to collect information from end-users of industrial control systems and use them for future attacks. Although traces from Duqu executables have been found in a limited number of organizations, it is confirmed that it was targeting industrial control manufacturing companies. As imposed by its nature, Duqu is considered to be an attack preparation malicious tool that aims to aid future industrial cyber-attacks, such as the Stuxnet case.

Another serious cyber-attack that could have catastrophic impact is the one reported back in 2008 (Krebs, 2008) related to a nuclear plant in Georgia, USA. The Edwin I nuclear plant (U.S. Energy Information Administration, 2012) was forced to make an emergency shutdown that was a result of some software updates from the control manufacturer. It is crucial to note with this example, that (malicious) maintenance activities is one among the most common causes for incidents, as compromised or manipulated equipment can interrupt critical systems' operations. For example, consider updating the firmware of a control device; the specific operation either involve a physical access to the device and installing the firmware through a dedicated laptop or – more recently – update remotely the firmware of the device via IP networks. Both cases raise cyber-security concerns as media being involved in the update can carry non-certified software, as well as firmware packages can be already wrapped with malicious code and located still on the firmware's company servers. In the Georgia case, the specific maintenance activity although driven by the software control manufacturer, resulted in a 48 hour disruption of the nuclear plant operation raising certain alarms and major concerns about the reliability of the operations, being applied to a critical infrastructure (U.S. Energy Information Administration, 2012).

McAfee's report in (McAfee, 2011) raises huge concerns related to the Night Dragon malware (Dragonfly, 2014). Focusing primarily on industrial control systems, its main objective was to launch attacks depending on a combination of techniques including social engineering and spear-phishing. Known software vulnerabilities found in end-user operating systems such as Windows, allowed the Night Dragon to obtain valuable information that spanned from financial reports to business deals and sensitive intellectual property data.

One of the incidents worth mentioning is the attack launched against the US electrical grid in 2009 (Zhang, 2013) which affected power distribution and transmission.

After a huge number of investigations from both electrical and ICT experts, the final outcome of the analysis of the incident was that hidden malicious software has infiltrated the facility. It was confirmed that attackers could use software backdoors to cut electricity at will.

Concerning AMI, at the US Black Hat conference 2009, Mike Davis, an IOActive security consultant, proved the weaknesses of the whole metering architecture and in particular of smart meters that were being deployed in those days (Cordova, 2010). By means of a proof of concept, he demonstrated that a cyber attack could be used to get remote control of about 15,000 out of 22,000 homes within 24 hours. To show that Mike Davis and his team created a simulator as well as a real piece of malicious software (i.e. a worm) capable of self-replicating and self-distributing across an area where all houses are equipped with the same brand of meter.

In August, 2012, Justin Clarke reported a security flaw in the operating system of RuggedCom's Rugged Operating System (ROS) (August, 2012). RuggedCom products provide ruggedized network timing and communications infrastructure for electricity transmission and distribution, as well as other industrial applications. Clarke's report asserted that a single key could be used to penetrate the inner workings of the ROS. Once inside, an attacker could easily view communication traffic without additional security barriers.

In July 2012, the top U.S. military official responsible for defense against cyber attacks, General Keith B. Alexander, reported a 17-fold increase in cyber attacks against American infrastructure from 2009 to 2011 (Gjelten, 2013). GlobalData reported in September 2012 that the cyber security market in China will increase from $1.8 billion in 2011 to $50 billion in 2020. Symantec observed spear phishing attempts in the form of emails with PDF attachments from February 2013 to June 2013. The email topics were related to office administration issues such as dealing with an account or problems with a delivery. Identified targets of this campaign were mainly US and UK organizations within the energy sector. In May 2013, the attackers began to use the Lightsout exploit kit (InfoSecurity Website, 2014) for attacks, redirecting targets from various websites. The exploit kit has been upgraded over time with obfuscation techniques. The updated version of Lightsout became known as the Hello exploit kit. A newer approach used by attackers involves compromising the update site for several industrial control system (ICS) software producers. They then bundle Backdoor.Oldrea with a legitimate update of the affected software.

To date, three ICS software producers are known to have been compromised. The Dragonfly attackers used hacked websites to host command-and-control (C&C) software (Symantec Security response, 2014). Compromised websites appear to consistently use some form of content management system. The current targets of the Dragonfly group, based on compromised websites and hijacked software updates, are the energy sector and industrial control systems, particularly those based in Europe. While the majority of victims are located in the US, these appear to mostly be collateral damage. That is, many of these computers were likely infected either through watering hole attacks or update hijacks and are of no interest to the attacker. By examining victims with active infections – where additional malicious activity has been detected – it is possible to gather a more accurate picture of 'true' victims. Dragonfly uses two main pieces of malware in its attacks. Both are Remote Access Tool (RAT) type malware which provide the attackers with access and control of compromised computers. Dragonfly's favored malware tool is Backdoor.Oldrea, which is also known as Havex or the Energetic Bear RAT. Oldrea acts as a back door for the attackers on the victim's computer, allowing them to extract data and install further malware. Oldrea appears to be custom malware, either written by the group itself or created for it. This provides some indication of the capabilities and resources behind the Dragonfly group. The second main tool used by Dragonfly is Trojan.Karagany. Unlike Oldrea, Karagany was available on the underground market. The source code for version 1 of Karagany was leaked in 2010. Symantec believes that Dragonfly may have taken this source code and modified for its own use. Symantec found that the majority of computers compromised by the attackers were infected with Oldrea. Karagany was only used in around 5 percent of infections. The two pieces of malware are similar in functionality and what prompts the attackers to choose one tool over other remains unknown.

10.1.2 EVOLVING SECURITY STANDARDS

The smart grid becomes the major litmus test for future Internet of things, proving ground for a network of millions of smart meters. In this way equipment and meter manufacturers must consider security as a critical, system-level requirement when developing smart grid devices. There is no doubt that multilayered, life-cycle hardware and software security is the best solution for keeping smart grids operational. For this reason, new security standards in an international manner have to be in place as living, upgradable documentation in order to secure grid operation and controllability from recent attack bursts.

Currently, a smart grid environment relies heavily on standards, mainly to guarantee interoperability among systems. Standards also play a key role in smart grid cyber security. Standards to develop smart grid cyber security are available today, although some enhancements and new materials will be required to reflect the evolution of the smart grid, its technologies, and threats. Some will also need to be specifically profiled for the smart grid environment. The challenge is to maintain these standards over time at an appropriate pace. This will require substantial effort, but the benefit of supporting the deployment of smart grid infrastructures that are secure by design will make it worthwhile (ECETS, 2012). The CEN-CENELEC-ETSI SG-CG/SGIS working group (ECETS, 2012) chose a European electrical grid stability scenario as reference to define security levels. These security level definitions help to create a bridge between electrical grid operations and cyber security. They provide guidance in helping to identify critical areas where security matters, mostly from a global electrical grid stability point of view, starting from pan-European supergrids down to microgrids in city neighborhoods.

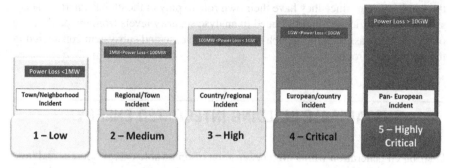

FIGURE 10.1 M/490 SG-CG/SGIS Security Levels

The last few years have seen an exponential growth of threats. In its fourth quarter 2012 threats reports executive summary document, McAfee says, "For the year, new malware sample discoveries increased 50 percent with more than 120 million samples now in the McAfee Labs 'zoo'". Cyber threats are also evolving and becoming highly sophisticated. Advanced persistent threats (APT) are good illustrations of this mutation. Also, attackers are no longer amateurs, but highly skilled and organized professionals able to launch complex and coordinated attacks using sophisticated tools. Information systems have always been targeted by cyber attackers. What is relatively new is the realization that industrial control systems are also vulnerable. This was demonstrated in 2010 with Stuxnet, the first discovered malware targeting industrial control systems. Electrical grids are valuable and critical targets that need to be protected from cyber threats. Smart grid layers require a system of systems approach with differentiated security needs. The smart grid includes different domains:

- Power generation
- Transmission
- Distribution
- Distributed energy resources
- Smart cities
- End consumers

It relies on a multitude of stakeholders, each with its own specific role and activity within a given domain. A smart grid architecture is a system of systems: a large and complex system made of smaller and simpler systems distributed and interconnected. Each smaller system has a different systemic impact on the global system stability and each must be assessed. Each smart grid subsystem and its associated assets require specific security functions and solutions. For example, the solution to secure a substation is not the same as the solution to secure demand response and home energy management systems. However, this does not mean that subsystems with "lower" criticality should not be secured. The security measures for each level must be sufficient to mitigate the risks. All subsystems would not necessarily need to align to the subsystem having the highest security requirements to effectively protect the whole system, since they have their own role to play in the global smart grid eco-system. Smart grid stakeholders need to analyse security levels from the perspective of a global risk assessment of each smart grid use case and subsystem considered in the end-to-end architecture.

10.2 SUSTAINABLE BUILDING INTEGRATED ENERGY TEST-BEDS

Distributed generation with a high penetration of renewable energy sources and low-carbon technologies is accepted as an alternative for traditional centralized power plants (Kroposki et al., 2008). The microgrid concept has emerged as the local-level integration and coordination of distribution energy resources, and enables the reduction of running cost and green house gas emissions, as well as guarantee availability of power supply, among other benefits (WBCSD, 2007). The microgrid concept can be extended to commercial and residential buildings, where there are growing opportunities for reduction of energy consumption and new market opportunities for stakeholders. Those sectors consume around 40% of total energy use in industrial societies (Scenarios for a clean energy future, 2000), and account for nearly one-third of greenhouse gas emissions. On the other hand, the security of microgrids increasingly comes as second priority. Especially when the integration of heterogeneous systems inside a building is rising, weak security implementations of the individual components cause critical vulnerabilities. To this end, different control strategies residing either in local embedded controllers of the components, or high level control up to the SCADA system can cause system instability, which can easily result in major grid faults.

We are going to describe common control strategies that are often implemented in smart grids. We select to focus on the test-bed microgrid (Valdivia et al., 2014) which is composed of different components all controlled through a SCADA system. Although it is a small-case system only, hierarchical control strategies assure the optimal operation of all of the sub-systems, and it applis a multidisciplinary approach consisting of information and communication technologies (ICT), power systems, power electronics, controls and optimization, and diagnostics. The electrical microgrid incorporates a 10 kW wind Turbine (Bergey Excelsys), a 35 kWh (85 kW peak) Li-Ion battery (Saft), a 50 kW electrical/82 kW thermal combined heat and power unit (CHP) by Sokratherm, a feeder management relay at the point of coupling between the microgrid and the rest of the building, and a set of local loads. Both the battery and the wind turbine are interfaced with the microgrid through power electronics converters (Triphase and Aurora, respectively), while the CHP is interconnected through a synchronous machine. This structure incorporates all of the major components in microgrids, such as renewable generation, Internal Combustion (IC) based generation, storage and different kind of interfaces. Thus, different control strategies on different hierarchical layers, stability issues (such as those resulting from synchronous machines interfacing controlled power electronics converters) and seamless transition from island to grid-connected mode, among others, can be evaluated. For further information the reader can refer to (Valdivia et al., 2014).

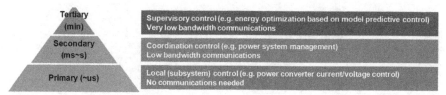

FIGURE 10.2 Hierarchical control of the building-level electrical microgrid and thermal system

Originally an integrated test-bed like the one described in (Valdivia et al., 2014) is controlled by following the hierarchical three-layer architecture illustrated in Figure 10.2. Similar approaches have been reported in (Lopes et al., 2006; Vasquez et al., 2010).

10.2.1 TERTIARY (SUPERVISORY) CONTROL LAYER

Tertiary control is performed by an integrated energy management system based on model predictive control. Recent efforts have focused on the application of predictive control to heating, ventilation, and air conditioning (HVAC) systems in energy efficient buildings (Ma et al., 2012; Samad & Kiliccote, 2012) thereby not including electrical local generation and storage. Here, the supervisory control considers the electrical microgrid components as well as heating system (including boiler, CHP, storage components), and computes the optimal set-points of them such that the running energy cost is minimized (Xiaohong et al., 2010). Electrical and thermal load forecasts as well as gas/electricity pricing and weather forecasts are exploited to achieve this goal. The problem is cast as mixed integer linear programming provided that all the equipment models are conveniently linearized.

10.2.2 SECONDARY (COORDINATION) CONTROL LAYER

The secondary control is used to perform coordination tasks and is implemented by two dedicated control units:

1. Programmable Logic Controller (PLC) and a Supervisory Control and Data Acquisition (SCADA) system: This system performs central control of the electrical microgrid. It performs tasks such as detection, seamless islanding transition and reconnection via a Feeder Management Relay (FMR), as well as load balancing under islanding conditions. This also receives set points from tertiary control for the different subsystems and sends them as inputs to the primary controllers via standard communications (Modbus) and analog/digital signals. This layer can also include provision of ancillary services to the utility grid. An overview of the SCADA Human Machine Interface is shown in Figure 10.3. under operation in islanded conditions.

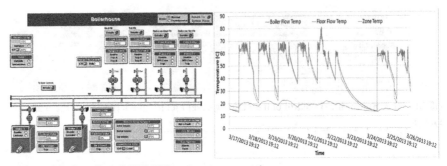

FIGURE 10.3 Overview of BMS HMI and system operation

2. Building Management System (BMS): Figure 10.3 shows also the BMS for the building heating system that implements the local controller algorithms for thermal system components. The two boilers that provide hot water to the main heater are controlled using an On/Off algorithm to regulate the flow temperature to its set-point. A PI algorithm is used to regulate the flow temperature for each mixing valve. The radiators are modulated by on-off thermostats to maintain zone temperatures close to the user-selected set-points. Figure 10.3 shows the BMS HMI for boiler management and experimental temperature profiles over one week. This is a simple operation example where the boiler and mixing valve are scheduled to be active at 7am and off at 9pm and during the weekend (3/23/2013 and 3/24/2013).

10.2.3 PRIMARY (LOCAL) CONTROL LAYER

The primary control layer is embedded in the generators and is responsible for assuring the stability of the electrical system and the correct dynamics and power quality. Thermal system local controllers are PI for mixing valve control, and On/Off for radiators and boiler control.

Figure 10.4 illustrates a detail of the power electronics converter for the battery. A multi-stage DC-DC converter boosts the battery voltage (360-480 V approx.) to

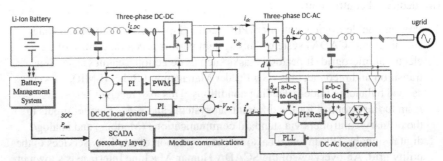

FIGURE 10.4 Battery inverter local controller (grid-follower strategy)

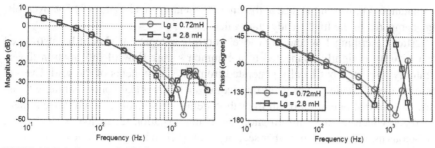

FIGURE 10.5 Influence of grid-impedance on inner plant dynamics (current-loop) in power converters

650 V approx. This converter also controls the DC link voltage using a multi-loop strategy. The three-phase DC-AC converter controls the AC-side current in d-q frame using a PI control plus resonators for harmonic compensation. This control structure for the DC-AC stage (herein shown for grid-follower operation) can be easily completed with an external voltage control for grid-forming operation. The set points for the grid-current are managed by the secondary control layer (the SCADA system), which receives inputs such as state of charge and maximum power available from the battery management system.

A critical issue related to system stability comes from the fact that the grid impedance in island conditions is significantly larger than that under grid-connected conditions. This can influence significantly the current control loop dynamics, so that a controller stable under grid-connected mode can be unstable in island mode. Figure 10.5 illustrates the plan of the current loop for different grid inductances (having feed-forward of grid voltage and considering digital delays). A substantial phase and magnitude drop is observed above 400 Hz with large inductance.

Figure 10.6 shows results corresponding to an islanding transition. At the time of islanding, the microgrid was exporting 18 kW at the point of common coupling. As can be seen, the microgrid remains stable with similar total harmonic distortion (THD) less than 2%. Load balancing algorithms are applied to compensate the

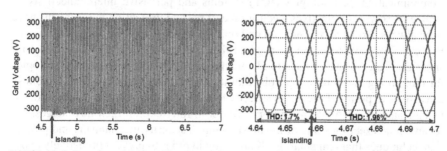

FIGURE 10.6 Experimental Transition from grid-connected (parallel) mode to islanded mode

instantaneous power unbalance at the time of islanding, leading to only 3% overvoltage compared to the final steady-state value.

After describing low and high level control strategies, it should be also noted that security is tightly connected to a common secure flow of information that is centrally inspected but locally generated from the components of the grid. Even in case of a small-scale power plant that requires a hierarchical control strategy to assure the optimal operation of all the sub-systems. This involves a multidisciplinary approach which includes information and communication technologies (ICT), that malicious users can exploit. Cyber security attempts can be sourced due to small alert deactivation that an intruder can perform. Notifications and fake true-positives (on the SCADA level) can be easily set up if an intruder will have access to the communication medium and deflect alert messages from its intended recipient. For example, if a smart meter is hacked, not issuing messages when the battery component of the grid is charging, the SCADA centralized decision algorithms can go ahead with legitimate but not authorized operations, bringing the battery component to danger, and thus the grid at risk.

10.3 SECURITY MEASURES AND PROTECTION MECHANISMS

With rising levels of automation in European electric power systems, the number of sensors and actuators in SCADA systems is increasing, making field-level control systems more and more powerful, while the smart-metering infrastructure seeks to converge with grid automation systems. Currently, there are several critical shortcomings in smart grid security technologies. For example, the resilience of systems for Supervisory Control and Data Acquisition (SCADA) to attacks is one such concern, along with cost-effective smart meter authentication and intrusion detection. While measures are in place for restoration of physical components of a grid in the event of an attack (CIGRE, 2007, 2008), fast restoration of the smart aspects of the grid remains overlooked. These deficiencies in smart grid security need to be addressed by the development of concerned technology. As the smart grid concept today depends heavily on increased use of Information and Communication Technologies (ICT) systems and pervasive interconnectivity to realize its services objectives, security measures and protection mechanisms have to be always activated, maintained and ready-to-react in case of suspicious events. However, we have to take into account that cyber security risks associated with smart grids are not well understood, and the most effective tools and technologies for monitoring and mitigating vulnerabilities are in their infancy. Such a premise can also be a 'point' of breach as security tools and mechanisms have to be utilized by educated SCADA administrators in order to fully exploit their advantages. We review in this section some of the most common security mechanisms and protection techniques that real smart grids are using in order to prevent proactively cyber security attempts.

10.3.1 **INTRUSION DETECTION SYSTEMS**

The operation of electrical utilities relies heavily on SCADA systems. Due to the demand for state-of-the-art means of communication in smart grids, the complexity of SCADA systems and their interconnections has increased, leaving them vulnerable to a wider range of cyber-security attacks. Even as the legacy components in the grid lack inherent countermeasures against cyber-attacks, the sophistication of attacks in this domain is increasing continuously, with declining need for resources to execute them. With the code for Stuxnet – arguably the most influential malware in the context of industrial control systems – in the public domain, its attack vectors and exploits can be adapted towards new targeted attacks.

The contemporary defences against such threats either rely on delayed or overdue security patches, leading to SCADA systems being forced to operate with known vulnerabilities, or the use of existing IT security methodologies that are not fully compatible with SCADA operations, so that even the most mature technology in the IT domain leaves gaping vulnerabilities specific to the smart grid environment. Intrusion detection and prevention tools specialized for SCADA systems are mostly unripe for implementation (Verba & Milvich, 2008; Coutinho et al., 2009; Carcano et al., 2011). While fiscal, legal and practical issues hinder retrofitting of smart grid SCADA networks, an alternative route which correlates temporal and physical status information with traffic and packet content could add robustness to smart grid communications, along with boosting capabilities for real-time monitoring of the network and connected devices and generating forensic logging data.

The Industrial Control Systems Cyber Emergency Response Team (ICS-CERT) has identified several design actions for intrusion detection and mitigation in control systems (ICS-CERT, 2012), such as SCADA application whitelisting to prevent intruders migrating within networks, implementing security zones for communications to slow down lateral movement through the rest of the network (Grimes, 2010), and firewalls/data-diodes to enforce one-way communication between network segments.

In summary, a novel mechanism that blends physical knowledge of SCADA and power systems with emerging network security skills is called for, one that unifies currently disparate approaches for IT security, such as stateful firewalls, data-diodes, application whitelists and behavioural analysis, to enable discovery of zero-day vulnerabilities through analysing behaviour and symptoms.

10.3.2 **PHYSICAL UNCLONABLE FUNCTIONS- PUFS**

A physical Unclonable Function (PUF) is a cryptographic function that generates a unique identity for a device based on the physical attributes of the device that cannot be cloned or mimicked by another device. A PUF embedded inside a smart meter can be exploited as a natural source of cryptographic keys used to protect the confidentiality of the meter data. While the concept of PUFs is well established, there exist only early proposal to apply it to smart meters.

The original PUFs were based on random optical reflection patterns, now classified as non-electronic PUFs (Tolk, 1992; Pappu et al., 2002). They gave rise to analogue-PUFs which measured various electronic attributes like threshold voltages, coating, power distribution and LC values. These were followed by intrinsic PUFs, which did not require special fabrication steps and could be integrated into the same chip as other functions. These measure either random delay deviations due to silicon process variability, or use the stable settling states of digital memory, but pre- and post-processing steps like error correction codes are necessary to ensure resilience and uniqueness of PUF-based keys, which still demand huge administrative effort and human intervention for generation and management in large-scale networks. Cutting-edge PUF classes include asynchronous or self-timed logic allowing fastest possible execution of complex functional blocks while increasing the robustness and entropy of PUF-based cryptography, without using complex blocks like error correction, reducing the cost of implementation on a device.

Fundamental strong authentication employing PUFs to generate cryptographic keys securely and automatically inside smart meters could reduce the attack points existing in the Advanced Metering Infrastructure (AMI). Authentication protocols using error correction services and new PUF designs could improve the stability of PUFs and economise on on-chip resources, making PUF-based authentication economically viable for hardware implementation.

10.3.3 ADVANCED SECURITY ANALYTICS

The primary objective of cyber-security risk assessment is to identify vulnerabilities and threats, and determine their impact. Risk assessment provides a structured process that identifies risks in terms of consequences, their probabilities and their effect on objectives, either qualitatively using threat graphs and game-theoretic models, or quantitatively by using metrics representing threat probabilities. There are many conflicting risk assessment methodologies, standards and tools (SISRAM, 2012). A repository is maintained by the European Network and Information Security Agency (ENISA), but none of those have a standard common framework to ensure a minimum level of harmonization, which prevents automation of security analysis methodologies. Current risk assessment frameworks are based on those designed for IT and traditional power grid systems such as those described by National Institute of Standards and Technology (NIST) (NIST, 2014), North-American Electric Reliability Corporation (NERC) (NERC, 2002), International Society of Automation (ISA) standards (ISA, 2007), thus not catering to the idiosyncrasies of a smart grid. This makes it an arduous task to apply one or more of these methods and techniques for any realistic risk assessment.

It is necessary to merge both cyber and power systems security approaches for risk assessment of a smart grid. The existing standards and best practices should be evolved to employ tools that provide significant insights into threats and security strategies, such as attack graphs and game-theoretic models, in tandem with enhanced algorithms for security analytics using machine-learning techniques to identify previously unknown patterns in the data.

10.3.4 RESILIENT CONTROL ALGORITHMS

With an increasing connectivity, control systems to the Internet and proprietary IT solutions becoming integral parts of such systems, the security and resilience of critical control systems to IT threats is a concern that is not completely addressed by incorporating traditional IT security in control design. Control systems utilizing closed-loop schemes, malicious data and actions can enter at any point inside the cyber-physical system and culminate in adverse physical effects on the infrastructure, even in the case of encrypted communications. Thus, while providing the necessary tools, conventional IT security cannot guarantee comprehensive security of a cyber-physical system. The fresh domain of resilient control systems attempts to develop a theory for control systems with performance that degrades gracefully under unexpected and malicious attacks. Automatic fault detection systems in control loops can allow dynamic reconfiguration and disconnection of attacked control loops to restrain the physical system within a safe operating state, but require detailed dynamic models, something that is not readily available for large-scale power grids. Even in case of exceptions, these tools are initiated from non-dynamic estimates of state, and are not designed to detect cyber-threats in real time. Bad Data Detection (BDD), which is commonly used by SCADA and Energy Management Systems (EMS), can be circumvented by an attacker with some knowledge of power systems, but the key idea of using data measurement redundancy can be applied to future smart grids making dynamic models and real-time fault detection an interesting avenue for control system resilience. To achieve this, the possibility of employing dynamic models of power grids to isolate cyber-attacks should be investigated for small- and large-scale and distributed implementation, along with developing methodologies and simulation tools that can be used to assess the sensitivity and relevance of various components in control loops in smart grids. Controller hierarchies and overlapping control authority can be exploited for defence against unexpected threats.

10.4 ANTICIPATED RESULTS: SMART GRID TEST-BED USE-CASES

In this section we review two use-case studies coming from the smart grid infrastructure. We describe network vulnerabilities in IEC 61850, which may be discovered by performing fuzz testing of system operations, and secondly perform security analytics in SCADA system data.

10.4.1 NETWORK VULNERABILITIES IN IEC 61850 SMART SUBSTATIONS

IEC 61850 (IEC, 2003) based smart substations have played a significant role in power system operation, becoming increasingly complex and interconnected as state-of-the-art information and communication technologies (ICT) are adopted. Although the IEC 62351 standard (International Electrotechnical Commission – IEC, 2007) has provided a framework for the cybersecurity design of the IEC 61850 protocol, problems remain and major manufacturers often do not implement adequate security in their intelligent electronic devices (IEDs) (Hoyos et al., 2012). In recent years, during the construction of smart substations, utilities and manufacturers have tended to pay more attention on the interoperation of devices and implementation of functions. As a result there has often been a lack of attention on cyber-security considerations and testing. Research on effective cyber-security for IEC 61850 based smart substations is still at an early stage, and the analysis of specific vulnerabilities and cyber-attacks is still ongoing.

10.4.2 IEC 61850 BASED SMART SUBSTATION

In order to realise the essential requirements of smart substation automation systems, i.e. control, monitoring, and relay protection, IEC 61850 divides the whole system into three logical levels (substation level, bay level, and process level) and ten logical interfaces, as shown in Figure 10.7.

In Figure 10.7, the meanings of the interfaces (from ① to ⑩) are as follows:

1. Protection-information exchange between station and bay level, such as protective action events.

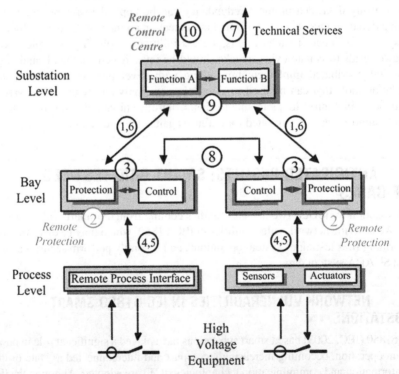

FIGURE 10.7 The logical architecture of SCADA systems in smart substations

2. Protection-information exchange between bay level and remote protection, for example, data exchange between fibre channels for differential line protection.
3. Data exchange within bay level.
4. Current transformer (CT) and voltage transformer (VT) instantaneous data exchange (especially sample values) between process and bay level.
5. Control-data exchange between process and bay level, for example, generic object oriented substation event (GOOSE) trip signals sent from intelligent electronic devices (IEDs) to intelligent terminals.
6. Control-data exchange between bay and station level, such as control commands sent from the monitoring system to IEDs.
7. Data exchange between substation (level) and a remote engineer's workplace.
8. Direct data exchange between the bays especially for fast functions such as interlocking.
9. Data exchange within station level.
10. Control-data exchange between substation (devices) and a remote control centre.

A typical network architecture of IEC 61850 based SCADA systems is shown in Figure 10.8. The architecture consists of the physical level, process level, bay level and substation level.

- The physical level includes electronic current transformers (ECT), electronic voltage transformers (EVT), and switchgear.
- On the process level, merging units (MUs) are connected in the SV/IEEE1588 network, and intelligent terminal (ITs) are connected in the GOOSE/IEEE1588 network. The process level networks are Ethernet switch-based fibre-optic networks.

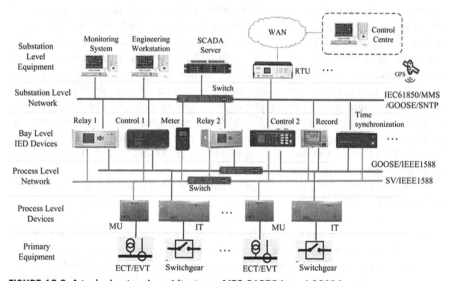

FIGURE 10.8 A typical network architecture of IEC 61850 based SCADA system

- The bay level IEDs include relays, measure-control devices, fault recorder, network analyser, and time synchronization IED. The bay level IEDs are connected in the process level networks and the substation level network.
- The substation level consists of the monitoring system, engineering workstation, SCADA database, and remote terminal unit (RTU). The substation level network, a switch-based cable network, supports MMS, GOOSE and simple network time protocol (SNTP). The control centre communicates with the smart substation using IEC 60870-5-104.

In conventional IT security, fuzz testing is regarded as one of the most useful techniques in finding vulnerabilities of software and protocol implementations (Kim et al., 2011). In protocol fuzzing, a fuzzer can send virtually unlimited test cases using invalid or falsely manipulated data, within the framework defined by a given protocol specification, to a protocol implementation. The effective test cases as input information can find security vulnerabilities of the application, which were not anticipated by the protocol designers or software developers. Therefore, fuzz testing is an effective approach to test and improve the security and reliability of protocol implementations (Sui et al., 2011).

Injected packets, including abnormal remote commands and set points, may bring a normal process into unintended states and/or cause an IEC 61850 server to freeze or other unexpected behaviours (Reaves & Morris, 2012). Malformed packets transmitted to IEDs may lead to denial of service by crashing an IEC 61850 protocol stack (Morris et al., 2011). One of the mitigation measures for the malformed packet attack is to test the robustness of IEDs using the fuzzing technology to identify potential vulnerable points.

IEC 61850, based on an object-oriented modelling approach, adopts state machines to define and delineate complex protocol service and functional behavior of IEDs. In terms of security and reliability testing for the IEC 61850 communication stack, the IEC 61850 protocol is more difficult to test than those without state machines. In addition, the IEC 61850 based IEDs to be tested in smart substations have complicated logical models, including numerous logical nodes, data, and data attributes. Current testing approaches for protocol security and reliability are based on capturing, mutating, and then replaying messages between the tester and the IED. However, due to the complexity of IEC 61850, conventional testing methods may be inefficient when replaying too many redundant packets. An additional issue is that when an IED freezes and does not respond to the client, due to a malformed packet sent by the tester, the test process has to stop.

In this case study an automatic fuzz testing approach is used to test the security and reliability of the IEC 61850 protocol stack, as well as the robustness of IEC 61850 based IEDs. The core idea of the IED robustness testing is to send test cases with malformed messages to the IED, and then check the communication status of the IED. The robustness of the IED depends on its response to the malformed messages. For test cases with the same malformed message, the more unhandled exceptions and unexpected behaviours there are, the worse the robustness of the IED. The proposed fuzzing approach used is a black box testing method, which only needs to know the IEC 61850 protocol, rather than the specific implementation of communication module inside the IED (Jiang et al., 2014).

In order to implement the above fuzz testing method, a test platform, such as shown in Figure 10.9, can be tailored for security testing of IEC 61850, using a fuzzing simulator, IEDs, a remote-controlled power strip, and a switch.

The fuzzing simulator runs the fuzz testing method as an IEC 61850 client. The IEDs are IEC 61850 based servers, such as real protection relays, as well as measurement and control devices. The Ethernet switch connects the fuzzing simulator and the IEDs. The power strip in Figure 10.9 can be remotely controlled by the simulator in order to turn on or off the IEDs. The fuzz testing steps may be executed as follows:

1. As an IEC 61850 client, the fuzzing simulator accesses the IED as an IEC 61850 server. In this case, the normal communication is built between the IEC 61850 client and the server in the test-bed, and normal communication packets are captured, e.g. via Wireshark.
2. In the fuzzing simulator, the collected messages are pre-processed by removing useless and redundant data, in order to generate a set of initial sample messages. A number of test cases with malformed messages are constructed from the sample messages, using mutation-based fuzzing methods.
3. During the fuzz testing process, the malformed messages are automatically sent to the IEDs one by one, and the malformed messages which cause the IED communication failure or status exception are recorded into a log file.
4. The fuzzing simulator should automatically detect the status of the IED tested. If the IED is crashed due to the test, the fuzzing simulator will send a control command to the remote-controlled power strip to restart the crashed IED, so that the fuzz testing can continue to test the next malformed packet after the IED restarted.
5. After the fuzz testing, the robustness reports of the tested IEDs are generated according to the ability of IEDs to addressing malformed packets.

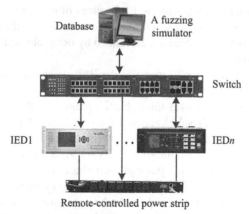

FIGURE 10.9 A test-bed for fuzz testing of IEC 61850

In general the results at the time of publishing typically show that most IEDs exist with cyber vulnerabilities with varying associated levels of risk. The common issues encountered for IEDs include:

- The human machine interface (HMI) of the IED tested has no response
- The communication programming of the IED is overflowed
- The IED cannot connect normally to the monitoring system
- The IED cannot communicate with the RTU
- The dispatcher in the control centre cannot remotely control the IEDs in smart substations

The clear consequence for control systems that use IEDs with the above vulnerabilities is that an attacker can severely disrupt the management and control of the underlying physical systems via a range of malformed packets. For mitigation, several steps should be taken. The first obvious step is the robust testing and patching of devices by manufacturers. For users, as has been covered in previous chapters, there is a requirement for protection and monitoring of the network environments in which the IED devices are used. Particular cyber-security mechanisms should include clear segregation of functionally different network domains, protected by firewalls, with devices such as IEDs contained in security zones with strict cyber-security policy enforcement. Zones containing with the most functionally critical assets, such as the IEDs, should also be carefully monitored with intrusion detection systems, tailored to the network and devices characteristics and security policies of that security zone.

10.4.3 SECURITY ANALYTICS IN SCADA SYSTEMS

Security analytics, at its heart, checks for consistency among the different variables accrued from a SCADA system. The key idea behind such a consistency check is that if only a subset of the sensors are manipulated by an attacker, the values that they communicate will not conform to the values measured by the unattacked sensors. When it comes to smart grids, smart meters form an axiomatic component of the grid. These smart meters communicate back values of dozens of variables at every time step. However, not all of these variables are measured — the meter measures a few values, and all other variables are calculated by using physical formulae involving these few measurements.

Most typically, the meter will measure the RMS values of the phase-to-neutral voltages (V_A, V_B, V_C), the RMS currents through each phase and neutral (I_A, I_B, I_C, I_N), and the average active power through each phase (P_A, P_B, P_C). From these ten measured values, Kirchhoff's Voltage and Current Laws, Ohm's Law, and other physical and geometrical formulae will allow the meter to calculate the remaining variables: The phase-to-phase voltages (V_{AB}, V_{BC}, V_{CA}), the reactive (Q_A, Q_B, Q_C) and apparent (S_A, S_B, S_C) powers through each phase, the total active (P), reactive (Q) and apparent (S) powers, and the total positive and negative active, reactive and apparent energies. Some meters also provide the aggregate power factor, albeit there being no uniform agreement over its definition. Some meters could even be designed to measure a few of the values which can be either calculated or measured (like the phase-to-phase voltages).

All this data, from all the meters can be collected and physical equations can be used to cross-check the reconciliation of their outputs (within a certain allowable error). Such verification can prove invaluable in the cases where one or more of the meters have been manipulated to measure incorrect values. There is room, however, for a simpler verification on a smaller scale.

In October 2014, cyber-security researchers managed to remotely shut down power supplies to households, tamper with meter readings, and insert malicious worms into the meters by hacking the reprogrammable chips inside smart meters in Spain (Illera & Vasquez-Vidal, 2014). In such an attack, the attacker has to modify the readings communicated by the meter to the utility. If the utility implements cross-checking equations for intra-meter values, the number of variables that the attacker needs to modify to maintain consistency multiplies.

As an example, consider just the voltages in the grid. The meter measures the phase-to-neutral voltages (V_A, V_B, V_C), and either measures or calculates the phase-to-phase voltages (V_{AB}, V_{BC}, V_{CA}). However, as shown in Figure 10.10, it is clear that these six values are not independent. In the phasor notation, they form four triangles. Geometrically, if each of these angles subtended by the three smaller triangles at the origin is calculated using the cosine formula, they should add up to 360° (or 2π radians). Thus, one of the consistency checks can use the equation:

$$\cos^{-1}\frac{V_A^2 + V_B^2 - V_{AB}^2}{2 \cdot V_A \cdot V_B} + \cos^{-1}\frac{V_B^2 + V_C^2 - V_{BC}^2}{2 \cdot V_B \cdot V_C} + \cos^{-1}\frac{V_C^2 + V_A^2 - V_{CA}^2}{2 \cdot V_B \cdot V_A} = 2\pi$$

However, it is unreasonable to expect the formulae to yield perfect agreement in nominal conditions, due to many factors such as synchronicity of measurements, accuracy, etc., which makes it necessary to allow for a certain error while cross-validation. The intra-meter equations are, more often as not, of an implicit form. In addition, several variables, such as currents and powers, could very well be zero at any time, and might cause divide-by-zero errors in some formulae. Thus, it is

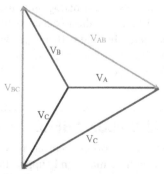

FIGURE 10.10 Phasor Diagram of Grid Voltages

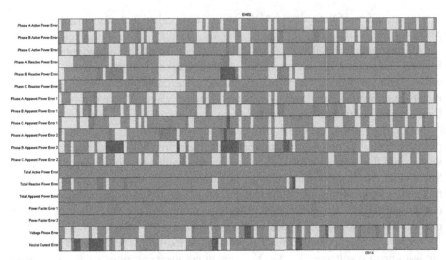

FIGURE 10.11 Intra-Meter Security Analytics

advisable to consider the distribution of the deviations of the actual values from the calculated values.

One method is to construct a histogram of historical data (when the system is known to have been in an unattacked state), and calculate the probability of the deviation experienced by the real-time measurements during cross-validation. If too many cross-validations yield discrepancies that have a low probability, it would be fair to assume that something is wrong in the meter firmware, most probably an attack. A security analytics display that checks this could look similar to Figure 10.11, where 19 cross-checking equations are calculated at each time, and coloured grey (probability > 68.63%), light grey (4.55% < probability < 68.63%), dark grey (4.55% < probability < 0.3%), or faded grey (probability < 0.3%), the values being chosen to match 1σ, 2σ, and 3σ normal variations even for other distributions for consistency reason.

This methodology also provides a way for multiple levels of security analysis. For example, at the end of the day, a comparison could be made between the day's distributions of errors with the historical histograms, using a measure of distance such as the Bhattacharyya distance. If the distance is higher than expected, there could be a problem with the meter. In Figure 10.11, this would correspond to checking whether 68.63% of the area is coloured grey, 26.82% is coloured light grey, 4.25% is dark grey, and 0.3% is faded grey.

10.5 CONCLUSION AND LOOK AHEAD

It is a clear fact that in the smart grid concept energy and security systems have been designed separately for both demand and supply. Industry today on the other hand, focuses on the development of next-generation integrated security and energy management solutions. The primary focus is controlling power on district level (buildings interconnections), where requirements are more specific, generally aiming to provide security, comfort, and secure and efficient energy supply, particularly for critical loads. According to real world implementation experiences, a known problem occurs in the grid when the demand side requires more energy than the maximum provided by the smart grid. This can, in the worst case, lead to a shutdown of all the demand loads and supply devices, including the critical demand systems. Such a premise can for sure raise security awareness of ICT people while smart grid control engineers on the same line, design resilient control algorithms for the individual grid components.

Nowadays smart grid control engineers face a new challenge when managing distributed energy systems; they have to minimize the total energy consumption without confining performance or security standards, while maintaining a certain level of functionality of the grid for safety purposes. Meanwhile, as ICT attacks and cyber-physical hacking is rapidly expanding composing a regular "top news" label in the security community blogs, newly introduced security mechanisms have to be validated with respect to realistic smart grid operating conditions, such as in test-beds with a focus on protecting communication infrastructures and, above all, human lives. First experiences on smart grid demonstrations reveal that new architectures emerge from the requirements of new use cases and actors, being expanded on top of existing grid infrastructures. This leads to interconnecting existing subsystems with new ones, which inherently implies an enlargement of the grid's attack surface, and so requires considering new risk mitigation measures. This must be done by taking into consideration the potential impact of an attack to the end-to-end electrical system stability for each use case. New approaches to manage cyber contingencies in a consistent way can be found in the domains of advanced intrusion detection systems, security analytics based on data mining and clever clustering techniques as well as physical unclonable functions for smart meter protection.

ACRONYMS

AMI	Advanced Metering Infrastructure
APT	Advanced Persistent Threat
BDD	Bad Data Detection
BMS	Building Management System
CHP	Combined Heat and Power (Unit)
CT	Current Transformer
ECT	Electronic Current Transformer
EVT	Electronic Voltage Transformer
EMS	Energy Management System
FMR	Feeder Management Relay
GOOSE	Generic Object-oriented Substation Event
HVAC	Heating, Ventilation, and Air Condition
IED	Intelligent Electronic Device
IC	Internal Combustion
ICS	Industrial Control System

ISA	International Society of Automation
IT	Intelligent Terminal
MU	Merging Unit
NERC	North-American Electric Reliability Corporation
NIST	National Institute of Standards and Technology
PLC	Programmable Logic Controller
PLL	Phase-Locked Loop
PWM	Pulse Width Modulation
RAT	Remote Access Control
RMS	Root Mean Square
ROS	Rugged Operating System
RTU	Remote Terminal Unit
SCADA	Supervisory Control and Data Acquisition
SNTP	Simple Network Time Protocol
THD	Total Harmonic Distortion
VT	Voltage Transformer

REFERENCES

August. (2012). Justin Clarke reported a security flaw in the operating system of Rugged-Com's Rugged Operating System (ROS).

Carcano, A., Coletta, A. G. M., Masera, M., Fovino, I. N., & Trombetta, A. (2011). A Multidimensional Critical State Analysis for Detecting Intrusions in SCADA Systems. *IEEE Transactions on Industrial Informatics*.

CIGRE C2.02.24. (2007). Defense plan against extreme contingencies.

CIGRE. WG 34.08. (2008). Isolation and Restoration Policies against System Collapse.

Cordova, R. (2010). *Enhancing network scanning for discovering vulnerabilities*. MSc thesis. University of Colorado, Dept of Computer Science.

Coutinho, M. P., Lambert-Torres, G., da Silva, L. E. B., Martins, H. G., Lazarek, H., & Neto, J. C. (2009). Anomaly detection in power system control center critical infrastructures using rough classification algorithm. In *Proc. 3rd IEEE International Conf. on Digital Ecosystems and Technologies*.

Dragonfly. (2014). *Cyberespionage attacks against energy suppliers*. Symantec Security Response, Version 1.21. July 7, 2014.

Duqu. (2011). *A Stuxnet-like malware found in the wild, technical report.* Laboratory of Cryptography of Systems Security (CrySyS). Report. Available at http://www.crysys.hu/publications/files/bencsathPBF11duqu.pdf.

Gjelten, T. (2013). First strike: US cyber warriors seize the offensive. *World Affairs Journal*, January.

Grimes, R. A. (2010). Isolated security zones yield stronger network protection. [Online]. Available at http://www.infoworld.com/d/security-central/isolated-security-zonesyield-stronger-network-protection-403.

Hoyos, J., Dehus, M., & Brown, T. X. (2012). Exploiting the GOOSE protocol: A practical attack on cyber-infrastructure. In *Proc. 2012 IEEE Globecom Workshops* (pp. 1508–1513).

ICS-CERT. (2012). *Targeted cyber intrusion detection and mitigation strategies*. Technical Information Paper ICS-TIP-12-146-01A, Update A, July 19, 2012.

IEC. (2003). 61850: Communication networks and systems in substations. Geneva: IEC.

Illera, A. G., & Vasquez-Vidal, J. (2014). Lights off!! The darkness of the smart meters. Black-hat Europe. Available at https://www.blackhat.com/eu-14/briefings.html.

InfoSecurity Website. (2014). LightOut is Latest Cyber Threat to Target Energy Sector. http://www.infosecurity-magazine.com/news/lightout-is-latest-cyber-threat-to-target-energy/.

International Electrotechnical Commission – IEC. (2007). Power systems management and associated information exchange – data and communications security. Technical Specification IEC TS 62351-1, May 2007.

Institute of Electric Efficiency. (2012). *Utility-scale smart meter deployments, plans & proposals*. IEE Report, May 2012.

ISA. 2007. *Security for Industrial Automation and Control Systems*. Part 1: *Terminology, Concepts*, and Models.

Jiang, H. T., Yang, Y., Huang, W., & Guo, Y. J. (2014). Robustness testing method for intelligent electronic devices. In *2014 Asia-Pacific Electronics and Electrical Engineering Conf.* Shanghai, China, December 27–28.

Karnouskos, S. (2011). Stuxnet worm impact on industrial cyber-physical system security. In *37th Annual Conference of the IEEE Industrial Electronics Society (IECON 2011)*Melbourne, Australia, November 7–10.

Kim, H. C., Choi, Y. H., & Lee, D. H. (2011). Efficient file fuzz testing using automated analysis of binary file format. *Journal of Systems Architecture, 57,* 259–268.

Krebs, B. (2008). *Cyber incident blamed for nuclear power plant shutdown*. The Washington Post Online, Washingtonpost.Newsweek Interactive, June 5, 2008.

Kroposki, B., Lasseter, R., Ise, T., Morozumi, S., Papatlianassiou, S., & Hatziargyriou, N. (2008). Making microgrids work. *IEEE Power and Energy Magazine, 6,* 40–53.

Lopes, J. A. P., Moreira, C. L., & Madureira, A. G. (2006). Defining control strategies for MicroGrids islanded operation. *IEEE Transactions on Power Systems, 21,* 916–924.

Ma, Y., Borelli, F., Hencey, B., Coffey, B., & Bengea, S. (2012a). Model predictive control for the operation of building cooling systems. *IEEE Transactions on Control System Technology, 20*(3), 796–803.

Ma, Y., Kelman, A., Daly, A., & Borrelli, F. (2012b). Predictive control for energy efficient buildings with thermal storage. *Modeling, Simulation and Experiments. IEEE Control Systems Magazine.*

McAfee. (2011). *Global energy cyberattacks: night dragon*. White Paper, McAfee® Foundstone Professional Services and McAfee Labs. February 10, 2011.

Morris, T., Pan, S., Lewis, J., Moorhead, J., Reaves, B., Younan, N., et al. (2011). Cybersecurity testing of substation phasor measurement units and phasor data concentrators. *The 7th Annual ACM Cyber Security and Information Intelligence Research Workshop (CSIIRW).* October 12-14, 2011. Oak Ridge, TN.

NERC. (2002). Security Guidelines for the Electricity Sector: Threat Response, Emergency Plans, Communications, Version 1.0, dated June 14.

NIST. (2014). Smart grid cyber security strategy and requirements, NISTIR 7628.

Pappu, S., Recht, B., Taylor, J., & Gershenfeld, N. (2002). Physical one-way functions. *Science, 297,* 2026–2030.

Reaves, B., & Morris, T. (2012). Analysis and mitigation of vulnerabilities in short-range wireless communications for industrial control systems. *International Journal of Critical Infrastructure Protection, 5,* 154–174.

Samad, T., & Kiliccote, S. (2012). Smart grid technologies and applications for the industrial sector. *Computers & Chemical Engineering, 47,* 76–84.

Scenarios for a clean energy future. (2000). Interlaboratory working group on energy efficient and clean-energy technologies. The Interlaboratory Working Group on Energy-Efficient and Clean-Energy, NREL/TP-620-29379; ORNL/CON-476; LBNL-44029.

Sui, A. F., Tang, W., Hu, J. J., Technology, M. Z. L. C., Nanlu, S. L. C. W. Z., & District, C. y., et al. (2011). An effective fuzz input generation method for protocol testing. In *Proc. 2011 IEEE 13th International Conf. on Communication Technology* (pp. 728–731).

Symantec Security response. (2014). *DragonFly: Cyberespionage Attacks against Energy suppliers.*

Tolk, K. (1992). *Reflective particle technology for identification of critical components.* Albuquerque, NM: Sandia National Labs.

Tweed. (2011). Katherine. Smart Grid Italy: What to Watch, GreenTechGrid.

U.S. Energy Information Administration. (2012). *State Nuclear Profiles, Georgia Profile: Edwin I Nuclear Power Plant*, Data for 2010|Release Date: April 26, 2012. Full report: http://www.eia.gov/nuclear/state/pdf/snp2010.pdf.

Valdivia, V., O'Connell, S., Gonzalez-Espin, F., El-din Mady, A., Kouramas, K., De Tommasi, L., Pesch, D. (2014). Sustainable building integrated energy test-bed, Power Electronics for Distributed Generation Systems (PEDG). In *2014 IEEE 5th International Symposium on* (pp. 1, 6, 24–27).

Vasquez, J. C., Guerrero, J. M., Miret, J., Castilla, M., & de Vicuna, L. G. (2010). Hierarchical control of intelligent microgrids. *IEEE Industrial Electronics Magazine, 4,* 23–29.

Verba, J., & Milvich, M. (2008). Idaho National Laboratory Supervisory Control and Data Acquisition Intrusion Detection System (SCADA IDS). In *Proc. IEEE Conf. Technologies for Homeland Security.*

WBCSD. (2007). Energy efficiency in buildings: Business realities and opportunities. *World Business Council for Sustainable Development.*

Xiaohong, G., Zhanbo, X., & Qing-Shan, J. (2010). Energy-efficient buildings facilitated by microgrid. *IEEE Transactions on Smart Grid, 1,* 243–252.

Zhang, Z. (2013). Cybersecurity policy for the electricity sector: The first step to protecting our critical infrastructure from cyber threats. *19 B.U. J. Sci. & Tech. L, 319,* 319–320.

FURTHER READINGS

ECETS. (2012). European Committee for Electrotechnical Standardization, CEN-CENELEC-ETSI SG-CG/SGIS working group "CEN-CENELEC-ETSI Smart Grid Coordination Group – Sustainable Processes," November 2012. Available at http://ec.europa.eu/energy/sites/ener/files/documents/xpert_group1_sustainable_processes.pdf.

FP7 iTesla Project: Innovative tools for electrical system security within large areas. Available from http://www.itesla-project.eu/.

Survey of Information Security Risk Analysis Methods. (2012). *Smart Computing Review,* 2(1).

Utility-Scale Smart Meter Deployments, Plans, & Proposals, IEE Report, May 2012, The Edison foundation, http://www.edisonfoundation.net/iei/Pages/IEIHome.aspx.

Subject Index

A

Abusive surveillance, 17, 40
Address resolution protocol (ARP), 132
Advanced measuring instrument, 12
Advanced metering infrastructure, 55, 114,
    117, 294
Advanced persistent threats (APT), 7, 258, 287
American National Standards Institute (ANSI), 117
AMI. *See* Advanced measuring instrument;
    Advanced metering infrastructure;
    Automated meter infrastructure
ANSI. *See* American National Standards
    Institute (ANSI)
APDU. *See* Application protocol data unit (APDU)
Application protocol data unit (APDU), 120, 123
APT. *See* Advanced persistent threats (APT)
ARP. *See* Address resolution protocol (ARP)
Attack surface, 59, 115, 225, 226, 303
Attack trees, 100
    example of, 101
    fault tree analysis, 68
    threat identification process, 227
Automated meter infrastructure, 256

B

Bad Data Detection (BDD), 295
BAT. *See* Best available techniques (BAT)
BDD. *See* Bad Data Detection (BDD)
Best available techniques (BAT), 25, 27, 31
BMS. *See* Building management system (BMS)
Building management system (BMS), 221, 290
Bus probing, 83–85

C

CAM. *See* Content addressable memory (CAM)
Case studies, 12, 60, 152
    advanced metering infrastructure (AMI), 60
    conclusion, 40
    data protection testing of smart grids, 25
    distribution grid management (DGM), 64
    EU light regulatory approach to personal data
        protection, 31
    European legal order, privacy and personal data
        protection in, 19
    false-data injection attacks on power
        transmission networks, 152
    IEEE 14-bus benchmark, 172
    minimum-resource adversary policies, 172

recommendations, 41
regulating smart grids in Europe, 25
smart grid roll-out neglecting individual
    interests, 12
wide area monitoring, protection, and control
    (WAMPAC), 62
CEN-CENELEC-ETSI Smart Grid reference
    architecture framework, 196
CFR. *See* Charter of fundamental rights (CFR)
Charter of fundamental rights (CFR), 20
Chemical mechanical polishing (CMP), 97, 99
Chip decapsulation process, 95
Cisco secure development lifecycle, 229
    Smart Grid solutions, 229
    static analysis tools, 229
CJEU. *See* Court of Justice of the EU (CJEU)
CMP. *See* Chemical mechanical polishing (CMP)
Common vulnerabilities and exposures (CVE), 230
Common weakness enumeration (CWE), 230
Communications, basic attacks on, 132
    ARP spoofing, 132
    denial of service (DoS), 132
    injection, 133
    MAC Flooding, 132
    man-in-the-middle (MITM) attacks, 133
    replay, 133
    session hijacking, 133
Content addressable memory (CAM), 132
Control-centric approaches, 156
    control systems, anomaly detection in, 156
        fault detection, model-based, 156
        fault isolation
            data driven, 158
            model-based, 156
        resilient control framework, 158
            active fault-tolerant control, 159
            robust control, 159
Control-centric risk assessment methodology, 152
Control-data exchange, 297
Control systems, risk assessment for, 159
    adversary goals and constraints, 162
    adversary model, 160
    disclosure resources, 161
    disruption resources, 161
    model knowledge, 161
Core root of trust for measurement (CRTM), 104
Court of Justice of the EU (CJEU), 21
CRTM. *See* Core root of trust for measurement
    (CRTM)
Cryptographic algorithm, 89, 94

307

Printed in the United States
By Bookmasters